INVALID FORMAT
AN ANTHOLOGY OF
TRIPLE CANOPY

Volume 2

SternbergPress

A NOTE ON INVALID FORMAT

by the Editors
of Triple Canopy
published September 27, 2012

WE BEGAN THE FIRST volume of *Invalid Format* by describing how Triple Canopy came into being in the summer and fall of 2007, as a flurry, then an avalanche, of emails between friends and strangers. At the time, we had only a vague sense of what we were after: an online magazine, an original framework for serious reading and viewing in a medium that seemed to resist such efforts. Our first four issues, compiled in volume one, are a record of our attempts to make that vagueness concrete. Online, we started to move, however haltingly, beyond text illustrated with JPEGs and placed within horizontally sliding pages. Offline, we worked to turn the ideas and experiments that had constituted Triple Canopy into nonprofit paperwork and grant applications; traded in a flattened power structure for a traditional masthead.

By 2009, where this second volume picks up, we were realizing ambitions once floated in Google Groups. This was something of a surprise, and a challenge: How could we continue to publish distinctive work, and just what did we mean by "publish"? Did we have a politics? Was Triple Canopy a job? What was it, really, that we were after? We had a sense of our relationship to technology—selectively enthusiastic about "innovation," skeptical of any libertarian endgame—and had all learned some HTML; we understood what our content-management system could and couldn't do. And so we settled into (tweaked, chafed against, abandoned) the structures we had in place. Our second four issues, compiled here, achieved

fuller expression: Typically, there were autodidactic and polymathic hydras, essays and reports too expansive to fit elsewhere, projects by visual artists translating their studio practices to the Web, video that wanted to live somewhere between a gallery and YouTube, literature that did *something else* on a computer screen besides beg to be printed.

For more than a year, we were consumed by two issues devoted to urbanism, approached from many angles and in many forms: a translation of an interview with a Chinese expert on underground cities, a multimedia presentation on "smart sprawl" by a fabricated eco-friendly development firm, a rumination on John the Baptist and cellular automata. Those issues, set against the backdrop of the foreclosure crisis and a deflationary failure of political will, incorporated academic thought and artistic license, parsed city zoning and experimental geography, rhymed Tijuana's slums with Dubai's McMansions. But perhaps more important, they helped define Triple Canopy's mode of turning outward while looking inward; our desire to have our publication annex public space.

We tested the urbanism issues in the Kitchen's black-box theater, punctuating the editing process with performances of articles-in-progress amid the band Zs' brutalist constructions and Nine 11 Thesaurus's rap about teen life in Brownsville. With the microcinema Light Industry and a circle of artists and academics, we organized a weeklong series of screenings and discussions radiating from Wang Bing's

THE EDITORS

documentary *Crude Oil* (2008), on view five times, from dawn to dusk—an exhaustively deep reading of art-time with work-time. As part of the NY Art Book Fair at MOMA PSI, we got dozens of once and future contributors to read, dance, project, and otherwise make present pieces from an issue of *Aspen*, the half-century-old magazine-in-a-box that's been our lodestar. Taken together, these experiences of Triple Canopy as a protagonist, moderator, facilitator, writer, venue, designer, historian, technologist, and entity about town pushed us to place ourselves in what we later dubbed "the expanded field of publication."

Invalid Format serves as a record of these widespread publishing pursuits, and as a translation of these activities, across forms, into print. Its design, by Project Projects, reflects this challenge of transformation. *Invalid Format* is built around templates meant to accommodate different kinds of material, while constraining the ways in which it might be represented. Last time, we called this "the book as content-management system," but that's not quite correct. The pages aren't generated automatically based on a set of parameters. Each layout reflects decisions about how works produced for the screen might be transposed to the paperback, shifting between vertical and horizontal orientation as your iPad (or an eighteenth-century botany treatise) might—yet no e-book's structure is so precisely responsive to such varied contents. And while the form (and introduction) of this volume may be partly recycled from the first, there's a greater sense of reaching to do things with print that we couldn't do with the Web—or that we *could* do with the Web but must redo on the page, if not revise, abridge, omit. How do you print an interactive exegesis of Latin American modernism? A memoir on Hinduism and electronic prayer that concludes with a Flash-driven puja? An MP3ed excursus on the sound of the rolled *r*? A YouTube essay on authenticity? A quodlibet on Prussian blue, when Web color isn't true color and, anyway, this book is in grayscale?

A book is also a preservation strategy. Think of the obsolescence of all new media: cassette tapes, LaserDiscs, Zip drives. *This* book is one of our preservation strategies, among many, because we want Triple Canopy to last. We want to run on more than charisma and fumes, to be able to pay our editors and contributors, and generally to behave like a new-model arts organization. We want to be collective in a sustainable way, not just as an appealing formal arrangement. It's one thing to talk about it, as we did in our first year or two; it's another to get $100,000 for "capacity-building" from the Andy Warhol Foundation on the condition of regular meetings with consultants and the generation of an "organizational narrative." We became a nonprofit. We conferred with lawyers and accountants, built a board of directors, started writing checks. We saved up for a redesign (see volume three). We started a Twitter account and thought we'd leave it to rot.

The correspondence concluding this volume attests to our long march to institutionalization. So many of our models refused to play the game: *Aspen* famously folded after the US Postal Service revoked its periodical mail rate, and we couldn't afford that either. So, from email flurry to paperwork. Triple Canopy began in September 2007 with thirty people packed into a living room (and others tuned in via Skype), speaking in and out of turn; staying up until 3 a.m. taking positions and making jokes, achieving and abandoning consensus, impressing and infuriating one another, feeling elated and nervous and always that something was at stake. After a long summer day in 2009, a dozen editors and cohorts—almost all of them having performed *Aspen* or illustrated an article or played a party—ate soup dumplings after an art opening for another contributor-friend (a category that now seems, inevitably, to include everyone we know). We paused midway for a ceremonial signing of Triple Canopy's articles of incorporation, a few hundred flimsy pages. And this past week, as Labor Day approached, a dozen more people cycled through our white-walled office in Greenpoint, Brooklyn, to edit, design, copyedit, and generally fuss over this book, in PDF and as sheafs of proofs, while others stole time from office jobs across town to chip away at this introduction, emailed from an Alpine village to comment on the cover, texted from LA with answers to fact-checking queries, or, in the case of Light Industry, now our roommates, went over layouts in between testing 16-mm prints and CD-ROMs for a marathon Chris Marker screening. Somewhere in that sentence, that week, those people; somewhere in those technologies and procedures and jokes and arguments—somewhere in there is the book you're holding. ⊠

ISSUE 5
IDOL TRAFFIC

published February 10, 2009

CANOPYCANOPYCANOPY.COM/5

INVALID FORMAT 2

ISSUE 5 2009

FLASH YR IDOLS

From Kolkata and the universe within Krishna's mouth to Vermont and the pleasures of virtual prayer. A memoir and a video game.

by Bidisha Banerjee
with George Collins
published February 10, 2009

In its original form, "Flash Yr Idols" features a Flash video game, designed by George Collins, that provides the reader with a virtual experience of the Sri Yantra. Here that e-puja is represented by images.

1. PERIMETER: FOUR DOORS TO INFINITY

*One day when the children were playing, they reported
to Yashodha, "Krishna has eaten dirt." Yashodha took
Krishna by the hand and scolded him and said, "You
naughty boy, why have you eaten dirt? These boys, your
friends, and your elder brother say so." "Mother, I have
not eaten," said Krishna. "They are all lying. If you
believe them instead of me, look at my mouth yourself."
"Then, open up," she said to the god, who had in play
taken the form of a human child; and he opened his mouth.*

*Then she saw in his mouth the whole universe, with
the far corners of the sky, and the wind, and lightning,
and the orb of the Earth with its mountains and oceans,
and the moon and stars, and space itself; and she saw
her own village and herself. She became frightened and
confused, thinking, "Is this a dream or an illusion fabricated by God? Or is it a delusion in my own mind? For
God's power of delusion inspires in me such false beliefs as
'I exist,' 'This is my husband,' 'This is my son.'" When
she had come to understand true reality in this way,
God spread his magic illusion in the form of maternal
love. Instantly Yashodha lost her memory of what had
occurred. She took her son on her lap and was as she had
been before, but her heart was flooded with even greater
love for God, whom she regarded as her son.*

—translated from the Bhagavad Purana,
a tenth-century Sanskrit text, by Wendy
Doniger in *The Implied Spider*

At first, I knew Hinduism only as an extension of family
life—full of order and chaos. Packed tight as atoms, transcendence, superstition, playful affection, and holy terror whirled about one another, clashing occasionally, like
hanging temple bells purifying the wind. If Hinduism is
the temple of civilization (as my great-grandfather loved
to argue), then its daily pujas and seasonal Pujas are the
candles, lamps, and fireworks that light up the altar.

At sunrise, like a martinet, before the city of Kolkata grew restive, my grandmother rang her hand bell; then she ground sandalwood into paste. With some of it she adorned our family pantheon, saving the rest for her cheeks. Fresh flowers were delivered along with the milk and reverently tossed at our idols. The day began. Commerce, gossip, traffic jams, cooking, and family feuds did, too.

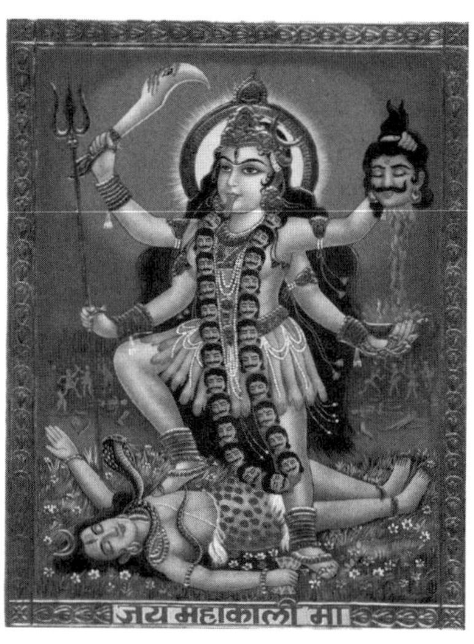

Artist unknown, Kali.

Everyone knew that on Thursdays between 2:30 and 5 p.m., subtle planetary movements rendered our own stirrings inauspicious; as the sun glared the world into submission, we loosened our pajama strings and fell into a deep sleep. These stupors were different from the siestas we took on other weekdays; on Thursday afternoons, we dared not do anything important, even in our dreams. Was it mere astrology, divine doctrine, or family predilection that also led to bans on trimming our nails after sunset and on learning to swim?

Every evening, when he sat down to eat, my grandfather put a tiny bit of food and water aside. He was a man of the world. He idealized the sixteenth-century Molgul emperor Akbar, cried when President Nixon, Mother Teresa, and Princess Diana died, and railed against Gandhi. As a young Communist enthralled with Subhas Chandra Bose, the Bengali nationalist who brought troops to support the Japanese during World War II, he had flung away his sacred thread. He still hated the stringy caste mark, with its pernicious branding of division. He never failed to feed our Brahman ancestors, but toward the end of his life, when illness prevented him from carrying out annual rites for his father, he smiled and said, "By now he's been reborn. He's playing somewhere—he doesn't need my devotions."

Evenings were the best. My grandmother lit incense, did her evening pujas, and supervised the cook, while my grandfather, still in his suit, drank Complan. The rest of us drank tea and ate fried plantains and banana flowers. Sometimes, many people came over, and we used banana leaves as plates. Afterward, we threw away the leaves, as if the banana plant weren't Kalabou, the wife of Ganesh, the elephant-headed god. We worshipped her during the festivals Durga Puja and Ganesh Puja (a puja is a private act of prayer, a Puja a public rite performed by priests), cladding the plant in a sari and smearing her leaves with vermilion paste. Then she became a polite, well-heeled stranger, and it was impossible to contemplate picking her fruit or spoiling her fronds. Who knew what she might do to us?

At night, my grandfather laid aside with his suit his worries about steel manufacturing, the stock market, and family crises. After a cold bath, he sat cross-legged on the bed, his lower body now swathed in white cotton, water droplets as shiny and surprising as untimely dew peeking out of his chest hair, specks of talc on his brown skin like aromatic dust. Beside him, quiet for once, I breathed in the peace he breathed out. I knew he was doing his puja, but what was he *actually* doing? To make me laugh, when things weren't going according to our wishes, he would scold his gods and goddesses, just as he scolded me. Is that all a puja was then? A chance to rebuke your favorite godlings?

After my grandparents had fallen asleep, I would lie awake, chattering with the goddess Kali, mother of death and destruction. Her vivid face, with its bloody stuck-out tongue, was emblazoned on a calendar across from my bed. She and I had a special bond—Bidisha is one of her 108 names, and one of my three. I'd beg her to tell me stories, and sometimes she would.

Kali was a fearsome aunt and easily provoked, but those skulls strung around her neck were endearing. It was sweet how she would suck on them absentmindedly, like lollipops, and she was always good for a bone-chilling story, long after everyone else was asleep. When I finally drowsed off in the dregs of one of these complex, gory tales (which always ended with Kali adding several freshly scalped, grinning skulls to her garland), I felt as peaceful as my grandfather after his bath.

2. FIRST CIRCLE: CLOSED OUT

Beef, biceps, and the Bhagavad Gita.
—Swami Vivekananda, on what Indians
needed to defeat the British

ISSUE 5 2009

If my rapt conversations with Kali were my first pujas, they were also very nearly my last. When I was ten, Hindu fundamentalists destroyed a mosque built by a Molgul ancestor of Akbar's. Two thousand people died in the ensuing riots. I had trouble reconciling my family's apparent obliviousness to the violence with my grandfather's stories of a syncretic Hinduism. That same year, my parents separated; it was unclear whether a culture that had so much room for warrior goddesses had any tolerance for a single mom. On her parents' urging, she chose to settle in the US rather than endure the raised eyebrows at home. Had I remained in India, or moved to Jackson Heights, perhaps I would have internalized more doctrine, perhaps attended a Hindu youth camp. But in Lawrence, Kansas, my pujas grew anemic. And what kind of Puja takes place in a basketball-sick high school gym or a yellowing Methodist church? A hundred-strong crew of displaced Bengalis assembled one lone day a year, each of us having come a long drive across the paved-over prairie, our tangail saris taken off mothballs, our *ras gollas* and Rabindra Sangeet defrosted.

An outlier herself, my mother devoted her life to teaching Kansans about standard deviation—painstakingly, she drew the box and whiskers, the stem and leaf; at night, Bhagavad Gita tapes helped her sleep. Before I drowsed off, my first year in the US, I would watch figure skating and practice my splits, then prostrate myself for puja. Bedtime prayers seemed somehow American. But afterward, as the year grew old and my mother slumbered fitfully, I would play country music or Super Mario 4 until dawn.

Transcendence, superstition, playful affection, and holy terror spun apart, their atomic bonds broken, the temple now locked. In high school, I ate beef for the first time (it tasted like stinky goat) and scandalized my grand-father by accepting a job at the Paradise Café, where I built my biceps by scrubbing dishes and toilets. I opened up to the Doors, Nine Inch Nails, and *The Doors of Perception*; my Bhagavad Gita stayed shut, a jumble of diacritics and morality.

As a girl, I was denied the sacred thread granted to Brahman males upon adulthood, and I was outraged. Yet, following my grandfather, I would never have worn the thread had it been given to me. I still remembered two all-purpose mantras he had taught me, and used them to fight off fatigue, financial worries, heartbreak, cockroaches, and poor road conditions. One, the ten-word *sarvamangala* mantra, is an invocation of the goddess Durga. The other is an eight-word zinger: *Maha Maya, Maha Medha, Maha Buddhi, Maha Lakshmi!* Great Illusion, Great Intelligence, Great Conscious-Awakeness, Great Wealth!

3. OUTER PETALS: CIRCLING

Today, in 2008, it seems the e-puja has always been there, on the Internet. Otherwise, some midwestern Indian pro-grammer with a freezer full of Ma's cooking would have had to invent it. It is not only Hindus who have constructed online facsimiles of reverence, but it's the Indian diaspora, nostalgic for drumbeats and flower petals, that has taken interactivity most seriously.

I cannot approach the e-puja historically. I am not interested in who created the ur-template from which each subsequent garland, incense burner, lamp, drum, and flower was copied for pasting the Web over, or in how the sham of interactivity developed, or in who holds the e-puja world record. *Click!* The lingam is wearing your garland! *Drag!* The incense is lit! *Click*, *click*, and *click*. The blessing is yours!

Where does the goddess reside? Is she happy to be clicked on and dragged, anytime, by anyone, in any state of mind? What relationship do those bodiless clicks bear to five thousand years of tradition, which dictate, down to the minute, how a puja should be performed? Or is the goddess moved by informality? Maybe she who would chat with me at night also enjoys appearing on computer screens to brighten the days of workers glued to their desktops?

I am most tempted to perform an e-puja in early fall, during the sensory explosion that is Durga Puja. For sixteen years, I longed to be in Bengal for this four-day festival, which marks Durga's triumph over the demon Mahishasura. It is simultaneously the most riotous and the most unifying moment in the Bengali Hindu's year: Muslims, Christians, and unbelievers get swept up in the fanfare. Writers and editors fuss over Puja editions of literary magazines. Artists labor for months to create neighborhood shrines out of bamboo and clay. The walls of one *pandal* might be decorated with the colors and designs of an indigenous tribe; another could feature a blood-soaked Mahishasura or an enormous replica of Hogwarts.

Every morning and evening, women's ululations goad the conch-shell wielders into higher frequencies while men with bulbous two-sided drums hanging like pendants from their necks square off against the gong players. Priests chant, then fall dramatically silent; the crowd lobs petals at the goddess; the mantras start anew. In front of Durga, wild dancing men and women brandish clay pots of tinder, camphor, and incense, which trail shimmying garlands of

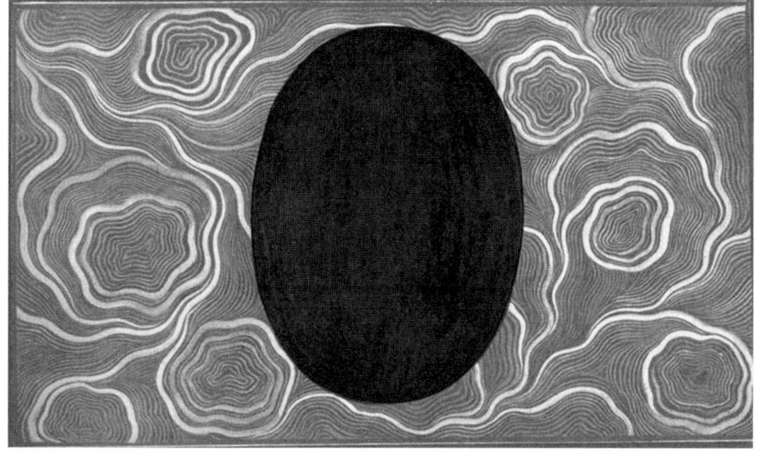

Kangra school, *Hiranyagarbha* painting, ca. 1775–1800, gold and tempera.

smoke. On the last day, everyone goes forth and showers friends and family with sweets and good cheer. Afterward, the idols from the shrines are driven to the river by exultant crowds and submerged, then left to frustrate fish and seep bright paint into the water. (Indian environmentalists, in particular, welcome e-pujas.)

4. INNER CIRCLE: CLOSING IN

"Humankind cannot bear very much reality," T. S. Eliot intoned. If divinity is the ultimate reality, why do we continue to seek it out? Yashodha couldn't bear seeing the universe in Krishna's mouth. But after her vision was forgotten, she returned to daily life with a redoubled love for God, whom she now held as her son.

October of a year ago, in rural Vermont, I missed even the diasporic Durga Pujas celebrated in Boston and New York. As I spent the week scrolling through the e-pujas out there, I realized that I had become willing to use whatever it took—contortions or incense, keystrokes or mouse clicks. Performing an e-puja is like being stranded on a virtual desert island and eating a coconut made of pixels. Once I lived on the real island; there I encountered not just coconuts but their tree's very own spire leaf, a tender and delicious heart of palm at its base. But so far from Bengal, placing stock in authenticity is a fundamentalism I can't afford. Reality can't wait.

I N V A L I D   F O R M A T   2

I S S U E   5   2 0 0 9

5. THE FOUR UPWARD-POINTING TRIANGLES: "MALE" ENERGY

I have known Hindu priests to cop a feel in crowded lines and to rush along the spiritual VIPs who have paid the most to the goddess fund. At the most awe-inspiring temple I know, Fullara Ma's in Labhpur, there's no idol—only a squat stone jutting out of the earth and covered in red ooze. (Another story: When an incarnation of Durga had her body sliced into fifty-two pieces and scattered throughout India, the goddess's lips fell here.) Fullara Ma resides in a tiny room, guarded night and day by mangy priests who bathe her in milk, throw hibiscus flowers, and chant mantras, all in exchange for money. Her temple was built by my great-great-grandfather. He is still remembered by the priests, who lose no opportunity to cackle about my family's peccadilloes and scandals; apparently, gossip is a solemn part of the oral tradition. I used to go to Fullara Ma's temple and sit by the adjoining pond, but I never made a formal puja because I didn't want to bribe those scoundrels to encounter the goddess for me. E-pujas evade most personal conflict. But the space that opens up can be terrifying.

6. THE FIVE DOWNWARD-POINTING TRIANGLES: "FEMALE" ENERGY

The first e-puja I made was representational. I did not stray far from the templates out there; I was interested in a hand-made look. Once, a village girl in rural Bengal slipped her hand into mine as we picked our way through flooded rice fields. "City people think they have it all. Well, they don't. I know that the real puja takes place here," she confided, as the warm mud squelched between our toes.

In the Bengali countryside, where I lived recently, Durga Puja remains the biggest event of the year. It is very much a harvest festival. All year, as farmers accumulate rice straw, they mold the leftover husks into faceless female figures, each of them Durga. The soon-to-be-goddess leans casually against bus stands and mud huts or slumps, as though she's tired of awaiting immanence and just wants a cigarette. She can be sodden or bulbous, alluring or merely scratchy. Occasionally, she sprouts out of herself.

Designing my own e-puja wasn't about giving old rituals an electronic face-lift. Perhaps those who use the e-pujas out there regularly go to temples or sit at the feet of a guru, and these experiences rose-color the crude Flash animations. I had no temple and no guru and no real expectations of the gods. Instead, here I was, my own guru, eager to induce epiphany. I needed concrete tools to expand with rigor my sense of reality, to pay daily homage to the incomprehensible Krishna within myself and all else. How could I touch divinity's spire leaf or, at the least, my grandfather's peacefulness? My hands were tied—I had to turn to the Sri Yantra.

7. CENTRAL DOT: PSYCHOGEOGRAPHY OF THE VERTIGINOUS *BINDU*

Mantra gives formula and equation; yantra, diagram and pattern; and what correlates both systems of rela-tions is Tantra. . . . A yantra then represents a particular force whose power or energy increases in proportion to the abstraction and precision of the diagram. Through such yantras or power diagrams, creation and control of ideas and physical forces are supposed to be possible. . . . It is not an arbitrary invention but a revealed image of an aspect of cosmic structure. . . .

Just as the musical string must be plucked in a par-ticular fashion to sound a certain note, so must the yantra line be mastered and mentally plucked to bring forth its image or power. Thus the yantra diagram of apparently static lines will, with mental application, vibrate in per-fect relation like a finely tuned instrument.

 —Ajit Mookerjee, *Tantra Art: Its Philosophy and Physics*

The Sri Yantra is, or appears to be, a diagram in which four doors open into two circles. The first has sixteen pet-als, the second eight. In the center, nine triangles blur into and out of focus. Four male triangles point up while five female triangles point down. Unlike yin and yang, the Sri

Yantra is imbalanced, and this asymmetry is hallucinatory. Although it has been read in many ways—it is an esoteric meditation aid to understanding nonduality; it is nonduality; it is an aspect of the Supreme Goddess; it is a union of male and female energies; it is the relationship between pentatonic scales and microtones; it is a coded map of the world; it is the cosmos itself—the Sri Yantra is not a symbol. Without the mantras to unleash it, without a guru to correct pronunciation of those mantras, the Sri Yantra is nothing. But what else is it?

In honor of my grandfather's playful religion, I decided to make a game of the Sri Yantra. I enjoyed the difficult task of visualizing it, and with the help of my partner, I created a Flash animation that would allow anyone to trace the diagram. I used an eighteenth-century drawing of the Sri Yantra from Rajasthan. (Since Tantra is a form of Hinduism akin to Gnosticism, my family in Bengal was unfamiliar with the diagram.) I recommend breathing deeply or listening to music or doing both while tracing it. According to tradition, the yantra should not be traced at night.

Remaking the yantra as pure geometry was a study in signal and noise, an attempt to tease out the vagaries of handicraft from matters cosmological. The Sri Yantra is, after all, the world; a quarter-inch gap might be the Bay of Bengal. The drawing's right gate was slightly narrower than the left (the careless hand of an eighteenth-century apprentice or a deliberate and significant choice?). Far more obvious was the extra line, tiny and meticulous, on the upper gate's left side. It couldn't possibly have been an error, but, orbiting asymmetrically on-screen, it would have seemed like one. (What if it were the pin that attaches the world to the sky—the very seat of consciousness, the entry point of the goddess?) I didn't include it.

The point of the first male triangle was slightly set off from the first female triangle's baseline. This might have been an unimportant imprecision—or did it bespeak a different mathematics, more complex than that of the gross body of bland, overbalanced modern yantras? It did, I decided, and I rewove the inner lines from a different skein of petals. The Sri Yantras out there showed four male triangles and five females—but no, in our ancient version the male shapes were dominant! Two hours of recalculation followed, accompanied by growing suspicions of concealment and conspiracy. Then I realized I'd scanned the book upside down.

As the days dragged on, the juddering and uneven rotation of the layers began to work bad mojo. During the day, my partner and I built little Taj Mahals of code. But by five or six in the evening, minor errors in construction would manifest in three-dimensional fields, wildly whirling outlines, and ghostly inversions. Fault-riddled code yielded nearly the right results; cleaning it up left things worse. The angular pull of the outer petals became more and more visceral—like being picked up and spun—and the triangles, half their points missing, resembled mismatched gears. Perhaps things were going so poorly because I was working at night. Sometimes, very late, it seemed the center would not hold.

That threatened a premise of the project—that the Sri Yantra could exist in an atomized way but still be pinned to the bindu in the center. But the bindu cannot be reached. It cannot be seen, and no path leads to or from it. Somehow I failed to see, until the piece was almost done, that I'd forgotten the bindu entirely.

After more than six months of working on the game, I visited an ashram in Rikhia, Jharkhand, with my yoga teacher. On the train, I savored my solitude in the ladies' compartment. I breathed in the locomotive's sooty, high-spirited rhythms and wished they could continue forever. But I arrived too late to receive *diksha* from the guru, and as a hundred people lined up to receive their personal mantras, I roamed the ashram alone. Suddenly, the Sri Yantra was everywhere: on tote bags and daily planners and dorm-room walls (reinterpreted, with the word *love* inscribed inside heart-shaped petals). No mystery surrounded the yantra's associated mantra, *Aīm Hrīm Klīm*. Everyone knew it and chanted it often. Bull's-eye! I was in the bindu, and a bit disconsolate. Stressed out, I left early. But an hour later, sitting again inside the clattering train, the wind off the brilliant mustard fields tearing the shawl from my body, I felt once more at peace on the axis leading toward and away from the Sri Yantra's ground zero. ⌧

On the next page, there are images of two versions of the e-puja. The first is meditative and, like most beginners' meditations, extremely boring. (If repeated use leads you to transcendence, we want to know!). The instructions: "You move through the yantra alone. You move by pointing yourself along the right path. If you get stuck, click. The yantra will not rotate. It will all be visible (as is traditional)."

The second version of the e-puja is a more traditional video game, and is difficult to navigate. The instructions: "Six others keep you moving through the yantra. Will you reach the end? You move by pointing yourself along the right path. If you get stuck, click. The yantra will rotate. It will become visible in stages. Don't get blanked by the devas chasing you! You win once the flatness of your computer screen explodes into multidimensionality inside your mind. If you get there, please make sure to have a raucous block party, complete with drums, flowers, incense, and good food. And don't forget to scold the gods on my behalf."

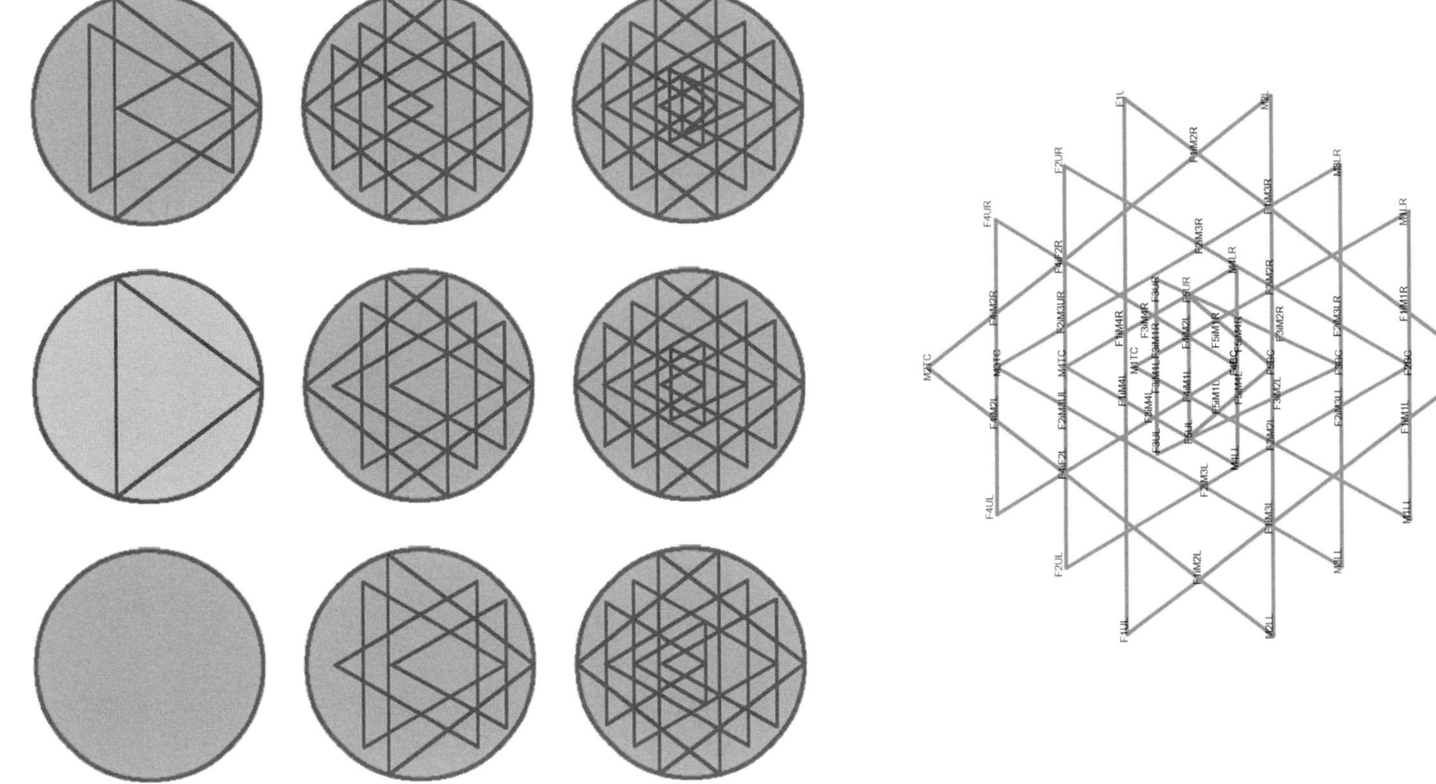

ISSUE 5 2009 INVALID FORMAT 2

BETWEEN SCANS

A video in two parts: human dancer and analog tools. Movements, voltage patterns, poses, signal processing.

By Anna Sperber and Peter Kerlin
published February 10, 2009

My wife, Anna, and I have been collaborating since we met in 2002. I make music, videos, and interactive work. Anna is a choreographer. She typically begins a piece by improvising with her dancers, with a form emerging gradually, honed and distilled over several weeks. My role in our collaborations has generally been to create sound or video to augment or accompany the performance. With this project, we set out to integrate video more fully into the process.

"Between Scans" is the product of five days well spent in residency at the Experimental Television Center in Owego, New York. After years of making videos with digital tools, it was freeing to return to the physicality of analog. We used synthesis (applying varying voltage patterns to the video signal), a seven-camera array, and a primitive video switcher to create states in which the effects of the image processing and of the captured movement amplified each other, states in which the humanistic presence was graphically abstracted or fractured while, simultaneously, the geometric nature of the imagery took on an organic quality.
—*Peter Kerlin*

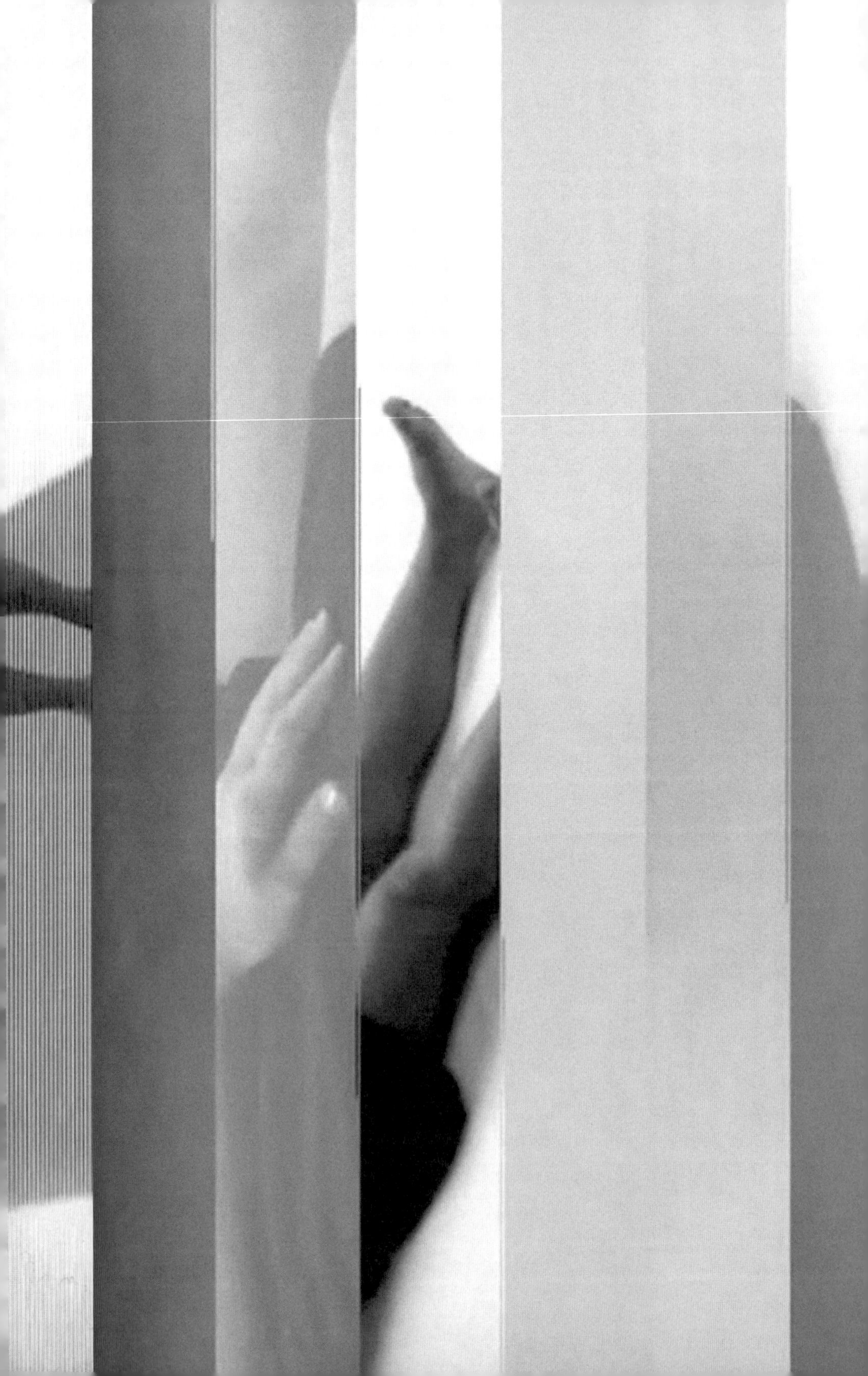

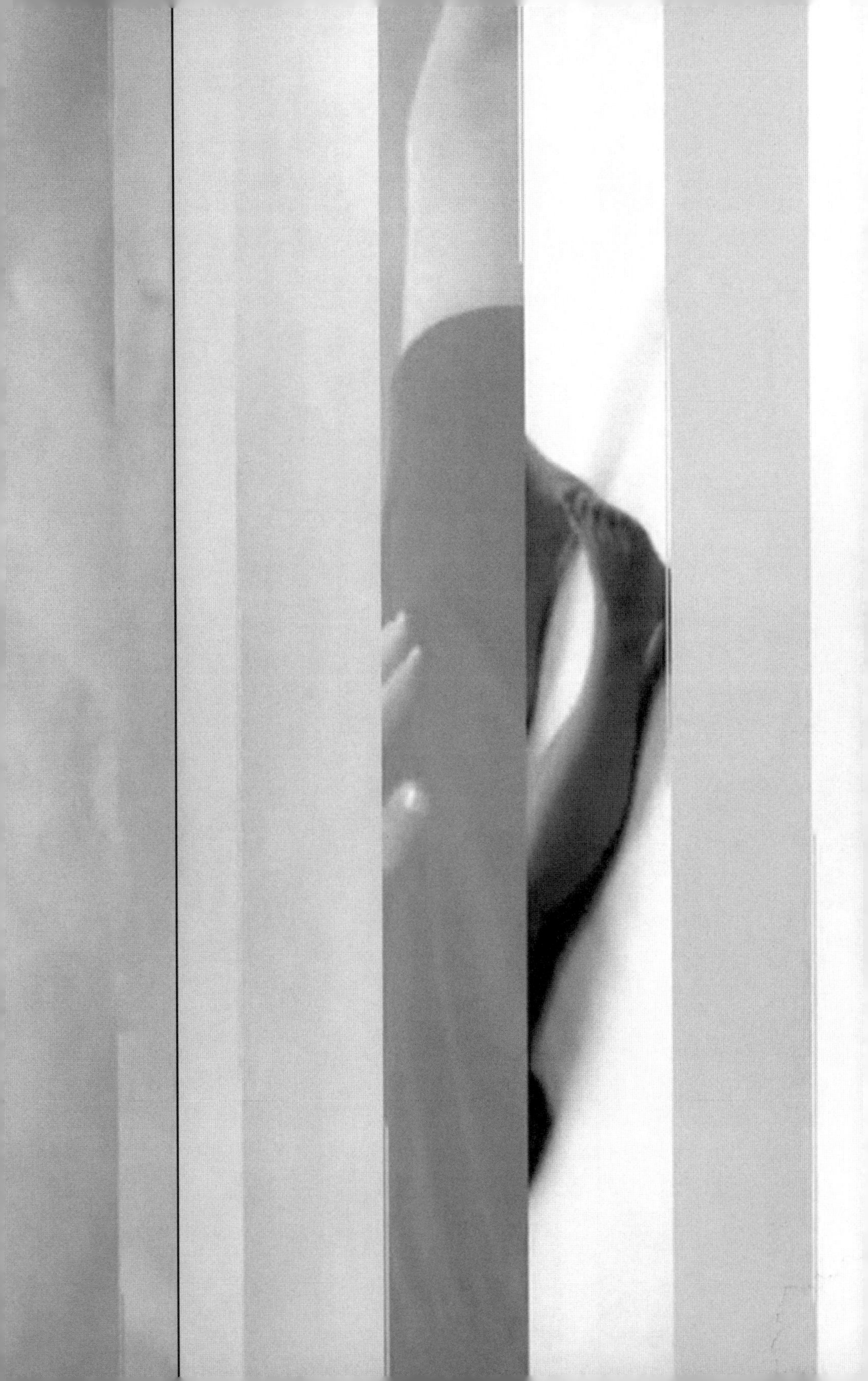

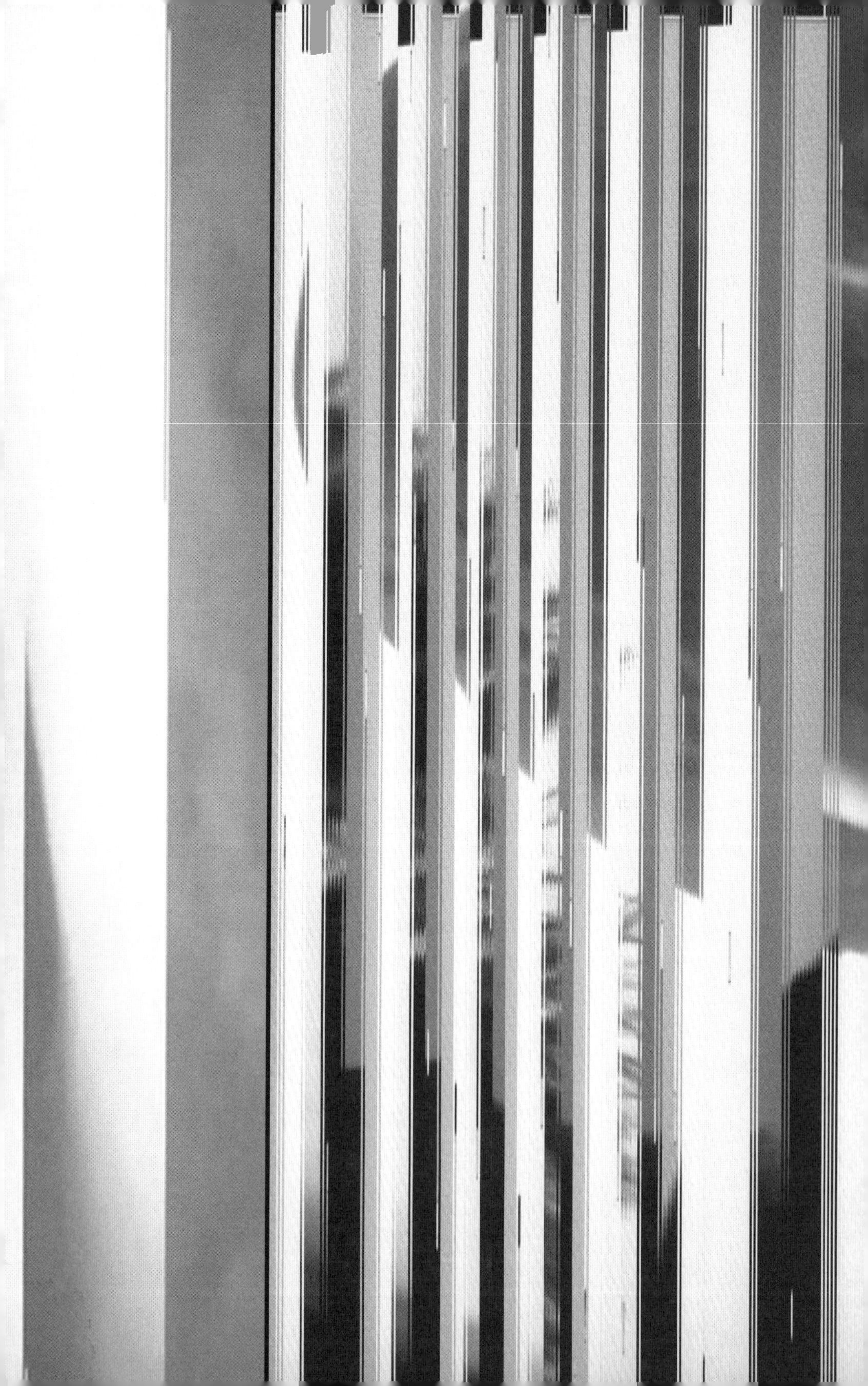

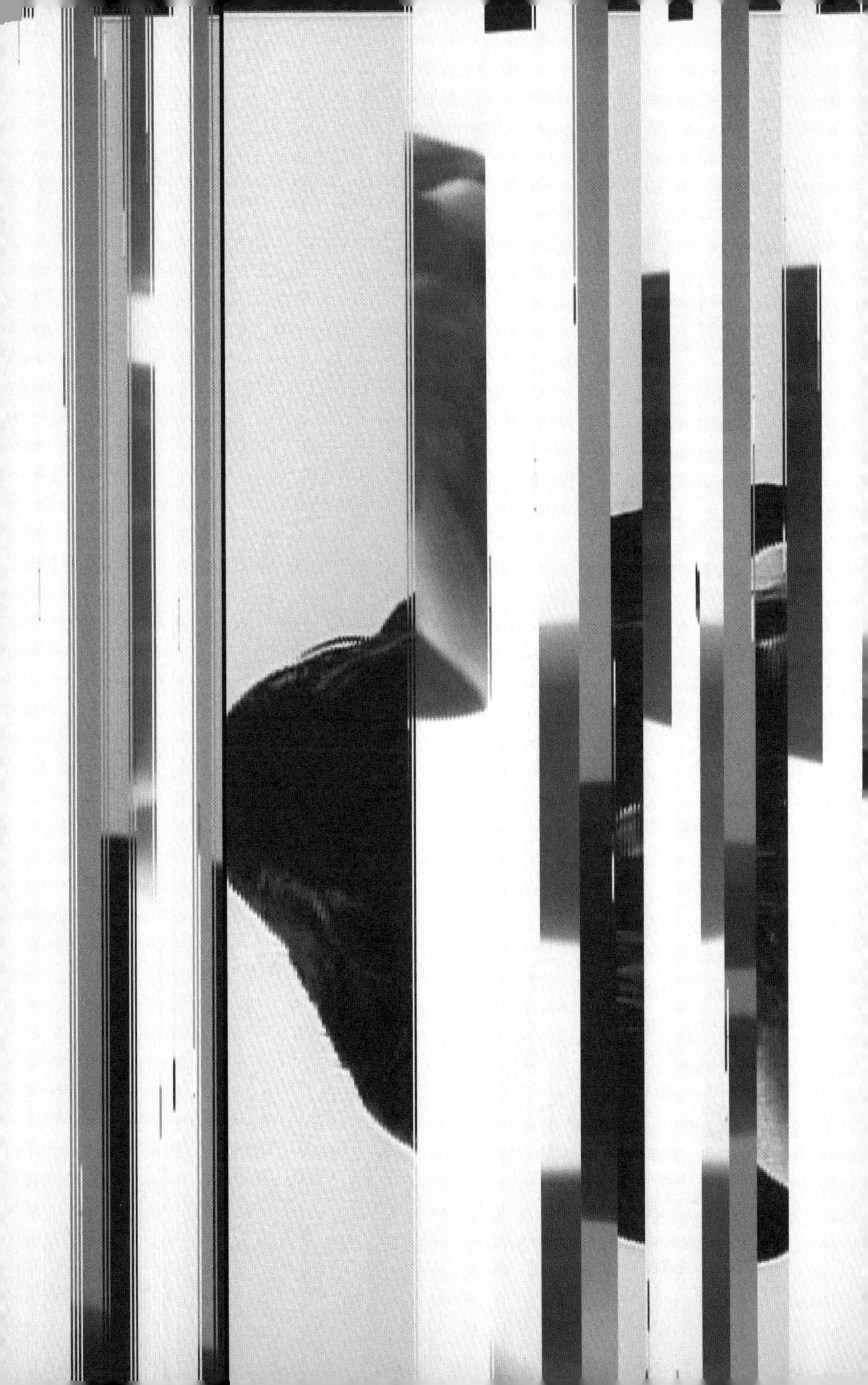

INVALID FORMAT 2 ISSUE 5 2009

HORROR FILM 1: SHANGHAI BLUE

A photographic serial approaching a cinematic genre; a deformation of one art form to infiltrate another.

by Leslie Thornton
published February 10, 2009

All kinds of snakes, centipedes and flies were living on every part of his body. Bees, wasps and uncountable mosquitoes were also flying round him and it was hard to see him plainly because of these flies and insects. But immediately this dreadful ghost came inside this house from heaven-knows-where his smell and also the smell of his body first drove us to a long distance before we came back after a few minutes, but still the smell did not let every one of the settlers stand still as all his body was full of excreta, urine, and also wet with the rotten blood of all the animals that he was killing for his food. His mouth which was always opening, his nose and eyes were very hard to look at as they were very dirty and smelling. His name is "Smelling-ghost."

This is a visceral description of a particular ghost found in Amos Tutuola's book *My Life in the Bush of Ghosts*, and it is an image of horror, partly because we can imagine it. It is not a possible being, still we can imagine it; all of the elements are familiar. Tutuola's image is fictional—not derived from our world, where true horrors occur. A worldly horror affects a different part of the brain, inducing shock, denial, and other forms of protective response. A fictional horror fascinates, attracts, cruelly absorbs us, and offers catharsis, or at least a promise of more entertaining helplessness. It relies heavily on anticipation, escape from the unknown; it offers up the misshapen—the familiar overwritten by excess and uncertainty.

I've been using photographic serials as a way to observe various cinematic genres. So far my focus has been on the horror film. I am circling around the genre, relying upon a strategy of feigned blindness, as if feeling it with my fingers or other senses to discern its shape beyond just a simple definition. I am deforming one art form, the photographic, to viscerally penetrate another, the cinematic.

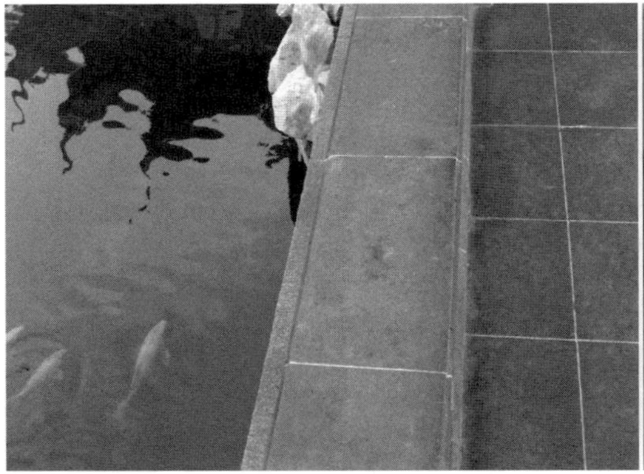

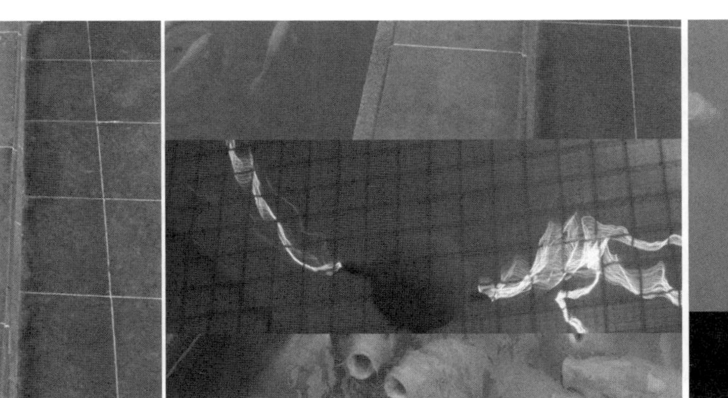

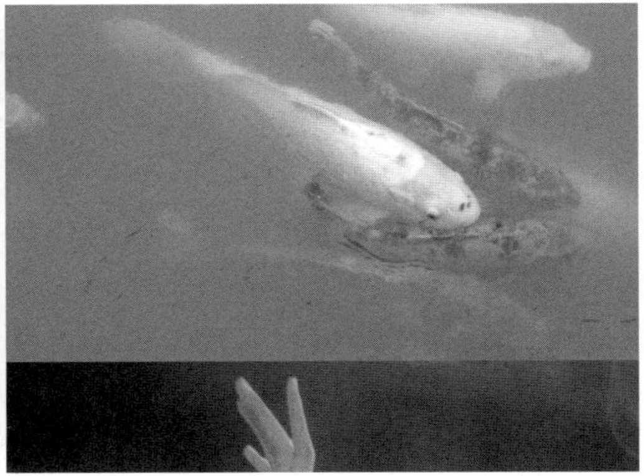

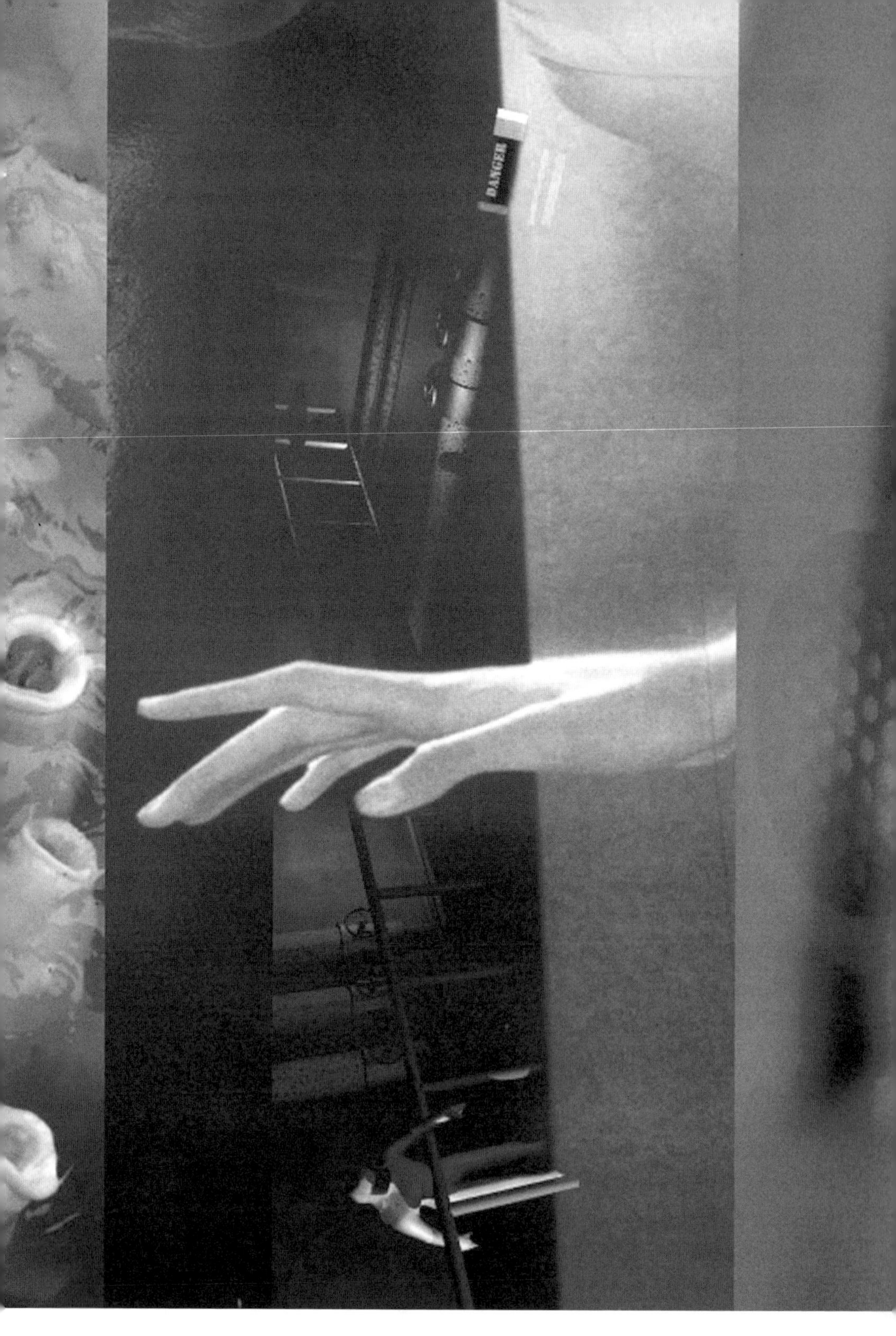
DANGER

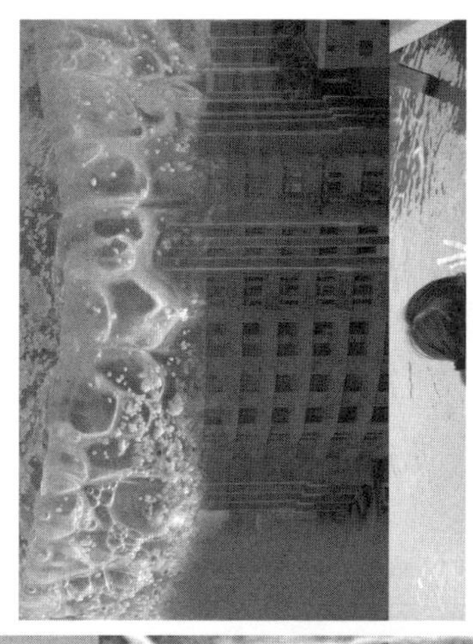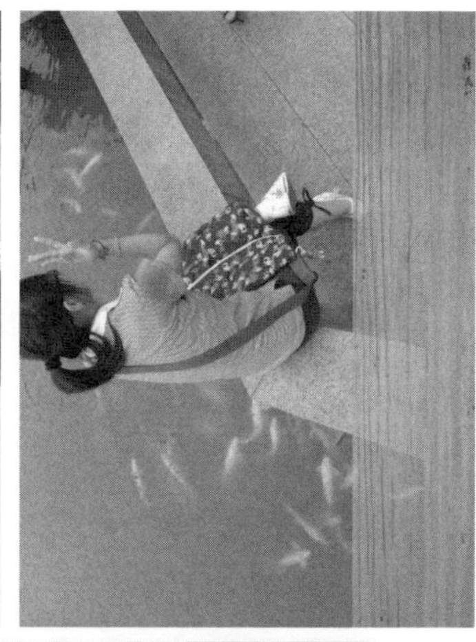

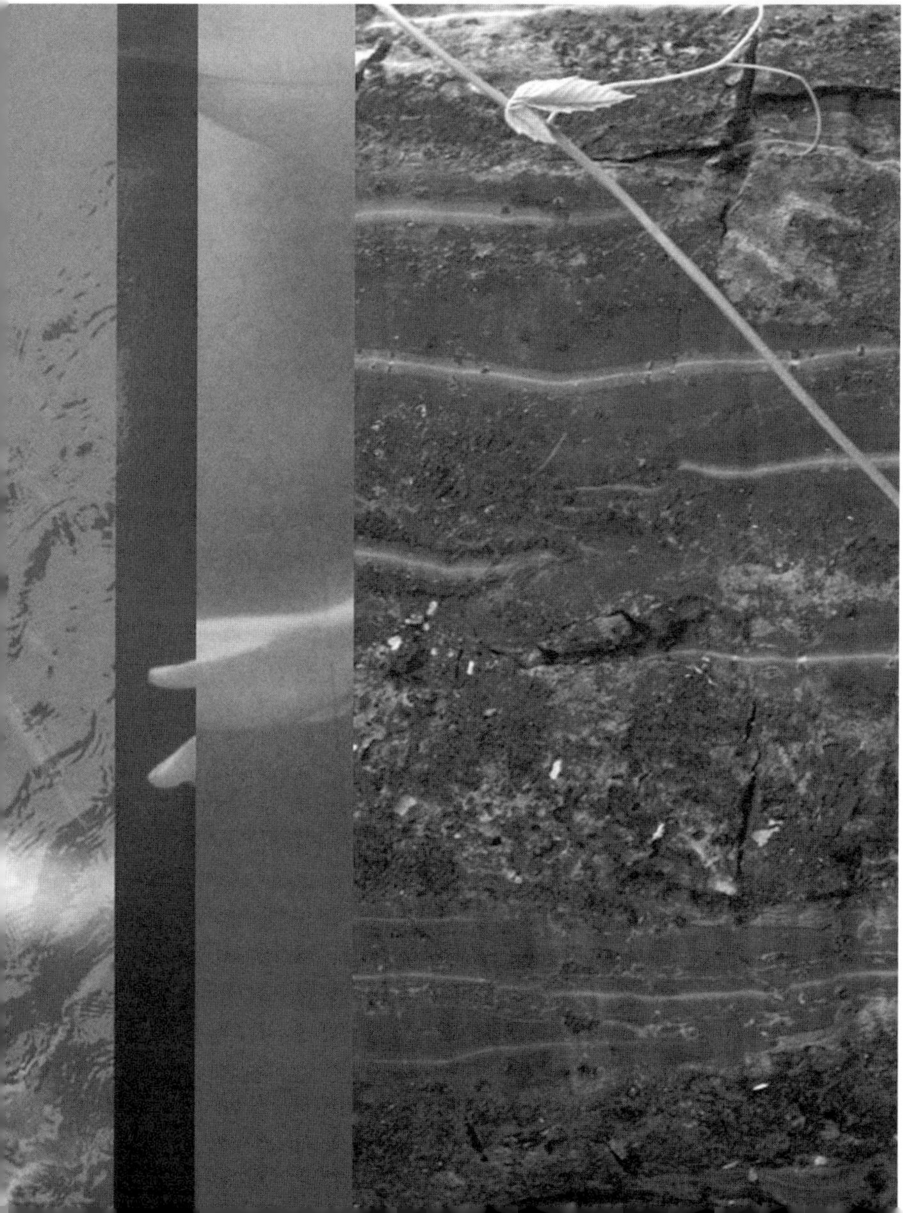

INVALID FORMAT 2

ISSUE 5 2009

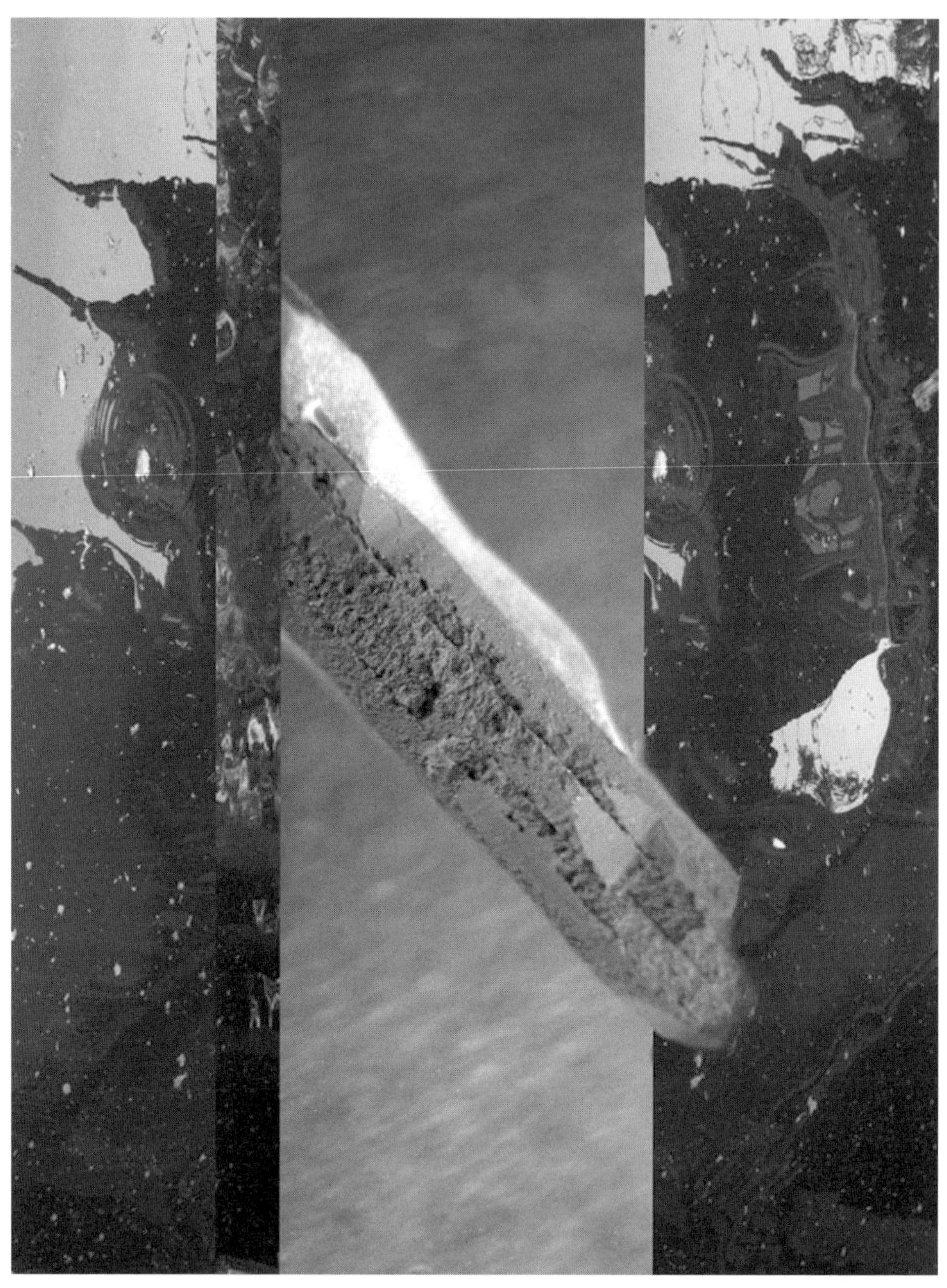

TELEVISION FOR THE PEOPLE

The fan-made world of Jeff Krulik, from public access to parking lots to proto-peer-to-peer.

by Ed Halter
published February 19, 2009

INVALID FORMAT 2

ISSUE 5 2009

HEAVY METAL RULES

In 1985, Jeff Krulik, a twenty-four-year-old station manager for a DC-area cable-access channel, met John Heyn, a young filmmaker who had worked in Baltimore as a production assistant on John Waters's film *Polyester* a few years before. Heyn contacted Krulik after reading about him in the *Washington Post*, in which he learned they both had worked on documentaries about dying local movie palaces. Bonding over a common love of exploitation films and other "weirdness and subculture," as Krulik later put it, the two soon made plans to collaborate.

Heyn had the idea to interview fans at a concert outside Maryland's Capital Centre arena. Seeing that a Judas Priest show was coming up in May '86, they decided to commandeer equipment from Krulik's television studio and give it a try. "It could have been any concert," Krulik has recalled. "We weren't metal fans. I had come from the punk, new-wave—whatever you call it—alternative-rock landscape. As did John, more or less. My favorite bands were the Cramps, the Clash, the Ramones, all that. So metal was the furthest thing from my record collection. I was never really dismissive of it. I just never patronized it or consumed it. But you didn't have to be a metalhead to know about it, since it was all around you, and bands like Judas Priest were filling arenas." Krulik and Heyn could never have known that their video would become one of the most legendary music documentaries of all time: *Heavy Metal Parking Lot*, a razor-sharp chronicle of teen headbanger folkways.

"We were worried that we would encounter some dangerous bikers doing drug deals," Krulik confessed to *Decibel* magazine years later, "but that couldn't have been further from the truth. People were falling all over themselves to be on camera." One probable reason was that the two resembled news reporters, given the bulky rig they toted: an imposing one-tube camera attached to a suitcase-size handheld U-matic recording deck—the local TV standard of the time. The two switched off interviewing and

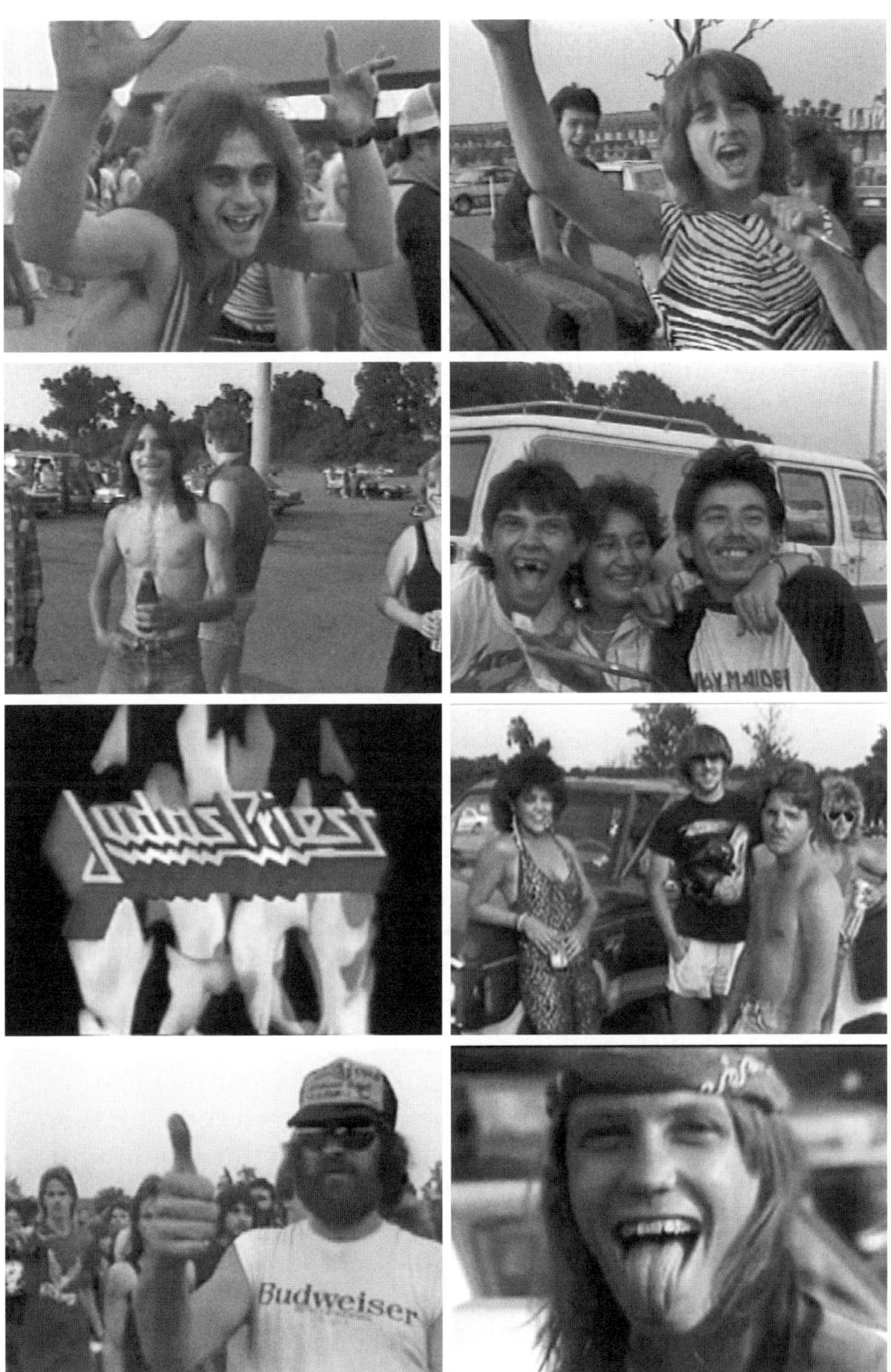

recording as they worked the parking lot. "I can't even imagine what people thought when they saw these two doofuses walking around with a three-quarter-inch camera and a separate deck and a microphone," Krulik says. "We certainly didn't look like the people in the crowd. I'm sure I was wearing a Lacoste shirt and a pair of OP shorts." The pair shot only an hour of footage on three tapes, then left without entering the concert. Heyn edited this down to a little over fifteen minutes, and Krulik gave the tape its title.

Many of the Priest fans who appear in the footage assume that Krulik and Heyn, barely a decade older than most of them, are professionals, shooting for television or the band itself. Looking into the camera, the metalheads tell viewers not to drink and drive, blurt out messages to band members Rob Halford and Glen Tipton, or simply wave and shout. But not everyone is so welcoming. "I was trying to explain what public access was. It was Channel 6A," Krulik remembers. "Nobody got it." At one point, an off-screen Krulik gives up explaining and simply claims to be from MTV, to which a fan replies, "Bull. Shit."

Since making *Heavy Metal Parking Lot*, Krulik has produced scores of documentaries, though only a few have been shown widely. While he's worked in television most of his life, the films he's made on his own have never been broadcast in that medium. His work is screened at galleries, festivals, and museums worldwide, but he's rarely described as an artist. Today an unassuming guy in his forties who could pass for a suburban dad, he's drawn to chronicling the fringes of entertainment, from rock demimondes to corny showbiz characters—accordion players and porn-industry conventioneers, record collectors and fading TV stars—with an incisive eye for the details of personality, equalizing the extremes he traverses with a notable lack of pretension. His work is sometimes pegged as comedy, yet it contains melancholic undertones. He claims he doesn't practice typical documentary gravitas, that he "doesn't do the serious stuff," yet one of his longest films deals with World War II and the Holocaust.

Despite this considerable body of work, Krulik's most famous effort remains *Heavy Metal Parking Lot*. The circuitous process through which this tape gained its renown was hardly one he could have predicted, much less controlled.

THE BOOTLEG NETWORK

Soon after *Heavy Metal Parking Lot* was finished, Krulik realized the video would never fly on Channel 6A: The swearing, drinking, and drugging by local teenagers wouldn't have been tolerated by the management, and he wanted to keep his job. So he and Heyn found other ways to share it. The first public screening, in October 1986, was at DC Space, an art gallery known for hosting local bands. Later, Krulik got a part-time job selling used vinyl, and he screened the video at a record convention in Silver Spring, Maryland. Then it became a staple of what Krulik calls his "living-room festivals": gatherings of friends watching the best—that is, the worst—clips culled from Channel 6A. He also gave copies to local record shops, which played it on monitors generally reserved for music videos and concert films.

Although there weren't many public venues for a short video documentary at the time, *Heavy Metal Parking Lot* had a theatrical premiere in 1988, when it was shown before the *Hail! Hail! Rock 'n' Roll* Chuck Berry documentary at DC's American Film Institute at the Kennedy Center. (Exhibiting videotapes in a movie theater was then uncommon, but the AFI was an early adopter of video projection.) In 1990, again at the AFI, Krulik programmed a one-shot series called the "Don't Quit Your Day Job Film & Video Festival," which screened works by himself, Heyn, and other locals, as well as bits of video ephemera. By that time, Krulik's career in community TV was over, and he had moved on to producing segments for commercial cable networks. He assumed "Don't Quit Your Day Job" would be *Heavy Metal Parking Lot*'s curtain call.

But the video took on a life of its own. Not long after completing the tape, Krulik and Heyn had begun handing out VHS copies to friends, colleagues, and anyone else who wanted one. "We gave it out like water," Krulik says. "We didn't sell it. We had totally appropriated Judas Priest music, hadn't gotten any releases. It was a totally underground thing. We didn't really have a plan." The tapes were copied, circulated, and copied again. Without either filmmaker's knowledge, *Heavy Metal Parking Lot* was replicating.

Passing around homemade videotapes at the time wasn't so unusual. The '80s and '90s were a golden age of bootlegging via audio and video cassette. The items circulated among friends would be familiar to YouTubers and BitTorrenters today: feature films and major-label albums, to be sure, but also a vast clutter of miscellany like celebrity porn clips, concert bootlegs, films transferred from 16-mm or 35-mm prints that had never received a proper video release, blooper reels, and unclassifiable footage that was funny or strange or both, often just tacked on at the end of a tape for laughs. Some of these clips became notorious in their own right. A mix tape might have included pilfered audio of Casey Kasem's verbally abusive in-studio tantrum from an *American Top 40* outtake; a VHS dub might have ended with a *Metallica Drummer* coda, from a home video of a Canadian slacker's consummate air drumming to selections from the band's self-titled 1991 album.

Today, we might think of this pre-digital phenomenon as a long, slow file-sharing system, a free-for-all black market in which audio and video ephemera traveled hand-to-hand and deck-to-deck rather than peer-to-peer. Tapes meandered through an analog Internet, one composed of clunkier technologies. The further a tape traveled, the more times it was dubbed, becoming fuzzier with each iteration. Connoisseurs boasted of having second- or third-generation copies of rarities like Todd Haynes's banned Carpenters biopic, *Superstar*, and Prince's long-unreleased *The Black Album*, reveling in their relative clarity.

Heavy Metal Parking Lot went viral through this network, and we may even have the identity of its Patient

Zero: one Mike Heath, a fixture on the DC-area rock scene whom Krulik calls "the Johnny Appleseed of *Heavy Metal Parking Lot*." Part of the evidence is a Christmas card with the following inscription, which accompanied a bootleg tape that found its way back to Krulik:

> Already an underground classic, one copy of this was given to me by Mike Heath, formerly of Washington, DC. It went on tour with Redd Kross, whose roadie Mike Dalke took it on tour with Nirvana. Redd Kross gave it to Evan Dando (Lemonheads) and it spread like wildfire. This is a second generation copy, and distributed in an edition of 10 for Christmas 1994, from Bill Bartell to my friends. Feel free to copy and spread the genius, as the filmmakers encourage this.

Of course, the anonymous holiday-card author couldn't have had any real indication that Krulik or Heyn encouraged the bootlegging, though it's likely this was part of the mythology developed by tape traders. Pat Fear, of the Los Angeles punk band White Flag, got a copy from Heath, and later told Heyn that Heath claimed "it was OK with you guys to make copies and distribute it as long as I wasn't selling it."

Fear gave a dub to Redd Kross, which got it to Dalke, Dave Grohl's roadie, who played it on Nirvana's bus during the 1993 *In Utero* tour. "That tour had different opening acts every few days, so a lot of opening acts picked it up," Fear told Heyn. "I was on the road with that tour while the Melvins were opening, and I walked into the Breeders' dressing room and Kim and Kelly [Deal] were doing lines from the movie. I was stunned, as I had no idea it was getting around to that degree." Traveling across the country's bootleg network, *Heavy Metal Parking Lot* had instigated a reversal of the fan-musician dynamic. When fans weren't watching them perform, indie-rock musicians got their kicks by watching fans perform for them.

Fear also gave copies as Christmas gifts to members

of Sonic Youth and other bands, even making his own box art with photos of three of *Heavy Metal Parking Lot*'s wasted youths, by then microcelebrities in their own right: the jumpsuited, shaggy-haired "Zebra Man"; the skinny fellow named "Graham, man, like 'gram of dope'"; and the hair-sprayed, redheaded girl who declares she wants to jump Rob Halford's bones. Fear wasn't the only fan to make unofficial box art for the tape: Another anonymous sleeve featured cartoon caricatures of Graham and two of his cohorts.

While rock gossip has preserved an oral record of the tape's most famous viewers, they're best understood

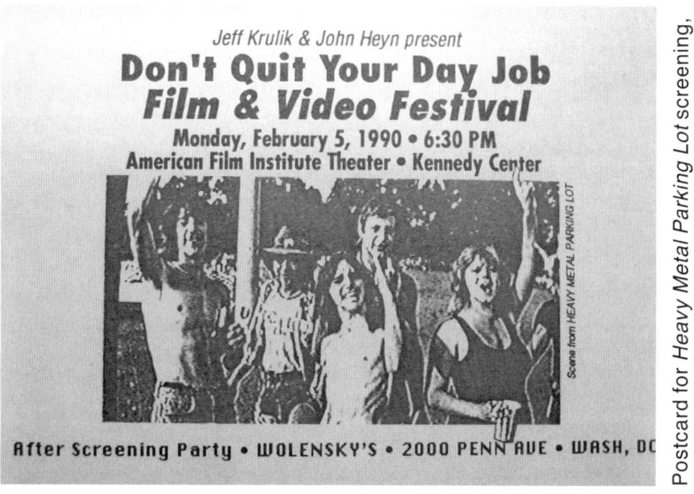

Postcard for *Heavy Metal Parking Lot* screening, 1990. Courtesy of Jeff Krulik.

as symptomatic of a larger phenomenon. For every Grohl or Dando who acquired a copy, an unknowable number of unremembered cultists passed it on as well. Heyn even once found a personal ad in the back of an undated alt-weekly in which a girl declares, "I hate heavy metal music, but I love *Heavy Metal Parking Lot.*"

Heyn and Krulik had no idea *Heavy Metal Parking Lot* had exploded until 1994, when Heyn received a call from Sofia Coppola, who had found his name in the DC phone book. Coppola, best known at the time for her role in *The Godfather: Part III*, was a fan: She had rented a bootleg VHS from Mondo Video in Los Angeles and given dubs of it to her boyfriend, Spike Jonze, and her cousin Nicholas Cage.

Coppola was producing a pilot for the short-lived Comedy Central series *High Octane*—a kind of Gen-X video-magazine show—and called Heyn to inquire about licensing *Heavy Metal Parking Lot* for broadcast. Though Coppola's show didn't last long enough to air the tape, Krulik and Heyn became inspired by their underground notoriety. They reunited in 1996 to shoot *Neil Diamond Parking Lot*: the same parking lot, ten years later, this time filled with middle-aged suburban moms chugging Diet Coke in their station wagons and humming "Sweet Caroline." In 1997, Krulik packaged a new version of "Don't Quit Your Day Job" around the two Parking Lot videos. He premiered them for the first time outside the DC area at the New York Underground Film Festival, then toured the program at numerous festivals and film venues over the following year.

Since then, *Heavy Metal Parking Lot* has reemerged every few years: a program at the Museum of Modern Art in New York for its fifteenth anniversary in 2001; a 35-mm blow-up to accompany the theatrical release of Chris Smith's documentary *Home Movie* in 2003; a *Parking Lot* reality show produced by Krulik and Heyn on the defunct Trio network from 2004 to 2006; interviews and ironic fashion shoots with the directors in *GQ* and *Visionaire*; and a legit DVD release in 2005, complete with a "Dub-O-Vision" version made from a tenth-generation VHS. The tape has also spawned numerous imitations and tributes, among them *Heavy Metal Sidewalk*, *Girl Power Parking Lot*, and *Raver Bathroom*.

In the first years of *Heavy Metal Parking Lot*'s existence, viewers may have been drawn primarily to the simple joys of laughing at shit-faced teens, but time has transformed the video from a mere stoner sideshow into a remarkably dense archive of a particular and increasingly distant moment—a pirate transmission from the past, reminding us how life was once lived otherwise. The video's broad comedy remains an essential part of the viewing experience, but now we're likely to appreciate finer details as well. The armed guard poised on top of the Capital Centre's roof; the haughty intonation with which one girl declares her preference for Dokken, subtly distancing herself from her peers; the oddly fey lilt to one hairy headbanger's dismissal of Rob Halford; the bleary-eyed hillbilly actually drinking from a mason jar; the girl's hand in a white lace glove, jutting in from the side of the frame, silently shooting us the finger. Anthropologists should savor the sheer number of hairstyles and fashions preserved from the summer of 1986—they couldn't wish for a richer ethnographic record.

Yet *Heavy Metal Parking Lot* isn't merely nostalgic admiration of an extinct hessian menagerie. Krulik and Heyn's interactions with each group of fans offer evocative fragments of whole lives, captured on the pivot of youth. We meet Dave, who's two weeks from shipping off to the air force, and then a gang of friends who've come to memorialize Timmy, a fellow fan who died in a car accident. Each interview is pregnant with a larger story: There are many worlds within the world of this parking lot, hundreds of young lives intersecting in a single ecstatic moment, then fanning off onto multitudinous pathways. Viewers of a certain age may recognize doppelgängers of themselves or of people they knew. No wonder Krulik once remarked, "Trying to dissect this film twenty years later is like dissecting the Talmud."

PUBLIC ACCESS GIBBERISH

Metal fandom isn't the only lost culture that *Heavy Metal Parking Lot* preserves. More obliquely, it stands as evidence from an earlier era of cable television, a milieu documented head-on in Krulik's compilation tape *Public Access Gibberish*. Edited in 1990, *Public Access Gibberish* is one of Krulik's earliest solo tapes. It was made for his first "Don't Quit Your Day Job" show at the AFI and compiled the video detritus he had culled for his living-room festivals in the late 1980s. Krulik worked for public access for only a few years, from 1983 to 1989, but the experience was crucial in

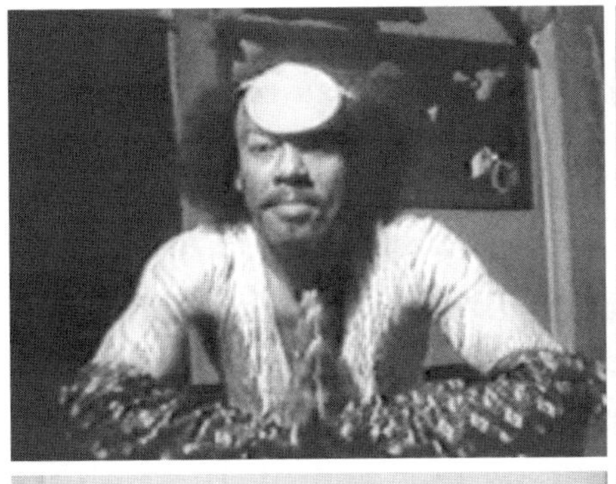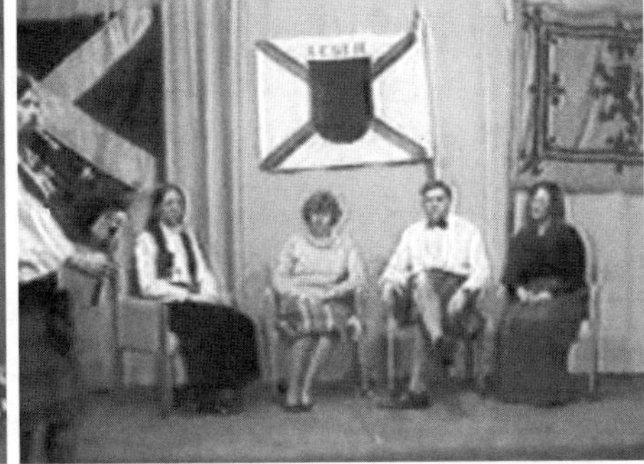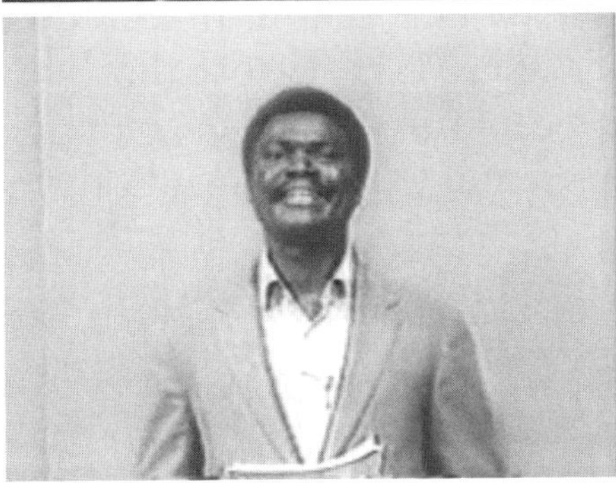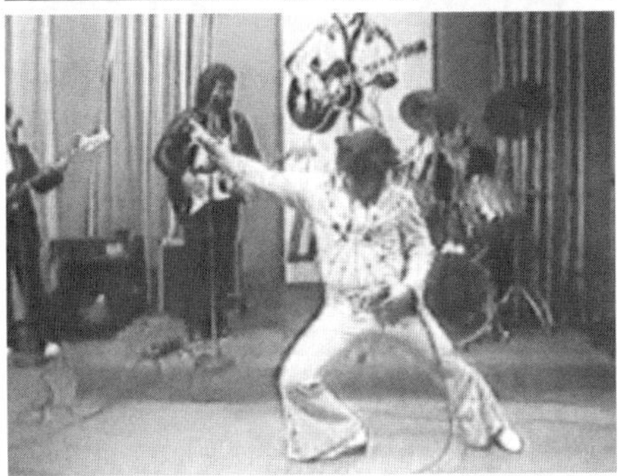

forming the aesthetic of *Heavy Metal Parking Lot* and the documentary work that followed.

Public access television in the United States has its origins in the 1960s. The earliest for-profit cable networks provided citizen-run airtime in exchange for use of the municipal roads and lands needed to run their cable lines. Along with public television, pirate stations, and art galleries, community-access channels provided a platform for the first wave of video activists. These artists' collectives formed in the late 1960s after the introduction of the Sony Portapak, the first truly portable video-recording system (and the direct ancestor of Heyn and Krulik's U-matic rig).

Early video artists' hopes for cable access were utopian—if corporate media was numbing America's consciousness, then citizen-run media would rouse it. "The basic business of cable is the cultivation of local culture," wrote Paul Ryan, a member of early video collective Raindance, in the journal *Radical Software* in 1970. "This does not mean stenciling national network type programming on a local setting. . . . The role of a cable system is

INVALID FORMAT

2

ISSUE

5

2009

to increase the community's awareness of their existing cultural system, thereby giving them more control over its development: to cultivate the local culture . . . cable can enlarge the capacity of the local culture to communicate about and control its development."

Ken Marsh, founder of the People's Video Theater, left New York City for upstate New York in the early '70s, where he brokered a deal with a local cable company to found Woodstock Community Television. In a pamphlet extolling the benefits of WCT, Marsh wrote that "community programming is a tool for vitalizing communications . . . in a time of complex and varying social values and problems."

Similar aspirations for community television can be found in other pockets of New Left discourse, especially among those inspired by techno-prophets like Marshall McLuhan and Buckminster Fuller. Abbie Hoffman's 1971 counterculture guide, *Steal This Book*, contains a section on producing and disseminating "guerrilla television." Raindance's Michael Shamberg produced manifestos on the dismantling of "Media-America." New, alternative forms of television would do much more than entertain: Advocates hoped they would transform the fundamental political structure of America, both democratizing technology and technologizing democracy.

Throughout the 1970s, only a segment of cable companies provided local access. In 1984, after Congress passed the Cable Franchise Policy and Communications Act—the bill requiring commercial cable companies to set aside a portion of their revenues for community use—community television spread to even the smallest towns. But granting widespread access to everyday people never caused the upheavals in political consciousness that Nixon-era activists dreamed it would, and when Krulik began working in cable during this era, he found the world of community TV far from heroic.

Right out of college in 1983, Krulik got a job selling cable TV door-to-door, which led to his appointment a year later as the director of the new public access studio in Prince George's County, Maryland, a suburb of DC. The community-television world he entered hardly threatened to overturn Maryland society. Krulik found himself overseeing Boy Scout celebrations, Sunday sermons, and PTA meetings. "Public access was a white elephant, a bribe to the counties to get cable franchises," Krulik later explained. "The studios were only one of the incentives, but the counties didn't care about production or having a studio for church services or community blowhards. That's why they'd even consider putting a twenty-five-year-old in charge. I was basically a community babysitter."

Whether or not community access served progressive political goals in other parts of the country, it certainly didn't aspire to much in Prince George's County. There, community access did indeed become a cultivator of local culture—as visionaries like Marsh had hoped—but largely of a banal variety. Yet Krulik found that even in this wasteland there were nuggets of excitement: shoddy magicians, outré Elvis impersonators, amateur hypnotists, hopeless Broadway wannabes, and living-room freak funkers. He hoarded tapes of the stuff, encouraging the most offbeat personalities to use his studio. A tape trader himself, he exchanged dubs with a handful of like-minded people across the country.

Despite his cynicism about the actual community value of cable access, Krulik did see it as a curatorial opportunity: "Working at a public-access station was great in this respect," he has said. "It was free, and it was immediate. It wasn't television by any conventional parameters; it was freewheeling, free-form, anything-goes. It was a lot like college radio at the time. There was a distinct parallel between the two, and I really embraced it." According to Krulik, his community-television captivity served as an incubator and an education. "I was always interested in filmmaking, but I had never taken filmmaking classes or even picked up a camera," he's said. "Public access was my production school. It's where I developed an eye behind the camera and really took to it."

But unlike college radio at the time, Krulik's cable-access scene didn't quite express resistance to mainstream entertainment. The fringe that Krulik gravitated toward as a station manager, and later showcased in *Public Access Gibberish*, wasn't about the subversion of mass media but rather the desire to become part of it. Public access became a low-rent fame-vending machine, pairing the logic of karaoke and the psychology of the talent show, the same impulses later commercialized by reality television. It gave rise to video-maker versions of the garage band, determined to burn off the boredom of the suburbs with momentary paroxysms of celebrity playacting. In this sense, form and content align: In the conclusion of *Public Access Gibberish*, when the local cable editor transitions through shots of the Elvis impersonator via an ostentatious series of analog wipes, it is clear that both the impersonator and the editor are aping the big-budget pizzazz of MTV with meager means. People didn't want to destroy mass media, they wanted to expand its reach so far as to include the masses themselves.

STILL OBSESSED

By the 1990s, Krulik's public access days were over, and he had moved on to freelance jobs producing segments for Discovery Channel and researching material for Errol Morris. Meanwhile, he embarked on a solo career as a filmmaker, making over forty documentaries ranging in length from seconds to nearly an hour. Though his work grows out of television, it shows mainly at noncommercial spaces, where he can get away with not clearing music rights or having signed releases from his subjects. In 1998, he launched Planet Krulik, a website that streamed all of his work to date for free—a cutting-edge notion at the time. More recently, he's shut down that site temporarily and begun posting odds and ends to his own YouTube channel.

According to Krulik, his primary inspirations as a director have been movies like Penelope Spheeris's *The Decline of Western Civilization*, which documents the early

Los Angeles punk scene, and the work of Chuck Statler, who made offbeat films for Devo to play along with on their tours and, fatefully, at DC's Hirshhorn Museum in 1979, when Krulik was a high school senior. But he also cites San Francisco comedian Mal Sharpe, who, with Jim Coyle, created a series of *Candid Camera*–style man-on-the-street segments for television and radio in the early '60s and a Sunday-morning DC talk show called *Capitol Edition*, which he describes as a "real local, folksy series of profiles of interesting people around Washington."

"Interesting people around Washington" could serve as a drastic understatement of Krulik's own overarching project. For his videos, he seeks out characters who pepper the seemingly unremarkable DC area, particularly its white Maryland suburbs. In *King of Porn* (1996), he profiles Ralph Whittington, an otherwise straitlaced archivist at the Library of Congress who's built a massive home collection of hard-core pornography and is eager to walk Krulik through its idiosyncratic organization: VHS boxes mixed in with his breakfast cereal in the pantry, his compulsion to collect outstripping his professional penchant for organization.

In *Obsessed with Jews* (2000), Krulik visits Neil Keller, an energetic accountant with a slight lisp who hoards trading cards depicting Jewish athletes, Jewish movie stars, and really, as Keller puts it, "anyone who's Jewish." In *First Edition Barbara* (2000), Krulik hangs out with an awkward middle-aged woman who sits right up front at any DC-area book signing—no matter the author, no matter the book—and later reveals a squealing passion for Beanie Babies. The personality parade of *Public Access Gibberish* marches on, but now Krulik seeks them out rather than waiting for them to come to him.

In other works, Krulik delves into the entertainment industry proper, albeit without the typical fawning or snark. For *Ernest Borgnine on the Bus* (1997), made with fellow television producer Brendan Conway, Krulik travels with the senior citizen movie star, who enjoys driving

INVALID FORMAT 2

ISSUE 5 2009

around the country like any other retiree—but instead of an RV, Borgnine rides in his own souped-up tour bus. In *Three Hour Tour* (2000), Krulik and Conway chronicle a charity boat ride with the aged survivors of *Gilligan's Island*, seemingly still stranded in the unglamorous trappings of B-level fame. Perhaps the finest of Krulik's behind-the-scenes work is *I Created Lancelot Link* (1999), made with producer Diane Bernard, which visits the elderly creators of the early '70s kids' series *Lancelot Link, Secret Chimp*—a *Get Smart*–style spy spoof set in a world populated by chimpanzees, with elaborate chimp-size sets, props, and costumes. Creators Mike Marmer and Stan Burns reveal themselves to be Krulik's kindred spirits, two guys who got away with something zany on the airwaves while management wasn't looking. (They relate that a network executive did visit the set once, but left quickly, never to return, after a male chimp bit him.)

Despite his focus on peculiar individuals, Krulik rarely comes off as exploitative. *Heavy Metal Parking Lot* and *Public Access Gibberish* might contain trace elements of freak gawking—an arguable tinge of disdain blended into their fascination—but most of the later works are unambiguously sympathetic. When we laugh, it's complicated: These are charming weirdos who sometimes remind us of ourselves, and there's often an undertone of pathos. One wonders what drives their compulsion to collect, and what happens off camera when the slight high of minor celebrity fades. Though Krulik's work possesses the engaging pace of television, he edits just a bit off the beat, letting shots linger slightly on his subjects after they've spoken, allowing for glimpses of an unguarded self: a rehearsed joke followed by a smile's retreat.

This bittersweetness is most fully on view in *Harry Potter Parking Lot* (2000), one of Krulik's Parking Lot spin-offs, in which he interviews geeky children awaiting an appearance by J. K. Rowling at a DC-area bookstore. But these nervy, introverted youngsters are little like the carefree metalheads of 1986. One girl tells Krulik frowny

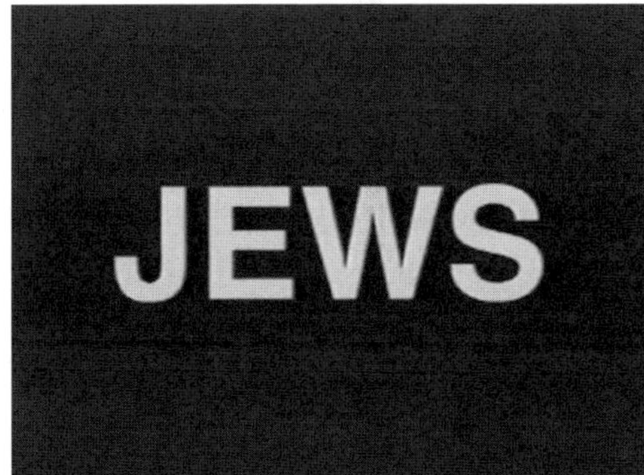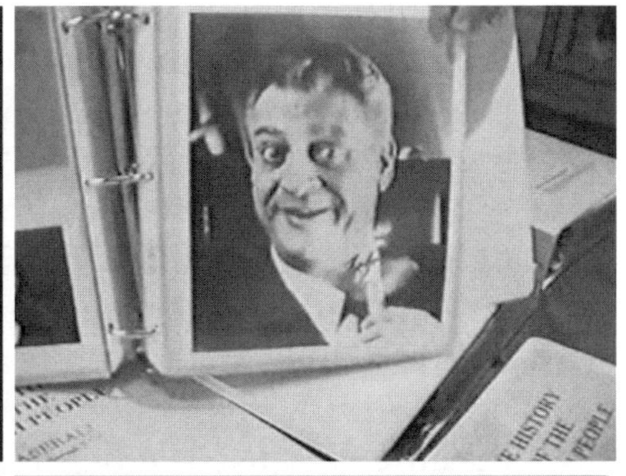
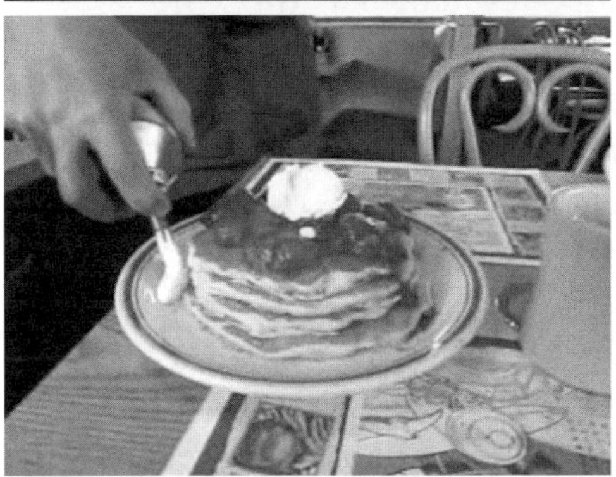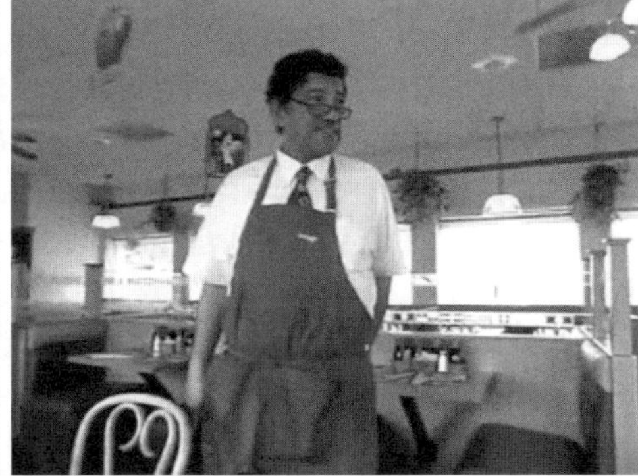
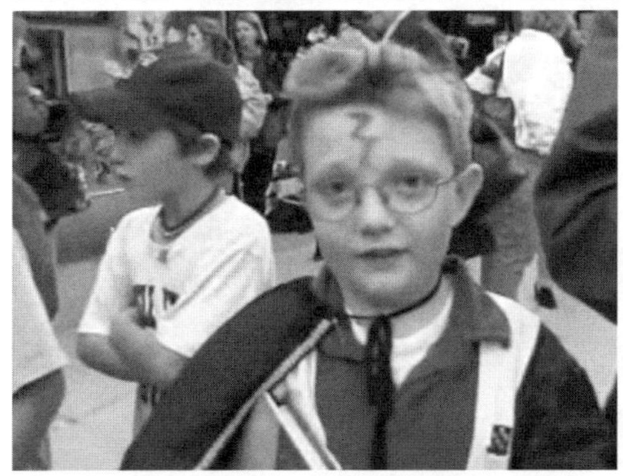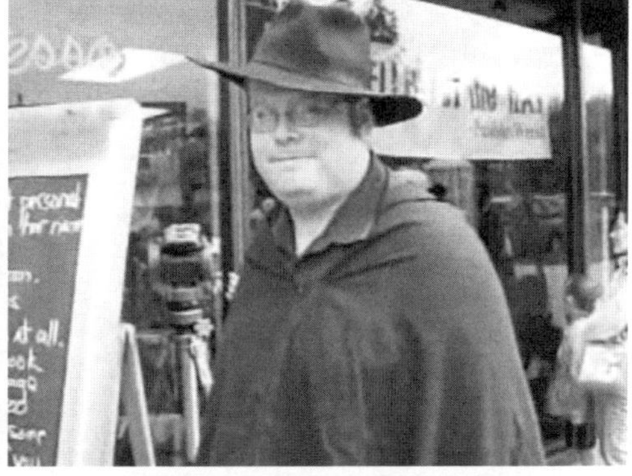
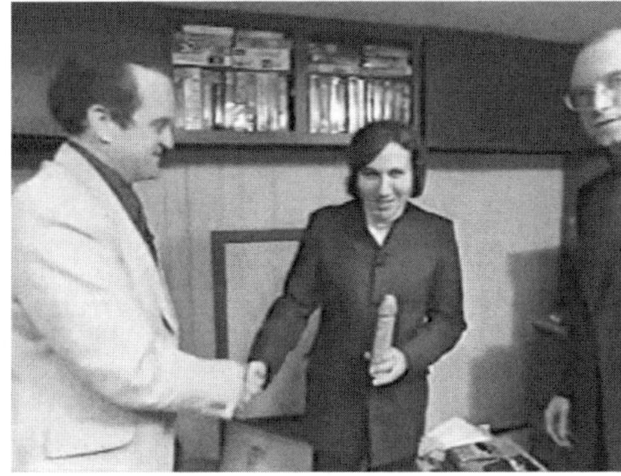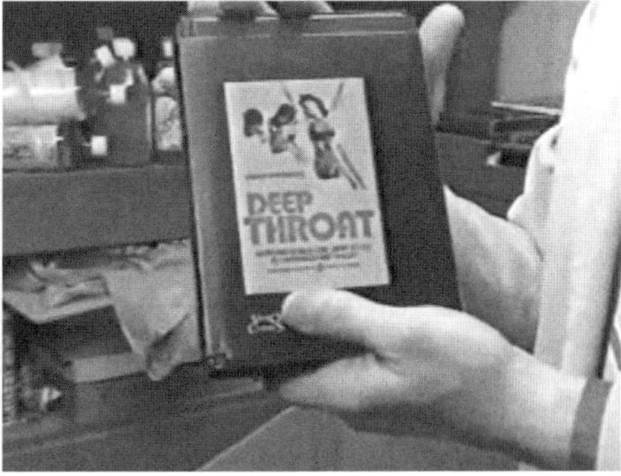

tales of her lonely camp summers, another kid anxiously attempts to show off the Harry Potter passage he's memorized (again a form of compulsive collecting), and an empty-eyed boy offers that "everyone has magic inside of them, in every little way"—an unsettlingly hollow echo of kid-vid platitudes. When Rowling appears, the children are shuttled past her with the cold efficiency of an industrial assembly line.

Krulik's work doesn't condescend to its subjects because he's just as much a fan or collector as those he pursues, a group he has taken to calling "Jeff's People" in the titles of his screenings. (Another common tagline is "The Obsessed World of Jeff Krulik.") Krulik provides a platform for his characters' desires, and his documentaries feel like collaborations, bereft of the gotchas we've

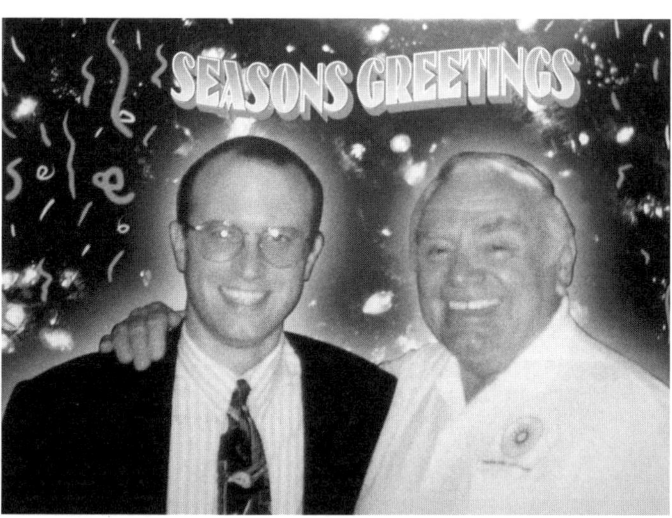

Postcard of Jeff Krulik with Ernest Borgnine, 1994. Courtesy of Jeff Krulik.

come to expect from the likes of Borat or *The Daily Show*. His people love the camera and are eager to entertain—Whittington and Keller could go on for hours. This egalitarian sensibility reaches an apogee with *Pancake* (2000), in which an IHOP waitress grabs Krulik's camera from him, then takes it on a tour of the kitchen while commenting on her coworkers, until she inadvertently shuts it off.

Occasionally, Krulik himself makes an appearance, always self-deprecating, as if teetering on the edge of failure: as the studio manager in *Public Access Gibberish*, hiding his face in shame; as an exasperated producer in *King of Porn*, collapsed on Whittington's bed after a marathon smut tour; as a seemingly lone cameraman in *Harry Potter Parking Lot*, failing to impress an all-too-media-savvy ten-year-old who wants to know where this video is going to show—the joke being, of course, that what Krulik does is something less than "real" television. One of Krulik's favorite directorial pretenses is to appear as if he doesn't know what he's doing, and his stylistic hallmark is an erratically wandering camera, easily distracted by some detail just outside its view, that suddenly veers to reveal a visual punch line: a chubby, caped Harry Potter–fan kid with lightning-bolt face paint.

The closest Krulik has come to creating a feature-length documentary is the forty-six-minute *Hitler's Hat* (2003). Though more conventional than his other work—it's the only piece with doc-standard talking heads and historical footage—it furthers his obsessions in less obvious ways. Venturing beyond his usual subject matter, he interviews surviving members of a World War II platoon who helped liberate a death camp at the end of the war, then raided one of Hitler's apartments, finding the führer's ceremonial top hat in a closet. Krulik allows each veteran to tell his own version of the story, keeping inconsistencies and gaps intact rather than forcing the accounts into false coherence. But they all remember one soldier impulsively stomping on Hitler's hat upon finding it, and the cathartic laughter that ensued. Here the celebrity brought down to earth is Hitler himself, reduced from world-threatening demon to an old top hat.

One could cite precedents and parallels for aspects of Krulik's work: Spheeris's rock ethnographies, the outsider theatrics of the Maysles brothers' *Grey Gardens*, the lost souls of Werner Herzog's documentaries, the small-town strangeness of Trent Harris's *The Beaver Trilogy*, the autobiographical eccentricities of George Kuchar's later videos, or the character-collecting impulse behind

Andy Warhol and John Waters. But Krulik's cable-access past may be the key to understanding the roots of his uniquely crafted, person-to-person aesthetic. It taught him to savor those special types who gravitate toward the camera in pursuit of their own rough-hewn self-realization. Once his cable-access wellspring ran dry, he began collecting these characters from the world beyond the studio.

Community TV as a format still exists, but it's long been overshadowed by the Internet; the rise of online video-sharing systems has democratized television far more than cable ever could. Notably, Krulik himself hasn't yet achieved a large following from his YouTube channel. Perhaps the attention-grabbing, instant-gratification quality of today's quick-spreading memes drowns out his more humanist comedy (or maybe he's just getting started). A TV-trained man who never picked up a film camera, Krulik has, ironically, had more success in theaters. His videos play best to live audiences, not solo webcrawlers.

Krulik may be public access's only true success story. He perceived the weird essence of the medium, then moved beyond it. Emerging from that 1980s no-zone, he has been able to create his own brand of television art: documentaries in the service of a unique screwball populism. Before community TV became outstripped by newer technologies, it gave us the obsessed world of Jeff Krulik, a guy who finds something remarkable in the unremarkable and sees everyday people as stars. ⊠

An earlier version of this essay was presented as a lecture at Art in General, New York, in January 2008. Quotes from Krulik are taken from records of his public discussions at Anna Helwing Gallery in September 2008 and Light Industry in January 2009, as well as the full text of a 2006 email interview between Krulik and *Decibel* writer Nick Green, provided by Krulik. Sources on the history of cable access include *Independent Video: A Complete Guide to the Physics, Operation, and Application of the New Television for the Student, the Artist, and for Community TV* by Ken Marsh (1974) and *Radical Software* magazine. Additional material on the history of *Heavy Metal Parking Lot* is taken from the video's official website, maintained by John Heyn.

TACKY SOUVENIRS OF PREINAUGURAL AMERICA

The crisis of authenticity in the age of immanent tinkering. An article in response to Ice-T vs. Soulja Boy.

by Ben Tausig
published February 18, 2009

Radio's a bunch of suckers. There's nobody there listening; they're just looking at numbers, and points, and what label you're on, and who's gonna put out the most payola and all that drama. Ninety percent of records out there—that you'll never hear, are better than the shit that's on the radio. These other records just tend to get on. There's a few good things out there, but a lot of that shit is straight garbage. "My lip gloss be poppin'"—get the fuck outta here. That shit is garbage. I mean, come on—Soulja Boy? What the fuck is that? Shit is garbage! And if dude don't like it, I'll punch him in his face. I mean, we came all the way from Rakim to "This is why it's hot, this is why it's not." I ain't feelin' it.

—Ice-T, interviewed in the YouTube video "First Shot Fired: Ice-T vs. Soulja Boy, Sunday, October 7th, 2007"

AS ICE-T IMPLIES, the thing called authenticity seems self-evident: obvious in its presence, glaring in its absence. As a question of being true—to beliefs, institutions, and traditions—authenticity strikes many as worth defending, or mourning. The epitaph "Hip-hop is dead," for instance, is almost as old as hip-hop. Typical is the reaction of Ice-T, a rapper since the heyday of beatboxing, against Soulja Boy Tell 'Em, who's still too young to drink. Soulja Boy, who

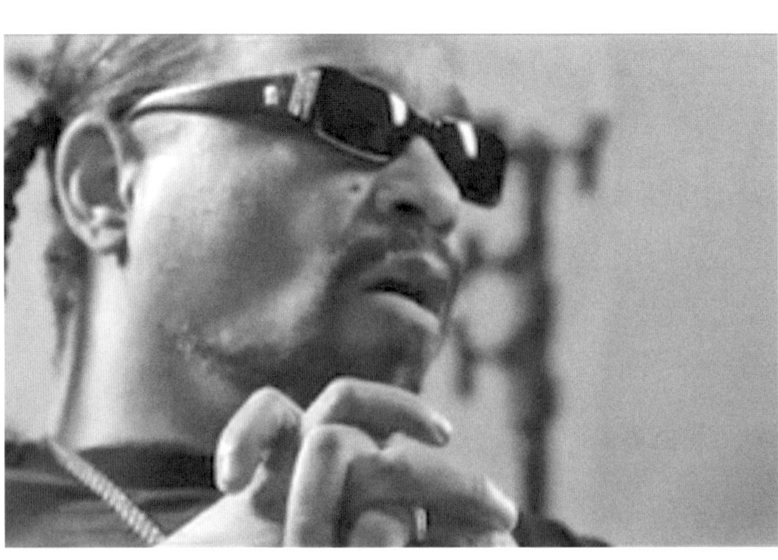

Rakontur, "First Shot Fired: Ice-T vs. Soulja Boy, Sunday, October 7th, 2007," still from YouTube video, 2007.

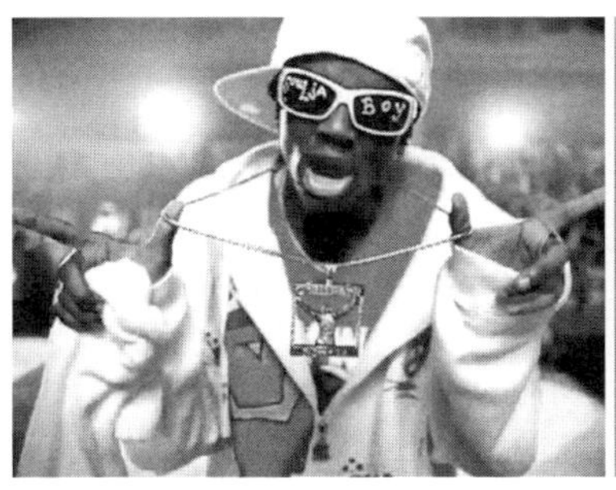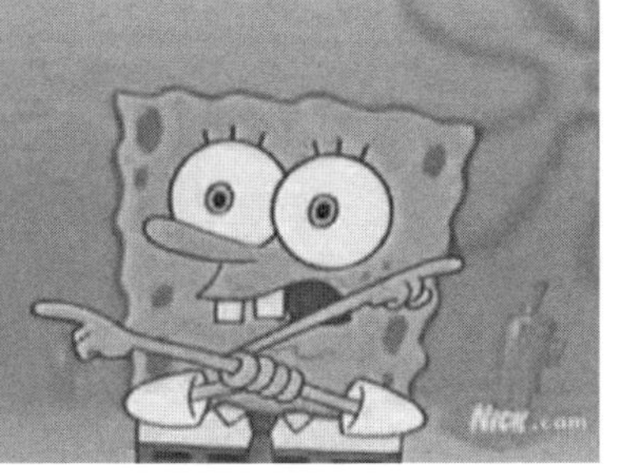

Soulja Boy, "Crank Dat Soldier Boy," and uzimakicody, "Spongebob Soulja Boy Dance and Song," stills from YouTube videos, 2007.

produced his breakout singles in a home studio and became famous through social-networking sites, is emblematic of a new and notably independent moment in musical promotion. But to Ice-T's aged ears, he's complicit in the desecration of hip-hop's authentic essence—the raw sound, the social message—in favor of the saccharine hook.

Many of us feel the sting when the authenticities that form us, personally and culturally, start to drift, generally in the breeze of technological change. As the argument goes, though we derive a sense of self in part through cameras, computers, recordings, and broadcasts, we also long for things that precede or avoid this mediation, or what we regard as *excessive* mediation. In response to this longing, we often look backward, in an attempt to recover authenticity in an earlier technological moment. This retrospection is at least as old as modernity. But authenticity today, in the expanded field of media, is more deeply in crisis. This crisis does not involve mere negation, but inversion. Inauthenticity, which looks a lot like the opposite of authenticity, is actually its successor—or its mirror.

Let's try taking an end run to sort out Ice-T's frustration. In sound, *fidelity* refers to the similarity—or lack thereof—between input and output, production and reproduction. To have fidelity is to play it again as it was played before; a high-fidelity recording will sound like it sounded live. From this, we can say a few things. First, that any instance of fidelity involves two points separated in time—an original and a copy. Second, that the earlier point is always an ideal toward which the latter orients itself. Third, that our understanding of fidelity will inevitably

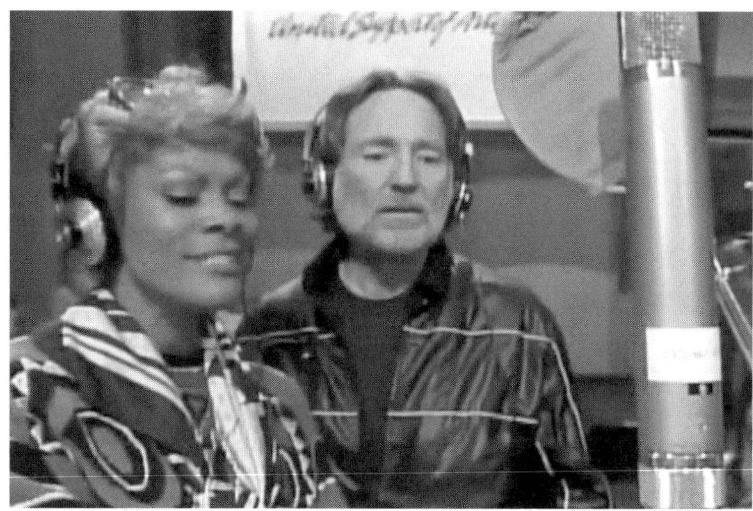

change in relation to the sophistication of technology. Even the most precise magnetic tape recorder is no match for today's digital devices: What was once high-fidelity now merely belies its own vintage.

Authenticity in any situation is judged on the basis of fidelity—but, considering the third point above, not always in terms of a linear relation. For instance, Bob Dylan's Basement Tapes sound authentic not because they reproduce Dylan's voice and playing but because of the recorder grot characteristic of amateur production at that time. Remastered editions with the tape noise scrubbed out therefore possess higher fidelity but perhaps less authenticity. Authenticity must entail the appropriate degree and kind of fidelity, inclusive of flaws.

That is to say, new kinds of flaws can generate new kinds of authenticity. Consider the following anecdote: In late November 2006, singer-songwriter Joshua Radin reported an embarrassing anecdote about Paris Hilton on his blog. The story, which was picked up by MSNBC.com, among others, described Hilton getting surreptitiously hammered on Grey Goose in the hours leading up to a brief performance at a club in Las Vegas. As she stood onstage, her backing track was activated, but Hilton herself was too drunk to sing along and promptly vomited, even as her disembodied voice continued to play through the speakers. Performance (art) over.

Do you like that? Enough of us do—or did at the time—that Hilton's career was not compromised; indeed, it has been premised exactly on such stunts. In a single drunken stroke, she showcased inauthenticity while authentically obliterating it; her profligate twenty-somethingness could not help but spoil the script. In her story, Hilton does not perform an authenticity that strives toward an archetype; instead, she enacts an utter destruction of inauthenticity through her infidelity to even a lip-synced Vegas gig: an infidelity to inauthenticity. And she didn't even mean it.

This double negation is itself a mode of authenticity, one that is increasingly common. It is accomplished by the decomposition of media rather than the avoidance of mediation. We will note that, expressed in terms of sound, it is neither a movement toward greater fidelity nor the reenactment of a specific, nostalgic moment of fidelity (as in the sampling of the "crackle" of vinyl). Instead, it is an active movement to pull representation into pieces.

Authenticity and inauthenticity do not stand apart, as they may have in a more modernist moment. Authenticity is, instead, conceived as a kind of gesture toward inauthenticity during performance. Nowhere is this schematic

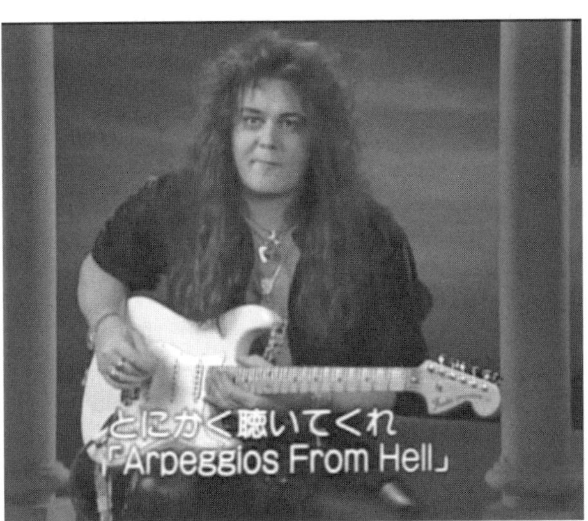

ATHOW, "Yngwie Malmsteen - Arpeggios from Hell," still from YouTube video, 2005.

Someone should flag this as inappropriate because that is some obscene AWESOMENESS. TheMetalguitarguy

WHY WASNT THIS ON THE RECORD!?!?!? TheShredder101

The best part is that there's hardly any improvisation. Great composision by Yngwie. MrStratocasterguy

Watching him play never gets boring. ZEBnet1

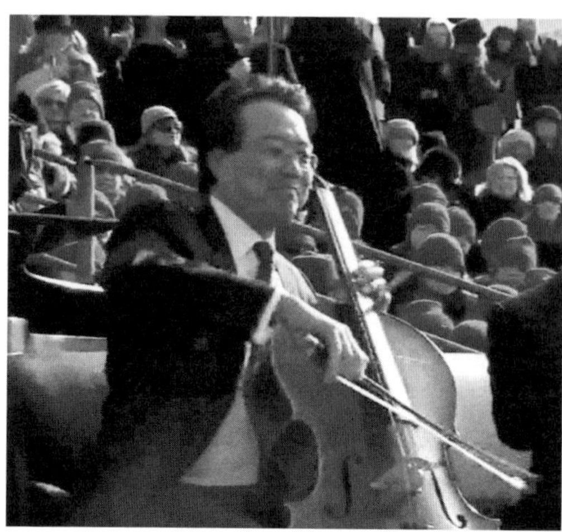

Boilingsand, "Yo-Yo Shreds at the Inauguration with Perlman et al," still from YouTube video, 2009.

I just laughed for 4:33 seconds straight. Hahaha! Classikev

ROFL! I always thought Schoenberg was trying to pull a practical joke on the entire musical world. chui101

Wow. Interesting how that remix messes with your sense of time. That moment seems to go on forever now. southpas

BRILLIANT!!!! Moved me to tears. So moving. John Williams is a genius! lstryer 3

demonstrated more clearly than in the rupture between sound and image. Pythagoras used the word *acousmatic* to describe pedagogy delivered to students from behind a curtain; novice learners were distracted by the true image of the teacher. Today, acousmatic sound is increasingly enabled by technology, every time we listen to recorded music, watch animated films, or receive orders from some Wizard of Oz. The absence of the image of the sound source can produce an uncanny effect, or a funny one.

Hilton's mishap is a great example of the disjuncture between sound and image, but such a splitting need not always be spontaneous or nonsensical. It can also be compositional. With editing tools widely available for dismantling and rearranging media, many viewers avail themselves of the chance to use circulating sound and video, copyrighted or not, as raw material for their own productions.

This approach is now so common as to be paradigmatic; in other words, one can express authenticity not only by harking back to an essence but also by destabilizing something already construed as inauthentic. The perfomer's—or the composer's—toolkit includes juxtaposition and destruction, humor and hostility. Ultimately, composition becomes a habit of looking, listening, and the exploitation of (re)sources. From the right angle, shit is gold. ⊠

THIS LITTLE LARD

Pygmalion and the pig for breakfast; Porky, Sun Ra, and suffering: an exchange on distraction and delay.

by Hassan Khan
and Clare Davies
published March 3, 2009

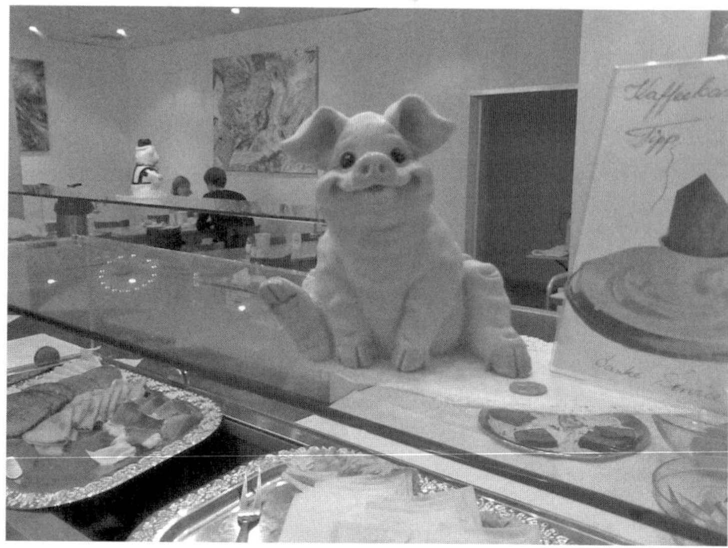

Hassan Khan, untitled, 2008 , printed cell phone photograph, 3 7/8 x 5 1/8". From the series "Lust," 2008. Courtesy of the artist and Galerie Chantal Crousel.

CLARE DAVIES: "The pig" seems to have a special place in your heart. First, we have this kinky porcelain piglet over cold cuts, then these pig cartoons, *stuffedpigfollies* (2007). Why pigs?

HASSAN KHAN: Well, the pig is anthropomorphized all the time. That's where my interest comes from: the method through which a culture speaks, the totemic figures it produces for this act of communication. I took this picture on my mobile phone while I was staying at the Agon Hotel in Berlin. The hotel itself had an eerie atmosphere because it was large and cheap and very '70s; the sculpture of a pig in the breakfast room to symbolize ham cutlets was irresistible.

This pig, through both its context, the hotel breakfast room, and its figurative affinity to what is human, is used to represent what we are going to consume; it therefore, ironically, becomes a marker of separation, difference, and distance. The distance between an inside (a contained, individuated unit with borders) and an undefined outside. It carves out a space between the diner, so to speak, and the object of the diner's desire. The pig is the "other," existing outside, to be ingested and consumed. This dynamic implies a set of limits and units—an idea of who we are, a unity that ends somewhere. All conditions necessary for a self-coming-into-being. (I tend to use the word *possession* to describe that operation.) The porcelain pig (or maybe the image of the pig) is a clue, a suggestion, as to what that operation might be about.

CD: The cartoon pigs in *stuffedpigfollies* seem to be possessed in an existential sense; or, at least, they have registered the way in which they are spoken through and are quite anxious about it. Cartoons or animated characters seem to lend themselves to the kind of self-awareness and accompanying anxiety that you grant the *stuffedpigfollies*.

This work seems to acknowledge the existential potential of "animated" images, as a general category. On the other hand, this little Agon pig is more oblivious, or more complicit: a porno pig (if pornography can be defined by strategic complicity).

HK: The sense of the "pornographic" comes from several sources. First, the nature of a totem: Its erotic significance must always lurk somewhere in the background. Second, the surrender to one's fate as material to be consumed: the ham and bacon symbolized by the pig. Third, the mass tourist experience and its gentle morning creepiness: young backpackers of both sexes congregating early in the morning for bad coffee.

So there is a connection, as well as a difference. The Agon pig is oblivious because it's plucked straight from the generic—it's an observation that I've framed. While the *stuffedpigfollies* pigs are actual propositions. I designed them and I wrote the sentences accompanying each panel. The cartoon pigs are possessed in the sense that they speak and perform a gesture—pointing, jumping, running.

The reference I use in *stuffedpigfollies*—the anthropomorphic Disney pig—is already symbolic of this cultural operation I refer to as possession. In using that ubiquitous pig but in a highly personal fashion, I'm learning something about how my imaginary operates from the generic and then allowing these deep structures to acquire or discover a specific form. Within that kind of logic, moments in the world suddenly start to speak.

A form is always a reference to a specific set of generic conditions. The generic is a collective history of the form and how it's been produced and utilized, how it's defined and identified. But a form is also always the result of a personal engagement with those conditions—that is, the process of the artist's work is that very engagement.

The most important question, however, is, Why take that image? Or, in other words, Why do I love it? What makes me think it's potent in one sense or another?

CD: I think cannibalism is a useful touchstone. The horror of what's pictured is the possibility that this very banal thing you're doing—eating ham cold cuts—is actually a horrific transgression that's been normalized.

HK: Cannibalism is the limit on the horizon: Without that ultimate taboo, the breakfast room would be a pool of dementia. I think what excites me is the idea that an image can speak in two tongues at the same time, be two (or more) entities simultaneously. That is, to me, inherent in the idea of an image but is clearer in some than others.

CD: Roland Barthes's essay "The Third Meaning: Research Notes on Some Eisenstein Stills" (1970) offers another way of talking about images that present themselves as unreadable, that engage something outside the logic of the accepted narrative: images that speak in two tongues, as you said, or three.

Barthes positions this sort of image in opposition to two other types of meaning: informational and symbolic. As I understand it, the third meaning is most visible in relation to disguise. It reveals itself negatively: "This looks wrong." Or it inserts another sense of conviction, maybe emotional, or intuitive, instead of "suspension of disbelief." I guess it raises the issue of what people react to when they look at something that is presented as an aesthetic work, a work of art or film.

Maybe trying to articulate this other category outside of information and symbol is just a way of making a space for "real art," you know, as in—it has something. Barthes is perhaps inevitably vague in the end. But I like his insistence on describing an experience of recognition that necessarily remains inarticulate. I suppose I understand your use of the totem in a similar way, in terms of our ability to recognize something that can't be articulated; it's why I can recognize that potency that you see in the image as well.

You shot this image of a television screen at the Agon Hotel, too, also with your cell phone. You've mentioned the way the woman is holding her hands. Does your interest in the image hinge on what is communicated by this gesture, whether intentionally or not?

HK: I'm actually only interested in the gesture itself, the woman's presence, rather than what kind of information this image might convey, what kind of critique of spectacle and capital. This is only a smoke screen; the animating force here is the woman's enigmatic gesture—which is what I can't carefully explain and file away. The off-screen slant of her eyes is more potent because this is an image of a TV screen: the surface of a daily transmission. But the associations of the TV screen are also undercut by the gesture. There's a casual, accidental distraction that's enough to puncture the whole edifice.

CD: The TV presenter relates to another operation of "animation." Your *stuffedpigfollies* seem to speak the voice of the artist who created them. They seem to be an animation in this very literal sense. On the other hand, the TV presenter, or rather her gesture, seems to have an unanchored or unauthored presence. The relationship of the artist as an animator of the artwork or animated through the artwork, and the way a work might originally or eventually exceed the artist's agency in that sense, seems to be a potentially anxious relationship. The work can be recognized before it is folded into an artistic process, or can seem to "get away" from the artist at some point in the process of its own creation.

Anne-Louis Girodet's *Pygmalion and Galatea* (1819) was meant to be his final masterpiece, to speak to the artist's lifetime of work, to present the artist as Pygmalion. But it betrays the anxiety involved in making such an assertion, mostly in the time it took to finish the painting. The painting was commissioned in 1813 and took five years to complete. Girodet only gradually introduced the work to the public, staging the application of its final touches for an audience of society ladies, hosting the king for a special viewing,

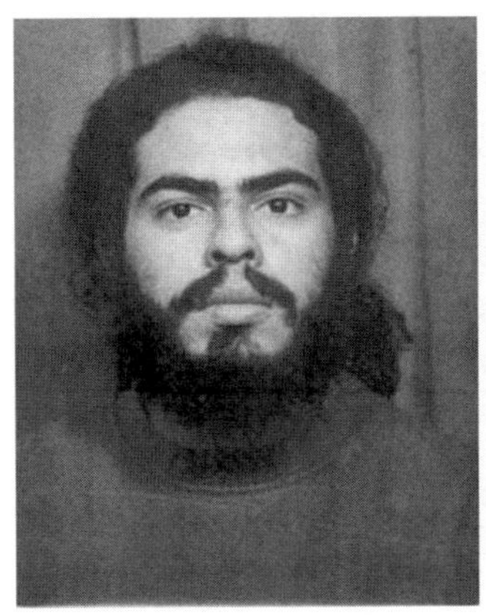 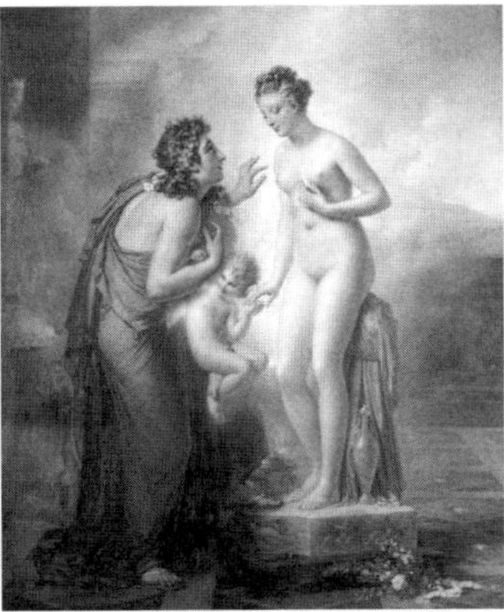

Photo-booth picture of Hassan Khan, age nineteen, ca. 1994; Anne-Louis Girodet-Trioson, *Pygmalion and Galatea*, 1819.

and then submitting it on the final day of the Salon of 1819—this delay, this distraction, and the foregrounding of his process in the service of what amounts to a portrait of the artist.

HK: What animates the work is the artist's activity. The question is, How do we escape the situation of illustration, where the work becomes merely a vehicle for the thoughts of the artist? Rather than expressing my own convictions through my work, I'm interested in what I might produce in spite of my convictions.

CD: Can this be applied to self-portraiture as well? Is it possible to produce an image of yourself in spite of your convictions? Or, what do you see in this photo-booth picture of yourself that exists in spite of your convictions? This claim to self-portraiture reminds me of the Romantic idea of the artist as having a closer relationship to what exists outside of language: the ability to translate it, present it, and, in the case of self-portraiture, make it coincide with the artist's own image.

HK: This image was taken in an automated photo booth, a piece of information that is pertinent here. It accidentally foreshadows two major interests, automation and portraiture. It is a document from a moment in my personal history, the time when a persona was being forged, tested, and then communicated as an image. Maybe this is part of what animates the artist's practice, the constant movement from source through process to product; there is both despair and demand. This is the artist fashioning himself as revolutionary, though even then I was quite aware that revolutions are only excuses for self-aggrandizement and posturing. Romanticism and nostalgia all have something to do with this choice.

CD: When you say that you're interested in what you might produce in spite of yourself, you're also partaking of a Romantic understanding of portraiture, one based on a certain illusion, a self-delusion, a self-willing—making something out of nothing, or not much.

HK: It seems that on some

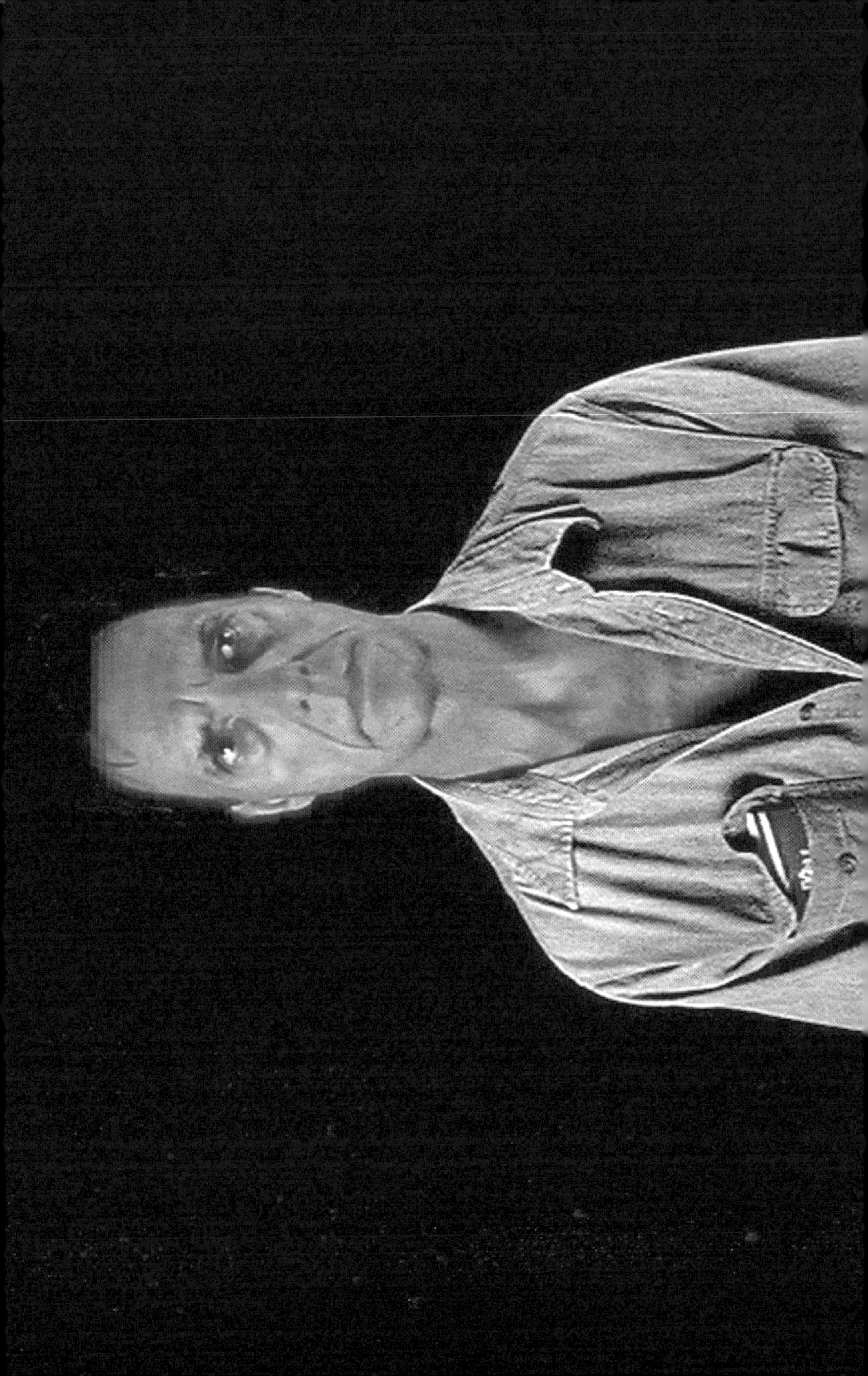

fundamental level I am unable to escape portraiture.

CD: Géricault's *Portrait of a Woman Suffering from Obsessive Envy* (ca. 1822).

HK: (*laughing*) Scary—nice title though. Looking is partly about being caught, trapped. I guess that's what disfigures the subject: The object of her gaze is reflected back onto her. And the look is transfixed. She's seeing something we're not.

CD: A critic, writing after the rediscovery of the painting in the mid-nineteenth century, claimed that the artist's friend, a doctor at the Salpêtrière who was interested in matching particular physiognomies to "corresponding" mental illnesses, commissioned a series of portraits of the insane intended as diagnostic tools, the idea being that a portrait can function as a scientific diagram of something intangible and invisible.

But, as you said, the sitter in *Woman Suffering* seems to be on the verge of becoming completely transfixed and "possessed" by her own vision. This is confirmed by the fact that the object of her gaze is out of the frame. What you call the totem functions in a similar way; it seems to be transfixed by something we can't see, as if that something is responsible for making it "insane."

HK: She is looking at something that she cannot turn into an explanation, something that does not "make sense." However, this is an active, almost aggressive, act of looking.

CD: The "mania of envy" title suggests that her gaze is directed outward, but what's pathological is this grasping for something perceived as "terribly" outside. That's the horror of envy, right?

HK: Yes. Exclusion, the limits of oneself. In Arabic, the words for one, lonely, unity, and limit or edge are all derived from the same trilateral root. But what interests me here is the challenge posed to the viewer to understand what she (the sitter) can't put together. (I only just now noticed that the word for challenge, amazingly enough, comes from the same root.) The inexplicable that lies outside needs to be challenged. Another way of understanding it is in terms of some kind of melancholic defeat. Maybe it's both a challenge and a defeat at the same time—again despair and demand.

CD: I was going to ask if you consider this and *Portrait of Hassan Khan, Aged Nineteen* in this way?

HK: Yes, as well as the letter *c* in *The Alphabet Book* (2006). *G.R.A.H.A.M.* (2008) is a portrait in time, one that also picks up these themes. But *G.R.A.H.A.M.*—a video rather than a still—possesses something extra. It consists of one continuous ten-minute shot of Graham sitting. The piece is silent, so the audience does not realize that I am interviewing him about his life. He is not allowed to answer back. Furthermore, I had asked him to keep his eyes trained on me as I moved up and down the studio. In a sense, the portrait is of a tension

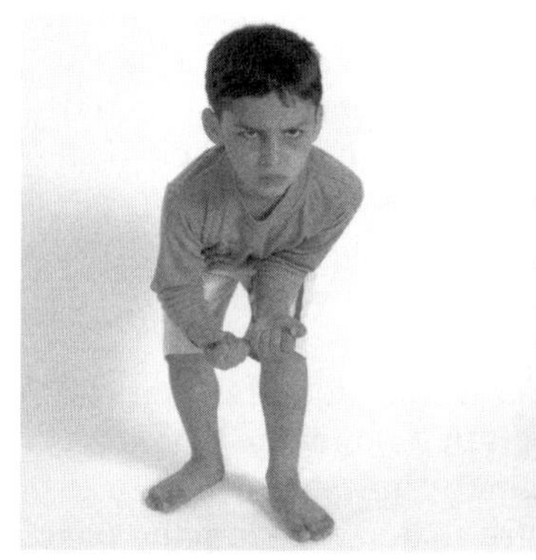 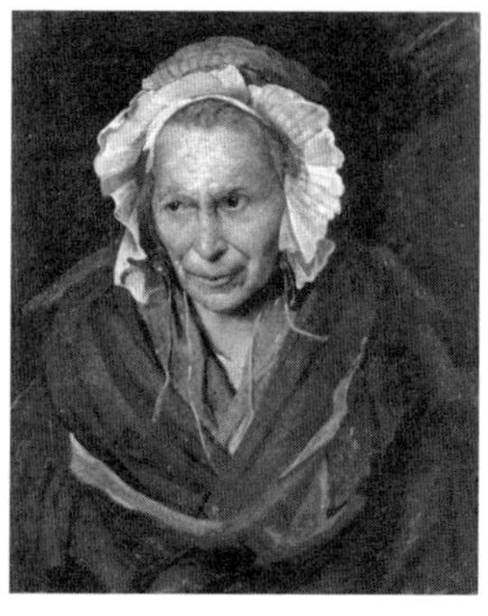

Hassan Khan, "The Letter C," from *The Alphabet Book*, 2006, 26-page book, 15 3/4 x 31 1/2". Courtesy of the artist and Galerie Chantal Crousel. Théodore Géricault, *Portrait of a Woman Suffering from Obsessive Envy*, 1819–20.

between a persona and its physical representation.

CD: As in the Géricault painting, the subject is responding to something outside the frame. In contrast, *The Alphabet Book* boy is just a mirror.

HK: Yes, a literal mirror: The kid models for advertisements. I hired him for a professional shoot; he was doing his job. I posed and he imitated me. I am not interested in his subjectivity, only in his ability to imitate me and thus channel something external. Inhabit something external. I could speak about this image in sculptural terms—it's about molding and channeling rather than representing. With *G.R.A.H.A.M.*, I am still seriously interested in someone else—in someone's presence. That's why there are dots between the letters. It's Graham as a logo of Graham. *G.R.A.H.A.M.* is a portrait of someone dealing with who he is.

CD: I don't see a logo as working in the way I think you're describing. The little boy in *The Alphabet Book* is more like a logo, I think. *G.R.A.H.A.M.* has more to do with your interruption of

Graham-as-subject from your position off-screen.

HK: Maybe *logo* is incorrect. Maybe what I meant was Graham as a corporation—something or somebody with an address and a headquarters. Which is slightly ironic knowing that Graham (the person) is in a sense quite dislocated and has been traveling around the world all his life.

CD: You seem to be making him visible as an individual, not a big, anonymous corporation.

HK: But an individual is a corporation. To capture his presence, it was necessary that he flag himself somehow. To do that is to possess an address, a location, even if it is tense like in that room when I felt he was going to stand up and snap my neck.

The situation creates a fragile tension—it's Graham sitting there being Graham. The idea of a corporation here has nothing to do with the banal understanding of the term (as a socioeconomic unit) but rather from the Latin root *corporare*, "to combine or form into one body." Separation, distance, and unity are the elements of this portrait. An understanding of what an individual is. At the end, he was actually very gracious after these pretty uncomfortable ten minutes of him sitting there being Graham. Ten minutes can be a very, very long time.

CD: I think that the Géricault portrait speaks to the threat that generated this tension on his part: You cornered him, made him reveal himself as pathological in some sense. In a parallel sense, Géricault's painting was made in the service of a kind of scientific vision: seeing the individual as an identifiable but ultimately mysterious "type."

HK: That's very interesting—the subject, even in science, remains mysterious even if identifiable. The sense of mystery surrounding the representation of the human figure remains, even if accidental and unwanted (in psychiatric hospitals, army files, police registers). It is as if in the very act of figuring the human needs to engage with that mystery. Is this enigma related to what an image is or to what human beings imagine about themselves? That is why I am interested in changing the rules of communication slightly—when you change these rules, it becomes possible to engage with that sense, if you will, on a different level.

CD: Capturing something, revealing that it's not necessarily true. Your interest in authoritarianism seems to inform the way you structure this relationship, in order to force a subject, as such, into view. Changing the terms of communication puts a different pressure on the possibilities for self-presentation, whether of the artist, the sitter (in this case), or the audience. Let's talk about your interest in authoritarianism.

HK: This is not an interest; it is an acknowledgment.

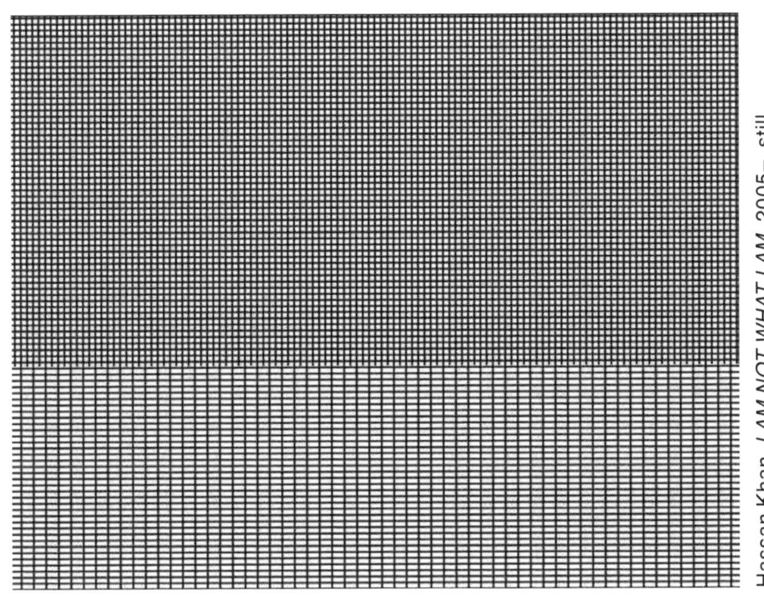

Hassan Khan, *I AM NOT WHAT I AM*, 2005–, still from a video projection, part of a synchronized live artist's talk, 60 minutes.

CD: It seems like you're using this acknowledgment, then, to talk about honesty. For example, in *I AM NOT WHAT I AM* (2005–) you present a performance of your own authority, as a speaker and artist, as well as a discussion of authority. The entire performance is exactly sixty minutes long. The accompanying sound and the images that appear behind you are coordinated with your own "live" discussion, down to the very second. There's no room for response or discussion, at least until after the work is through. You allow the audience to observe the latent authoritarianism that is normalized or explained away in everyday life. In that sense, it's a bit moralistic and antiauthoritarian empowering.

HK: *I AM NOT WHAT I AM* does not shy away from the authoritarianism latent in the aesthetic gesture and the spectacle—in the dynamics of communication. I reject the idea of art practice as having anything to do with a specific, more "empowering" model; the relationship is already fraught with tension and manipulation. I don't think the work is anti- or proauthoritarian. It just refuses a knee-jerk, placating antiauthoritarian pose.

CD: Still, you seem to be making a claim for the performative nature of authority. The depth of a "totalized sculpture/environment" depends on absenting or making invisible what is powering it. When you perform *I AM NOT WHAT I AM*, you are clearly putting yourself at the center of it all. Making the artist visible and also presenting an authoritarian performance as visually (as well as aurally) available might function as an unveiling, might be antiauthoritarian in a sense? Are you able to be equally invisible, in a sense, when you are visibly present during the performance?

HK: Authority has no specific nature. It's the matrix through which communication is made possible. Your statements still imply a morality that I am attempting to step away from, at least in my practice. The important thing is quite simple: not to be boring.

CD: OK, how do you avoid boredom? How do you define boredom in relation to authority? Are we bored if we don't sense the authority of an image over us?

HK: The important thing for me is not to fetishize your raw material, but rather to engage with it. Fetishizing your sources ironically transforms them into something else. And that's what I find boring. For example, Jonathan Meese fetishizes the icons of a specific fascism as well as the gestures of that fascism's subversion; that, to me, is boring. Matthew Barney, repetitively, proposes a symbolic representation of narrative processes as the source and charge of the work's power—that is, theater in the most reductive fashion. I'm interested in a less expressionistic acceptance of and engagement with what we're calling authority here—whatever that is.

CD: Can you point to anyone who is also interested in what you are talking about: an artist, filmmaker, et cetera?

HK: Let's take for example two nonartists: Werner Herzog and Sun Ra.

CD: To take Sun Ra: He developed an approach to musicmaking that relied on unusually extended and frequent improvisation sessions, with all elements of the rather unwieldy Arkestra coming, in a certain sense, "independently" to an understanding of their own roles. Does this speak to an invisible center, that could be "authority"—the depth of a specific culture? What about comparing this approach to the extravagant outfits and parading that characterized live performances? Is the latter "expressionistic"? Does it fetishize icons of authority—however campy the approach? The performances seem to make a satiric nod to traditions of formalizing control adopted by Southern Baptist ministers and ancient Egyptian pharaohs, among others. He seems to fail and fail spectacularly, but the music and musicmaking are in a sense removed from all that.

HK: Sun Ra's theater is not theater at all; it's a disguise for something else. The invisible center you mention unifies Ra's activities into a whole. It is what he is constantly orbiting. It might be necessary at times to believe in things that are unknowable to be able to produce forms. The spectacle does not rely on the crutch of half-baked psychoanalysis.

I would like to compare Matthew Barney with Sun Ra and show how Sun Ra is, for me, so much better. First of all, Sun Ra's spectacle operated within a paradigm, set its own rules, and created its own interpretative community. Although lyrically Ra seems to be discussing a whole worldview, the spectacle still manages to escape from the position of speaking about something—Ra's spectacle is an associative barrage fueled by the intensity of the music. In comparison, Barney's carefully constructed images (especially in the post-"Cremaster" phase) seem to be precious and inflated. While Barney seems to be interested in making pronouncements about a culture, Ra is consciously engaging with a wide popular repository of icons to produce an understanding of who he is in relation to his public. The irony, of course, is that Ra is the one with the prophetic pronouncements: the one who seems more fascistic on the surface.

CD: Judging from your examples earlier—Herzog and Sun Ra—it seems that you're working with an intuitive (not to say illogical) approach to association. Images have a force because they recall something that is familiar, related to other images, but without its own referent. There's something clear and persuasive in this relationship that eludes explanation.

HK: Association is definitely at play. And association can be pretty persuasive because it can outrun you and leave you breathless at any moment and that's also what images can do. I guess at a certain point all of this started happening when I decided to stop speaking about things and to try to work with what things are about.

CD: What things?

HK: I was speaking about things like society—bourgeois Egyptian culture, class, cities, et cetera. You know, stuff like that.

CD: When did that happen specifically?

HK: It was a period in between two periods. The first half of the '90s with music and in collaborations with Amr Hosny, for example: We were interested in a sort of intoxicated, surreal state—it meant that intensity was valued above meaning or speaking about things. Later on, when I started working in journalism and teaching for a couple of years, my work became much more "documentary" in its orientation.

CD: I remember a video you made in collaboration with Amr Hosny called *lungfan*. There's this surrealist idea of convulsive beauty, of transformation.

HK: Yes, I think we were also informed by metaphysics, somehow: a sort of yearning for loss. Something like that was at work, too. However (which is maybe surprising), the work managed to stay very abstract. We never descended into wallowing in our subjectivities. Expressionism was also out. I guess we were lucky not to operate in a cultural environment where self-expression was fetishized.

Lungfan was about hyperventilation. (The Arabic title was *nafas*, which can mean "breath" or "self,"

depending on how you pronounce it.) It aimed at some kind of ecstatic experience. I think that's why the Cairo Atelier audience reacted by accusing us of brainwashing and being agents of Israel. It's the typical paranoid reaction by an audience to forms that they are not familiar with. The Cairene audience (especially then) was both more invested and more suspicious. In a sense, their suspicion stems from a belief in the power of the work—maybe a healthier environment than all the liberal museums of the world.

CD: Who was making the accusations?

HK: All middle-aged, failed Egyptian intellectuals and artists.

CD: The Israel thing, resorting to that, indicates hysteria; it's like a signpost.

HK: Sure, but I think it's more tired than this. It's just a convenient way to insist on what you know and to shut everything else out. And to also break down anyone with whom you disagree. ⊠

FROM 'THE EVERYDAY'

"Oil, sexual fluids, animosity, tubs, / A raincoat, 'pages of illustrations.'" Debris from a hundred-day daybook.

By John Latta
published March 4, 2009

Another way is to obstruct
The way with debris; snack-
Packs, empties, CD jewel cases,
Magazine supplements, CPUs,
      pink cartridges,
Caulk guns, roofing tar, fluorescents,
Freon canisters, catalytic converters,
      syringes,
Tin foil, tape dispensers, detergent
Jugs, junk mail, AAA batteries,
Lawn chairs, road salt, Alka-
Seltzer, bromides, Clearasil, binder clips,
Blister packs, ointments, jockstraps,
      winter
Clothing, Post-Its, three-ring
Binders, tires made by Pirelli,
Yard refuse, mop handles, cooking
Oil, aerosol cans, insect repellants,
Rubbing alcohol, "dead soldiers," paper-
Back-novels, tree limbs, catheters,
Fanny packs, bicycle chains, candy
Wrappers, antidepressants, potato
      peelings, toasters,
Sharpies, Crayolas, floppy discs, cordless
Phones, lawn mowers, filing cabinets,
Vitamins, latex-based paints, grief
Pools, refrigerators, ambulances,
      varnishes, wood
Preservatives, nautical knickknacks,
      sloughs of

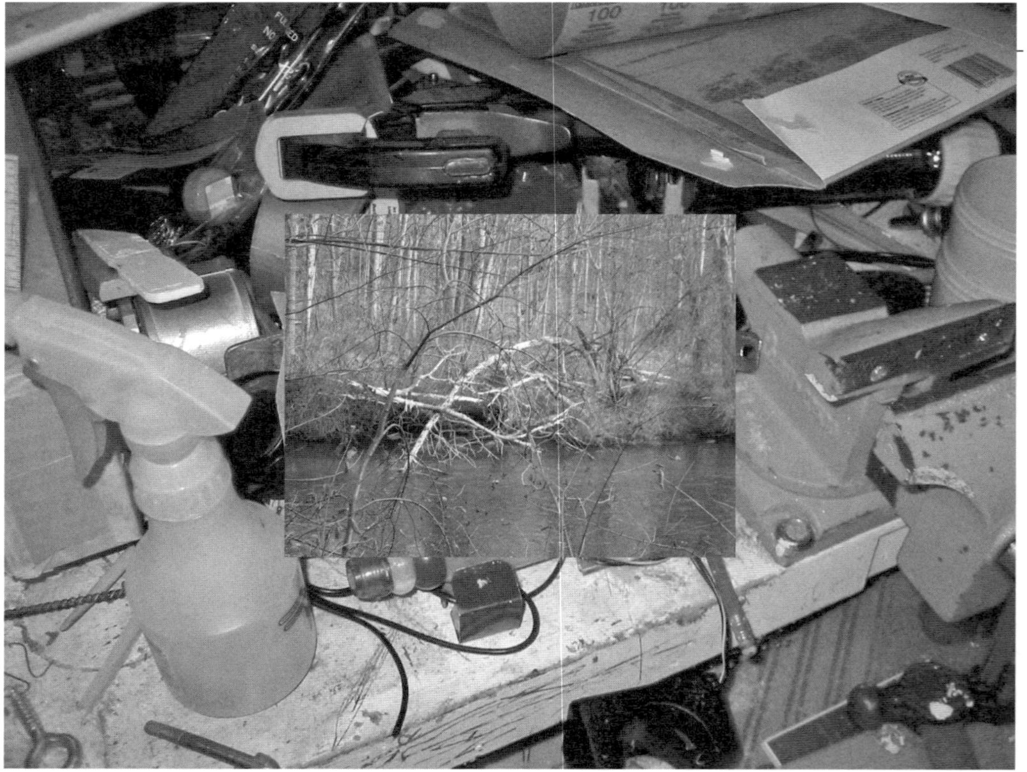

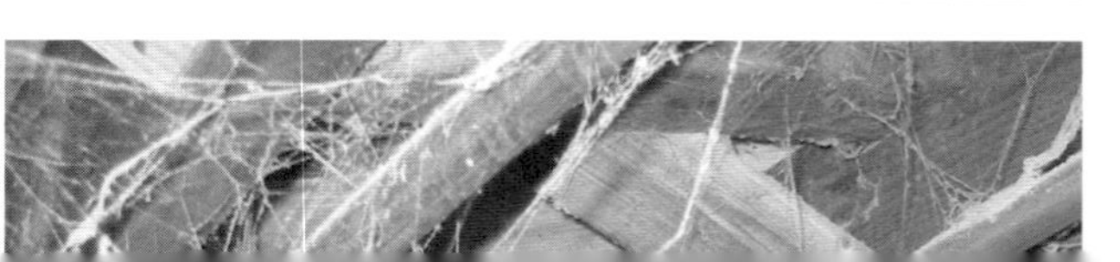

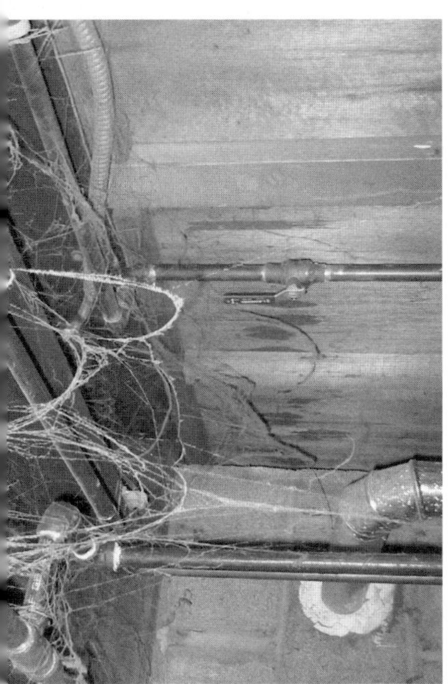

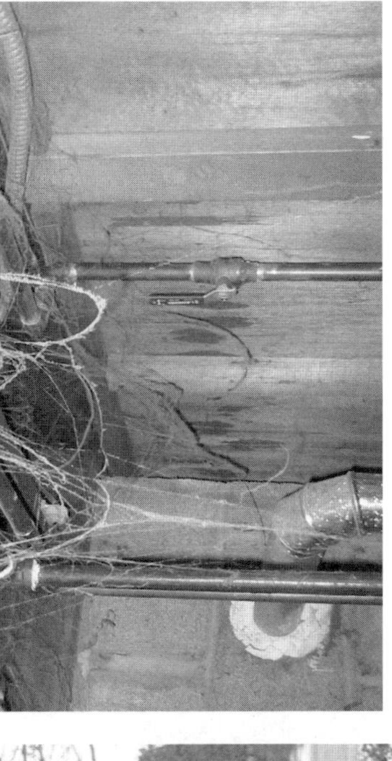

Despond, mercury thermometers,
    phosphorous-based
Fertilizers, the winter months, motor
Oil, sexual fluids, animosity, tubs,
A raincoat, "pages of illustrations,"
Blotting paper, aluminum boats, nylon
Stockings, lasagna noodles, Hostess
    Twinkies,
Paint thinners, antifreeze, barn siding,
Kodalith prints, Super 8 stock,
Modeling clay, pencils, a leather
Cowboy hat worn by Phil
Oohs. Razor blades, a gold
Lamé suit, a complete run
Of Decca 45s. A monitor,
A curb-dump'd brokwn monitor. ⊠

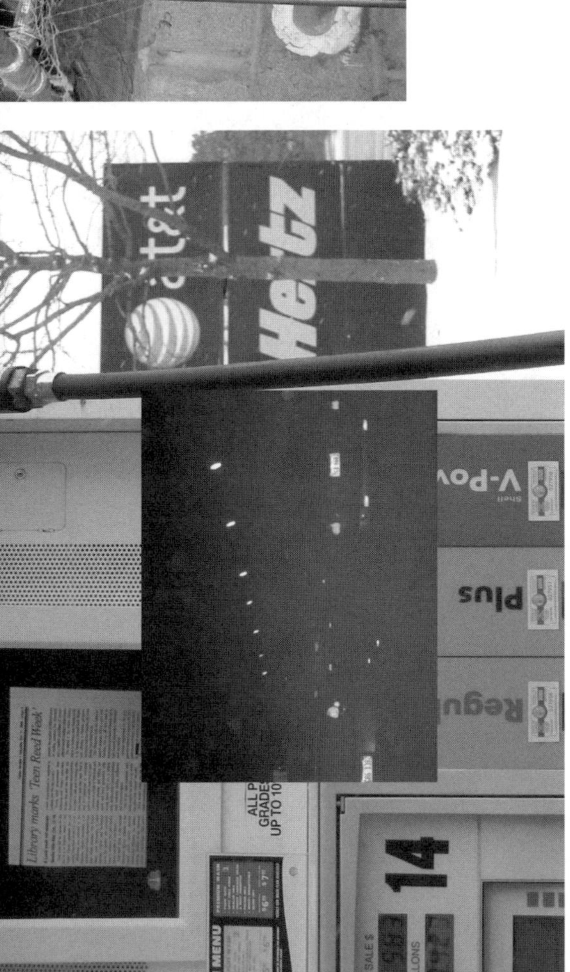

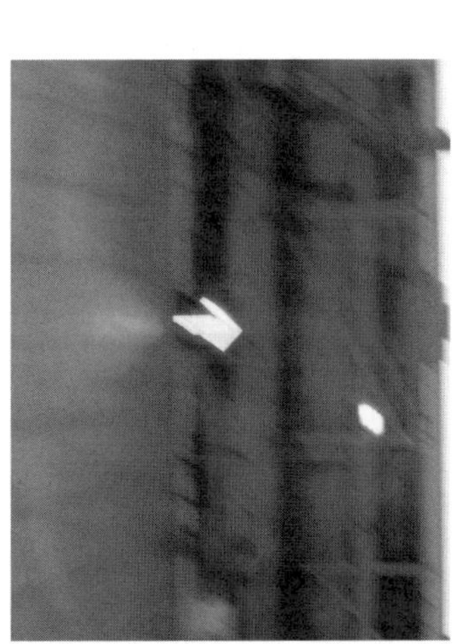

MORE TALKS ABOUT BUILDINGS

AN EVENING WITH TRIPLE CANOPY
THE KITCHEN, 512 WEST 19TH STREET,
NEW YORK, NY
APRIL 7, 2009

FOR THIS EVENT, expanding on an issue devoted to new and old forms of urbanism, Triple Canopy excavated real, unrealized, and potential spaces: The VPL Authority sold a planned mega-eco-city in the desert Southwest. Lucy Raven presented views and sounds of a grand Utahan suburb nurtured by copper-mine tailings. The Center for Land Use Interpretation screened scans of the architecture of Texas oil fields from above. Melanie Smith tracked the spiraling sprawl of Mexico City. Joseph Clarke analyzed the coincidences of megachurches and office spaces. Zs played sound constructions and Nine 11 Thesaurus performed raps from Brownsville. José León Cerrillo debuted *Wrong Place, Right Time* (2009), a digital print in an edition of 100.

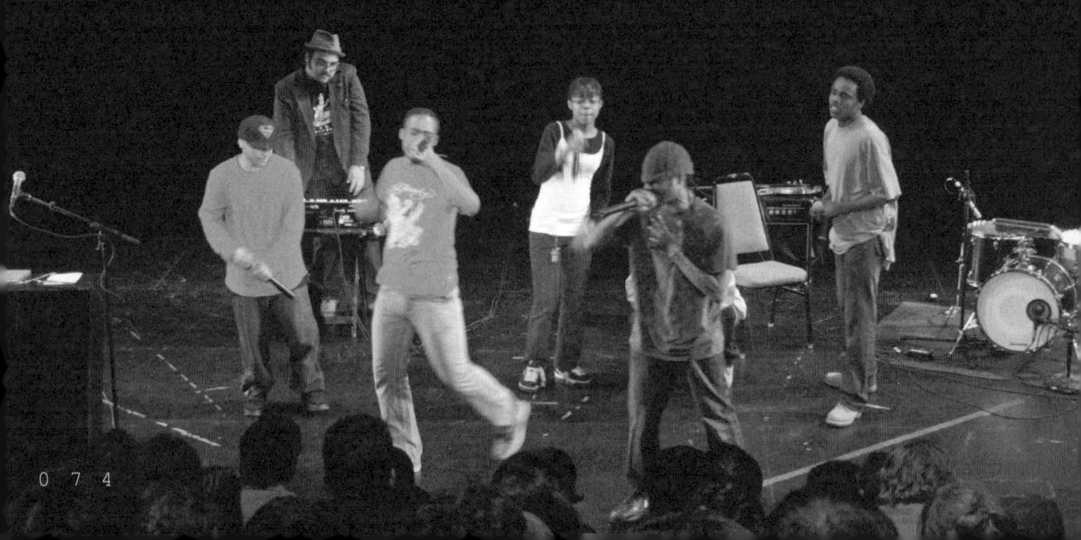

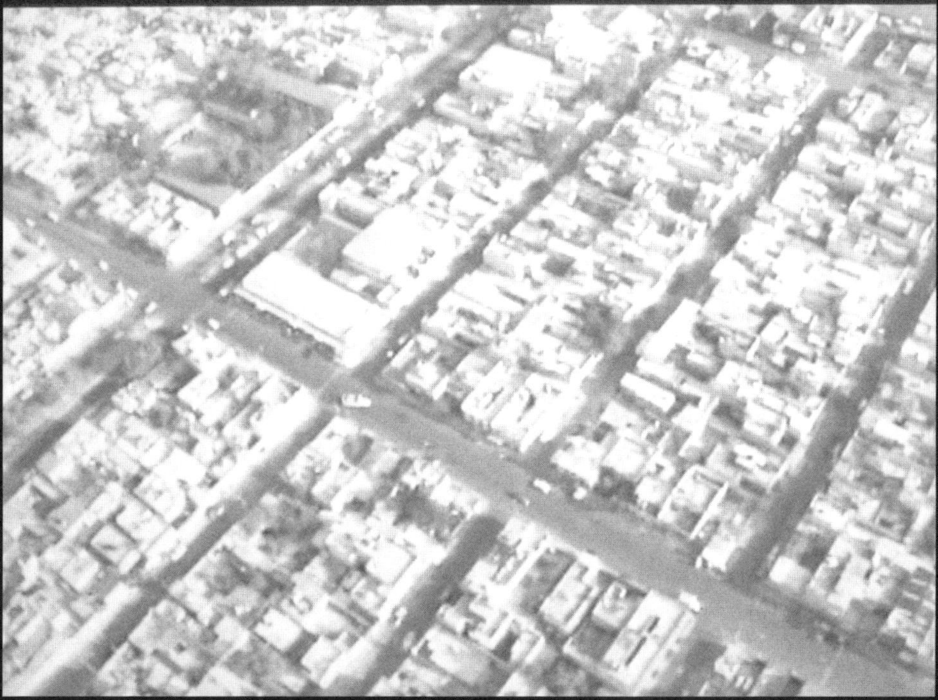

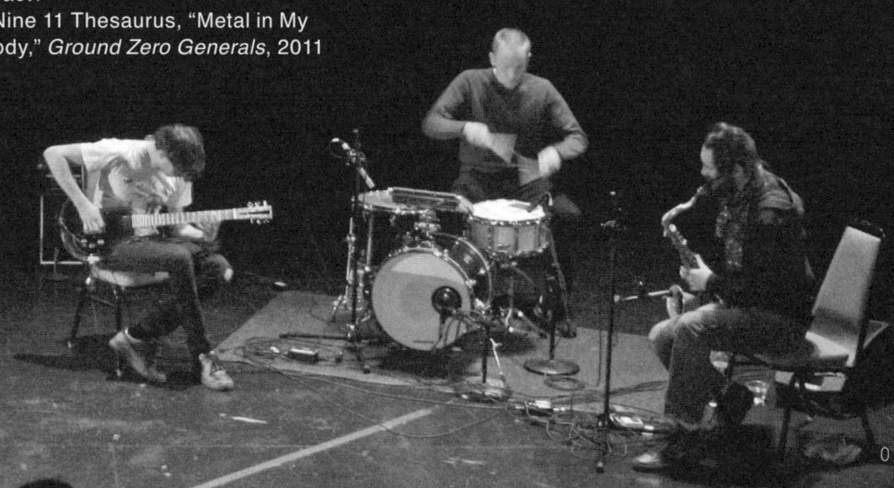

*What they fail to understand is that we're
students, not convicts / How we sup-
posed to function when everything that we
touchin' / is capable of mass destruction /
You still think that I'm bluffin'?
And I'm pretty sure it only happens to
Latinos and Blacks/What's up with that? /
You treat us like animals/how you expect
us to react?*
 —Nine 11 Thesaurus, "Metal in My
 Body," *Ground Zero Generals*, 2011

ISSUE 6
URBANISMS:
MODEL CITIES

published May 5, 2009

CANOPYCANOPYCANOPY.COM/6

A NOTE ON URBANISMS

An introduction to two issues examining our current urban situation and what lies beyond it: the city's past and its future; the suburban, the exurban, the frontier.

by the Editors
of Triple Canopy
published May 5, 2009

AS THE ECONOMY HAS COLLAPSED, the foreclosure crisis has metastasized, and the systems of finance that powered the global construction boom have degenerated, we've come to see the past few decades as an agreeable daydream—of what could be bought, what could be built, and what could be justified. For so many people in America and elsewhere, those years were a reverie of easy credit and adjustable rate mortgages, masking stagnant wages and yawning inequality.

All that fictitious money left its factual mark in the soil; the scaffolded remainders of hallucinated wealth surround us. Of course, the built environment is irreducible to a single point or a single analysis: Cities are accretions of what is designed and what is improvised, what is chosen and what is received, what is imagined and what is experienced. Likewise, the concept of urbanism now exceeds any fixed notion of the twentieth-century city, encompassing informatics and third world slums, modular megachurches and modernist office towers, master-planned eco-cities in the American Southwest and Midtown Manhattan-themed condos atop the rubble of old Beijing.

In the course of this issue and the following one, Master Plans, Triple Canopy will address these tensions and the spaces and lives they've produced, examining our

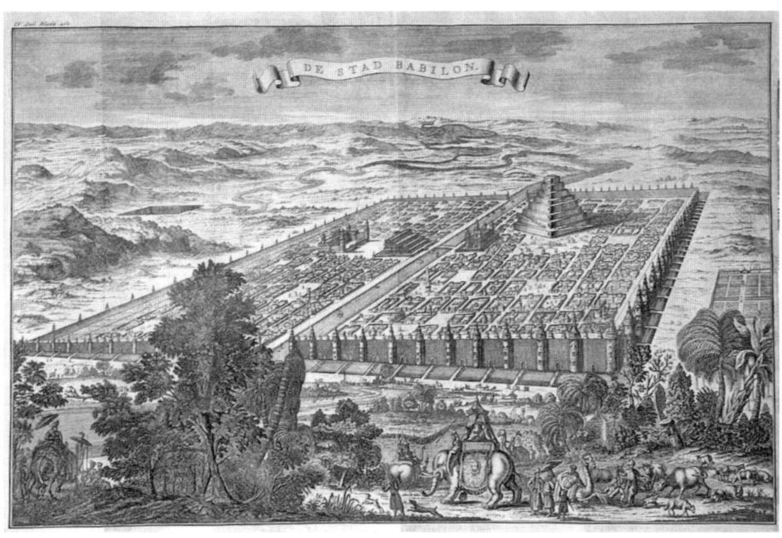

Engraving of the city of Babylon, ca. 1735, source unknown.

I
N
V
A
L
I
D

F
O
R
M
A
T

2

I
S
S
U
E

6

2
0
0
9

current urban situation and what lies beyond it: the city's past and its future; the suburban, the exurban, the frontier. Model Cities and Master Plans focus on the origins, products, and relics of planning, and its possibilities for the future. As the reign of ego architecture and its hyper-capitalist financiers comes to an end (or merely changes regents), we will offer alternative forms of and perspectives on urbanism, from artists, researchers, writers, and musicians, as well as architects. More than ever, we need a sense of urbanism that looks backward to move forward, that looks forward to see the present; an urbanism that considers the voices of those without the power to build, and the ideas of architects and planners who have built modestly, critically, or not at all.

Our cities have their foundation in elaborate fictions, but then so does all architecture; what are models and blueprints but stories waiting to be told? Surely, the hallmark of the age has been an untrained and unbridled will to creation in the guise of "growth." But now that the resources required for dreaming in steel and glass have been momentarily exhausted, the time has come for reckoning, for reimagining the walls with which we've built our world and the windows through which we see it. ⊠

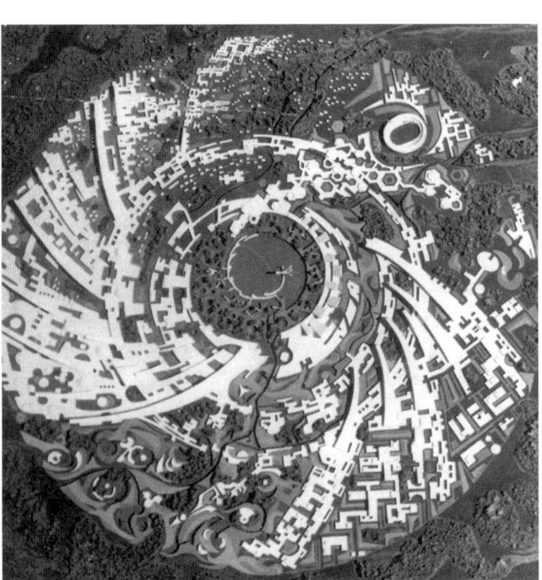

Aerial photograph of Auroville, the galaxy-shaped South Indian intentional community designed in the mid-1960s by French architect Roger Anger.

HE IS FRESH AND EVERYONE ELSE IS TIRED

In 1966, New York's new mayor, John Lindsay, launched a series of far-reaching plans to transform the city, most of which were never realized. The authors recover that vision and its lessons for the present day.

by Ian Volner
and Matico Josephson
published May 5, 2009

IN JANUARY OF 1966, in the midst of a debilitating transit strike, the recently inaugurated mayor of New York, John Lindsay, vowed to take on the city's "power brokers." He defined them as "a group of special interests . . . who for long years have sought to control the engines of government." While Lindsay's target that day was the Transport Workers Union, New York's "master builder" Robert Moses, was in close range.

At the time, Moses was still New York's most celebrated planner and the chairman of the mighty Triborough Bridge and Tunnel Authority. Highways were his chief endowment to the city, but they were also his curse. As the '60s waned, and as the city slipped into economic and social turmoil, it became apparent that Triborough's legacy would be a metropolis with a decaying physical plant and a declining quality of life. In place of Moses's racially partitioned New York, Lindsay, elected under the banner "He is fresh and everyone else is tired," promised a new city that would be integrated and equal, dense in population and activity, accommodating to people as well as to automobiles.

Robert Moses did, after a fight, step down from Triborough in 1966, but not before making a final bitter pronouncement: "That goddamned whippersnapper . . . will come and go; Triborough is going to be around for a long time."

The prediction today seems clairvoyant. "Fun City," as Lindsay's vision was sometimes called, came and went with the mayor who championed it, while the Moses legacy lives on. Moses suffered a long period of disrepute following the publication of *The Power Broker*, Robert Caro's damning 1974 biography. But he has since been recuperated: Hilary Ballon and Kenneth Jackson's 2008 book, *Robert Moses and the Modern City*, describes Moses as the sole individual capable of grasping "the city as a whole," dramatizing the opposition of antiplanning and master planning, neighborhood and metropolis. This narrative opposes Moses to writer and activist Jane Jacobs and her

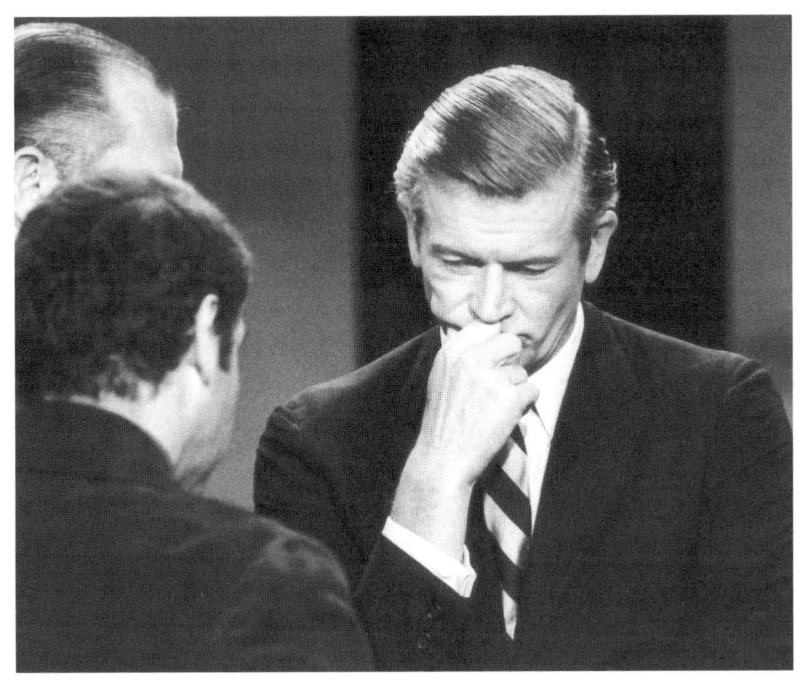

New York City Mayor John Lindsay.
Photo: Emilio Grossi.

supposedly antiplanning cohort (whom Moses derided as "nobody but a bunch of mothers"). In doing so, it obscures the long, varied history of "metropolitanism"—a combination of political culture, planning strategy, and architectural style—in New York. Moses's metropolitanism aimed to integrate New York into the landscape beyond its borders, slicing the urban fabric with throughways channeling rush hour traffic; the residuum, particularly housing, was displaced and relocated to the periphery. This approach to planning succeeded in inserting the city into a highway network but produced social divisions that would fester in later decades. Its failings would prompt a remarkably cogent, if less wildly prolific, response in the reforming urbanism of Mayor Lindsay.

Lindsay, elected as a Republican reformist in 1965, took cues from Moses and the organic poetics of the neighborhood fostered by Jacobs but refused to merely triangulate them. Immediately after assuming office, Lindsay sought to establish a third-wave metropolitanism. He would remedy the ills of the cannibalizing urbanism

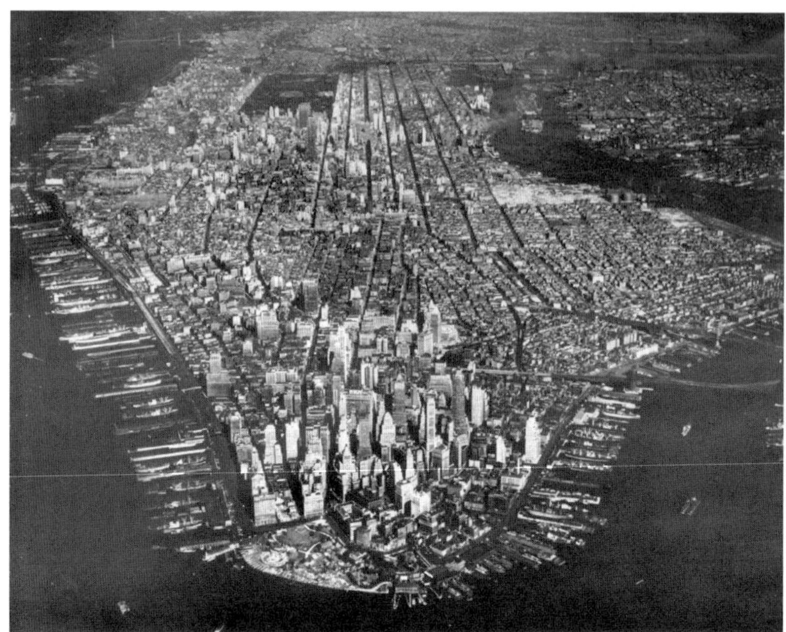

Aerial view of Manhattan, 1945.

undertaken by his predecessors and by then discredited—not by curtailing planning projects, whether housing developments or highways, but by dramatically expanding them into a singular planning ethos. He promised to thread infrastructure around the urban fabric rather than having it cut through the tenements, markets, smaller streets, and parks that were the warp and weft of New York's neighborhoods. Citizen participation would defuse the generally fraught planning process, granting a sense of empowerment and autonomy to previously disenfranchised communities. The focus of the planner was to engender a harmonious social order through the construction of green-fringed civic monuments, opening up the city for residents whose proper habitat was the entire metropolis.

The Lindsay interval has been largely forgotten, in no small part because of the painful memories of the social upheavals that marred his tenure—the Columbia student occupation, the Brownsville teachers' strike, the Knapp Commission on police corruption—as well as the popular perception that Lindsay's urban approach failed to address those upheavals adequately. Yet it remains pertinent to anyone interested in how New York and other major cities throughout the country might be improved.

Our present moment of economic crisis, with all it portends for the nation's crumbling infrastructure, would seem an ideal one to look back to a time when the dire need for the government to renew its compact with citizens compelled it to cast aside ideological and reactionary models alike, in favor of an ambitious program to remake New York and ensure its future. Perhaps most pertinent of all is the story of a young, cultured, and charismatic politician, as confident in the power of the people to effect change as in the ability of government to keep pace with their needs, who promised to usher in a new era for a city plagued by political gridlock, institutional malaise, and an insurmountable deficit, and who was elected under the banner "He is fresh and everyone else is tired."

Lindsay's election was the product of a skillfully orchestrated media campaign, the main theme of which was urban reform. The past decade had seen the first population decline in New York's history. Previously thriving neighborhoods in the western and southern Bronx, northern Manhattan, and central Brooklyn were beset with economic depression, gripped by racial tension, and rent by major roadway projects. Something had to be done, and the attractive, vigorous Lindsay, whom many could hardly refrain from comparing to John F. Kennedy, seemed the man to do it.

While many of Lindsay's projects bordered on the fantastic, his overall strategy was formulated and implemented by an array of decidedly grounded bureaucrats. But Lindsay and many in his inner circle were plagued by a peculiar variety of cultural provincialism, having never lived or worked in (or thought too much about) bedroom white-ethnic commuter communities in the outer boroughs. Lindsay endorsed a plan for Greater New York but took little interest in the facts on the ground anywhere outside Manhattan. Even with all the "contextually sensitive" and "vest-pocket" projects—small constructions on vacant lots in otherwise built-up blocks—proposed and built by Lindsay's planners in mid-rise, middle-class neighborhoods in Brooklyn and Queens, the intricacies of those communities often seemed lost on them. The plan for a Linear City in central Brooklyn was killed by local opposition when funding for an attached educational complex disappeared; a low-income public housing project proposed for Forest Hills, Queens, was altered beyond recognition by angry middle-class neighbors, who preferred that it be a retirement home for financially solvent seniors.

The local opposition to these proposals came in direct response to the perceived elitism of the Lindsay cadre—either by minority groups who resented the intrusion of white interlopers, as happened in Brooklyn, or by white ethnics who felt the liberal administration favored the interests of minority groups and the poor, as happened in Queens. Ironically, local opposition was often facilitated by the administration's insistence on community involvement in the planning process. For all Lindsay's moral uprightness and commitment to the impoverished and oppressed, his understanding of social conditions was limited; his breezy liberalism earned him derogatory nicknames such as "Mr. Clean," "Captain Marvel," "Sir Galahad," "Prince Valiant," and "The White Knight."

Lindsay's character aside, the mayor's urban program might have been more fully realized were it not for the wretched state of the city's finances. Well before October 29, 1975, when the front page of the *Daily News* accused President Ford of telling the city to "drop dead" after it asked for a federal bailout, the municipal coffers were alarmingly depleted. In 1973, President Nixon declared a moratorium on federal public housing expenditure, effectively ending New York's program of public housing construction. The situation was not improved by Lindsay's relatively poor understanding of the machinations of state government. He was routinely outmaneuvered by Governor Nelson Rockefeller, who channeled state money toward his own pet projects in the city, such as the World Trade Center, Battery

Park City, and Roosevelt Island.

The money dried up at almost the same instant that local opposition, strengthened by the popularity of Jane Jacobs's antiplanning philosophy, gained the upper hand. Lindsay's planning apparatus had tried to respond to Jacobs's criticisms of second-wave metropolitanism, but the mayor's technocratic idealism was ultimately quashed by communities that had, by nature of living with the consequences of Robert Moses's projects, become resistant to the very idea of urban planning. The promise of John Lindsay went unfulfilled, and his departure from city hall sounded the death knell of large-scale planning.

Nevertheless, that promise lives on, though buried under the patina of late '70s urban decay, the vulgar commercial projects erected en masse in the '80s and '90s, and the more recent vogue for speculative luxury condos and gaudy renovations of older tenements and townhouses. In examining a few of the projects built under the Lindsay administration, it is possible to discern the traces of other, unrealized proposals, the palimpsest of a master plan— elements of which might well be resurrected to address our own needs.

In what follows, we elaborate on the four spheres of Lindsay-era planning, detailing a number of realized and unrealized projects. One can glimpse in these projects— especially in the two major unbuilt proposals in Brooklyn and Harlem—the receding horizon of the late-modernist avant-garde in architecture, as reflected in megastructuralism, New Brutalism, neo-Futurism, linear cities, and, most significantly, the revisionist modernism of Paul Rudolph and Louis Kahn.

1. UPTOWN PUBLIC HOUSING

With its leaky ceilings, broken windows, and inadequate heating, the tenement at 311 East 100th Street became an emblem of the decay of New York's northern neighborhoods in the 1950s. Lindsay's housing expert, Woody Klein, joined the mayoral campaign because of his conviction—detailed in his 1964 book, *Let In the Sun*—that no wealthy metropolis should have a 311 East 100th Street on its conscience. By 1966, a band of blight stretched from 96th Street in Manhattan as far uptown as Inwood, hopped the University Heights Bridge at 207th Street, and followed the Grand Concourse south again, through the Bronx and all the way to Hunts Point. The causes were familiar: eminent domain demolitions, freeway construction, white flight, official neglect, arson, and an influx of black and Puerto Rican families seeking low-skill industrial jobs that were no longer available in the postwar city. Both northern Manhattan and the South Bronx were identified by the Lindsay administration as areas in need of major rehabilitation. Many housing projects for the area were proposed, and, despite funding difficulties, a number were constructed, among them the best of the Lindsay administration's revisionist take on urban renewal.

In 1967, an exhibition at the Museum of Modern Art called "The New City" featured work from the architecture graduate programs of Cornell, MIT, Columbia, and Princeton. All addressed as their theme the urban crisis as it affected Harlem and the South Bronx, and each proposed a solution: Cornell called for extensive demolitions along

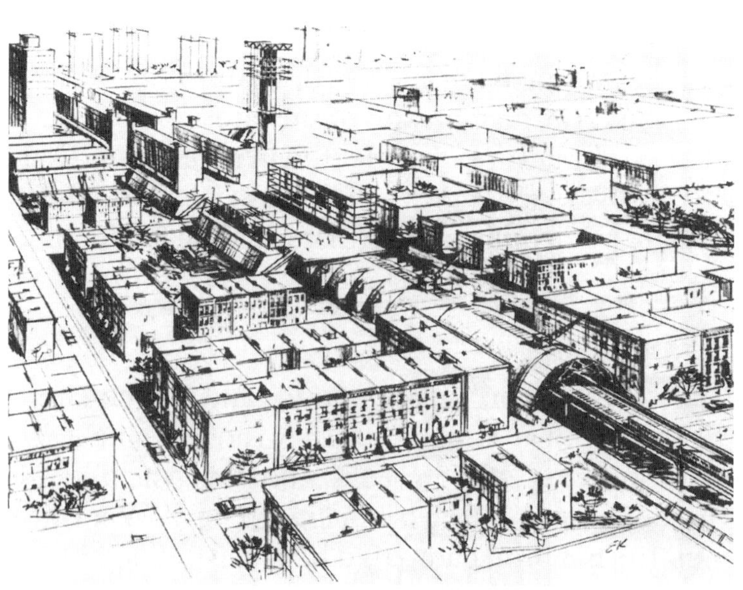

McMillan, Griffis & Mileto, *Linear City,* 1967–69, Brooklyn. Rendering.

the spine of central Harlem to create housing blocks set in vast, interconnected parks; Princeton imagined a massive public facility in the form of a pier jutting out from the Hudson waterfront, connected to Harlem by a string of new parks; MIT exhibited a plan for a series of land bridges and pedestrian walkways that would span Hell Gate, the strait on the East River separating Queens and Randall's Island. Given their scope and extravagant cost, none of these plans were ever seriously considered, save for one: Columbia's proposal to construct a two-mile-long housing, retail, and transit corridor along northern Park Avenue via a concrete vault placed over the Harlem Rail viaduct between 97th and 135th streets.

That this extraordinary proposal got as far as structural soundings on the new Metro-North elevated track owes as much to its design as to its designers: The Columbia team was led by the architects who were to become the core members of the influential Urban Design Group, which came to epitomize the Lindsay administration's belief in progressive architecture as an agent of urban improvement and sensitivity to the city's traditional character. In the exhibition catalogue, the team described the challenge they faced as one of providing "housing and other kinds of renewal without relocating the people for whom such improvements are intended." The solution was to build on the urban margin, making habitable the otherwise-empty transit corridor. The vault was to deploy a concrete truss system that could be laid in sections: Within it, new roadways for city buses would be laid over the existing Park Avenue roadway and the rail lines; outside, residential towers and parks would be built beside and above the vault. Park Avenue North, as its designers called it, was a breakthrough, applying a largely untried megastructural conceit—an enormous, multifunctional aggregate of modular elements—to the very local problems that had thwarted New York planners in the past. Transit would complement rather than disrupt housing. "Planner's blight," in which the announcement of renewal demolitions actually hastens a neighborhood's decline, would be avoided by doing away with demolitions altogether.

Unfortunately, early feasibility studies revealed Park Avenue North to be prohibitively expensive. Elsewhere uptown, however, some of its principles were put into practice. The Twin Parks neighborhood in the North Bronx was to see the first and most competently executed example of the vest-pocket-housing approach. Twin Parks was an area dotted with abandoned buildings, some of which had already been cleared, either by the city or by fire. In consultation with the UDG, architect Giovanni Pasanella began designing one of the sites, Twin Parks West, in 1967; construction was completed in 1973. The project consisted of five buildings ranging from ten to eighteen stories, their profiles reflecting the scale of the neighborhood without sacrificing the objective of a high-rise, high-density development.

As with many uptown projects of the period, Twin Parks was executed under the authority of the Urban Development Corporation, a public-private corporation created to issue bonds for housing construction, directed by former Lindsay adviser Ed Logue. The design approach shared by Logue and the UDG planners was borne out by another project in the Bronx that bears a remarkable resemblance to the unexecuted Park Avenue North. In 1970, Logue's UDC commissioned an ambitious plan from M. Paul Friedberg & Associates for rehabilitating the marginal Harlem River waterfront in the Morris Heights section of the Bronx, just west of the Major Deegan Expressway and Metro-North Harlem Line railroad. The firm proposed connecting the neighborhood to the east with a state park on the river, via planks laid over the road and rail. The project was christened Harlem River Park Towers and completed in 1975.

River Park Towers was the plan's residential component, and it presented an opportunity to realize in miniature what the UDG had envisioned for Park Avenue North: a major piece of housing placed over working infrastructure, with parking facilities, a school, stores, and Roberto Clemente State Park all attached. Visitors strolling along the complex's central walkway, which is beside the train tracks, are flanked on one side by textured stone storefronts, which evoke a typical city street, and on the other side by a sheer wall of forty-four-floor towers with no setbacks, their cutaway corners giving way to protruding blocks on the uppermost levels.

Another UDC signal project, Arthur A. Schomburg Plaza, can be found only a few blocks west of the unrealized Park Avenue North, at the corner of Central Park North and 5th Avenue. The Gruzen & Partners design features a midblock play area constructed over a low-rise parking structure, slung between two thirty-five-story towers. In accordance with the Lindsay mission of community-led renewal, the UDC entered into protracted and at times heated negotiations with Harlem residents, which resulted in an anodyne design, but one that included retail space, daycare facilities, and a child-development center (and delayed its completion until 1975). Schomburg Plaza is a mere ten blocks from 311 East 100th Street. In 1968, as Woody Klein was preparing to leave the mayor's office, he paid one last visit to the address. Despite the administration's efforts to turn the neighborhood around, 311 East 100th still stood in very much the same condition as Klein had found it seven years before. What had been a signpost for urban decline had become a measuring stick for the shortcomings of urban policy.

2. THE DEVELOPER FIX: MIDTOWN AND DOWNTOWN

Against the general impression of a city in peril, with a shrinking population and a deteriorating economy, stands the glaring fact of commercial development in Manhattan during the Lindsay years, during which some fifty million square feet of office space were built in two distinct spheres, Lower Manhattan and Midtown.

Lower Manhattan had long since been eclipsed by Midtown as the preeminent business district, even as it

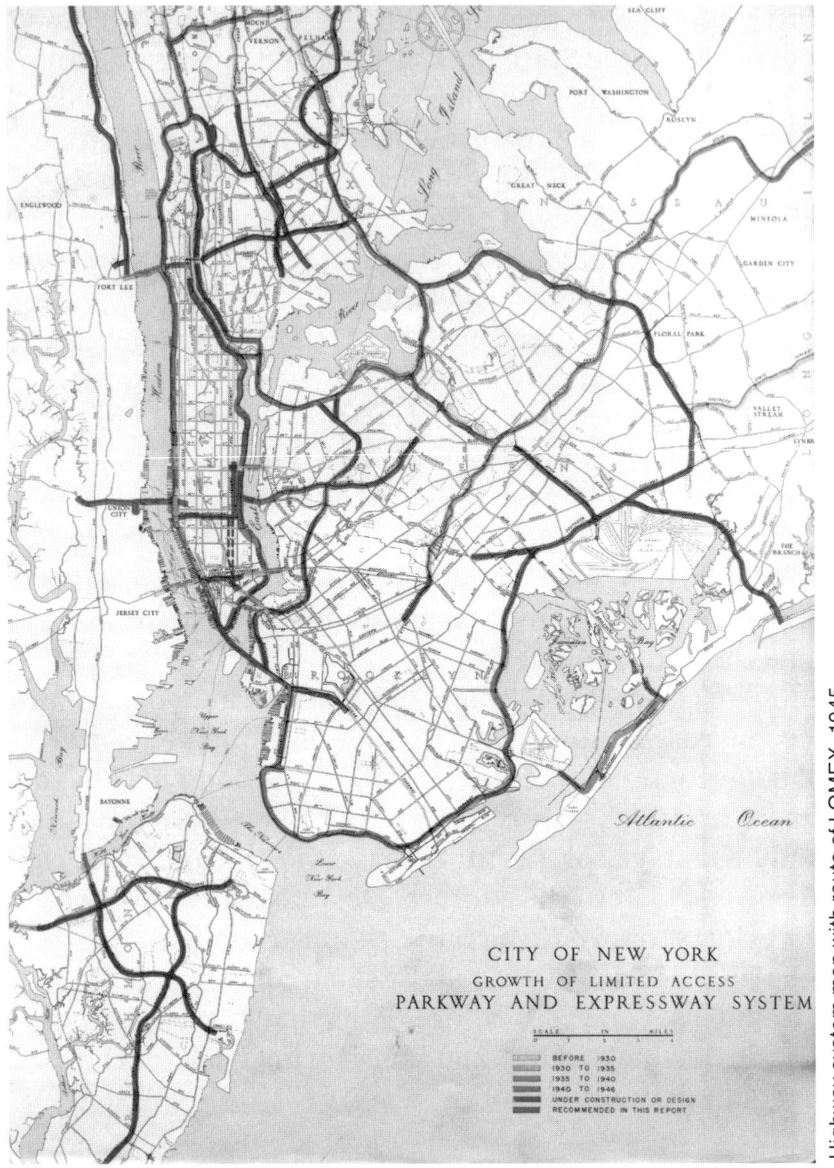

Highway system map with route of LOMEX, 1945.

remained home to the New York Stock Exchange. New construction had stood at roughly nil for nearly a generation; at night, workers fled the area. The Rockefeller family, which still had considerable real estate holdings in the area, was naturally interested in seeing it revitalized and combined forces with local business leaders to push for the construction of the World Trade Center, which was shovel-ready by the time of Lindsay's election.

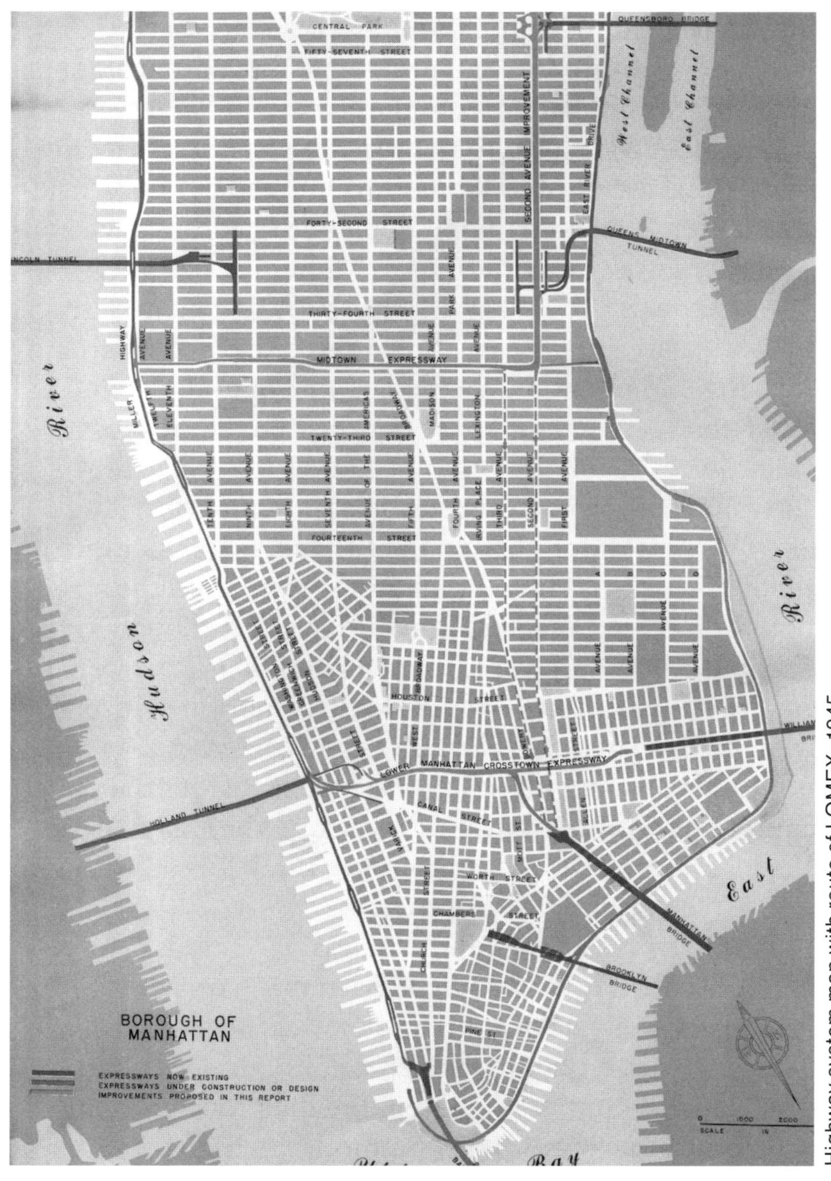

Highway system map with route of LOMEX, 1945.

Midtown, meanwhile, had seen steady growth since the end of the war, but the buildings constructed since were widely disparaged. The city's 1961 zoning revision encouraged the tower-in-a-park model of corporate architecture, first seen in Mies van der Rohe's Seagram Building, built at 53rd Street and Park Avenue in 1958. The tax-incentive structure of the zoning law allowed developers to build taller skyscrapers so long as they provided

INVALID FORMAT

2

ISSUE 6 2009

plazas at the ground level. Soon Park Avenue was lined with these corporate towers; drab expanses of marble separated anonymous facades from the street.

In Lower Manhattan, the UDG negotiated with developers to integrate new construction spurred by the World Trade Center. The instrument of choice was "creative zoning." In exchange for including such amenities as porticoes, overhead pedestrian walkways, and subway entrances, developers were allowed to boost their overall floor area by building higher and by increasing lot coverage. The UDG also instituted mandatory building envelopes requiring that towers reach their lot lines, creating consistent street walls that framed long, unbroken sight lines. The strategy was intended to turn the Financial District into an area where workers could lunch in the sun, cross the street without braving traffic, and descend into the subway without stepping outside. Too often the result was a warren of concrete precinct walls and unsightly marble planters. But the increase in public space has had a hand in Lower Manhattan's transformation into a hub of residential development, and the wider building envelopes helped restore the visual effect of the skyline—now a thick forest, rather than a sparse patch, of skyscrapers.

While Lindsay's planners worked to regulate development downtown, they lavished attention on Midtown. Following an analysis of foot- and car-traffic patterns, the UDG put forward a plan to totally reconfigure Manhattan's highest-density commercial area. It called for widening select crosstown routes to accommodate a higher volume of automobiles, restricting automobiles on other streets by expanding sidewalks, and closing Madison Avenue to cars altogether, creating a pedestrian-shopping promenade. This radical traffic retooling never happened. Nevertheless, the efficacy of Lindsay's planners in both encouraging and controlling private development can be seen in the thriving Theater District and on 5th Avenue, where commercial towers were induced to include theaters and shopping; in the porticoes around Lincoln

Square (pale imitations of the porticoes at Lincoln Plaza);
and in the bridges spanning lower West Street, which connect the skyscrapers to the east and Battery Park City to
the west.

One component of the UDG's ambitious traffic fix
was in fact realized: North-south pedestrian arcades,
appearing midblock and cutting through office buildings,
were made possible by the same trade-offs as were made
with developers in Lower Manhattan. The main sequence
of arcades is located between 6th and 5th Avenues, allowing one to walk from 51st Street to 57th Street without
recourse to the main thoroughfares. The arcades are a
mixed bag, attesting to advantages gained by developers
without offering evidence of meaningful public amenities
created in return. Without the proposed comprehensive
changes to car and pedestrian traffic in the area, these
dwarfed arcades, suffocated by packed crosstown streets,
are more symptom than reprieve. Those anonymous towers, pierced by dimly lit passages lined with cookie-cutter
minicafés and traversed by hurrying office workers, are
hardly inspiring works of architecture, and the district
only hints at the dynamism and livability envisioned by the
Lindsay planners.

3. LINDSAY'S LOWER MANHATTAN EXPRESSWAY

In Robert Moses's first sweeping schemes for new highways, devised before the Second World War, the mile-and-
a-half-long roadway stretching from the Holland Tunnel
to the Williamsburg and Manhattan Bridges stood out
as a potential link between land masses. Connecting the
proposed East Side and West Side highways, the Lower
Manhattan Expressway, or LOMEX as it came to be called,
would obviate the need for traffic between New Jersey
and Long Island to circumnavigate the southern tip of
Manhattan. By Moses's own estimate, construction of the
elevated highway would have entailed the displacement
of some 1,972 households and 804 businesses, and opposition from residents and elected officials stalled LOMEX

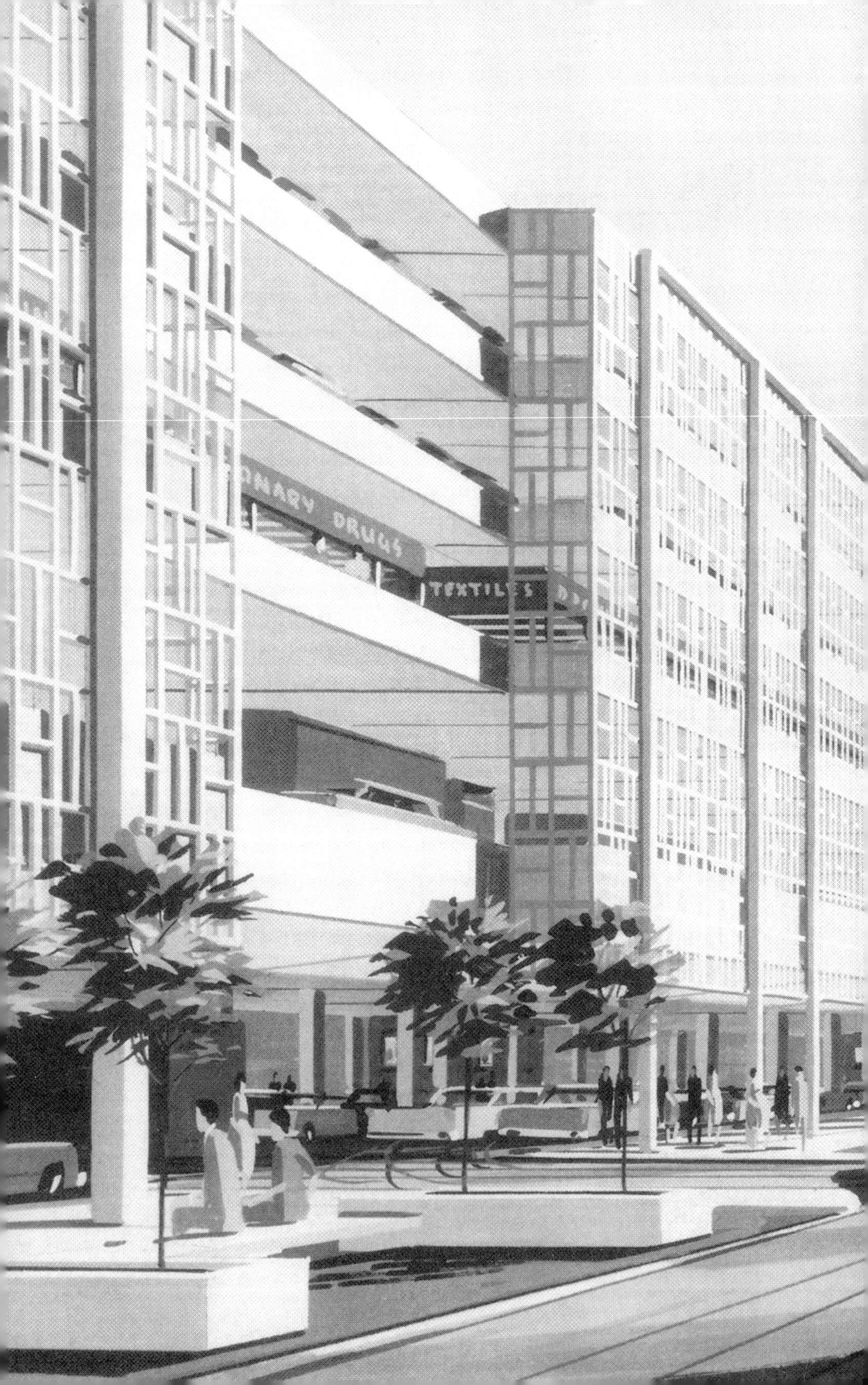
DRUGS
TEXTILES

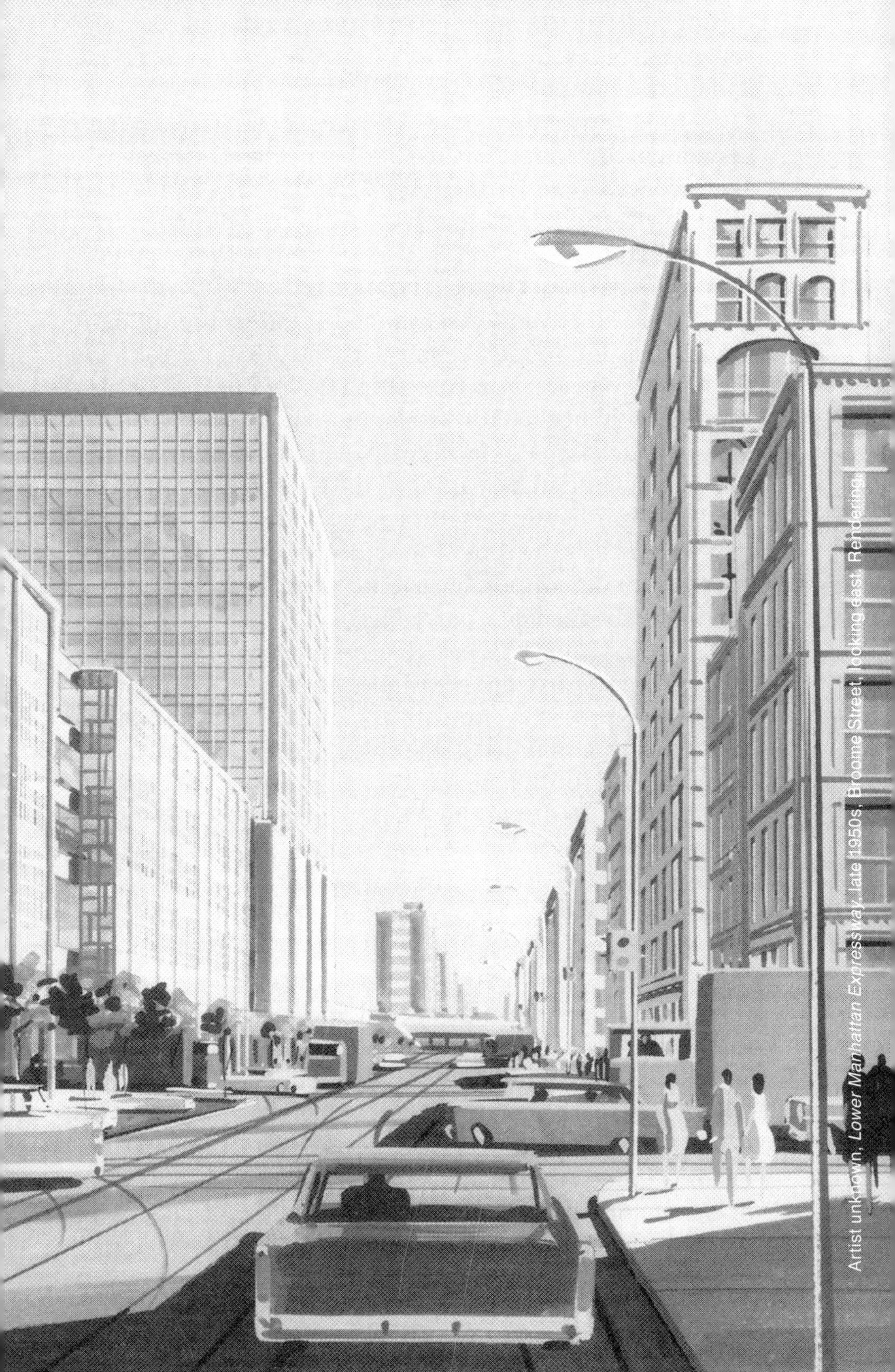

Artist unknown, Lower Manhattan Expressway, late 1950s. Broome Street, looking east. Rendering.

throughout the 1940s and '50s. Moses produced several revamped plans, but by 1965, LOMEX had very few friends and quite a few enemies.

John Lindsay was one of the latter—at first. During his campaign, Congressman Lindsay declared himself "anti-LOMEX" and came out for what the press termed the "Lindsay Loop," a belt highway tracing the perimeter of Lower Manhattan. After he was elected, however, the mayor took a second look at LOMEX and by May 1966 had retreated. He now disapproved of the "route" of the expressway but found no fault with the project in toto. Over the next two years, two competing LOMEX proposals circulated. The first called for a strip-and-cover tunnel, roughly on the model of the 1963 Trans-Manhattan Expressway in Upper Manhattan (leading to the George Washington Bridge). Another imagined an eighty-foot-high skyway that would clear the tops of the adjacent buildings, reducing need for demolition. Feasibility studies showed that a version of the former, a partially covered, partially tunneled route, would cause the least disruption and cost the least money. But the attempts of Lindsay's planners to build a sensitive expressway, one that took into account sensibilities of local communities, was thwarted by political momentum. In April 1968, Jane Jacobs, by then a minor celebrity, was arrested for disrupting a hearing on LOMEX. Jacobs and her supporters tore up the stenographer's record, crying, "There's no tape! There's been no meeting!" An official responded, "Arrest this woman!" and Jacobs was soon cuffed. Though she eventually pleaded guilty to disorderly conduct, her arrest galvanized the movement against LOMEX. The locus of the opposition was the neighborhood that would soon be branded SoHo, densely populated with artists and other white, educated, middle-class residents whose preservationist instincts could not brook an expressway, however sensitive. Facing a tough reelection in 1970, Lindsay quietly dropped the project, against the wishes of Governor Rockefeller; the mayor could only silence his protestations by hanging up on him.

The Confucius Plaza Apartments, a looming ensemble containing a tower and smaller outlying structures, is one impressive remnant of LOMEX. Completed in 1975 by Horowitz & Chun, Confucius Plaza is bounded by the Bowery, Division Street, and the Manhattan Bridge at what would have been the eastern terminus of LOMEX. With its facade gracefully sweeping around a U-shaped plan, the tower marks a conspicuous break with the boxy high-rise housing projects built in previous decades on the Lower East Side. Though Confucius Plaza's bulk threatened to obliterate street life, planners compensated for the intrusion by building a shop-lined portico along the western side of the building and a school along the street. They also included an arcade that allowed pedestrian access from the Bowery through to Divison Street, by way of an ample courtyard tucked into the building's horseshoe-shaped footprint. Confucius Plaza can be seen rearing up far Canal Street, a stark visual endpoint punctuating the long urban prospect. The tower would have set up a remarkable approach for cars moving eastward along LOMEX—an obelisk marking the route to Brooklyn—while its curvature would have perfectly accommodated the sweep of LOMEX's entry ramps.

4. THE MID-BROOKLYN EXPRESSWAY AND LINEAR CITY

As early as 1941, Moses had called for two major east-west thoroughfares in Brooklyn. The Bushwick Expressway would track the present route of Bushwick Avenue from the Williamsburg Bridge to East New York. The Cross-Brooklyn Expressway would connect the Verrazano-Narrows Bridge to the Nassau County line by building a road atop an underused section of the Long Island Rail Road. Though he didn't take an explicit position on the Brooklyn freeways during the campaign, his motto, "Cities are for people, not for automobiles," revealed his preference for the Cross-Brooklyn Expressway. Accordingly, in his first year in office, Lindsay rejected Moses's proposal to first complete the Bushwick

INVALID FORMAT 2

ISSUE 6 2009

Expressway and asked the state legislature to redirect funds to the Cross-Brooklyn.

As Lindsay was battling the conventional model of freeway construction in Brooklyn, another issue that had long divided the borough came to a head. The problem of school integration in New York had been a cause for controversy since the Supreme Court's *Brown v. Board of Education* ruling of 1954. The city's board of education had stumbled time and time again in its integration efforts and by the mid-'60s had managed to earn both the mistrust of black parents and the contempt of the white-ethnic anti-busing contingent. In Brooklyn, the debate centered on Brownsville, a low-income, predominantly black neighborhood directly adjacent to the white enclaves of Canarsie and East Flatbush. Within months of Lindsay's election, Brownsville parents were complaining that the city's plan to build four elementary and three intermediate schools to serve these discrete communities would effectively segregate the area's children. As an alternative, they proposed an "educational park" consisting of several schools housed in a central campus, which would draw a diverse mix of students from the area.

Lindsay became increasingly determined to scrap the Bushwick Expressway in favor of the Cross-Brooklyn, but could hardly fail to recognize that the LIRR line on Brownsville's southern perimeter sat precisely on the area's racial divide. The Cross-Brooklyn would be a de facto border between Brownsville's white and black populations—unless, as one of Lindsay's planners put it in a meeting with community leaders, the educational park could be placed "in such a way as to knit together rather than separate the communities on either side of the roadway." On February 25, 1967, Lindsay announced that Linear City, a five-and-a-half-mile-long city within a city, would be erected atop a central segment of the Cross-Brooklyn Expressway. The structure, like the unrealized Park Avenue North, was to be part of a platform covering the rail line and highway; it would include an educational park, housing, and industrial

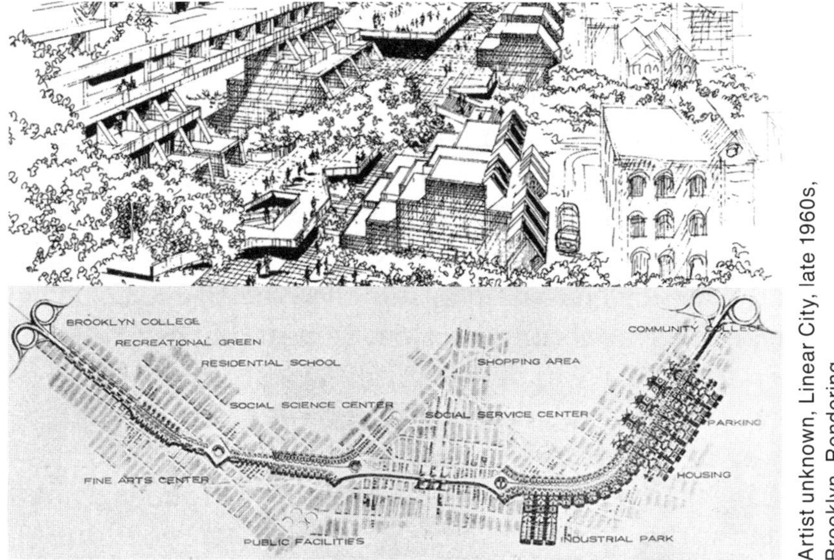

Artist unknown, Linear City, late 1960s, Brooklyn. Rendering.

facilities. Linear City would run in an L-shape from the beginning of Flatbush Avenue near the Manhattan Bridge, east to Canarsie, and then north to East New York along the rerouted Cross-Brooklyn's Queens-bound spur. Its planned terminus would have produced a cloverleaf interchange near the present juncture of the Jackie Robinson Parkway and Atlantic Avenue.

One can imagine what central Brooklyn might have been like had Linear City been built. For a driver cruising northeast along the Cross-Brooklyn from the Verrazano-Narrows Bridge, the landscape would unfold like something out of one of Antonio Sant'Elia's Futurist sketches: The platform would loom, hovering in the driver's frame; under the platform, a great torrent of automobile traffic would pass, disappearing from the view of anyone standing atop the plinth. Meanwhile, students and residents of Linear City would emerge from their homes, take an elevator to the public-transit express corridor just beneath their houses, and be conducted swiftly by bus or tram to the educational facilities. The surrounding neighborhood would be enriched by the low structures of the new development, with its shops and aboveground parks. Such, at any rate, was the dream of its planners: a synchronous and seamless city-within-a-city, an architectural fantasy drawing from the Japanese Metabolists and English neo-Futurists but adapted to the problems of race and class in New York.

In early 1968, Linear City was projected to be completed in four years' time. But the state government began to have second thoughts: State highway officials left Lindsay out to dry, despite having previously approved the project. The subsequent delay impelled the city to go ahead with planned school construction, eliminating half Linear City's raison d'être. In the meantime, local opposition to a highway-only project intensified, and the Cross-Brooklyn Expressway was abandoned altogether in 1969.

Linear City, though it left no lasting residue, may be regarded as the Lindsay project par excellence, exhibiting every major feature that distinguished the administration's planning ethos, its innovative architectural sensibility, and its political scruples. The major urban interventions of today—the myriad miniprojects of Mayor Bloomberg's PlaNYC2030, the Hudson Yards redevelopment, the Atlantic Yards project—certainly evidence a more pragmatic, if more cynical, approach to urban design, one lacking in idealism and rooted in profit motive. Perhaps a wariness of idealism is a worthwhile lesson of the Lindsay years, especially for our times. But one can't help but wonder: Do we still have the imagination, as Lindsay's planners did, to conceive a comprehensive urban vision in which every part of the city is the proper domain of every one of its citizens? ⊠

BOOM, BUST, BURN, BLAME: THE STORY OF FAKE OMAHA

From CyBar Stadium to Soapbox Yards: considering the evolution of a paper-and-ink city.

by Neil Greenberg
published May 5, 2009

I won't bore you with a detailed account of Fake Omaha's history. It is, after all, unsurprisingly similar to the basic life cycle of other American cities: boom, bust, burn, blame. What differentiates Fake Omaha is the amount of time it spent lingering between "burn" and "blame." While other cities struggled to redevelop and reinvent themselves in the 1980s and '90s, Fake Omaha was static; it seemed incapable of advancing the narrative it had created for itself, as if its identity had finally solidified around political morass and urban blight. Only in the past five years has Fake Omaha made a break with its past—as well as the politicians and builders who have defined it—and begun to piece together a plan for revitalization.

Today, Fake Omaha has a lot of catching up to do, but few would deny that it is finally catching up.
—*Larissa McClaine, Chief Planner and Development Director*

The following documents have been selected from the Fake Omaha archives in order to provide a sense of the city to outsiders and illustrate its redevelopment efforts, with the hope that other struggling municipalities can learn from its mistakes and recent successes.

In addition to transit schedules, redevelopment reports, internal memoranda, intraoffice communications, and remarks prepared for public officials, we have included aerial views of the city, so that readers may better orient themselves while navigating the city and its inner workings.

From an internal memorandum.

TO: All Planning Managers
FROM: Nick H. Curtis, Director of Planning & Economic Redevelopment Commission
DATE: August 12, 1998
RE: New Development Projects Meeting

My office has received numerous comments regarding the wave of new projects proposed for Downtown, The Felix, The Reserve, and Seis Sur. Some residents have praised these ideas as "innovative" and "badly needed." However, others have raised concerns over the feasibility of these projects.

My immediate staff has compiled a list of 14 proposed projects; we'll review all of these privately. Before we do that, I am calling a mandatory meeting for all staff to go over two projects that are of particular concern:

1) The Albright Pier development (810–870 North Fountain Street), which is already under construction. Past studies have shown that people can be enticed to visit Downtown if they know they will encounter a safe, clean, family-oriented environment. Historically, Downtown redevelopment projects have failed because of the city's inability or unwillingness to restrict and monitor public spaces in such a way as to assure this experience.

2) The Soapbox Yards development (main project office at 2621 Nearslope Place), which is currently caught up in the permitting process. Here, the developers are proposing extensive renovations to old warehouses that we've targeted for demolition. The city's own redevelopment plan for the area, formulated and presented to the community last year, proposed a big-box retail center to create a commercial core in the area; it was to be accompanied by a gated townhouse-style residential development. That plan was challenged by community organizations that lobbied for the preservation of the historic mill complex, chief among them New Day Development. The plan they support, submitted by Wagner Bros., is for a mixed-use facility with storefronts on the street level and a combination of market-priced and low-income housing on the upper levels. It aims to "take advantage of the site's location at the crossroads of three historic and culturally vibrant neighborhoods"—one black, one white, and one Hispanic.

In the past, such projects have been undermined by existing tensions between these groups, which has discouraged interest among young professionals, and as of yet I have no reason to believe this will not be the case with Soapbox Yards. Furthermore, the project banks on the notion that an expensive renovation of historic architecture will be more appealing to the desired inhabitants than the use of generic architecture (the success of which has been proven elsewhere), and disregards proven draws such as abundant parking, family restaurants in the proximity, and the presence of national retailers.

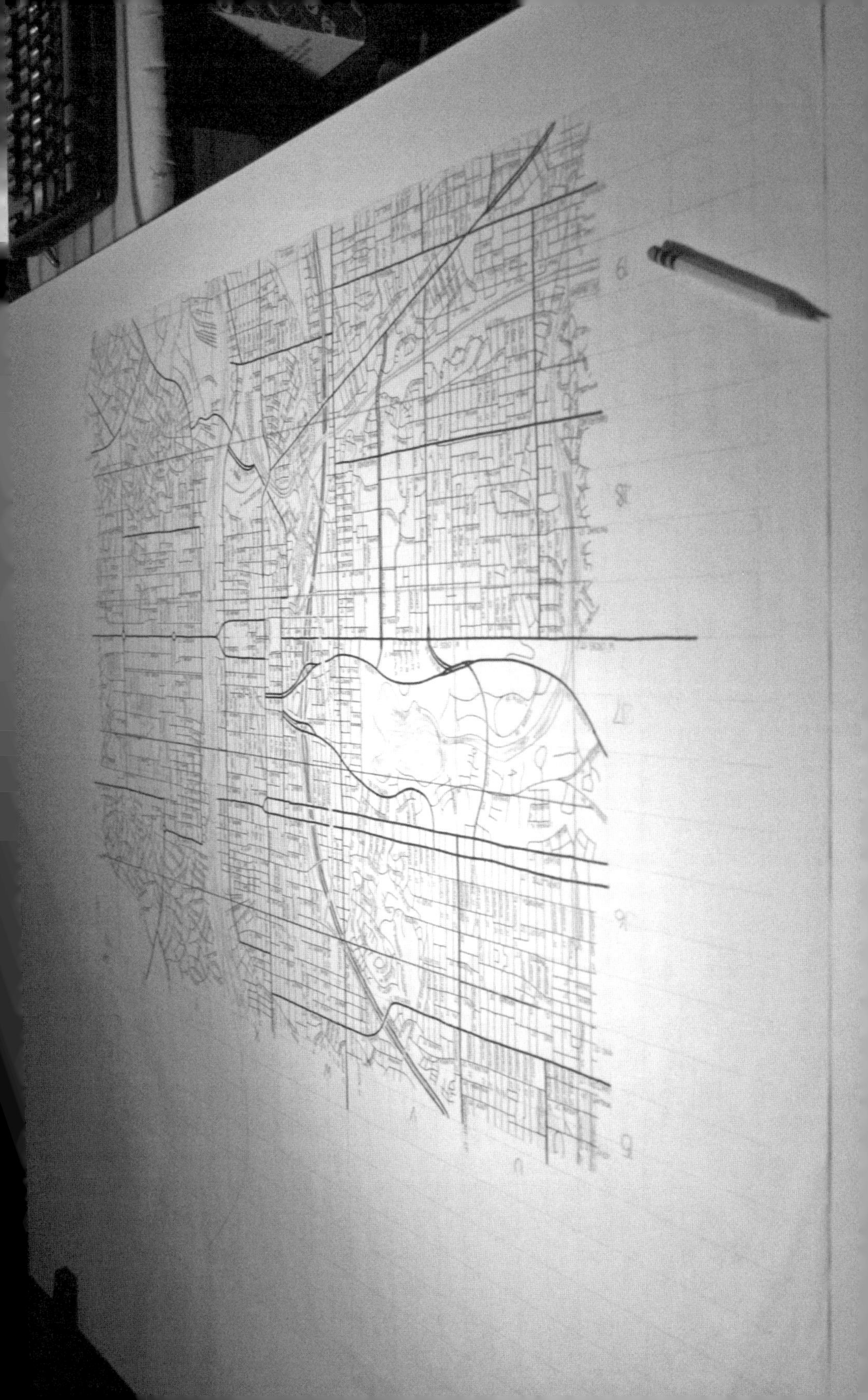

You are all required to attend a meeting regarding these projects. It will take place on Monday, August 17, at 12:30 pm in Room B031 (next to the cafeteria in the basement). No food is allowed in the conference room, so you'll have to take your lunch on your own time. Due to the recent court injunction, I am required to open this meeting to the public. However, I don't expect many members of the public to attend.
—NHC/km

From an email between planning managers.

FROM: Wurzburg, Gary <wurzburgg@staffmail.city-fo.net>
SUBJECT: Planning Mtg Follow-Up
TO: Spence, Kyle <spencek2@staffmail.city-fo.net>
DATE: Monday, August 17, 1998, 5:33 PM

Kyle,

I think Curtis was looking at you and me when he mentioned community outreach near CyBar and Soapbox. Maybe we should meet for a minute after lunch tomorrow and figure out how to tackle this? I don't know about you, but I've done a few meetings in that neighborhood. They're always talking about sidewalks and low speeds and kids playing outside—and they like Wagner/New Day's version of Soapbox Yards more than they like ours. They have a sentimental attachment to some of the local businesses that are still open there, but I don't think any of them even go there.

I mean, have you ever seen them at the pupusa place? They talk about how great the pupusas are but I bet they've never even been there. What is a pupusa, anyway?

In any case, we need to figure out how to convince them that the Soapbox plan isn't going to work, regardless of how good it makes them feel. We need to look into that lady who came to the meeting to see if she's working with New Day. Please find out more about her. I think she signed in on the clipboard. Talk to Karen and see if she held on to the sign-in sheet. And tell me ASAP what time you can meet tomorrow.
-Gary

PS: I think Curtis's diet is actually working. He kept pulling up his pants in the meeting.

PPS: Drinks at The Paddywagon Weds. at 8. Are you ever gonna ask that bartender for her number?

From an internal memorandum dated April 5, 1995.

TALKING POINTS FOR CYBAR STADIUM OPENING PREPARED FOR LT. GOVERNOR CAROLYN MCNARY

• This isn't just a stadium. It's a linchpin for rebuilding the entire city.

• We're pleased to enhance business in the neighborhood with the addition of 11,000 new parking spaces.

• We're hoping for several million dollars in spin-off development. We envision that the good energy created by CyBar Stadium will encourage entrepreneurs to take new chances. (No specific plans for new business development, so skirt issue!) Mayor Bowman has told me that he already has letters of interest from Hooters, Best Buy, and T.G.I. Fridays.

• The whole state is proud of the City of Fake Omaha and Hastings County, which together pulled in $30 million in public money to make this dream a reality.

• We weren't able to locate a suitable site near any freeway, but I'd like to remind all fans that CyBar is less than ten minutes from three different freeway access points.

• This project is a great public-private partnership.

• This project is the first proof of our urban redevelopment strategy with its focus on landmark projects that will establish the city as a destination.

• Many challenges remain. But the innovation of Mayor Bowman and the commitment to promoting Fake Omaha will keep us moving forward. ⊠

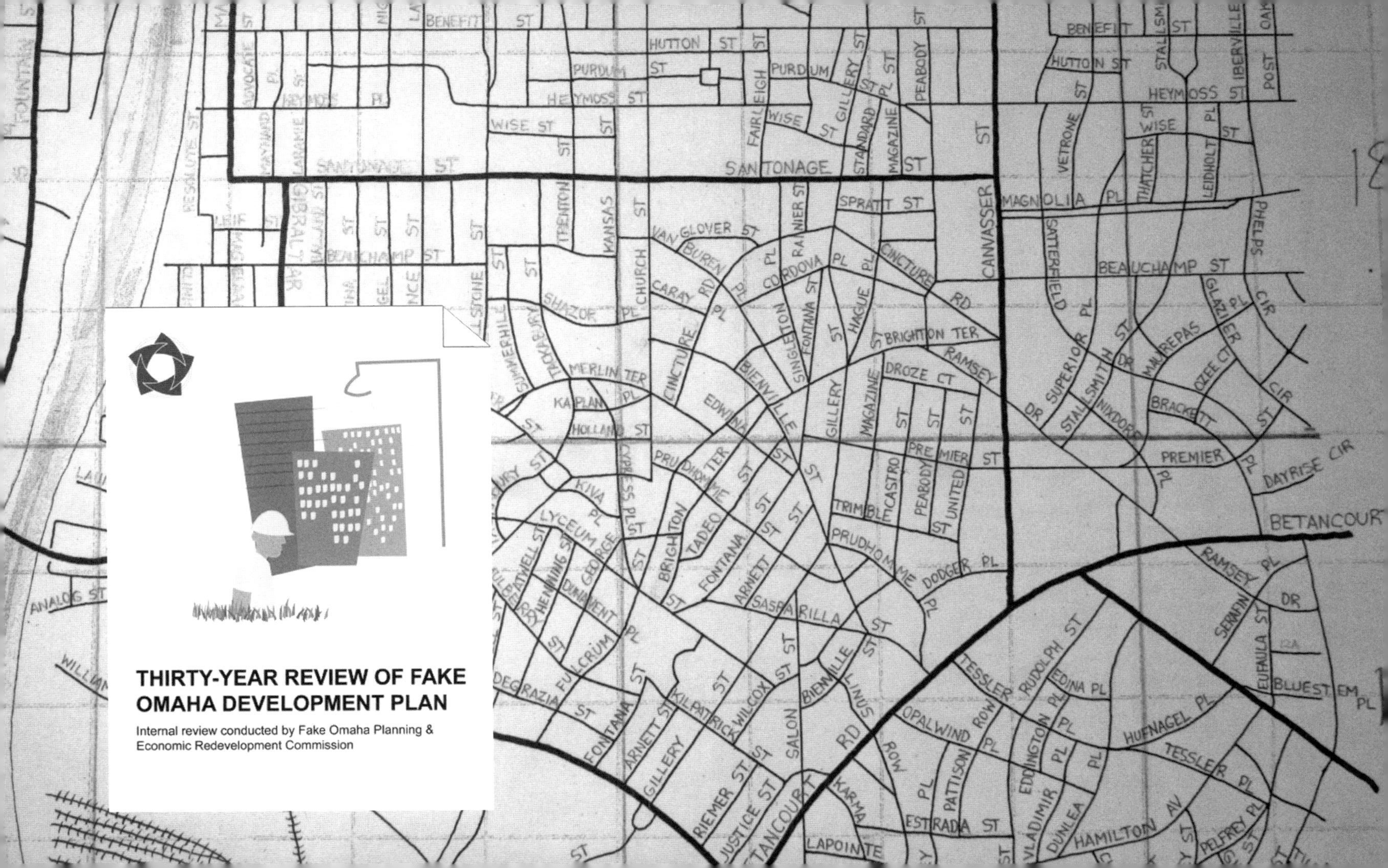

THIRTY-YEAR REVIEW OF FAKE
OMAHA DEVELOPMENT PLAN
Internal review conducted by Fake Omaha Planning &
Economic Redevelopment Commission

INVALID FORMAT 2

ISSUE 6 2009

INDEX OR CONSTRUCTED BY WAY OF EXPERIMENT

Supreme geometries and densely packed buildings: an artist project cannibalizing the sites and structures of modernism in Mexico City.

by José León Cerrillo
with Peter J. Russo
published May 5, 2009

In its original form, "Index or Constructed by Way of Experiment" features a Flash animation that enables the reader to cycle through a series of overlapping images of archetypal abstract and architectural forms. Here Cerrillo reconfigures that animated palimpsest for the page.

*Só a Antropofagia nos une. Socialmente.
Economicamente. Filosoficamente....*

*Foi porque nunca tivemos gramáticas,
nem coleções de velhos vegetais. E nunca
soubemos o que era urbano, suburbano,
fronteiriço e continental. Preguiçosos no
mapa-múndi do Brasil....*

*Contra o mundo reversível e as idéias
objetivadas. Cadaverizadas. O stop do pens-
amento que é dinâmico. O indivíduo vitima
do sistema. Fonte das injustiças clássicas.
Das injustiças românticas. E o esquecimento
das conquistas interiores.*

Cannibalism alone unites us. Socially.
Economically. Philosophically....

It is because we never had grammar
books, nor collections of old vegetables.
And we never knew what urban, suburban, frontiers and continents were.
We were a lazy spot on the world map
of Brazil....

Down with the reversible world and
against objectified ideas. Cannibalized.
The curtailment of dynamic thought.
The individual as victim of the system.
Source of classical injustices. Of roman-
tic injustices. And the forgetting of
interior conquests.
—Oswald de Andrade, "Manifesto
Antropófago" ("Cannibal
Manifesto"), 1928

*index or constructed by way of experi-
ment* was conceived by José León
Cerrillo as the Internet-based
variation of an existing sculpture,
*having to do with suspended symbolic
efficiency* (2008). First exhibited
at Dispatch Projects in New
York, that work is composed of a
rack of posters emblazoned with
archetypal abstract and architectural forms, drawn from the
modernist idiom and the cities of
Latin America, respectively. The
posters are semitransparent, and
as viewers flip the windows of the
rack, they obliterate images as
others emerge.

Those posters are repurposed
in *index* along with additional animated motifs that lead the viewer

through momentary negotiations
of the tenuous and torn relations
between the past century's utopian
structures and the culture of those
people meant to be stored in them.
The step pyramid of Chichén Itzá
runs up against the endlessly repetitive hues of low-income housing in
Ixtapaluca; Lizardi's *El periquillo
sarniento,* published in 1816 and
purported to be the first American
novel, speaks through the 1968
"Black Power" Olympics and con-
current massacre of three hundred
demonstrators in Mexico City;
Mario Pani's massive Nonoalco-
Tlatelolco housing projects sit atop
Le Corbusier's Modulor propor-
tional scale.

Andrade's manifesto is a touchstone for Cerrillo. The Brazilian
poet suggested, ironically, that
in order to develop their own
literature, his countrymen should
learn from the natives who had
cannibalized the first European
colonists in order to acquire their
strengths. If Brazilians were to
apply that method to the arts,
surely they would soon have a
respectable national style. Of
course, this parodic proposal
predicted the shape that Latin
American architecture and urbanism would take over the course
of the twentieth century.

Cerrillo's work echoes these
cannibalizations and acquisi-
tions. "Tudo esta visto," reads the
text cascading down one frame
(a quotation from Augusto de
Campos's revision of the cannibal
figure from Andrade's manifesto):
Everything is seen, but no orientation emerges. The work is,
in Cerrillo's words, "a map with
which to read another map."
—*Peter J. Russo*

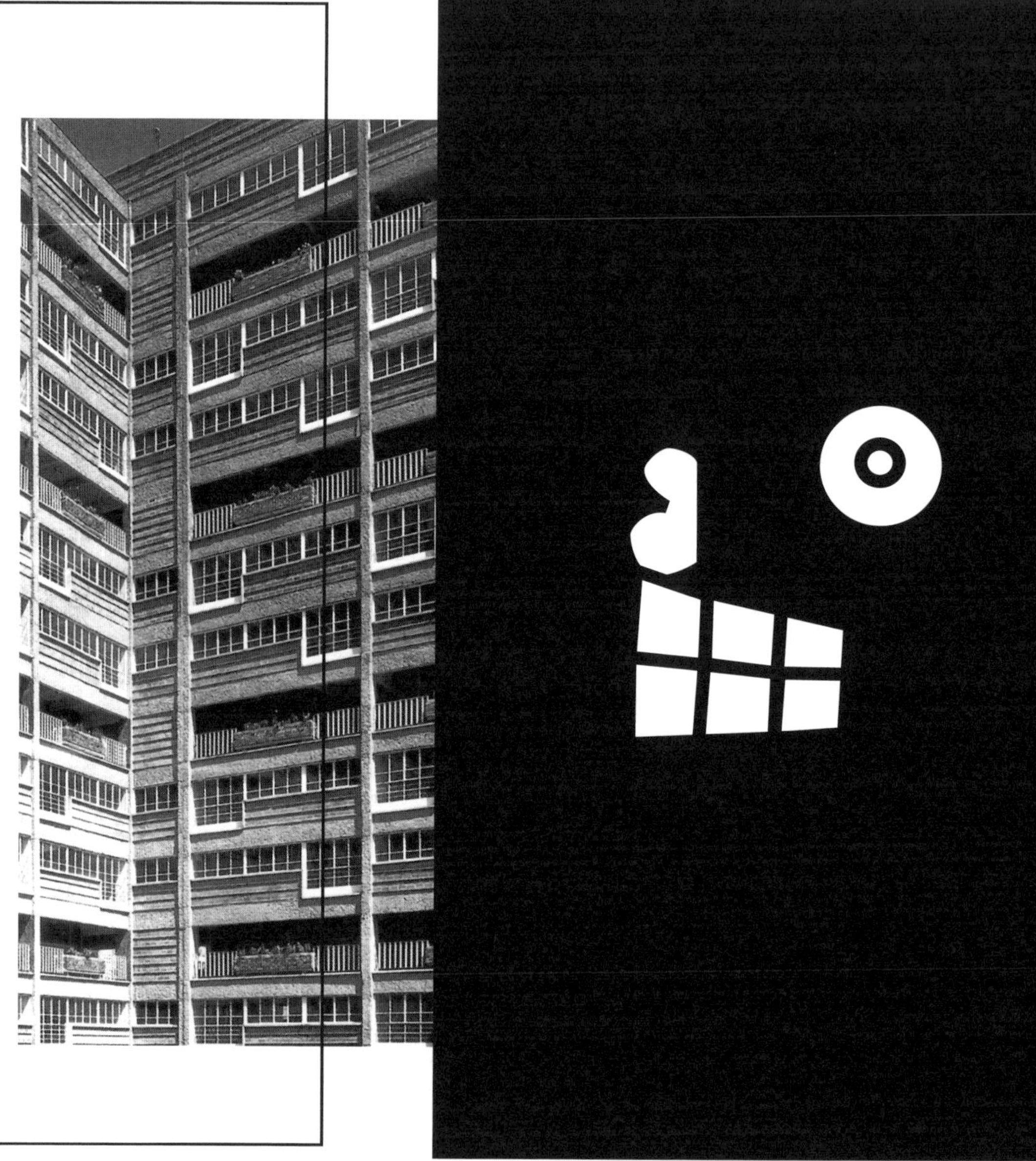

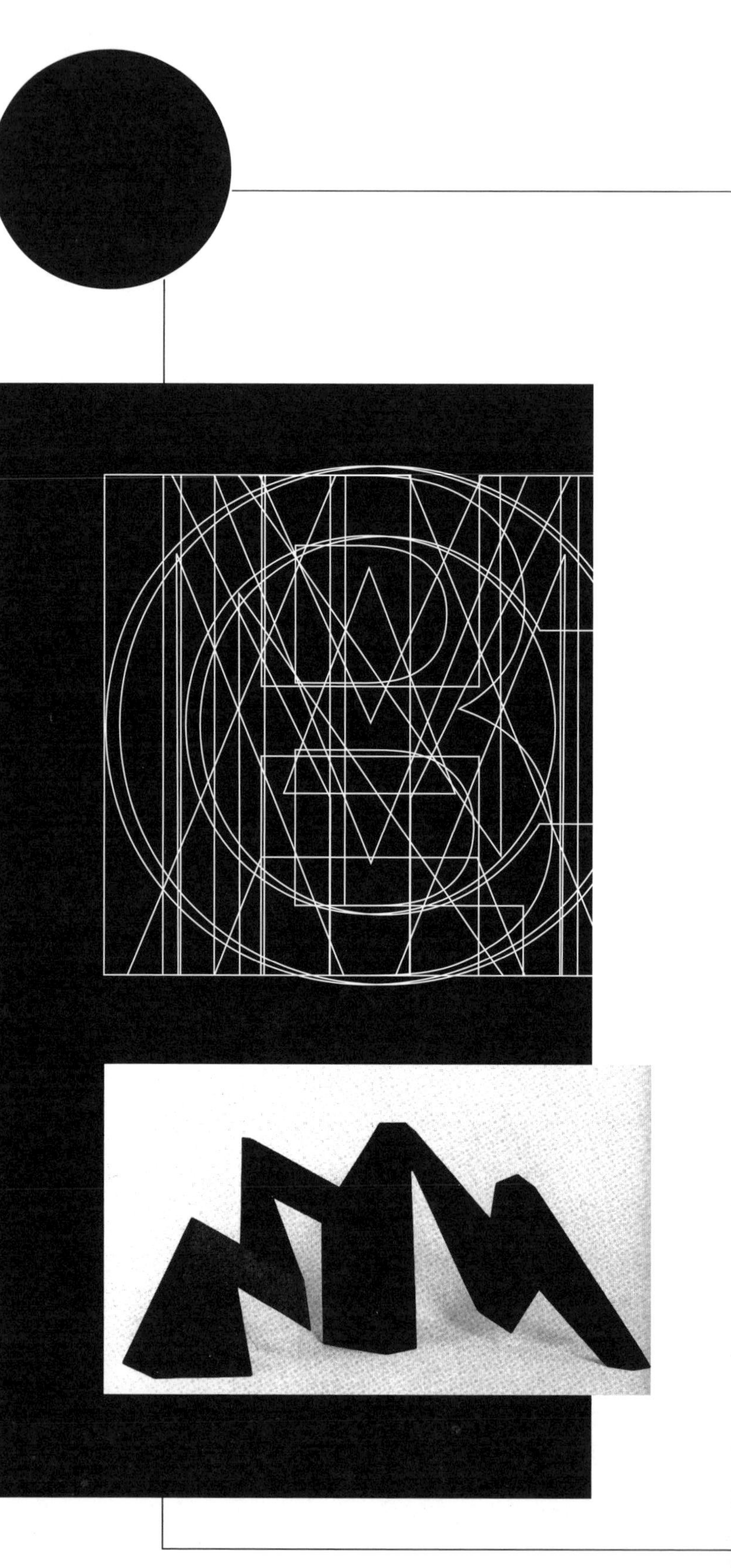

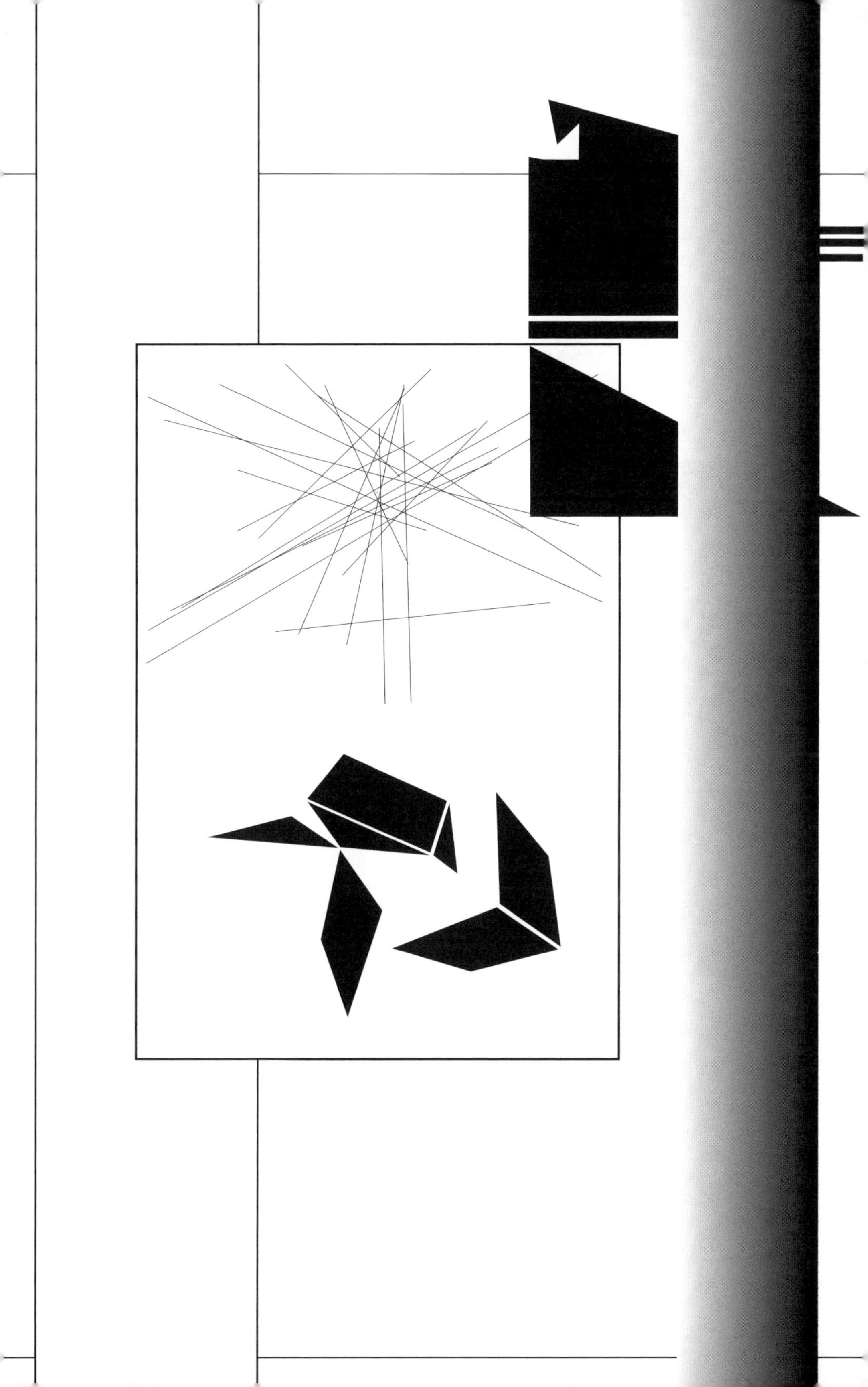

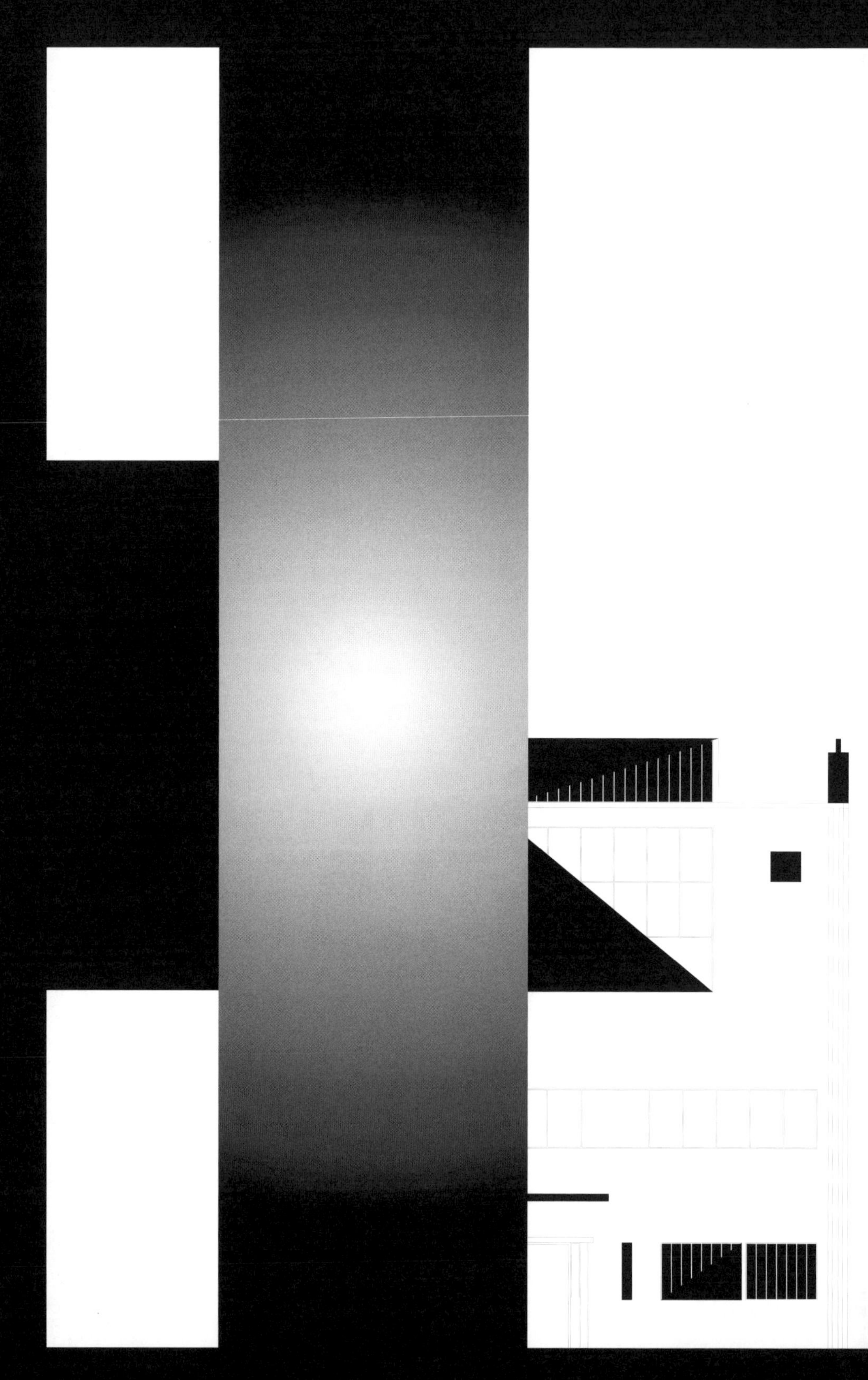

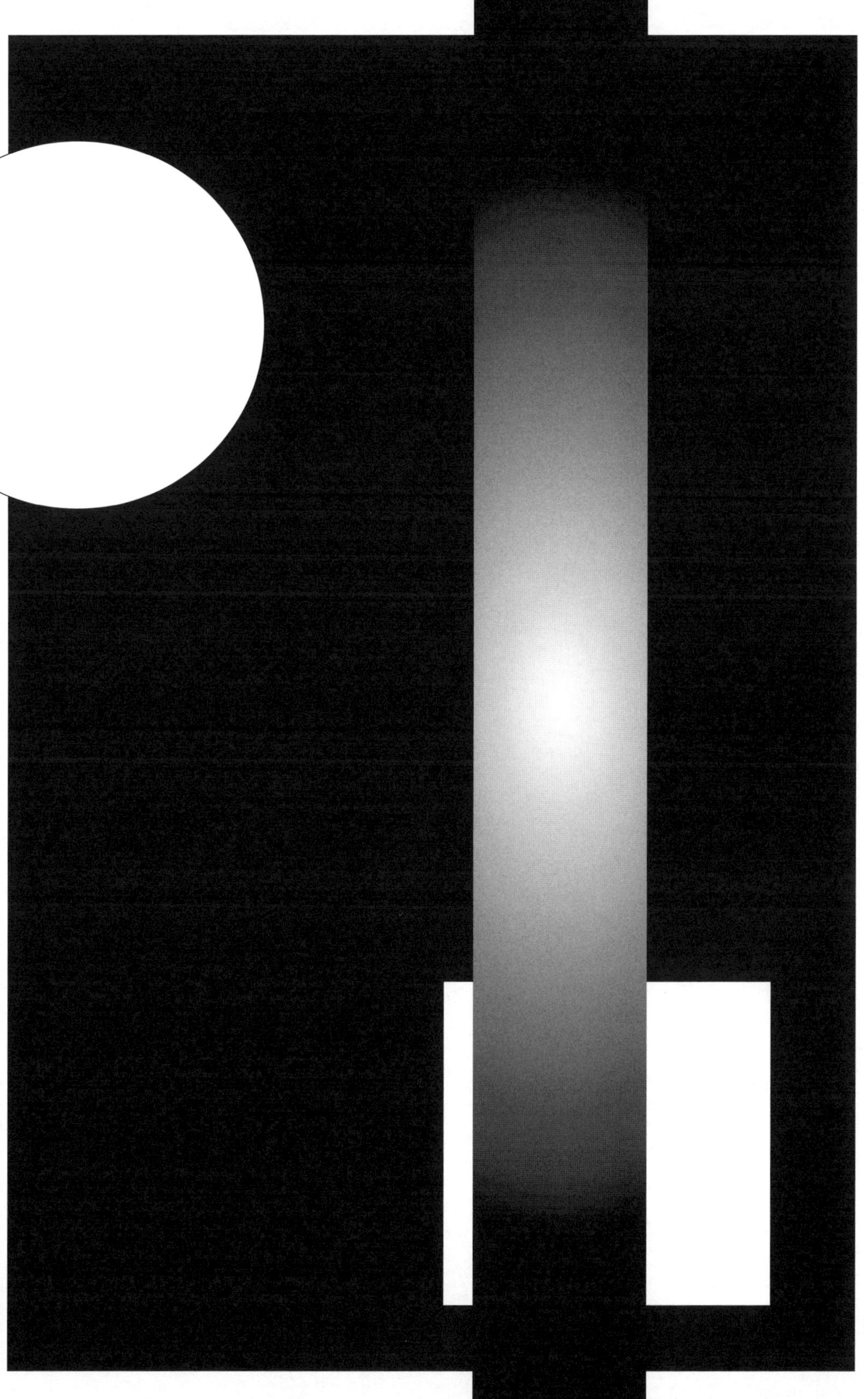

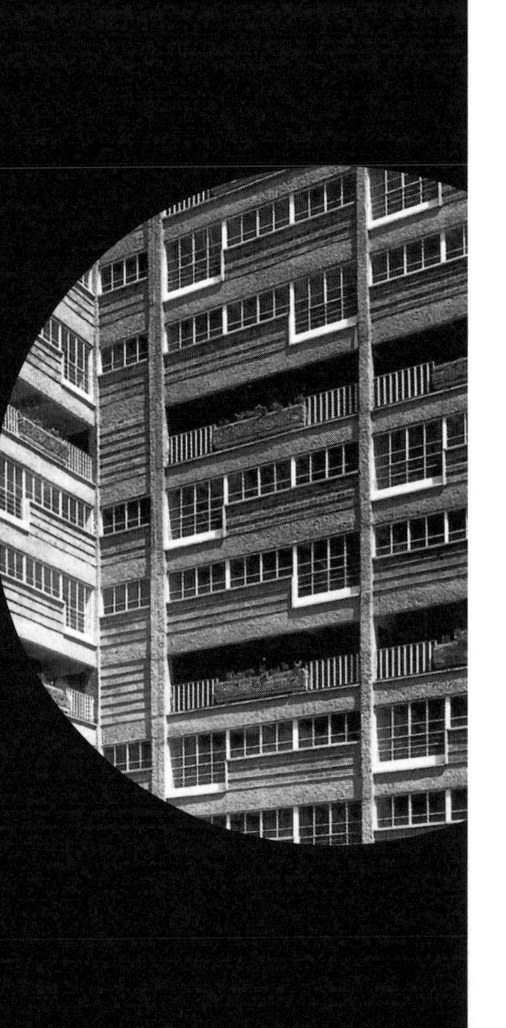

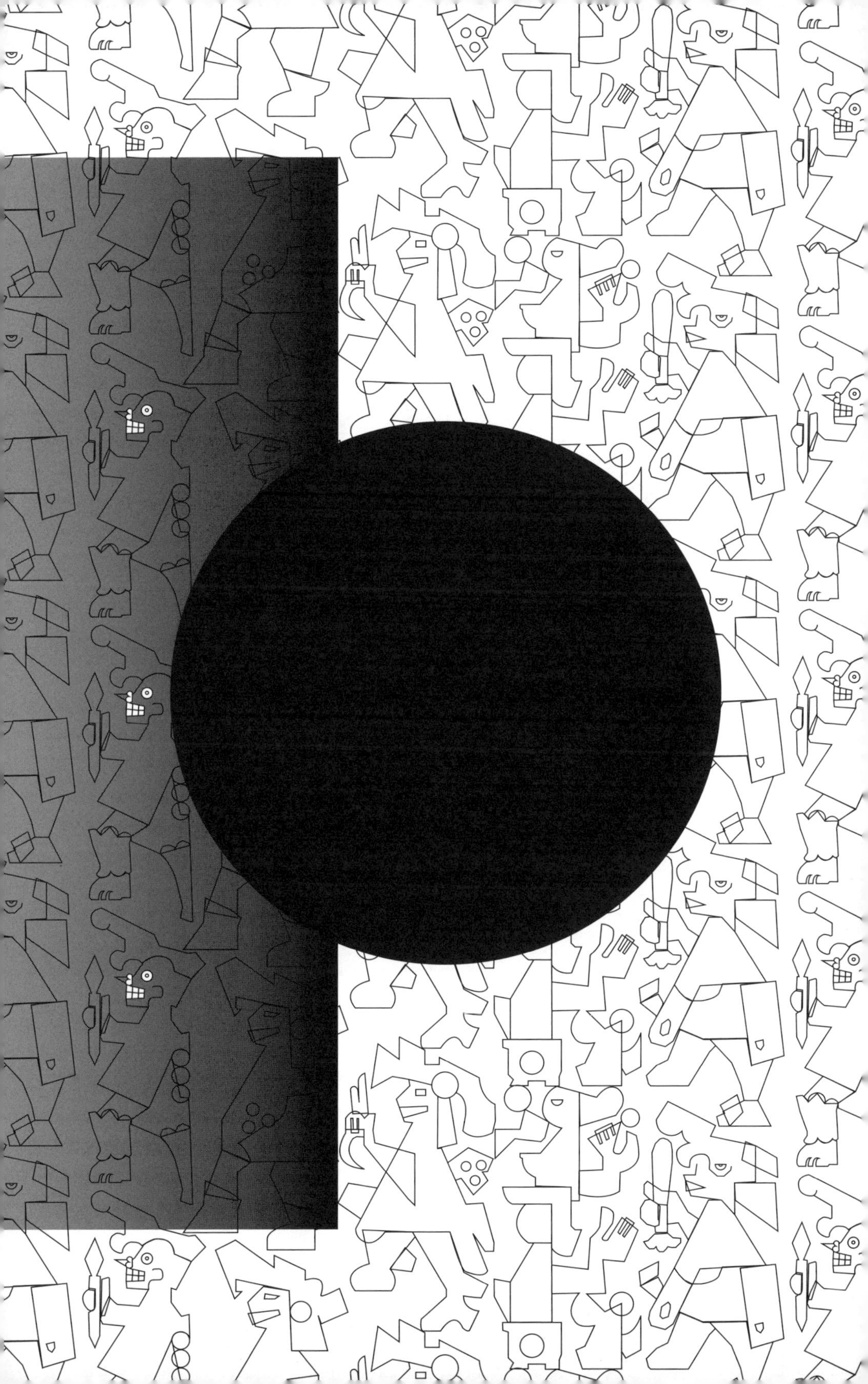

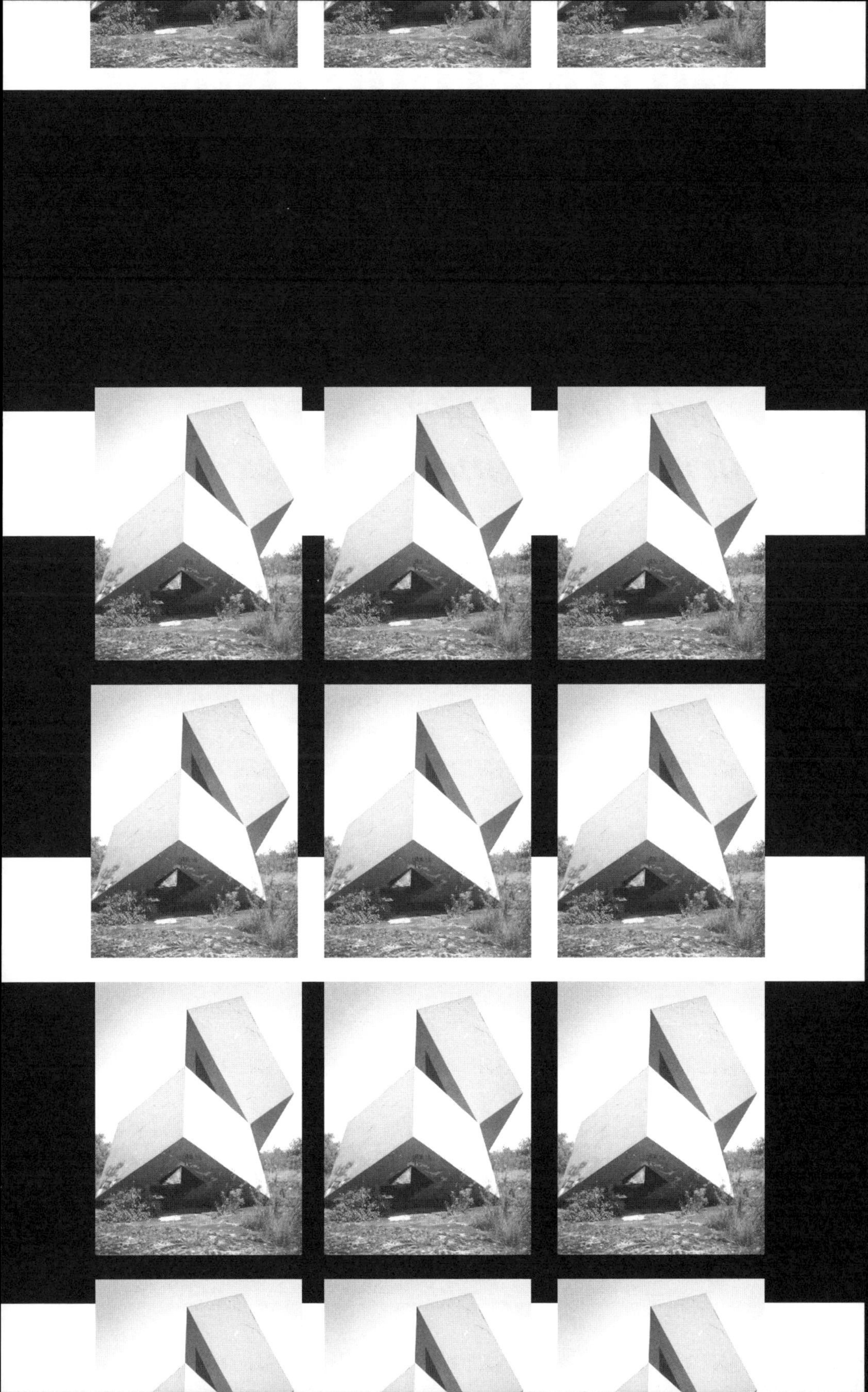

INVALID FORMAT 2

ISSUE 6 2009

INFRASTRUCTURE FOR SOULS

Tracing the parallel histories of the American megachurch and the corporate-organizational complex.

by Joseph Clarke
published June 2, 2009

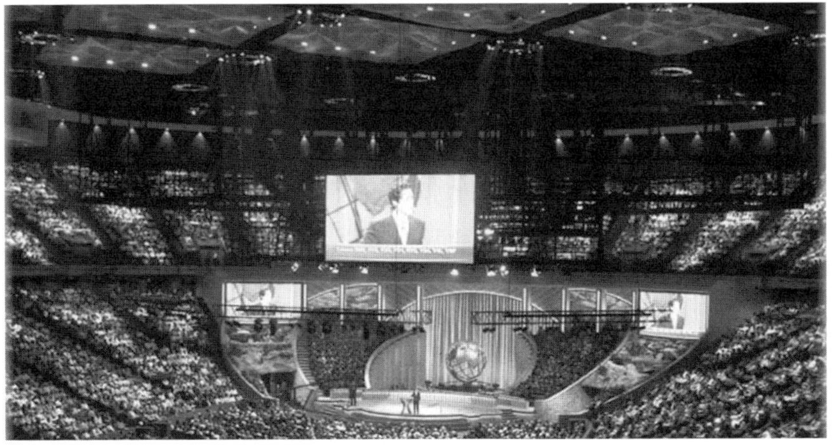

Pastor Joel Osteen, Lakewood Church.

WHEN PASTOR JOEL OSTEEN STRIDES ONSTAGE at Lakewood Church in Houston, klieg lights strobe, the Jumbotron flashes his perfect smile, and sixteen thousand worshipers roar their approval. It is an entrance worthy of a pro athlete or a pop star. Megachurches are often compared to big-box sports-and-entertainment venues, but Lakewood is one of the few that actually inhabits one: In 2003, the nondenominational church moved into the Compaq Center, a twenty-nine-year-old arena that had hosted the NBA Finals, bull-riding championships, and concerts by Paul McCartney and Kiss. The building, which came equipped with state-of-the-art A/V equipment, seemed like the most logical setting for the nation's largest religious congregation.

And yet, Lakewood and America's twelve hundred other megachurches—congregations that draw between two thousand and fifty thousand people per weekend—are not simply vast machines for passive spectatorship. Sunday services are convergences of worshipers who spend their weeknights at prayer groups, Bible studies, ministries, and missionary-training sessions. Successful megachurches are like well-run companies, with intricate corporate structures devised to keep each member personally engaged; their pastors are like chief executives, maximiz-ing the productivity of laborers in the evangelism enter-prise. Jumbotron notwithstanding, the architectural and organizational tropes of the megachurch are best compared to those of the modern white-collar workplace.

LARGE CHURCHES HAVE EXISTED since a few centuries after Christ, but the modern megachurch has its roots in nineteenth-century British and American Protestantism. This was the era of Christian camp meetings, forerunners of modern revivals that brought hundreds of enthusiastic worshipers out to the countryside, where they passed their afternoons listening to the harangues of charismatic men of God. England's top evangelical leader in the 1850s was Charles Spurgeon, pastor at a London Baptist church that eventually outgrew its building and moved into a converted music hall. Spurgeon's self-proclaimed forte was "soul-winning," and every aspect of his ministry was tailored to attract and accommodate masses of people.

For a national day of prayer in 1857, he preached to a crowd of over twenty thousand in the Crystal Palace, the enormous pavilion built for the Great Exhibition of 1851 to showcase commodities from around the globe. (It was later moved to the bucolic suburb of Sydenham Hill, where it served as a venue for occasional exhibits and performances until burning to the ground in 1936.) Constructed of iron, wood, and nine hundred thousand square feet of glass, the Palace was an early example of the use of industrial techniques to create an interior environment that could accommodate the most diverse contents. Spurgeon's flock paid a shilling each to stand amid horticultural displays and Assyrian statues as he preached.

THE INDUSTRIAL ECONOMY and its workers came to dominate American cities at the dawn of the twentieth century, and many middle-class whites escaped to new suburban developments. Their churches followed, but the architecture changed. Protestant worship services, once consisting almost entirely of preaching, had begun to include more elaborate participatory singing, recited exchanges between congregation and minister, and musical performances.

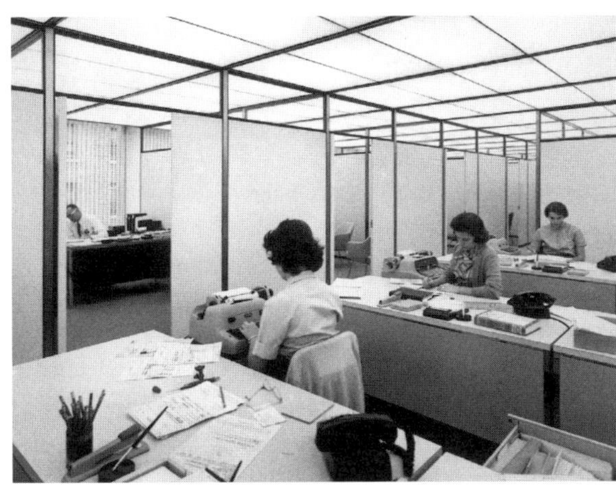

Union Carbide building, 1960.
Interior of Union Carbide.

Church architecture underwent a corresponding shift, from rectilinear designs modeled on early meeting houses to amphitheater-like layouts with radial seating and stages with elaborate pulpits and pipe organs.

As churches relocated to the outskirts, skyscrapers supplanted them as the most prominent buildings in large cities. (Presiding over the dedication of Manhattan's Gothic-style Woolworth Building in 1913, the Congregationalist minister Samuel Cadman nicknamed the edifice the "Cathedral of Commerce.") After World War II, corporations began erecting towers sheathed in metal-and-glass curtain walls, symbols of technological progress that harked back to the Crystal Palace. Under the sway of new management practices laid out in the pages of journals such as *Harvard Business Review*, corporate leadership strived to create a new kind of work environment: a modular office that could be transformed to fit any arrangement of workers or space that management desired.

THOUGH OFFICE TOWERS might have suggested an ever-greater concentration of workers, the key organizational principle of the new corporation was actually decentralization. (The opening up of office space was echoed by the delegation of responsibilities to semiautonomous division managers.) Fittingly, the postwar office paradigm was

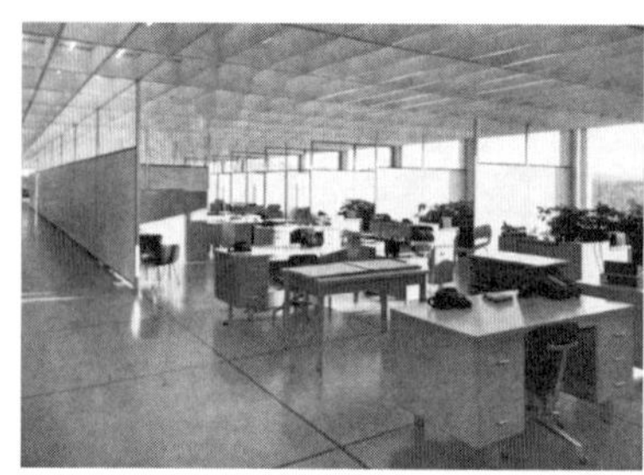
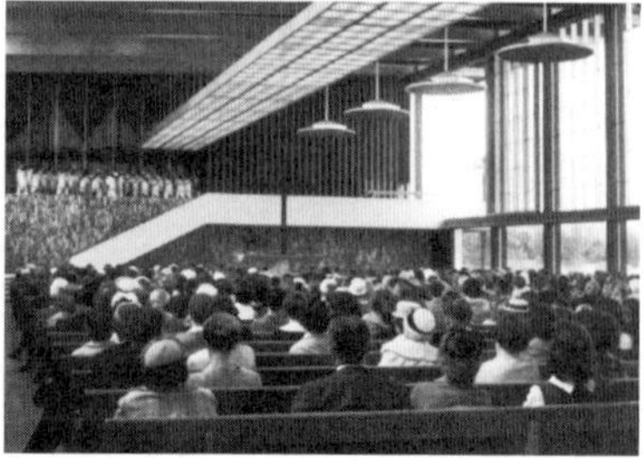

most cogently realized not in the central city but in smaller corporate offices in the suburbs, which proliferated after President Eisenhower established the interstate highway system in the mid-1950s. The General Motors Technical Center opened in 1955, in Warren, Michigan, twelve miles from downtown Detroit. Architect Eero Saarinen situated the 330-acre campus along an eleven-mile roadway circuit; the low-slung blocks of gridded glass and steel evoke the triumph of industry while remaining linked to the natural world via expansive lawns, thick stands of trees, and an artificial lake. Saarinen said that the best view of the complex was not from a static position, but from the seat of a car driving by it at thirty miles per hour. The same year, the preacher Robert Schuller—today best known as the host of *The Hour of Power*—began renting a drive-in theater in suburban Orange County, California, where he delivered Sunday-morning services from atop a snack stand. Worshipers would park their cars and watch Schuller through their windshields.

THE MIDCENTURY EMBRACE of car-friendly, arcadian settings for work and worship drew on a sense of the uprightness of the rural that had been cultivated by prominent Americans from Thomas Jefferson to William Jennings Bryan. Even after Schuller's congregation moved into a new building on the same site in 1961, it maintained its connection to the drive-in church: Richard Neutra, its architect, made the signature feature a floor-to-ceiling glass wall with panels that slid open during services, merging the sanctuary with the parking lot outside, giving worshipers

in cars and pews an equal view of the pulpit. A similar aesthetic emerged in office design. The Connecticut General
Life Insurance Company, wishing to move away from
downtown Hartford in order to expand its headquarters,
hired Skidmore, Owings & Merrill to design a new structure in the idyllic suburb of Bloomfield. The result was a
low, crystalline block set on two hundred acres of farm-
land. "The magnificent mechanical efficiency and smooth
flow of this building is economically important," said one
speaker at the building's 1957 dedication, "but the lake, the
swans in the lake, the green grass, the trees, and just plain
space, lift the souls of the people who work here and the
company for which they work. Compare it with the steel
and concrete, the grim, impersonal jam which represents
the city. Which is closer to God?" The inside of the building was laid out according to an open plan influenced by the
increasingly popular "office landscape" paradigm, which
was meant to create a sense of spaciousness and encourage
communication. Both the exterior and the interior of the
office building had become landscapes, with architecture
as a thin glass wall mediating between them.

THE IMAGE OF RURAL AMERICA as the paragon of morality and social harmony was buttressed by the specter of
a nuclear attack on a major city. In the 1950s, municipal
governments went out of their way to locate train stations,
hospitals, shopping centers, and other critical infrastructure beyond the anticipated blast radius. While most mainstream religious leaders responded to the atomic threat
with sermons denouncing nuclear weapons and grappling

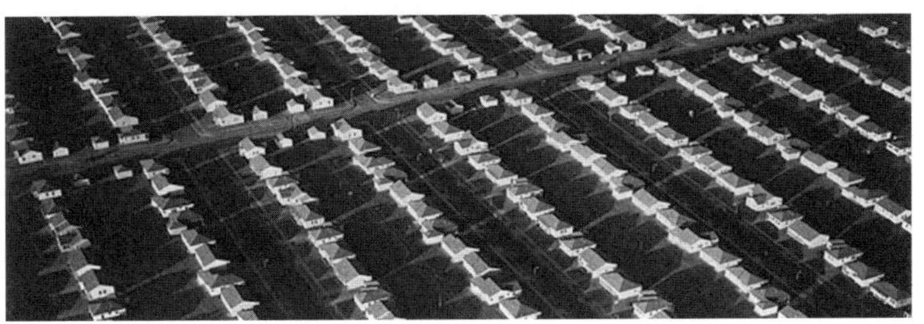

Tract housing, Lakewood, CA, 1950.

with the morality of war, many evangelical preachers exploited the apocalyptic mood to further demonize cities. Two days after President Truman announced the first Soviet atomic test, a young Billy Graham warned in a fiery sermon: "Do you know the area that is marked out for the enemy's first atomic bomb? New York! Secondly, Chicago; and thirdly, the city of Los Angeles!"

After World War II, the mass-production technologies used by wartime factories were employed to churn out prefabricated houses, as American families migrated by the hundreds of thousands to fields of tract housing that now ringed most major cities. The church was essential to suburbia, as it provided a sense of purpose for residents who might otherwise feel consigned to anonymity as they commuted between far-flung offices, commercial strips, and residential subdivisions. Corporations addressed the same problem by adopting the doctrine of "human relations," which sought to boost productivity by giving each employee—each "organization man"—a sense of his personal value to the company.

FOR THESE DUAL INSTITUTIONS to minister effectively to suburbanites, they would have to be subdivided; they would have to adopt organizational and spatial frameworks capable of reducing their perceived size and conveying their appreciation for the individuality of workers and worshipers. In 1968, David Yonggi Cho, pastor of Korea's

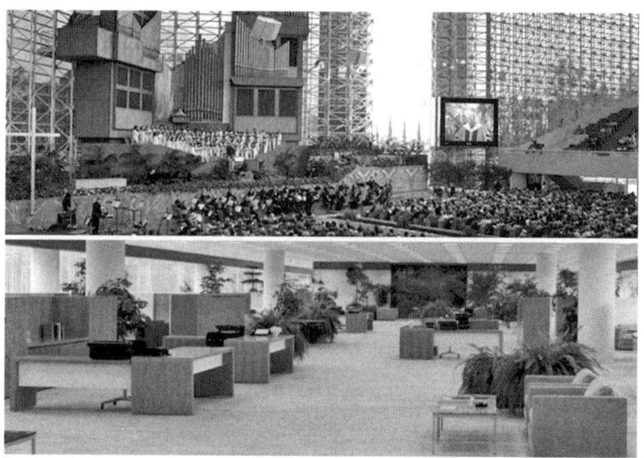

Crystal Cathedral, 1980.
Weyerheaeuser buiding, 1971.

Yoido Full Gospel Church, restructured his ten-thousand-person congregation by dividing the city of Seoul into small groups, or "cells," that would each meet on a weekday in a member's home. Members were encouraged to invite their friends, and when a group reached a certain size, it would undergo what Cho called "cell division." Within a decade, the church was the world's largest, with two hundred thousand members. The cellular model quickly migrated to the US, where it fostered a new breed of churches.

They began pushing Bible-study groups, teen groups, young-professional groups, single-parent groups, addiction-recovery groups, motorcycle-enthusiasts groups, bowling groups, and ballroom-dancing groups. The church experience no longer revolved around the Sunday service. That same year, the Herman Miller furniture company created the Action Office, the forebear of the modern cubicle system. It has since sold five billion dollars' worth of "systems furniture." Businesses loved cubicles because they enjoyed favorable tax status as compared with conventional enclosed offices. Workers would love cubicles too, the theory went, because the structures would provide them with personal space while promoting communication and collaboration.

IN 1977, SCHULLER'S CONGREGATION, having outgrown Neutra's building, began construction on the Crystal Cathedral. The Cathedral, designed by Philip Johnson, would hold three thousand people and serve as a sound stage for the pastor's TV show. It sits in the middle of a parking lot, and from the outside appears to be a mute, symmetrical, reflective object. But the inside feels like a giant greenhouse: Worshipers look through the space-frame structure directly out to the surrounding woodlands and the sky above. Audiovisual equipment clings to the metal struts above the pulpit; behind it is a section of wall that swings opens during services. "After I am dead and gone, the development will outshine the preacher," Schuller told the *Christian Century* in 2002. "The real

Weyerhaeuser building, 1971.

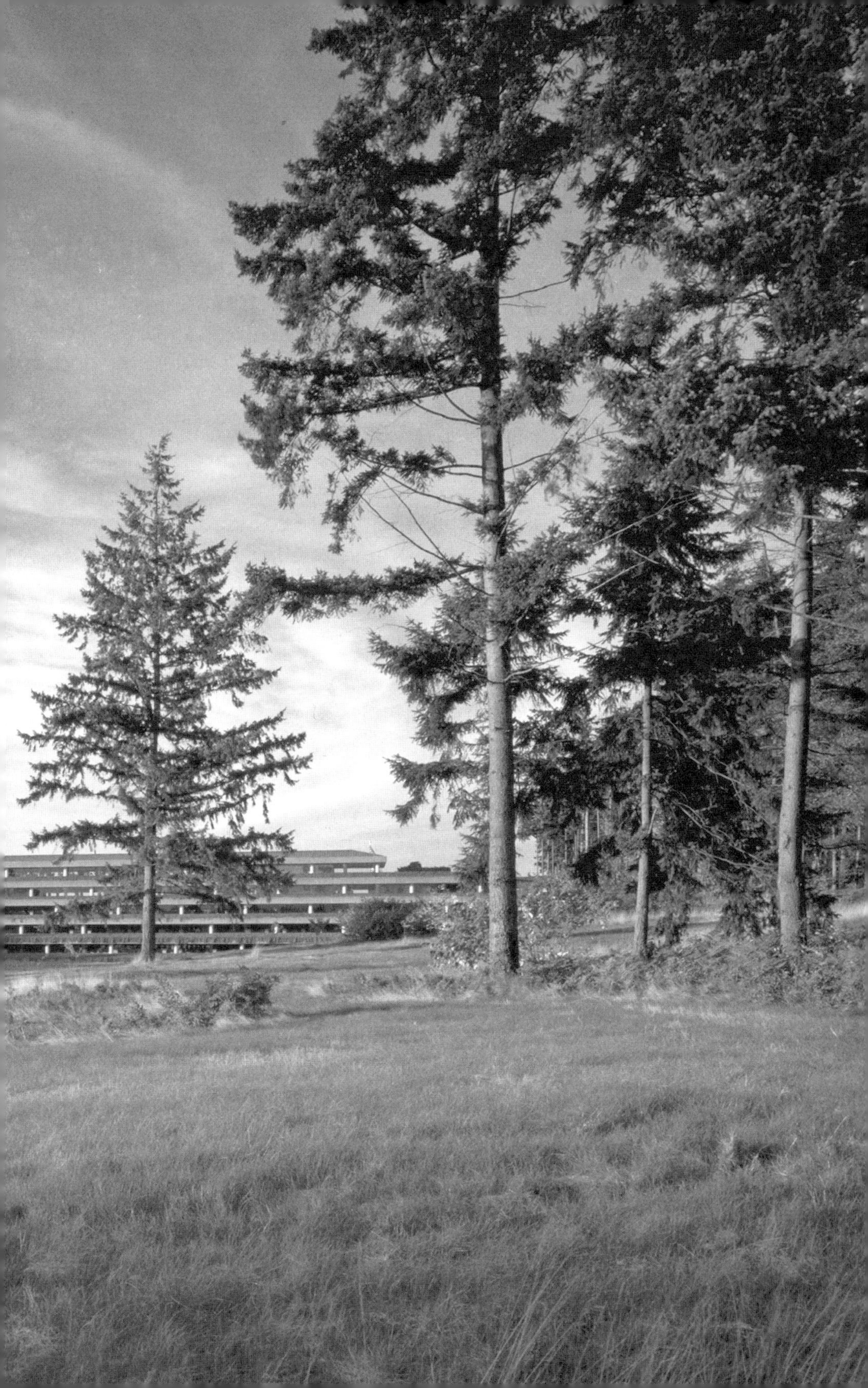

preacher that attracts people and ministry is going to be the structures, the grounds and the landscaping."

In the same decade, the headquarters of the Weyerhaeuser forestry company, designed by Skidmore, Owings & Merrill, was built near Tacoma, Washington. Weyerhaeuser deliberately selected a site with a rural feel that was nevertheless in full view of an interstate highway, using the pastoral setting as a marketing tool. To create a collaborative, democratic ethos inside the building, the company adopted an open floor plan and gave every employee a view of a window, if not a window view. (Here, too, communications technology was fully integrated: Telephone and electric lines were buried beneath the floors, and speakers continuously broadcasting white noise allowed workers to have private conversations.) Whereas the Crystal Cathedral's glass walls stood in for divine illumination, here each pane symbolized corporate transparency.

THE 1980S AND '90S SAW THE RISE of so-called seeker megachurches, which targeted those disillusioned with religion. Rather than enforcing traditional worship styles, they embraced counterculture and youth rebellion. Chief among them is Rick Warren's Saddleback Church, in Orange County, California. Built in the '90s, Saddleback plays down crosses and other conventional Christian signifiers and avoids mention of its Southern Baptist denominational affiliation. Instead of a massive auditorium, the church occupies multiple midsize structures scattered across a lush 120-acre campus. Visitors customize their worship experience by choosing from a range of services: Saddleback Classic in the main Worship Center, OverDrive for youth, and Praise! for gospel-music lovers. As Warren's model gained traction, the ideology of the democratic office was taken to new levels by management theorists associated with the Quality of Work Life movement. They recommended radically open office environments that would give workers control over their environment and dissimulate corporate hierarchy. "Office facility planning should be a systematic process that encourages employee participation, promotes innovation, and champions mobility," advised a 1985 article in *National Productivity Review*. Corporations paid millions for the advice of consultants like Peter Drucker, whose thirty-nine books include *People and Performance* and *Managing for the Future*. Drucker argued that "knowledge workers"–people who are productive with their minds, not their hands–need progressive workplaces that minimize authority and make them feel like they can express themselves freely.

DRUCKER'S PROTÉGÉS HAVE GONE ON to head GE, Proctor & Gamble, Intel, and other companies, and his influence has been felt in countless new workplace designs–nowhere more than the Googleplex, built by Studios Architecture in 1997 as the headquarters of Silicon Graphics and acquired in 2006 by Google. Its designers conceived of the space as a "destination office": Though it is densely packed with workstations, one does not go there merely to work, as evidenced by the Ping-Pong tables, lava lamps, exercise balls, and nap spots provided by the company. The correspondences between the Googleplex and Saddleback are remarkable. Rigid building models were broken down into amorphous, disaggregated masses, screened from their parking lots by trees and artificial hills; both campuses include plush lounges, landscaped paths, beach-volleyball courts, and cafés (with "outdoor seating for sunshine daydreaming," Google's website boasts). The architecture is meant to persuade church members or secular employees—especially younger people—to spend their most productive time there. As Google CEO Eric Schmidt has said, "Knowledge workers believe they are paid to be effective, not to work 9 to 5." It's no coincidence that Saddleback mirrors the top office environments of its day. Warren was a good friend of Drucker's (the consultant died in 2005), and the books he has written for pastors quote Drucker

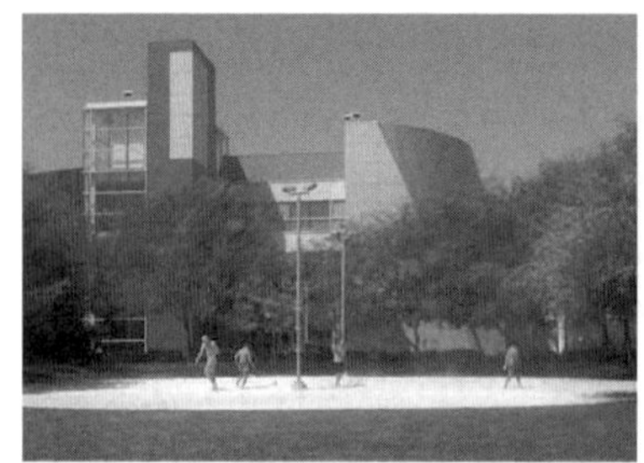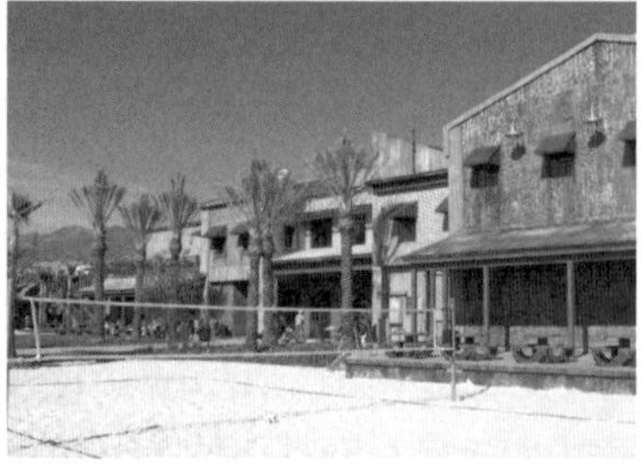

liberally. Drucker, in turn, was so impressed with the business acumen of evangelical leaders that in 1998 he declared the megachurch "surely the most important social phenomenon in American society in the last thirty years."

RECENTLY, SOME MEGACHURCHES HAVE ANNOUNCED that they are extending their reach back to the secular urbanized areas they had left behind. Before being ousted for "sexual immorality," Ted Haggard, the pastor of Colorado Springs' New Life Church, exhorted members to practice "grid praying"—canvassing a town block by block until it had been covered in prayer. Other churches are expanding their physical presence by building or buying shopping centers and mixed-used developments that will attract the unchurched. Some evangelicals have started preaching the virtues of New Urbanism, the urban-design movement that aims to mitigate the feeling of placelessness induced by *Alphaville*-esque developments by grafting them with brick facades and privately owned "public space." Pastor Randy Frazee's 2001 book, *The Connecting Church*, encourages the faithful to "rediscover neighborhood" and "implement a common place" in order to win souls in what has become "the loneliest nation on Earth." Workplace designers have taken up a similar meme. In a 2004 article for a company publication, two Herman Miller executives suggested that New Urbanist ideals of walkability, increased density, and commingling of social and work life might be applied to office design to create "a work environment that could approximate the richness and vitality of the urban experience." Along the same lines, an architect with the design and consulting firm Gensler announced in an article last year: "Place-making is back in the corporate vocabulary." It is unclear whether or not these moves represent genuine engagements with the city. But megachurches' and corporations' embrace of the idea of the urban is the logical next step in their colonization of everyday life, part and parcel with the ever-more-diffuse protocols they have developed for managing souls. Evangelical congregations now publish books and brochures and offer courses to help members navigate their lives beyond the church; with attendance increasing as the recession has deepened, the church has been charged with offering consolation as well as guidance.

In the corporate world, even in the midst of today's layoff campaigns, companies strive to maintain an image of caring, and human resources departments cultivate the psychological well-being of their employees by providing depression and anxiety counseling, online databases of relationship and parenting advice, and referrals to life coaches. Modern-day management acts as an organizational superego, struggling to order the behavior of employees and keep existential terror at bay. The corporation achieved the status of legal personhood more than a century ago (and enjoys this benefit without having to suffer the frailties of the human body). But the underlying corporeal metaphor for an all-pervasive organizational infrastructure had been established long before the advent of modern companies. As Paul's Epistle to the Ephesians says: "No man ever yet hated his own flesh; but nourisheth and cherisheth it, even as the Lord the church: For we are members of his body, of his flesh, and of his bones." ⊠

INVALID FORMAT 2 ISSUE 6 2009

VIRTUAL BOWERY

Rebuilding the Bowery in one adequate descriptive system, with Lower Manhattan circa 1997 as a flock of digital swans.

by Dan Torop
published June 16, 2009

In 1999, I dreamed I was drifting over the Bowery at sunset. The street was covered by a red fog laced with yellow-orange fumes. Cars wove heedlessly between lanes yet never collided. I spun and circled through the air above, watching the silent passage below. When I awoke on the couch at my studio, a few streets east of the Bowery, I resolved to replicate the vision.

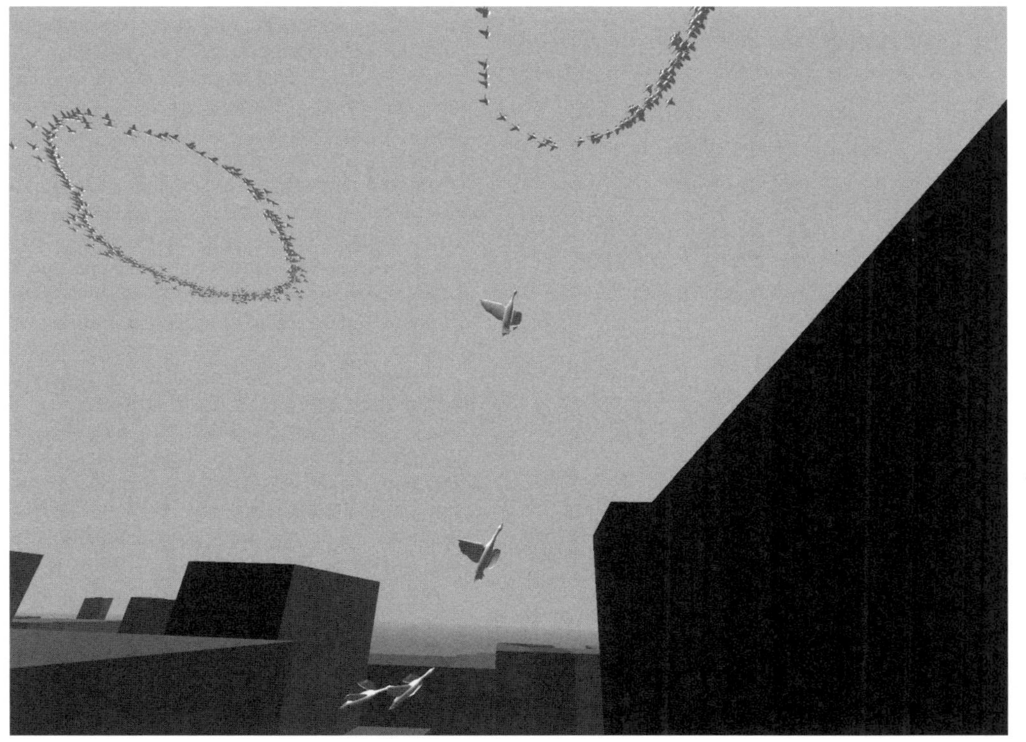

This picture shows the length of the Bowery that I flew over in my dream. At 190 Bowery is a graffiti-covered 1898 Beaux-Arts mansion that has housed a single family in its seventy-two rooms since 1966. At 222 Bowery, William Burroughs had an apartment known as "The Bunker." He died in 1997, a year after this photograph was made. Since then, the pincers of prosperity have grasped the street. Where there once were parking lots, condos called Avalon and NoLIta Place stand; between them rise the stacked silver boxes of the New Museum, whose facade is stamped with rainbow letters spelling "Hell, Yes!"

Summer evenings in 1997, I'd wander down Bleecker Street to the newly named NoLIta, just west of the Bowery. Every storefront on one stretch of Elizabeth Street below Houston was occupied by shops stocked with esoteric merchandise. In the windows of butchers I'd see sparkly pinwheels, model ships, and papier-mâché castles. In the evenings, the grates would come down, and the block's residents would unfold card tables outside and chat. At a bar up the street, performers would play an electronic music newly named "illbient." I would look in for a minute, then amble past, too shy to walk inside.

The year before, I had begun hanging out with swans. I found them along the Connecticut shore and off the A train beyond Howard Beach. I made repeated visits to a favorite swan couple in New Haven's East Rock Park, always bringing a loaf of Italian bread. Cajoled by crumbs, the birds would come close enough for a photograph, or even to nip my outstretched hand. They were, to me, a thread of magic in the mundane.

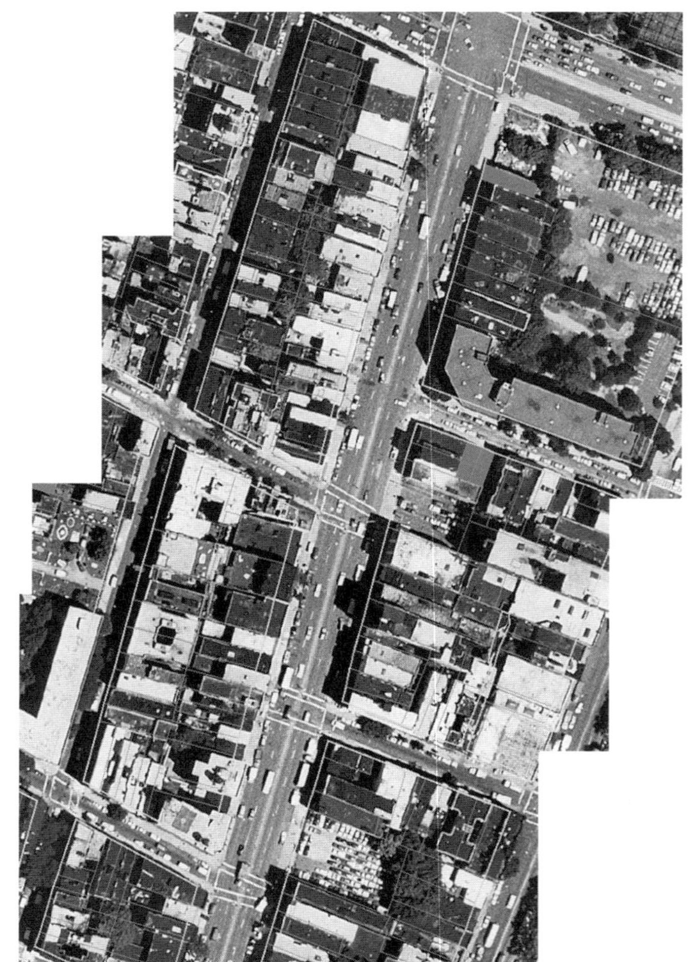

I took the release that year of a swan-themed postage stamp as a sign of the importance of my work. I began researching the swans of America.

Mute swans, I discovered, come from Europe, where they are kept as "ornamental" birds. They're found in the eastern US and are gradually spreading westward, into the habitat of native trumpeter swans. Agents of the Wisconsin Department of Natural Resources have shot hundreds of encroaching mutes in the past decade to keep the West safe for the native species.

Trumpeters summer in Alaska, nesting one family per lake. If humans intrude on their territory, the swans depart to a more isolated lake, traveling overland for the sake of their unfledged cygnets. (If the cygnets don't learn to fly by winter, the entire family will remain and freeze into the ice.) Walking swans are easily killed by predators. Even a few noisy interlopers can destroy a trumpeter population.

I went to Alaska in the summer of 1997 to seek the native trumpeters. I stayed in Fairbanks, where, in the university library, I discovered a paper on the nesting habits of North Slope trumpeters. The article's authors had set up time-lapse Super 8 cameras with telephoto lenses in the tundra to record the behavior of nesting trumpeters. The paper included some lovely drawings, which I scanned for future reference.

I found no swans in Alaska, but I did fall in with a community of far-northern artists whom I thought to be as strange and beautiful as the birds. In 1997, electronic music made a lot of sense, and the University of Alaska had an Internet connection. Fairbanks's young musicians were trading Mouse on Mars songs and sequencer patches with correspondents in Berlin and Antwerp. I went on a car trip with a few new acquaintances and a forged dip-net fishing license. We camped alongside streams filled with so many spawning salmon that they jostled against one another like the traffic on a New York avenue. When we arrived at the Chitina River, it was fast flowing and gray with mud swept down from the mountains. We caught no fish. The next morning we were barely able to light a smoky campfire.

I got back from Fairbanks and found a place to live on lower Mulberry Street. One night I met some friends at their West Village apartment, which had just been visited by a pot-delivery man. I stayed until the Prodigy CD playing on the stereo overcame me with nausea, then excused myself and—barely able to walk—hailed a cab home. The lights streaked as we drove down the Bowery, like the hyperspace effect in the original *Star Wars*; I resisted asking the driver to turn down the slinky jazz music pulsing from beneath the seats.

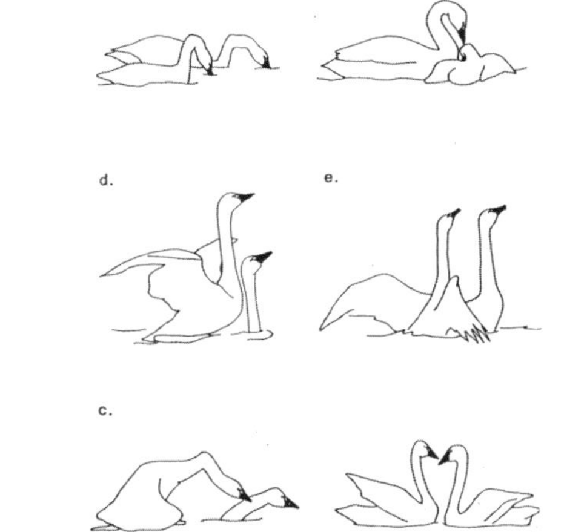

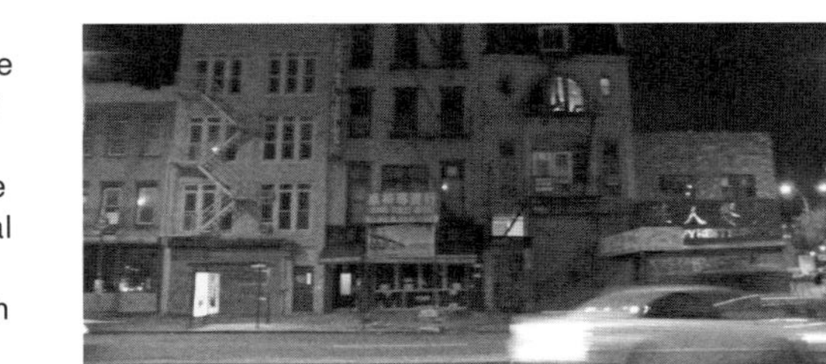

It had the red Bowery dream a year later. I wrote a few notes about it, then carried on with some photographic projects. I left the Mulberry Street apartment and moved east to Allen, to Ludlow, across the East River to Greenpoint, to Williamsburg, then finally south, by way of Red Hook, to Gowanus. The blocks in the dream were painted over and faded into boutiques, galleries, and baby stores.

The more photographs I made, the more I thought of the unphotographable dream. Finally, in 2007, I wrote a proposal to create a computer program that would simulate the Bowery circa 1997 and submitted it to Eyebeam, a digital-arts space:

The camera swoops down over the Bowery's double lanes of traffic. Cars jostle and turn, brushing each other, while on the horizon the sun sets smoky orange. Birds veer through the hazy air, as if traversing a rough torrent. As we drift above Houston St., Prince, Stanton, Eldridge, and Spring, the buildings stutter, altered in aspect. The sidewalks and windows expand and contract. We dive into the street and the cars part ahead of us. We are ghosts in this city. Time slips as we yaw past the house in which William Burroughs once lived. It's no longer 1997. We plunge into a dirtier, grimier Bowery Bum past. Time appears as double-exposed images, taking us back to 1897, 1797, to when the Bowery was a lane, a path, a forest, a swamp.

The proposal was approved. I was grateful for the chance to revisit the Bowery and redeem the years I had spent in its orbit.

Eyebeam is housed in a ramshackle West Chelsea building that feels like a drafty submarine. It's a determinedly antimarket, anti-commercial institution that time (or at least the recent prosperous decade) has nearly forgotten. The artists there make either really amazing or really awkward things. Sometimes both at once. Generally, the Eyebeamers work with electronics or computers. I decided that my Bowery had to be written in Lisp, a programming language as odd as the street had seemed to me until recently.

A computer scientist named John McCarthy created Lisp in the late 1950s, and in the years since it has roosted at research universities, flickering into and out of use. Lisp was the language of choice for artificial intelligence until that obscure quest for self-knowing machines was swept away by personal computers; many hard-core programmers still write their code with Emacs, a text editor created with—and sinuously modifiable by—a 1970s Lisp variant. Whereas most contemporary languages have practical goals—solving math problems, or constraining the imagination of corporate programmers so that when one is fired the next can easily take over—Lisp was designed to be the quintessence of a computer language. Its original definition could be written out in half a page—in Lisp.

```
(defun where-bird-wants-to-go (bird dead-ahead
                          neighbors-vel neighbors-pos neighbors-colors)

  (declare (a-bird bird)
           (v3:vec-averager dead-ahead neighbors-pos neighbors-colors))
  ;; FIXME: use neighbors-vel match velocities with the neighbors!
  ;; FIXME: keeping more of weighting in mind -- if there isn't much
  ;;    likelihood of hitting a bird dead ahead, still dodge a little but
  ;;    aim towards center of group?
  (cond
    ;; go away from the birds which are dead ahead
    ((plusp (v3:v-avg-count dead-ahead))
     ;; FIXME: the closer these birds are, the faster it should want
     ;;    to go away!
     ;; FIXME: perhaps just combine negative of this vector, which is
     ;;    heavily weighted with the neighbors-desiring vector!
     (v3:setv3 (bird-role-color bird) color:+red+)
     (setf (bird-role bird) 'avoid)
     (v3:with-averager-result (dead-ahead avg)
       (v3:v- (bird-pos bird) avg)))

    ;; if too far from origin, then let's go back home!
    ;; FIXME: could birds potentially just wander off forever if they
    ;;    were in a circular bunch?
    ((or () (abs (v3:x (bird-pos bird))) (* 1.5 *max-bird-wander*))
         () (abs (v3:y (bird-pos bird))) (* 4.0 *max-bird-wander*))
         () (abs (v3:y (bird-pos bird))) *max-bird-wander*))
```

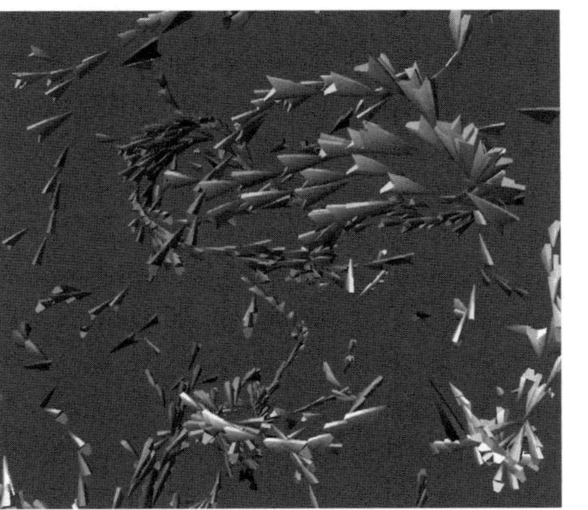

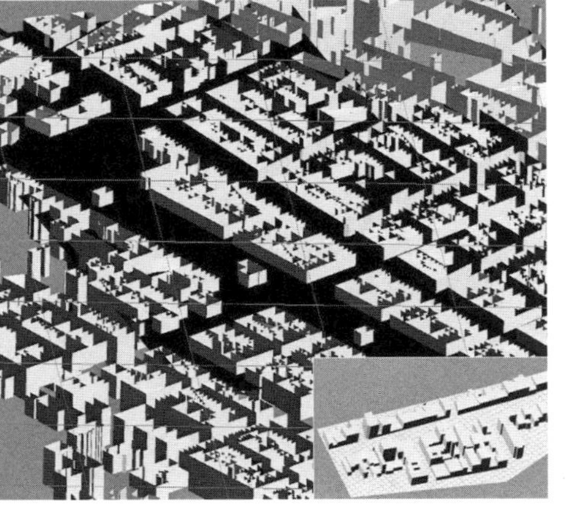

Eyebeam gave me a computer that looked like a cast-off from the spaceship in *Alien*, and a corner in a skylit room that rattled with the wind gusts from the Hudson and crackled as the spring storms blew through.

While thinking about my raw 3-D graphics, I revisited the computer scientist Craig Reynolds's influential 1987 paper, "Flocks, Herds, and Schools." Reynolds sets out three rules for a "flock": Its members attempt to avoid collisions with, match velocity with, and stay close to nearby flock mates. Depending on how far its creatures can see and how fast they can turn, the flock changes from a swarm to a line to a chaotic assembly.

I started to think of the cars on the Bowery as flocks, sharing behavioral rules with the birds above. But then, I thought, its buildings were also flocks over time, going up and down in something like unison. Creating a flock in Lisp seemed a good way to start my project.

I programmed a covey of triangular birds in accordance with Reynolds's rules. (I later learned that he wrote his own first flocking program in Lisp.) While showing the birds to a visitor, I adjusted the program a bit, enter-ing the relevant Lisp into Emacs while the flock was spinning in a neighboring window. In most languages, the program must be restarted for changes to register. But to my surprise, the flock responded to the new commands immediately. Lisp, with its self-encompassing nature, sees no difference between itself and the program it is running.

I started leaving my primitive flock flying for hours and days on end; I wrote and rewrote the program as the triangles swarmed and circled in response. In the movie *Dark City*, space aliens experiment on humans by inducing artificial sleep, implanting them with new memories, and altering their physical environment. In *The Matrix*, glitches occur when the computer makes changes to the simulated human world. For my Lisp birds, as for our own dystopian Manhattan, the rules could change in midflight.

None of this had much to do with the Bowery. I had thought of the street as one of the secret roots of the city, a place truer than the grid of streets and avenues it sunders, and so, when I began biking it daily en route from Gowanus to Eyebeam (over the Manhattan Bridge, up the Bowery, then across Prince Street to the West Side), I was disappointed at how little relation it bore to the old-fashioned clarity of Lisp. Maybe these two relics of the past would not intersect. Perhaps the Bowery was just unsavory and wretched.

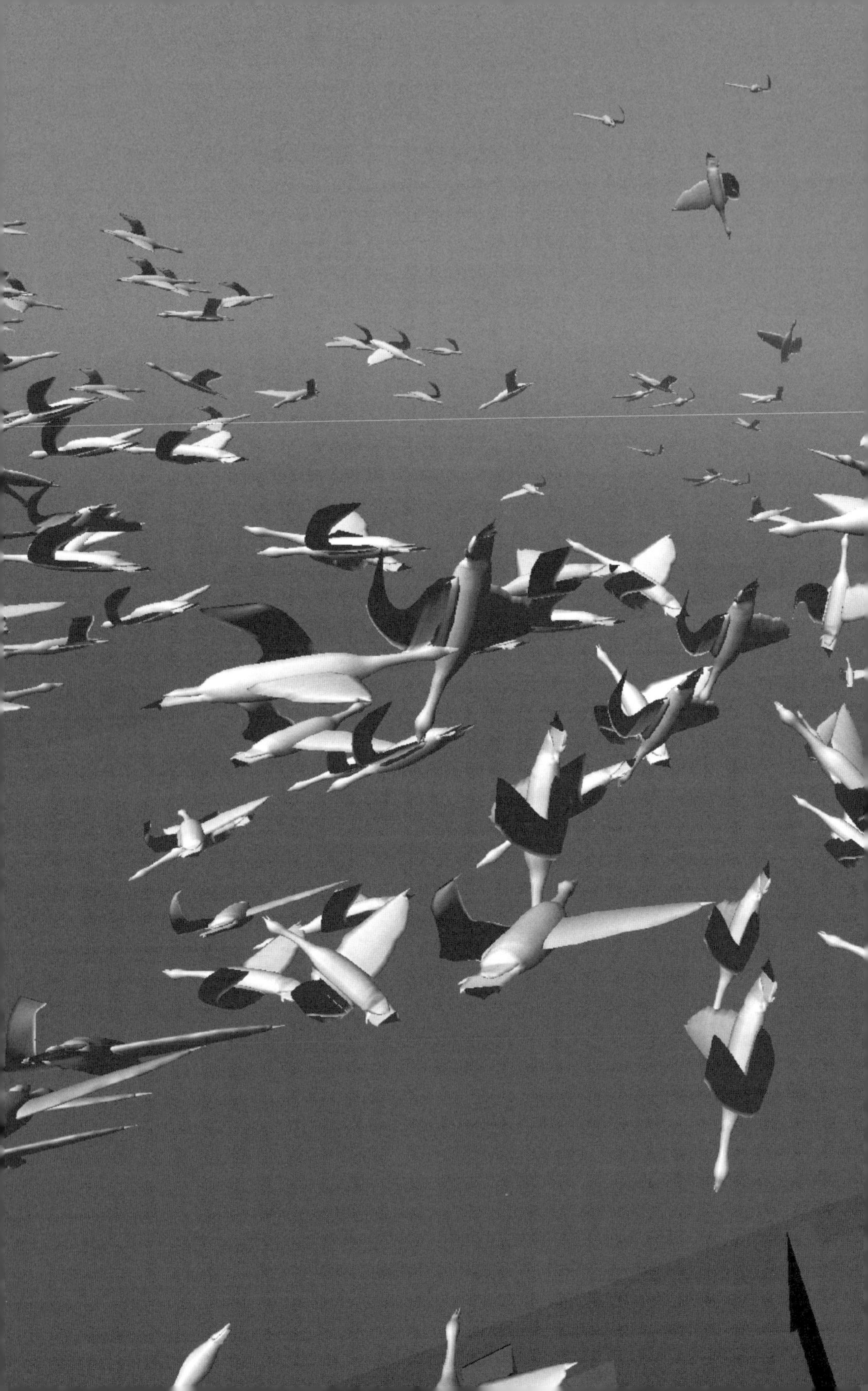

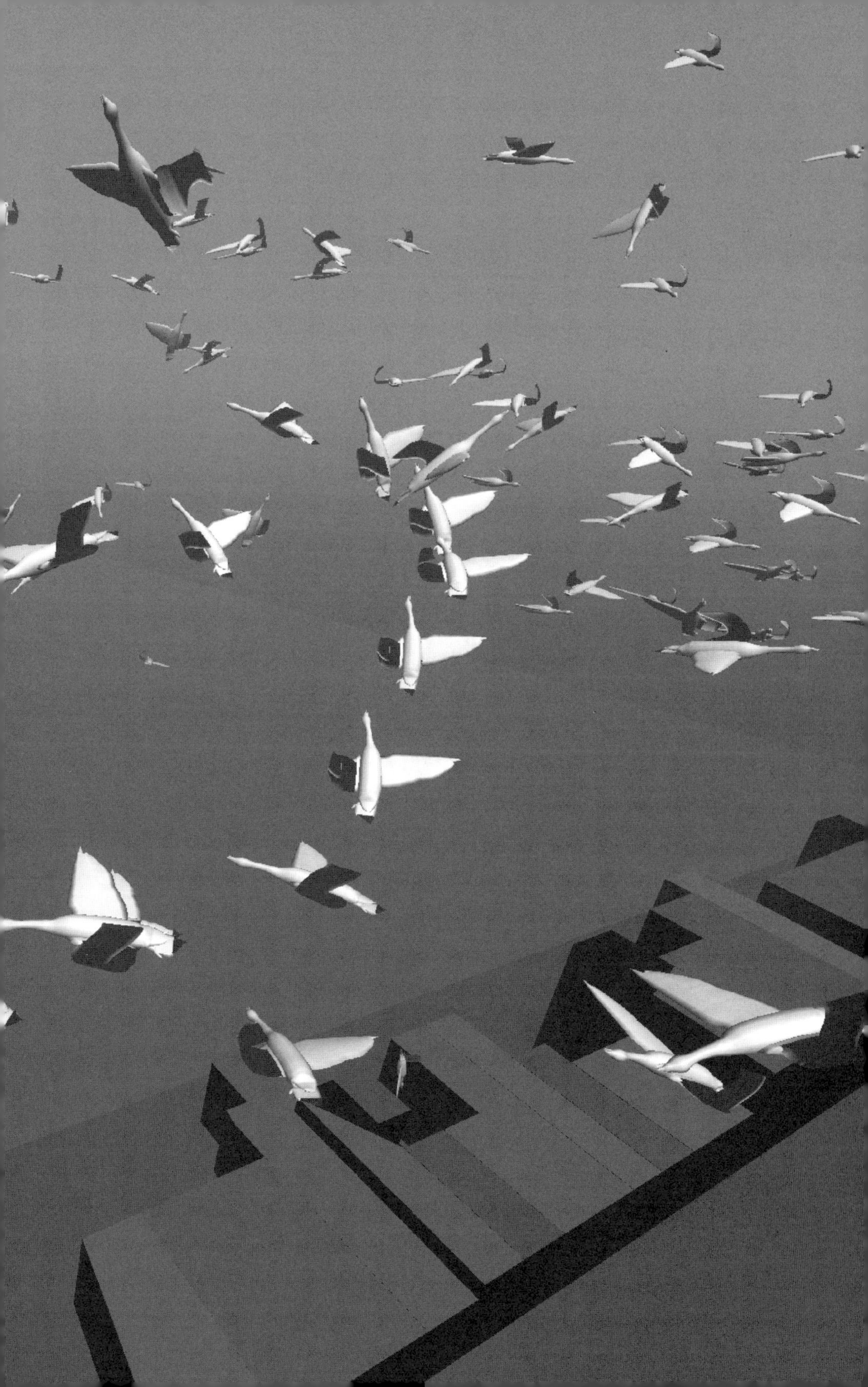

I was even more put off when I came across a flyer (by the redoubtable cartoonist Matthew Thurber) promoting a new collaboration between *Vice* magazine and MTV: the Virtual Lower East Side. This VLES seemed to be the cross-breeding of indie-rock nostalgia and a shoddy multiplayer video game. What would my Virtual Bowery be now but a cheap follow-up to a cynical rehash?

I decided that the Virtual Bowery should only be birds, no street. It should express the purity of algorithm and language, not the drabness of the urban marketplace. After a few bicycle accidents, I started taking the subway to Eyebeam, bypassing the Bowery altogether.

Lost in Lisp, I concentrated on creating a dubious system of virtual invisible buckets to hold the flock. Then, just when I'd convinced myself that elegantly spinning triangles were all that I needed, a friend at Eyebeam, mindful of my departure from reality, presented me with a 3-D model of Lower Manhattan appropriated from Google Earth. Not wanting to disappoint, I isolated from it the three blocks of my Bowery vision. After a day's work, I had laid the model Bowery under the flying triangles.

What was interesting, I realized, was not some abstraction of flock motion, but the streetness of the street and the birdness of the birds. I rendered a 3-D version of one of the Alaskan swan drawings and pretty soon replaced the triangles with swans swooping over the Bowery.

Summer arrived, my time at Eyebeam ended, and I moved on to other things. I walked down to the Williamsburg waterfront, where I had moved soon after losing my apartment off the Bowery and had one day seen a swan swimming in the East River. The road, which used to have an open view of the water and the Manhattan skyline, is now hemmed in and shadowed by condos.

I saw two swans browsing the muck of the Gowanus Canal, the toxic byway near my apartment in Brooklyn. The EPA had just announced plans to make the Gowanus a Superfund site. The mayor's office opposes the plan, for fear that developers will not want to build condos in the area. Three anonymous, glossy anti-Superfund flyers were slipped through my apartment's mail slot as I wrote this.

At a housewarming party for ex-Williamsburgers who had moved to Ridgewood, Queens, I met a man from British Columbia, and we got to discussing trumpeter swans. "Something I have often heard repeated is that the earth is a gong," he said, "that all creation is a frequency of sound . . . . Perhaps you re-created the tonal resonance of their wetlands."

I haven't yet put cars into the Virtual Bowery. For now, it's just blocky buildings frozen in the late '90s, with swans hovering overhead. I haven't worked with Lisp much recently, either. But I feel happy when I fire up Virtual Bowery and see the stiff-winged trumpeters circling above the red street. ⊠

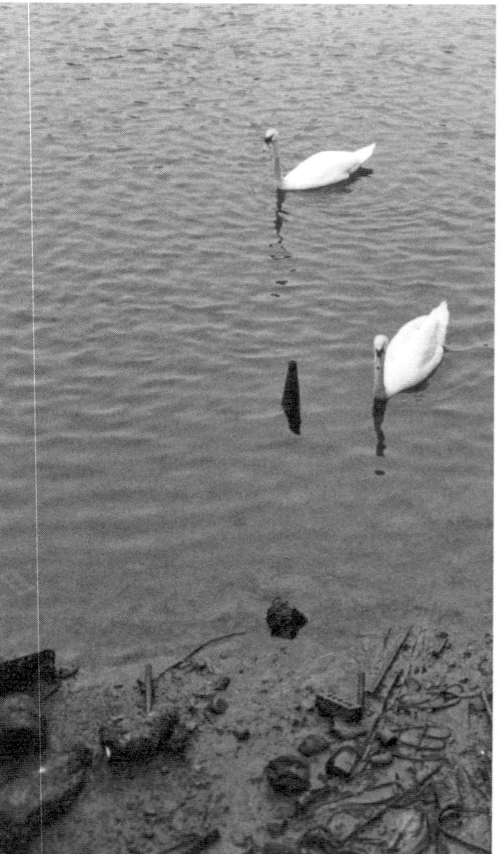

WIEDERHOLUNGS-ZWANG

The trauma of lost histories and the joys of JPEGs. A webcam atop the highest hill in Portland, Maine, transports one public place to another, and another.

by Gil Blank
with Caleb Waldorf
published May 27, 2009

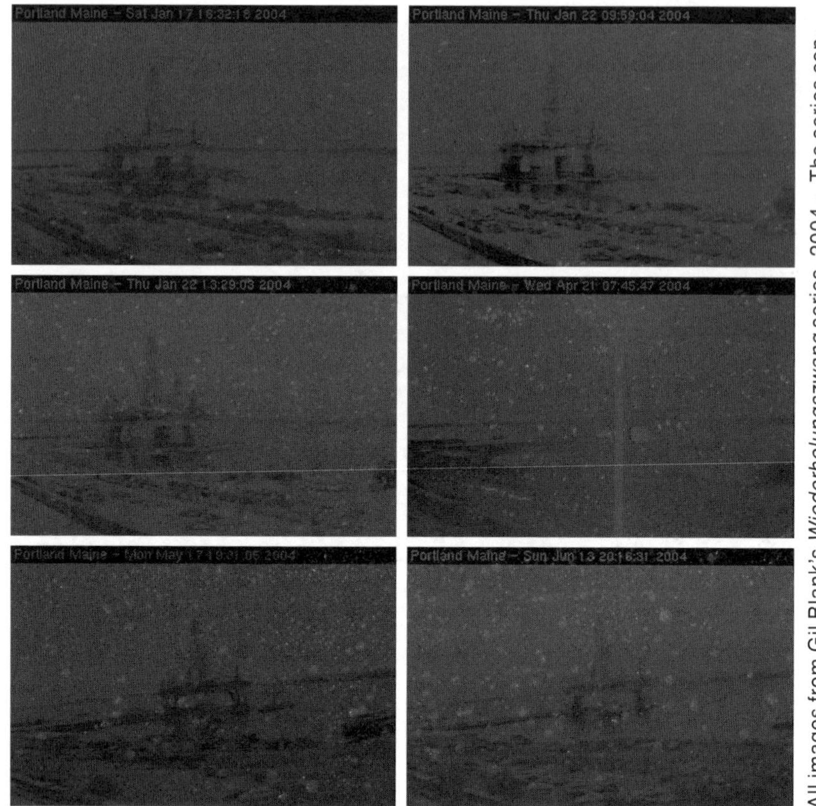

All images from Gil Blank's *Wiederholungszwang* series, 2004–. The series consists of various works derived from the feed of a webcam in Portland, Maine.

I S S U E   6   2 0 0 9

CALEB WALDORF: Can you explain where and how you obtained the original images for this project?

GIL BLANK: The images come from Portland, Maine. Even the name of the city conveys that singularly American sense of hope; it's a euphonic conjunction of earth and sea, of nature and possibility. Portland is flanked by landscaped promenades that provide views out onto the approaching maritime lanes, and at its highest point, atop Munjoy Hill, there still stands an observatory tower, now defunct beyond its service as a tourist attraction. The tower today is magnificent and forlorn, forever looking out onto a view that will never again correspond with it.

At some point, the local landmarks commission decided to place a webcam atop the tower's cupola, presumably in an attempt to renew its relationship to reality. To me, this gesture is as beautiful as it is pathetic; it also verges on the absurd, considering that a much higher-resolution unit with an only slightly lesser view is broadcasting from a car-rental agency closer to the waterfront.

Over the course of 2004, when I first visited the tower in Maine, I found myself returning to its Web feed again and again. I was living in New York and suffused with the effects of an urban technological center, and I began to live to some degree through these vicarious images.

cw: It seems to me that the same drive that motivated the city to place the camera in its current location may also have compelled you to look at the images.

gb: The webcam's lo-fi appearance certainly amplifies its democratic affect, as once was true of Brownie camera snapshots and Polaroids. Planted within each of those vernacular forms, though, is the ineluctable depreciation of the earlier idealistic notions of omniscience, harmony, and consummation that led Portland's settlers to orient the town in such a way as to provide that "Best General View" over the bay.

cw: In the end, you selected only thirty-five images from a year's worth of footage.

gb: I didn't plan the time frame; I simply downloaded the first JPEG in January 2004 out of plain interest in it as a picture. I continued downloading just as impulsively over the next twelve months.

Cianbro, an industrial construction corporation, was at that time in the process of building the Amethyst offshore oil-drilling platform down by the docks. One wholly unintentional aspect of my recording was to inscribe the platform as a central figure in most of the pictures. It was nearing completion during the period that I was watching, and was towed away several times for preliminary deepwater testing, which is why the port appears empty in the pictures from May. It was completely gone by September, shipped to its final destination off the coast of Brazil.

I suppose the drilling platform might evoke for some viewers the dominating influence of industry and capital, the displacement of natural and public areas, the worldwide circulation of petrodollars, and so on. Every one of these points is relevant, and indicative of the inherent generosity of photography. But none of them was primary in my thinking during the process, and the platform's presence only manifested itself to me emblematically, as one more transient feature of the landscape.

cw: Since 2004, this group of images has been exhibited several times, in multiple formats; over that time, you've continually rewritten and reprocessed the same images, oftentimes degrading them in the process. The end point seems to be their complete disintegration.

gb: I'm not sure that the singular or "complete" end you mention pertains. I print the images by a variety of means, with technologies as recent as an ink-jet printer and as outdated as gravure. The impulse has been to resist the abstraction of the image, while always acknowledging the impossibility of any such effort. Because the printing is performed in successive generations—each new process begins with the already-degraded image left over from the process before it—the effects of reproduction and circulation are slowly overcoming whatever vestige of "original" presence the pictures once had.

One term I've often thought about in relation to the photographs is *Wiederholungszwang*, which translates as "the compulsion to repeat." This term was coined by Freud (and later refined by Lacan) to describe a natural response to traumatic experience. If one workable definition of trauma is a missed encounter or lost history, it follows that such an experience can never be adequately recovered or re-*presented*, only endlessly repeated, even as each iteration carries you farther away. Looking at these images reproduced again in a different form—because every JPEG carries within it the code for its further disappearance—each viewer experiences another new but diminished event.

CW: The webcam is often viewed as a form of "personal media"— we glimpse a bedroom, a closely cropped face, flat lighting. A dock does not conjure up a sense of intimacy or personal space.

GB: The use you mention for the webcam—transmitting a picture of the self out into the world, with all the connotations of low-grade celebrity and annihilation of personal privacy that it implies—was precisely the opposite of anything that motivated me. I was on the receiving end of the view, and never had any intention of projecting any aspect of myself or my personal life onto the image. But your question is about a much deeper issue, which is where the self—as the embodiment of that original experience we keep coming back to—exists.

The view depicted doesn't show just any public space, but was considered at one time to be *the* singular public space, the town's great vantage. That possibility of some grand vista that would connect and clarify and consummate is why I first looked northward to Maine. It's important to understand that I didn't begin saving these pictures with any artistic motivation in mind at all; they were never intended to become an artwork. I accumulated them out of need, to reckon how exactly the stable sense of self is formed amid a life experience that is at all times on the verge of atomization.

CW: What do you find significant about recycling, reusing, and multiplying images whose currency tends to lie in their immediacy?

GB: It is, of course, impossible to speak of "originals" in these images. The placement, direction, framing, and subject—all the classical criteria by which a pictorial composition is defined as having some correlation to subjective experience—were out of my control. The camera was recording around the clock (and still is); my only remaining determinative criteria were whether to accept the gaze as I found it and when to commit it to memory by downloading its electronic traces. Even as first-generation downloads, the files were already abstractions of a view that itself was formed beyond my control. And yet that urge to make some sense out of a shattered history persisted, if only to form a model that could parallel the secondary experience of that dissolution.

CW: The original images you captured (which picture a nonplace) have been processed, distributed, and redistributed, as has the project as a whole. I get the sense that your work visually maps the erosion of the traditional role of the camera, and its replacement by technologies that have been instrumental in constructing the image of the nonplace.

GB: Or maybe my work implicates photographic vision as having carried the germ of this alienation all along.

CW: I'm curious what you think this piece would be without the multitude of (re)printed images. Can we capture something about them through their own erasure?

GB: I wouldn't consider the process an erasure, which implies a deliberate negation and a fatalism that has no place in the pictures. I think the way that you described it earlier, as disintegration, is more apt. The process then becomes a matter of witness, and of allowing the images to register another unexpected and ancillary index.

I think what you're rightly seeking is that secondary layer of meaning, which you can think of as the way that the photographs function, rather than what they simply portray. Despite the fact that they depict a certain time and place and social circumstance, all of which carry their own intrinsic interest, I grant you that my own reasons for looking at that early Web feed may have absolutely no bearing on your own experience of the images.

So then what possible operation could such images perform beyond solipsism? If there is any persistent meaning to be found in them, it has to be because the process of their dissemination—of the earlier downloading, of their further reproduction and dissolution, and of your eventual and momentary custody—becomes an ongoing model of contemporary social experience, rather than its mere illustration. ⊠

INVALID FORMAT 2

ISSUE 6
2009

THE CITY THAT BUILT ITSELF

Utopian modernism turned on its head in Caracas, where residents have made fifty-year-old superblock housing projects into the locus of sprawling improvised settlements.

by Joshua Bauchner
published May 12, 2009

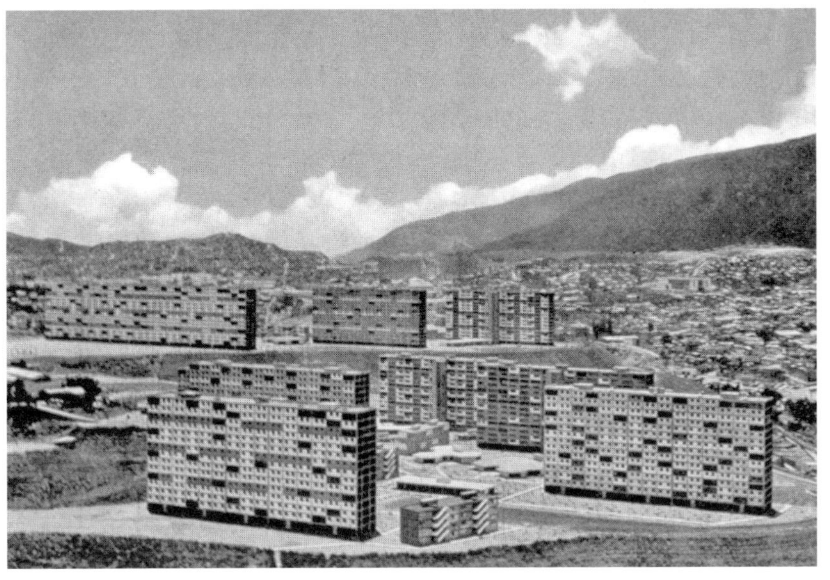

ON MANY MAPS OF CARACAS, the *parroquia* of 23 de Enero appears as empty space. A few roads are shown traversing the northwest corner of the city's central valley, spreading like ivy tendrils as they join together the jumbled street grids to the west, north, and east. But the space where the parish should be is blank. As you enter Caracas on the new elevated highway that channels traffic into the city through the northernmost tail of the Andes, it is these unmarked areas of the map that you first encounter. Beneath the highway, red cinder-block houses with corrugated tin roofs cascade down the hillsides. The *ranchos* closest to the highway are painted in the stereotypical bright colors and pastels of the tropics. Those that sit farther away were spared the old, cheap trick of rehabilitation and retain the rusty hue of dust and aged cinder block.

In the city's San Francisco Valley, these slums, where nearly half of Caraqueños live, dramatically run up against a series of gargantuan buildings with punchy red, yellow, blue, and white facades cut out from the hillside—*superbloques*. Each of these housing projects is forty meters tall and over eighty meters long. Nearly swallowed by ranchos, they are vestiges of modernist urbanism long since colonized by the realities of twentieth-century Caracas.

I
N
V
A
L
I
D

F
O
R
M
A
T

2

The last Venezuelan dictator, General Marcos Pérez Jiménez, oversaw the construction of the superblocks. The project was the concrete centerpiece of the New National Ideal, an ambitious renewal program intended to foment "the rational transformation of the physical environment." In the capital, this entailed a massive endeavor to rid the city of its metastasizing slums. Between Pérez Jiménez's fraudulent election in 1952 and downfall in 1958, the state built 28,763 housing units, many of them contained in Caracas's eighty-seven superblocks. The jewel was 23 de Enero, host to thirty-eight of them. Inaugurated in 1955 with the moniker 2 de Diciembre, in celebration of the dictator's assumption of power, the parroquia was rechristened 23 de Enero in 1958, to commemorate his flight from the country. It now stands as an ironic monument to the dictator and a continuing refutation of his legacy.

Because of Pérez Jiménez's tendency toward self-glorification, two-thirds of the blocks in 23 de Enero were still empty as of January 1958, years after their completion,

I
S
S
U
E

6

2
0
0
9

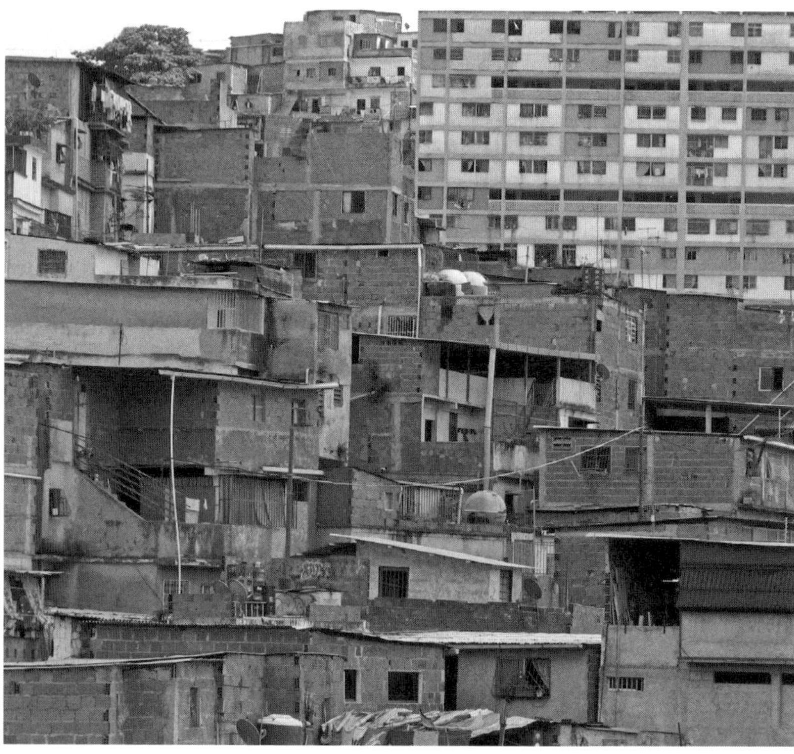

Bloque 52 and ranchos in Sierra Maestra.

waiting to be dedicated on the next anniversary of the
dictator's ascension. But on the twenty-third of the month,
as Pérez Jiménez was overthrown, rumors spread through
the subsequent citywide celebration that plentiful, free
apartments were available in the partially uninhabited
project. The rush on apartments carried over from the
superblocks to the open land surrounding them, where
Caraqueños began building houses out of urban refuse,
establishing clusters of makeshift ranchos that would soon
become full-fledged *barrios*. The dictatorship's greatest
symbol of regimen and progress was taken over and folded
back into the Caracas it was to have replaced.

This admixture of Latin America's two most prevalent forms of shelter, modernist housing blocks and improvised slum dwellings, is not unique, but the scale, site,
history, and density of 23 de Enero—over eighty thousand
residents live in the parroquia's superblocks and ranchos—
make it exceptional.

IT IS DIFFICULT TO IMAGINE Olga Marí Lugo building
anything. She is around five feet tall and eighty years old,
with a compact, weathered face and a frail body tented by
a knit sweater. When she picks up her cup and saucer, they
rattle softly in her hands. We are sitting in her living room,
the center of the house she has been building in 23 de Enero
for nearly fifty years. In 1961, when she arrived in the barrio Brisas de Primavera with her grandmother and three
sons, a friend gave her a small parcel of land on a hillside,
which had been neatly sculpted into a green incline by
government planners. The house, one of the first to be built
in the barrio, started like all ranchos: cinder blocks and
tin planted precariously on the incline. "I had to leave my
children here alone to go work," she remembers. "We lived
in a marginal situation. But I continued working, working,
working; I made the walls of the house little by little, little
by little. This lasted twenty-two years."

Originally, *rancho* denoted a rural farmer's house,
a basic structure contiguous with the land itself and

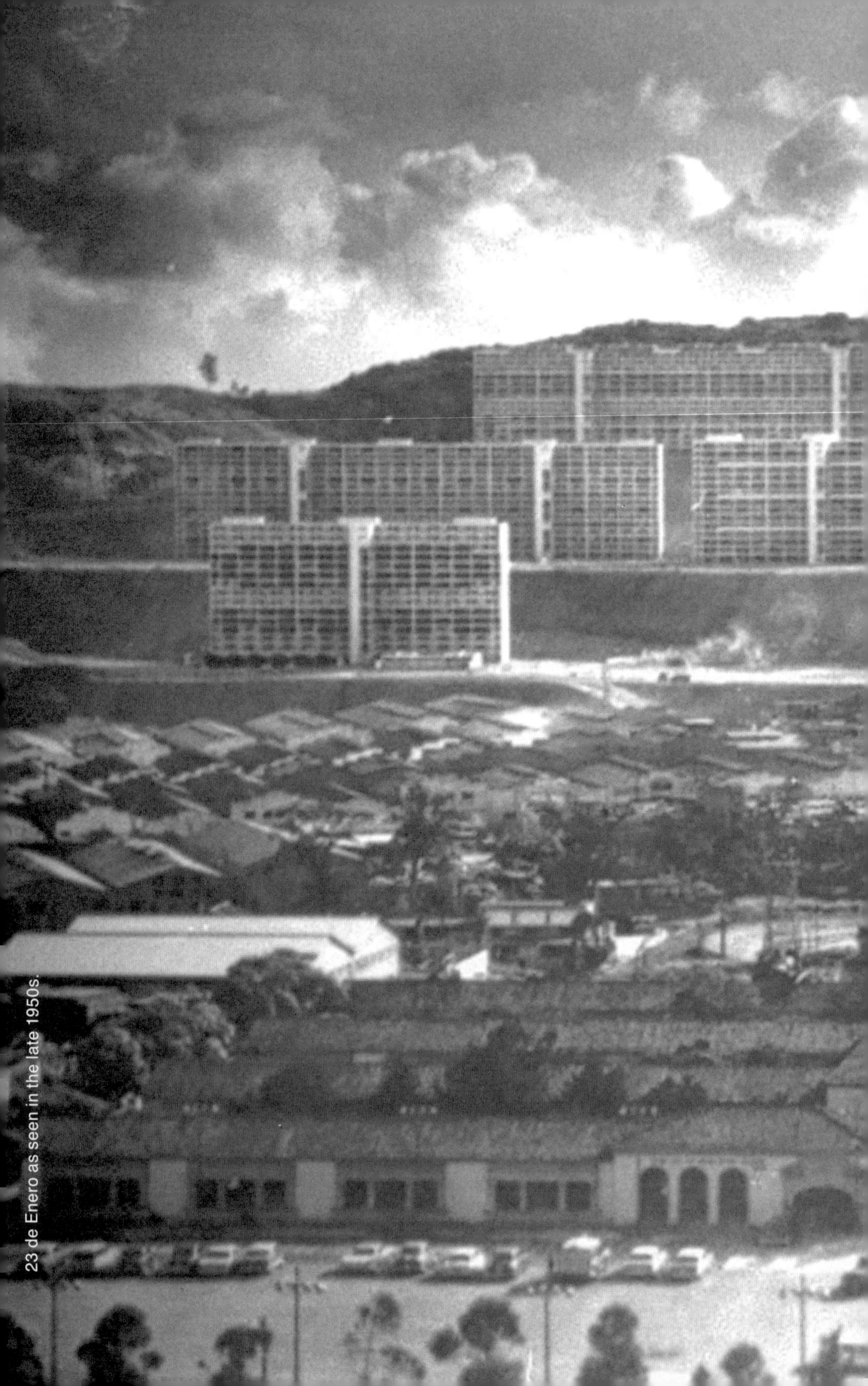
23 de Enero as seen in the late 1950s.

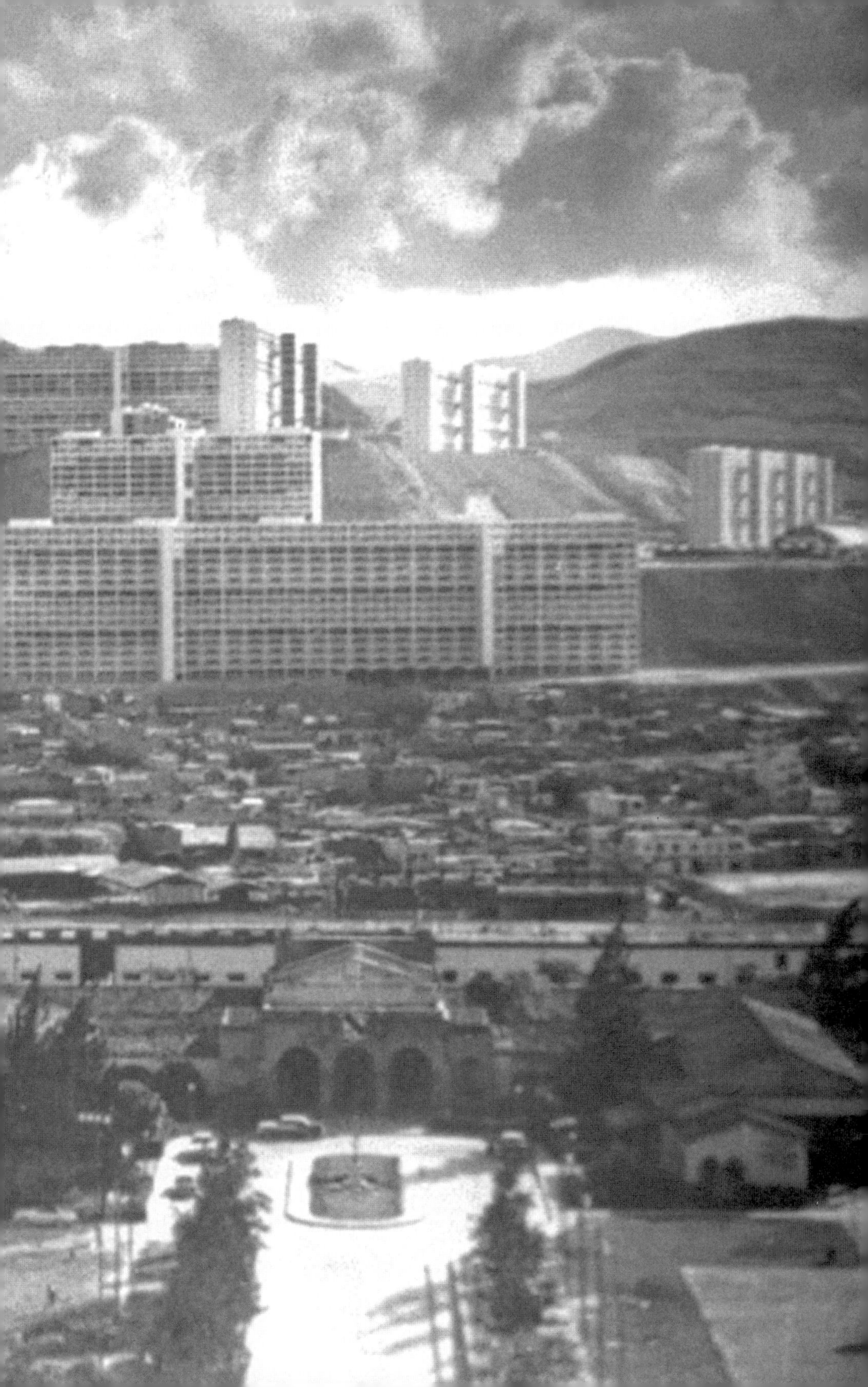

constructed out of necessity. In the early twentieth century, legions of rural migrants transported the rancho with them to the city. But unlike their rural counterparts, urban ranchos are constructed from the detritus of the city's growth: zinc, iron lattice, cardboard, rusted tin, cinder block, and cement. The ranchos in the newest, poorest barrios at the city's edges still exhibit these elements, with packed-earth floors and steps, tin roofs resting on risers, and basic square openings in the walls for windows. In older barrios, including those of 23 de Enero, such basic structures are rarer, while more "finished" ranchos prevail.

Though Olga has long since retired from construction work, her sons have continued to build, and the family's three-story home is now one such "finished" rancho. A covered entryway leads to a naturally cooled high-ceilinged living room, which is flooded with light entering from the nearby kitchen windows. The house is spacious, with a great sense of scale. On a clear and temperate morning, Olga and I look out from the balcony at a layer of red cinderblock additions crowning the houses of the surrounding barrio Sierra Maestra. As she tells the history of her house and family, there is a subtle transition in pronouns, from the masculine *lo*, referring to *rancho*, to the feminine *la*, referring to casa. Though Venezuelan housing statistics locate the distinction between rancho and casa in the type and finish of the walls, the transition from the former to the latter is neither linear nor teleological. The architect Teolinda Bolívar describes the rancho as "never finished, simply stopped." With births and marriages come new rooms and floors. The latest addition to Olga's house is a third-floor shop for her youngest son's carpentry business.

As the barrio is constructed rancho by rancho, individual housing needs are satisfied and replaced by collective needs: roads, water, schools, stores. Individual building efforts are subsumed by collective ones, which not only determine the physical shape of the neighborhood but define daily life in the community. Bolívar describes the resident of the barrio as neither *homo economicus* (economic man) nor *homo faber* (working man), but rather *homo convivalis*, a being constituted by human relationships that persist irrespective of the government in power.

During the few months I spent in Caracas last year researching and exploring parroquia 23 de Enero and talking with its residents, I often passed Friday evenings in a parking lot overlooking the barrios with my friend Maricarmen. We ate fat slices of dense pound cake and drank bottles of the ubiquitous Polar beer as twilight settled over the hills. The massive polychromatic boxes hovered before us, engulfed at their bases by a hive of burnt-red ranchos, each buzzing with laundry lines and water tanks, linked by tangles of black cable that arced through the sky from one row of ranchos to the next. The thump of reggaeton and the slap of dominoes on nearby tables filled the air, puncturing the city's dull rumble. As darkness arrived, the blocks and ranchos melted into the far-off handmade street lamps flickering from barrios across the ravine, weaving a pattern of faint lights mirroring the dim stars above.

ON THE EDGES of Spain's Nueva Granada viceroyalty, Caracas grew in the mold of most European colonial cities, with preordained norms instilled in its gridded street plan and central plaza. The tranquil weather and slow pace of life gave "the city of red roofs," as it was commonly known among its upper class, an abiding gentility.

By the mid-twentieth century, the sleepy capital city had become a burgeoning metropolis rapidly outgrowing its old colonial infrastructure. In his 1966 history of Caraqueño architecture, *Caracas in Three Periods*, Carlos Raúl Villanueva, the primary architect of 23 de Enero, declared Caracas "no longer properly a city, but a formation of different molecules." Between 1935 and 1961, with the country's agricultural sector moribund and ever-increasing oil profits flowing into the capital, the population of Caracas quintupled, while Venezuela's as a whole merely doubled. Nearly a million rural migrants and southern European immigrants flocked to the city, transforming it into a sprawl of tin- and zinc-roofed ranchos. By 1948, when Pérez Jiménez took power as part of a military junta, the barrios had become so widespread in Caracas that the formerly rural *rancho* had become an official designation in federal urban-housing statistics. Within three years, it became the name of the enemy. The government issued a study condemning the barrios as "a threat against the morals, health, and security" of the nation, and its 1951 housing plan declared "war against the rancho."

Tasked with prosecuting this war and solving the so-called housing problem, the public housing bureau hired Villanueva to lead TABO, its new architecture studio. TABO's cheap, long-lasting housing was to be the central front in the New National Ideal's fight to regenerate the nation's moral and intellectual character by force of blueprints and poured concrete. Following the populist strains of modernist architecture dominant in postwar Europe, Villanueva designed a superblock modeled after Le Corbusier's Unité d'Habitation (which was itself inspired by a Soviet communal-housing project).

Pérez Jiménez and his architects adopted much of Corbusier's utopian vision and rhetoric. The superblocks were designed to synthesize different classes, values, and lives into "an organic community." They were to be part of a radical master plan to reconstruct all Caracas with the balance and order craved by modernist architects and dictators alike. Villanueva adapted Corbusier's design for the Venezuelan climate by including open-air passages; he accommodated the country's population explosion by expanding the proportions of each superblock to include 160 apartments on sixteen floors and by building double and triple superblocks.

Ultimately, though, the superblock lost much of its utopian character in the construction process. As the Caraqueño population grew, so did its discontent with the dictatorship, which was manifest in the growing number of fractured oppositional organizations. Pérez Jiménez

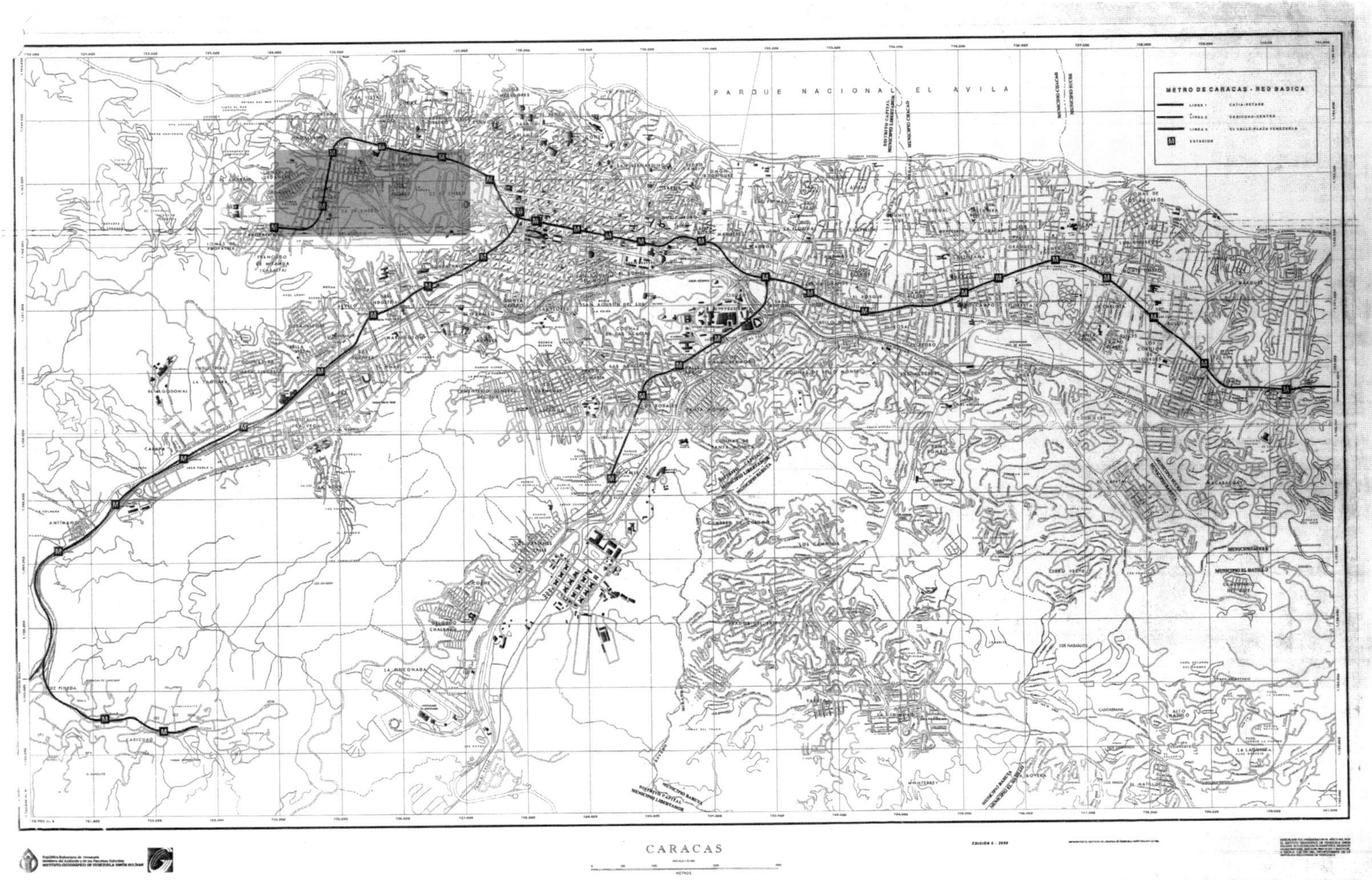

PARQUE NACIONAL EL AVILA
METRO DE CARACAS - RED BASICA
LINEA 1   CATIA-PETARE
LINEA 2   CARICUAO-CENTRO
LINEA 3   EL VALLE-PLAZA VENEZUELA
M   ESTACION
CARACAS
República Bolivariana de Venezuela
Ministerio del Ambiente y de los Recursos Naturales
INSTITUTO GEOGRAFICO DE VENEZUELA SIMON BOLIVAR
EDICION 4 - 2008
METROS

redirected this pressure into his already intense public works projects, rushing 23 de Enero from early sketches to breaking ground. His demands halved the total footprint of the project and brought the superblocks to construction without many of the features originally proposed by Villaneuva, including pilotis and loggia, north-south orientation, duplex apartments, interior trash chutes, and large common spaces on every fourth floor.

In the transition away from dictatorial whim after January 23, 1958, disarray presided in the city and the government. Student volunteers haphazardly began adjudicating disputes between new residents of 23 de Enero regarding their apartments and land. Delivering services and collecting rent became increasingly difficult as the population skyrocketed. Amid all this, construction by the state's housing bank was halted. Burdened with the debt left over from the dictator's many public works projects, the government steered its public housing resources toward smaller-scale projects. Three years after Pérez Jiménez fled, an in-depth state study of 23 de Enero called for the cessation of "all types of construction of superblocks."

ALTHOUGH THE SUPERBLOCKS failed to transform urban life in the ways predicted by modernist planners, they have fostered community. At one point, Olga spoke of El Caracazo, a violent upheaval in Caracas surrounding government incompetence, failures, and antidissident crackdowns in February 1989, during which one of her sons died. The violence in the parroquia was particularly acute, but she recalls a "sentimiento de pertenencia" (feeling of belonging) persisting throughout the chaos.

This feeling extends to the heights of the superblocks as well. Deprived of necessary funding and functional administration by a succession of governments, the superblocks are sustained both apartment by apartment and in small, ad hoc organizations. Impromptu organizing has been the hallmark of 23 de Enero, with committees tackling problems from physical infrastructure to gun violence

and drug use. While the collapse of the modernist promise
of cheap dense housing for the poor has followed a similar
course in decrepit clusters of towers everywhere from
Saint Louis to the former Soviet republics, here the community has managed to stanch social deterioration.

When I first arrived in Caracas and met with a group
of community organizers who lived in 23 de Enero, I asked
them how residents see the distinctions between different superblocks and barrios. Like the ranchos that surround them, the superblocks are always being renovated,
and they are in vastly different states of repair. Some have
peeling facades and trash-strewn front yards. Their elevators require full-time operators, and the exterior trash
chutes disintegrate as they descend from the top floor.
Others have luscious gardens and functional chutes. Their
elevators run smoothly on their own, and the paint is brilliant. I heard rumors that a few large families had even
connected vertically aligned apartments into duplexes.
The physical conditions of the structures seemed to me
to reflect distinct traditions of collective maintenance or
neglect. But everyone I asked evaded my questions with
a quizzical look and told me I was missing the point. They
felt at home throughout La Veintitrés, not only in particular barrios or blocks.

"Veintitrés de Enero is, and always has been, revolutionary," ninety-two-year-old Francisco Egañez told me
when I visited his home in Bloque 50. For Francisco, who
wore a red flannel shirt and a red hat bearing the logo of
his union, the parroquia was always a site of resistance, an
oppositional stronghold within the city of the government.
Even today it maintains its reputation as both a bastion of
Chavismo and the home of a handful of remaining radicals
independent of the president. But in a city supersaturated
with the word *revolución*—Ipostel, the dysfunctional postal
service, is, by its own account, "revolutionizing the mail"—
it's nearly impossible to parse such pronouncements.
Nevertheless, the interdependence of life in 23 de Enero
does seem to represent a more enduring, more difficult

form of collective politics than that offered up on President Chávez's weekly *Aló Presidente* talk show.

Birthed and orphaned by the state, 23 de Enero is now home to residents who have spent years struggling to preserve the lives they have created for themselves. Ligia Martínez de Elías, one of the first residents of Bloque 20–21, said to me, "I lived through Pérez Jiménez, I lived through Caldera, and now I live under Chávez. Regardless of the government, if you don't work, you can't eat. One doesn't live by the government."

OFFICIALLY, JANUARY 23, 1958, marked the Venezuelan democratic revolution. But the actual role of the state changed very little. The 1958 pact of Punto Fijo led to a political system dominated by two centrist parties dedicated to taming the dual exigencies of oil wealth and population growth, as the state had done since the emergence of a worldwide market for petroleum in World War I.

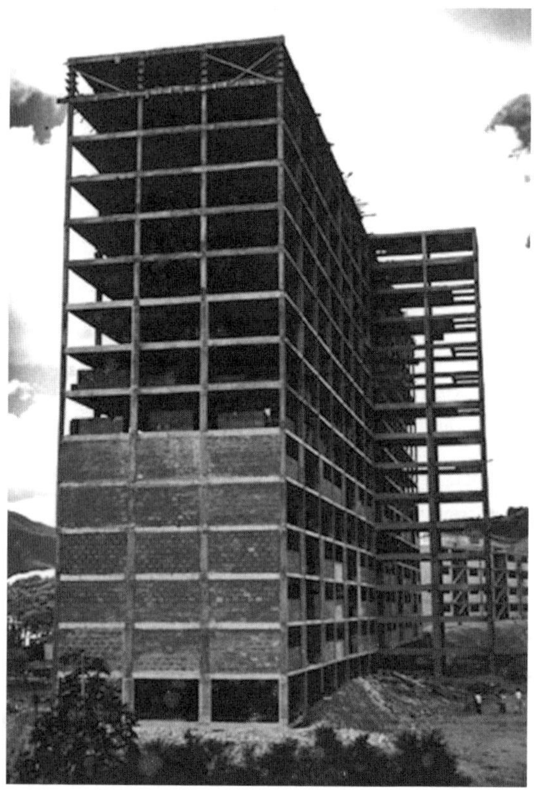

A superblock under construction in the late 1950s.

Like the dictator, the parties facilitated the extraction of crude oil from the country's subsoil; but after 1958 the people were allowed to cast ballots affirming the legitimacy of the system every five years. This arrangement endured until Hugo Chávez's 1998 campaign, which promised and delivered a break with *partidocracia*. It is less clear whether Chávez has altered the state's essential character. In Venezuela, "the state has nothing to do with reality," asserted the playwright José Ignacio Cabrujas in a mid-1980s lecture sponsored by the Presidential Commission for State Reform. "The state is a magnanimous sorcerer" buoyed by oil, which "is fantastic and induces fantasies"—first among them the fantasy of progress.

Historian Fernando Coronil terms Cabrujas's conception of Venezuela "the magical state" in his book of the same title. Under Pérez Jiménez, who was convinced Venezuela could will itself to modernity, the state produced a series of ostentatious performances that promised miracles but delivered little more than sparks from a wand. The repudiation of the state's ultimate magic act, the eradication of the city's slums, was not confined to January 23 or its immediate aftermath, but has been lived out over and over in the construction of the parroquia by its own residents.

On one of my first visits to the parroquia, a friend of a friend asked whether I had been to Monte Piedad, a barrio on the parroquia's eastern tip. I had. "Did you notice that there is no Bloque 8?" he inquired. I shook my head, and he proceeded to tell me a story I would hear many times during my stay in Caracas, though I could never confirm it: In an act of immense generosity that Latin American dictators tend to perform only for one another, Pérez Jiménez gifted an entire superblock to Colombia's dictator, General Gustavo Rojas Pinilla—Bloque 8. The polychromatic facade, exterior elevator column, endless square cutouts in the concrete balusters, and huge rooftop water tanks were all replicated thirteen hundred kilometers southwest of Caracas in Cali, Colombia. He smiled wryly and said, "The Colombians call it 'El Venezolano.'"

Today, the parroquia that encompasses the super-blocks is, to its neighbors, as prominent a symbol of Venezuela as the buildings themselves. Chávez has clearly learned something from 23 de Enero: The federal government now funds community councils directly, empowering them to make decisions about infrastructure improvements and social programs. These community councils are buttressed by *misiones*, federal programs to increase access to healthcare and education in the barrios, and they have begun to foster "sentimientos de pertenencia" in other parts of the city. Yet in Caracas, as in so many global megacities, the question of housing remains essentially unanswered, and the high rhetoric of modernism has yet to find a successor.

The physical lessons of the barrio can and must be learned by architects and planners in Caracas and beyond, where slums and superblocks are now integral parts of the built environment. The recent incredible barrio-rehabilitation projects in Medellín, Colombia, demonstrate progress

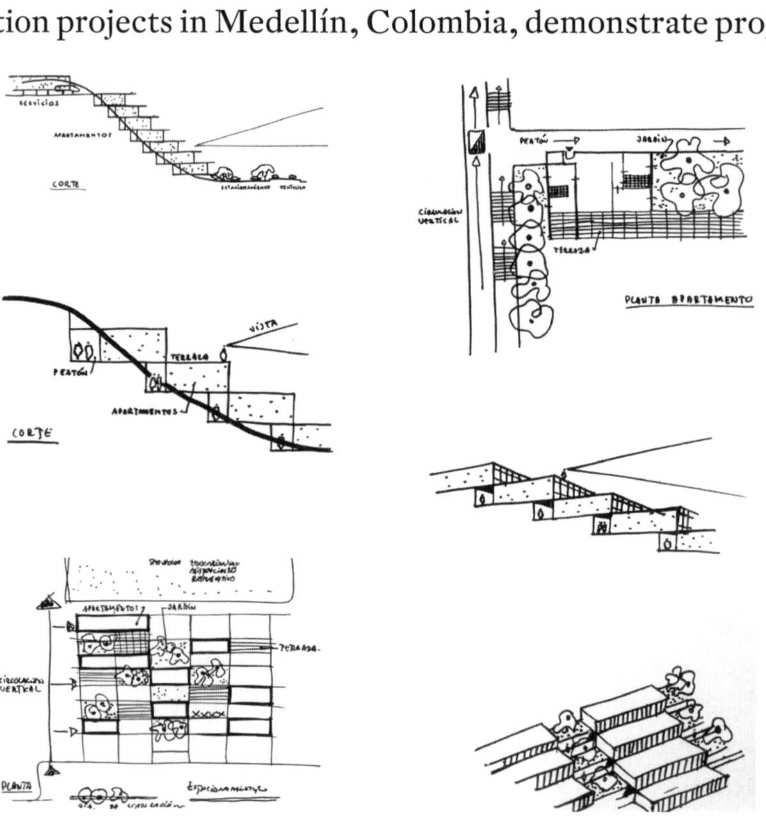

Sketch for a modified superblock by Jorge Romero Gutierrez, 1955.

in this vein. Chávez, however, may not have fully processed the lessons of 23 de Enero. Separate from his progressive and successful community councils and misiones, he has begun construction on an entirely new city called Caribia for the residents of the capital's poorest barrios just outside Caracas—a project squarely in the tradition of the magical state.

In a 1955 issue of *Integral*, Venezuela's leading architecture and urbanism review, Jorge Romero Gutierrez proposed a modified superblock that "would incline along the plane of the hill." In the accompanying sketches, each apartment has a garden covering its roof and a room built into the hill in back. They resemble a mass-produced barrio, but with additional niceties. The article only mentions the real architects of this modified block, barrio residents, to criticize their way of life as being incompatible with "well-planned housing."

Ironically, the same demographic and political pressures that inspired Gutierrez's design eventually led to the dissolution of the state agencies that would have funded its realization, and the plans never left the page. Nevertheless, the homemade model has thrived. Just several hundred meters from the presidential palace, 23 de Enero sits on its hill, baldly exposed to all those entering the city from the sea and the air, a living testament to Venezuela's legacy of housing built well, if not planned. ⊠

GYPSY MANSIONS

The Roma build their palaces just like the rest of us, one cinder block at a time.

by Lev Bratishenko
published May 27, 2009

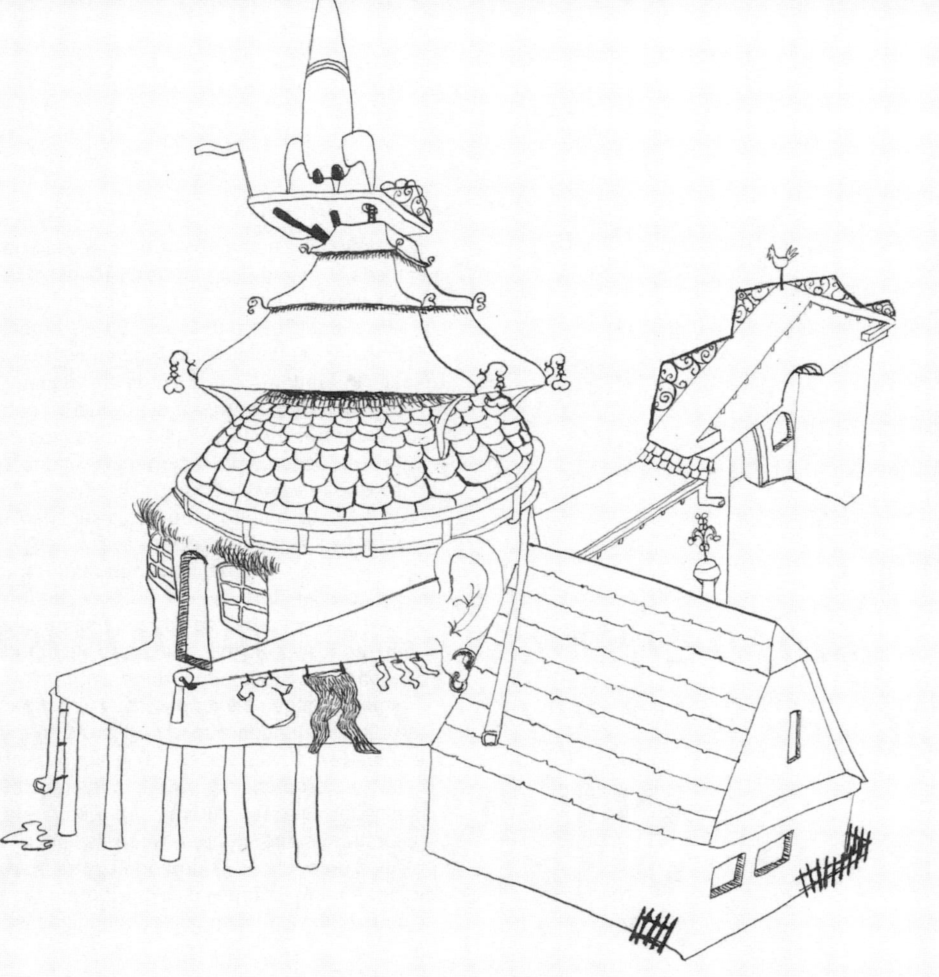

TIMIȘOARA, ROMANIA Like Saint Petersburg before she was operated on for her three hundredth, the brie-colored streets and decaying facades have a dusty continuity. Against this backdrop, the Roma build their Disneyland.

Forced by the Communists to settle in the '60s, they have embraced a style of permanent renovation. Their mansions, in primary colors, stick like fingers in the dead dictator's eye. But this provokes nothing beyond tourists snapping photos and locals shaking their heads.

"How do you think they pay for them?" they ask me and then spit.

Gypsy mansions are confusing. Though they are decorated with wild variation, their structural similarities are apparent. The mansion plans are essentially standardized: All rooms branch off a central corridor, and none have direct access to any others; but there the standardization ends, and this is not so surprising. Mansions are primarily structures of one-upmanship; eternal construction sites of dubious habitable value (they are often abandoned, though this could be because the settlement policies went with the Communists) that rise as barometers of personal (male) status, they are intensely decorated sheds with few interior complications.

They all have fences, and this isn't their only concession to the economic realities of living in palaces: Their paroxysms of decoration hide quality Soviet-bloc construction. Though the modest ones might be only three stories of stucco on cinder block with simple roofs, their architects—the family chiefs—apparently design them all the same way. Ornamental details are collected during travels until the stash is sufficient to sustain construction, or at least addition to an existing structure. I'm tempted to speculate on an obsession with competitive architectural bricolage.

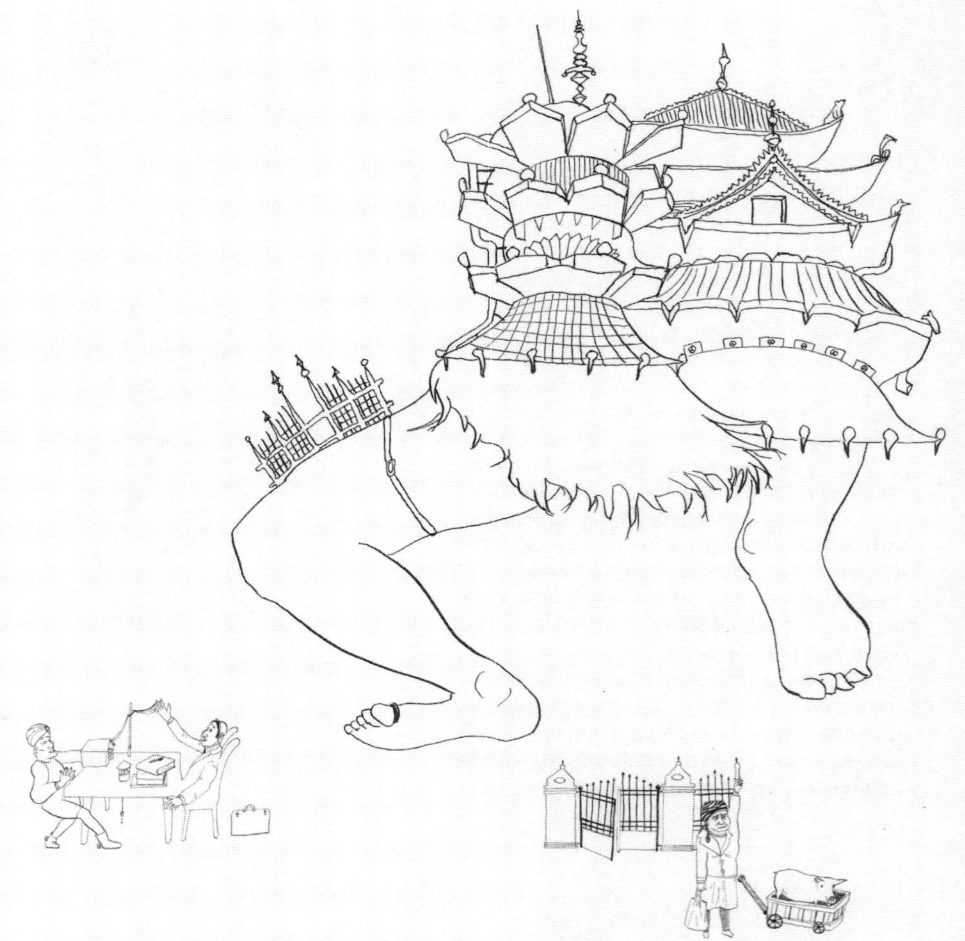

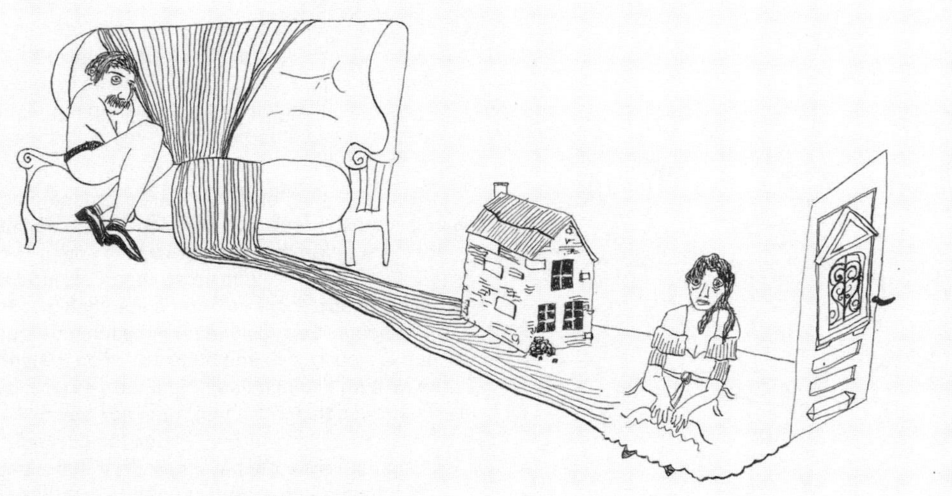

The chief is usually the fellow you'd expect him to be, the one with a solid-gold necktie, a round belly, and an enviable mustache. But there must be others: wise women and wrinkled bullies, drug dealers and car salesmen who've become rich, then powerful. Their mansions probably look the same, right down to the golden cutout of a Mercedes on the roof catching the dusk light.

A style defined by reaction cannot sustain agglomeration. Build too many examples near one another and it becomes hard to take any of them seriously. This makes it difficult to imagine villages of these mansions, such as Bărăgan to the south of Bucharest, where the difficulty of producing sufficient contrast engenders some really wild solutions. Or so I hear.

Everything I know is hearsay colored by Romanian discomfort with the Roma. The Timișoara mansions were isolated, silent, and dark—except for garage lights. It could be the gypsy equivalent of a suburban porch light, meant to deter burglars, though each house already has an iron gate with a crest of orderly spikes. What are they worried about?

The Romanians I met liked to speculate on mansion fund-raising. One friend's theory: The money collected by pan-European begging is funneled through secret underground channels to build empty palaces in eastern Europe. Families who return from working abroad spend all their savings on a new house and must live in one destitute room to save on heating and electricity. This would require a vast, highly organized network.

Once you learn that the gypsies probably came from India, the buildings take on an Eastern cast. Towering hunks of concrete and bulky columns become minarets and colonnades; even the characteristic stamped-tin roofs cry out for South Asian sun.

Inside are floral prints and bright wallpaper, maybe plastic-covered couches. The music and the dresses I have to imagine. ⊠

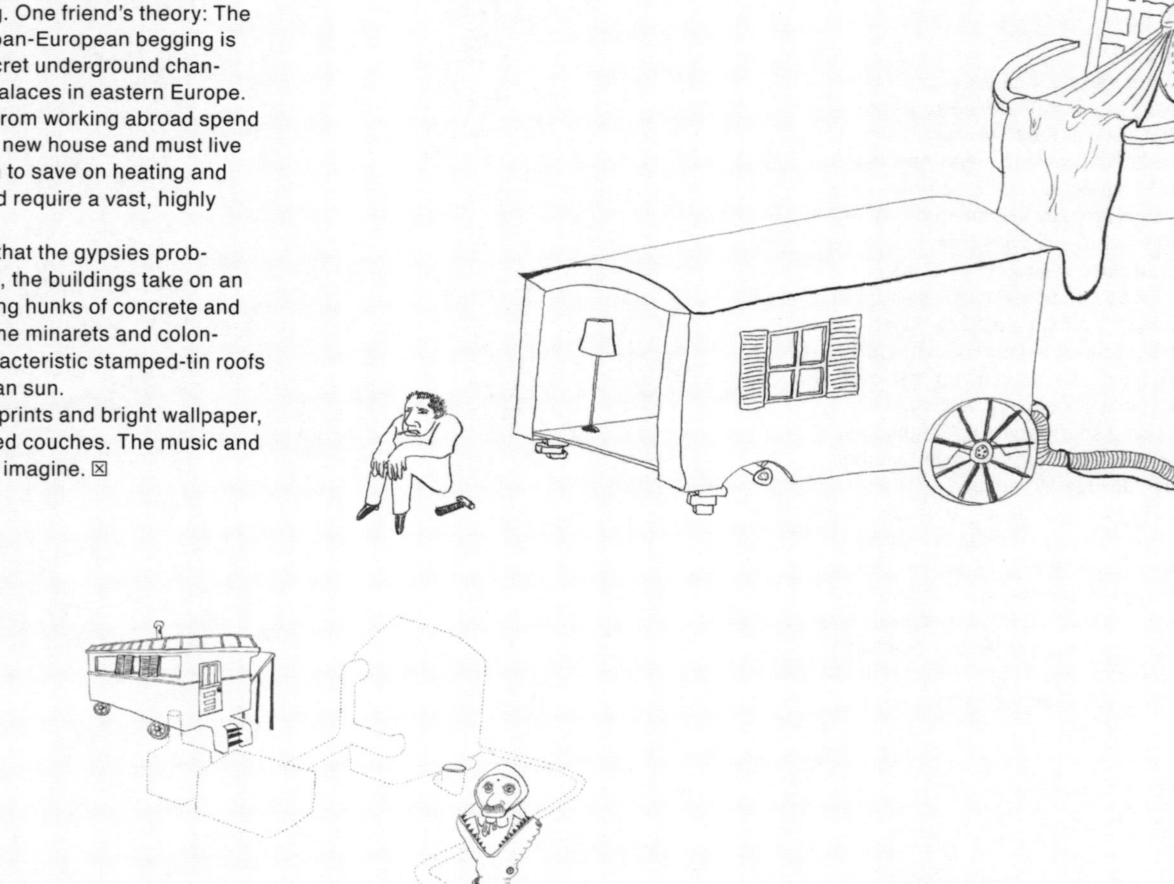

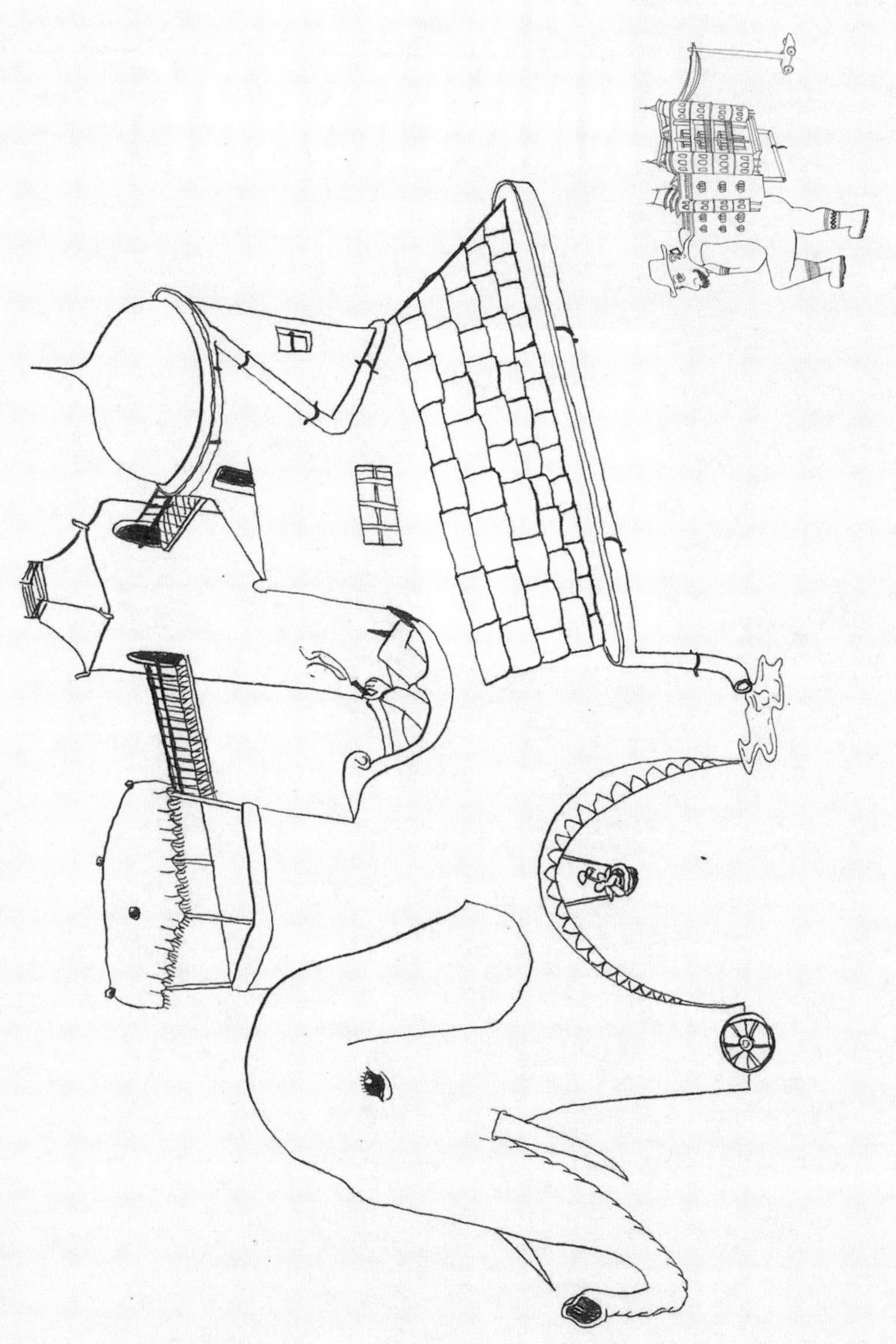

ONE-YEAR ANNIVERSARY

& ISSUE SIX RELEASE PARTY
GOWANUS STUDIO SPACE, 119 8TH STREET, BROOKLYN, NY
MAY 16, 2009

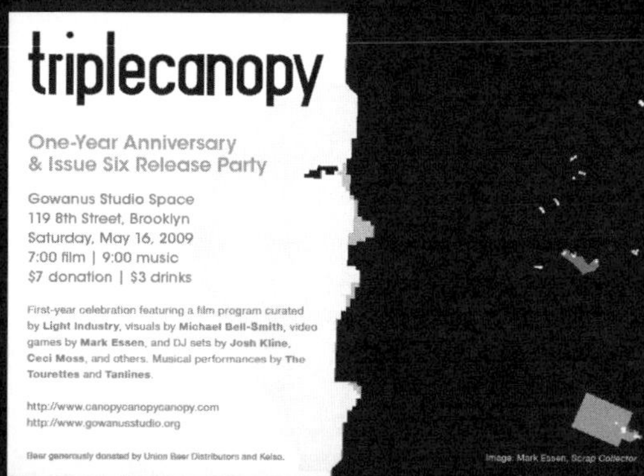

Image: Mark Essen, Scrap Collector

TRIPLE CANOPY CELEBRATED one year of existence and the publication of its sixth issue with a film program curated by Light Industry, visuals by Michael Bell-Smith, video games by Mark Essen, DJ sets by Josh Kline and Ceci Moss, and musical performances by the Tourettes and Tanlines. Light Industry presented *Reductions*, a screening of digest films, which were created for home viewing and transformed theatrical features into short subjects, bumping down the originals from 35 mm to Super-8. Digests often stripped the original films of color and sound and reedited the narratives into a concise ten to fifteen minutes, in the process changing their meaning in subtle, strange, and surprising ways. Light Industry's selection included a range of miniaturized movies, among them Jerry Lewis vehicles, horror films, kung fu pictures, and '70s disaster epics. Mark Essen showed Scrap Collector, a game about making money, and the Thrill of Combat, a game about flying a helicopter and collecting organs. "On your home video system you can play different games," Daniel Cohen writes in *Video Games* (1982). "It is 'programmable.' Each time you want to play a new game you put in a new cartridge. The games stir elemental passions. The adults who love the games most of all are those who make them. Video games mean big, big bucks. If someone offers you stock in Atari or gold—take the Atari. It's better than gold."

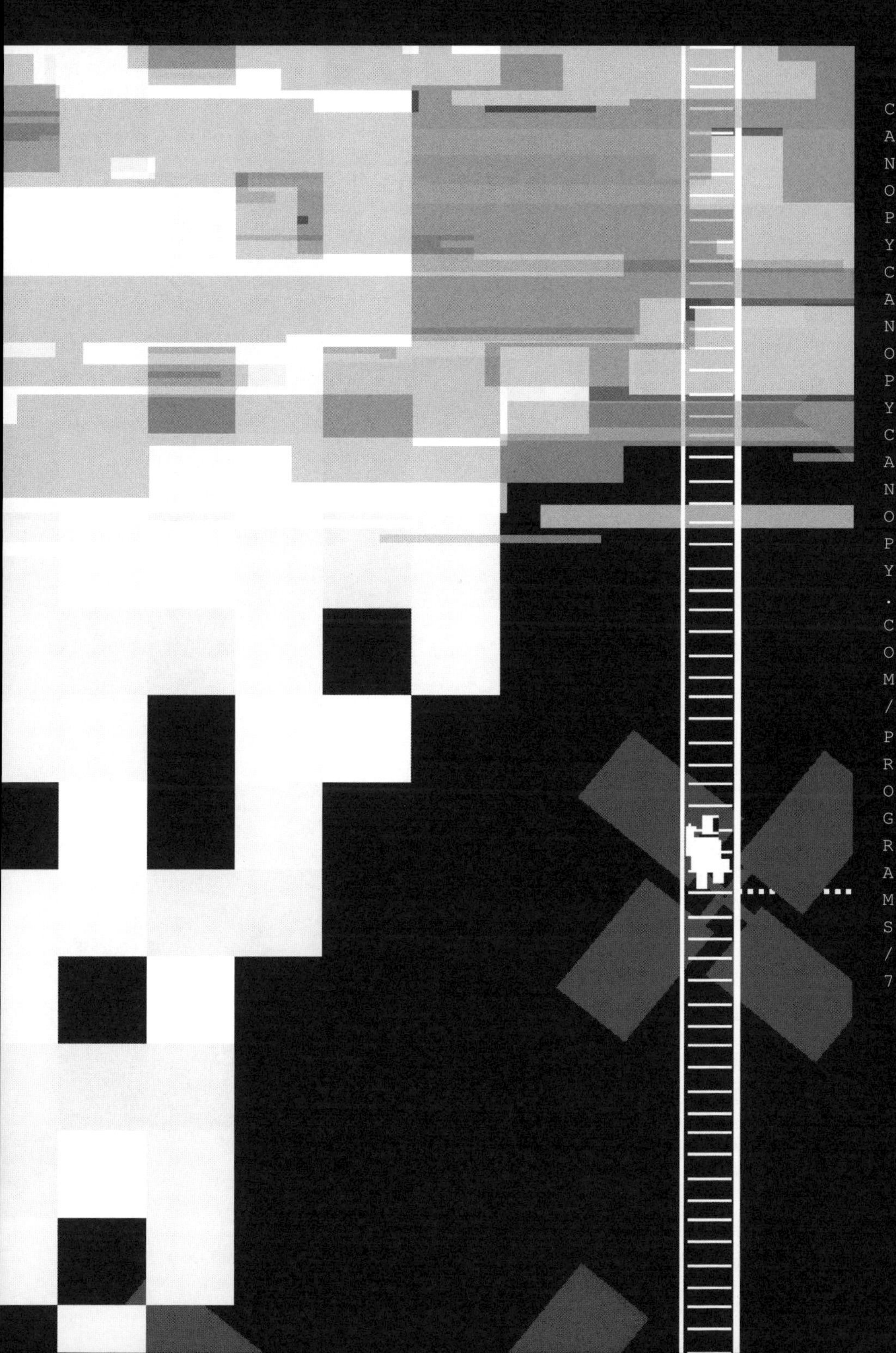
CANOPYCANOPYCANOPY.COM/PROGRAMS/7

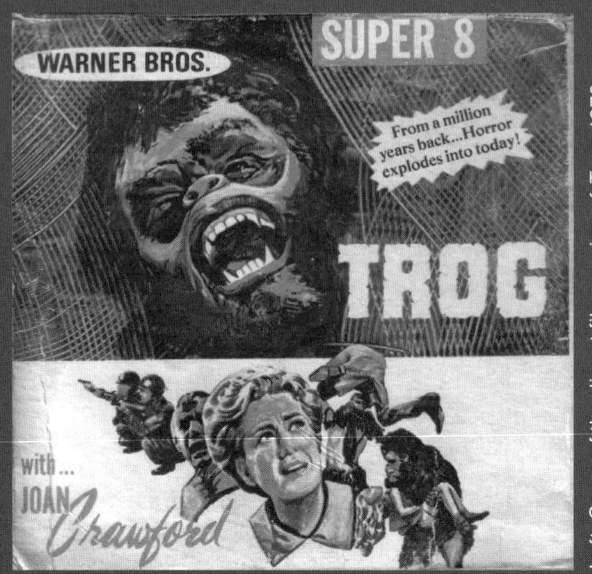

Left: Cover of the digest film version of *Trog*, 1970.
This page: Still from The Thrill of Combat, by Mark Essen.

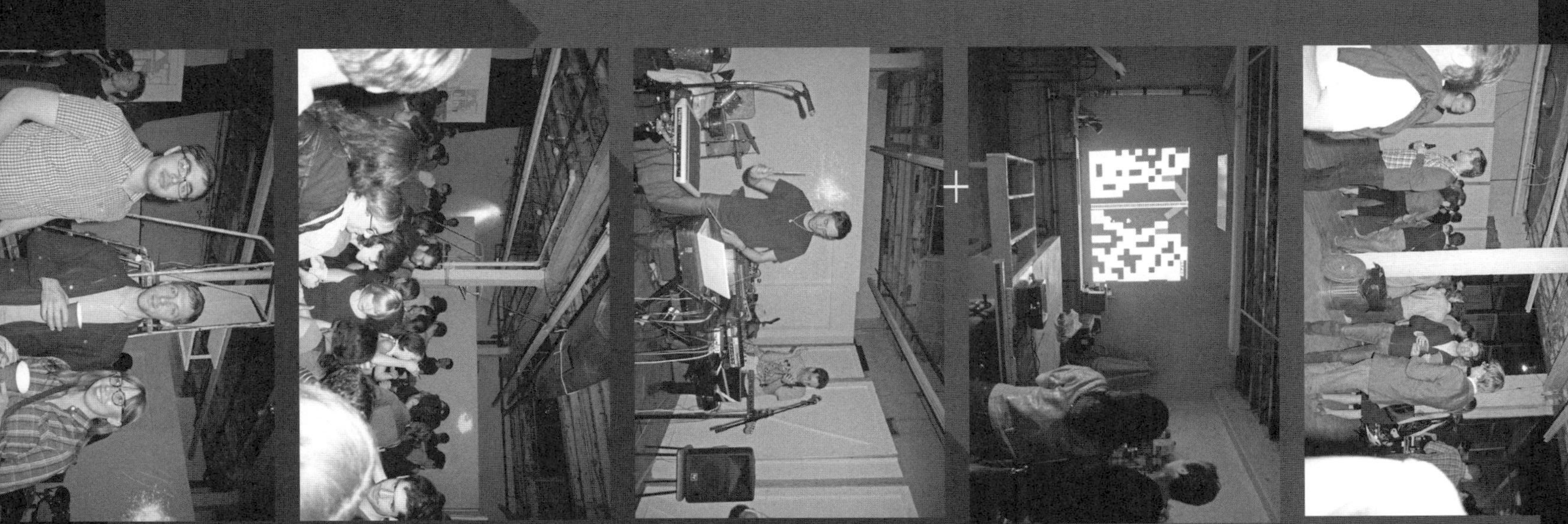

From Top: Thomas Beard of Light Industry and other attendees; Mark Essen's Scrap Collector; Tanlines; the crowd; Colby Chamberlain of Triple Canopy with friends.

ISSUE 7
URBANISMS: MASTER PLANS

published October 27, 2009

CANOPYCANOPYCANOPY.COM/7

DAYBREAK

In Salt Lake City's suburbs, the newest great dead American economy lies in wake atop the rumblings of the last one.

by Lucy Raven
published October 27, 2009

VILLAGE ONE

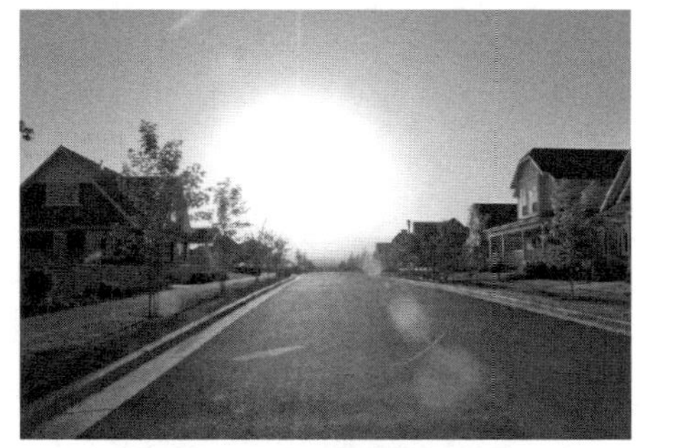

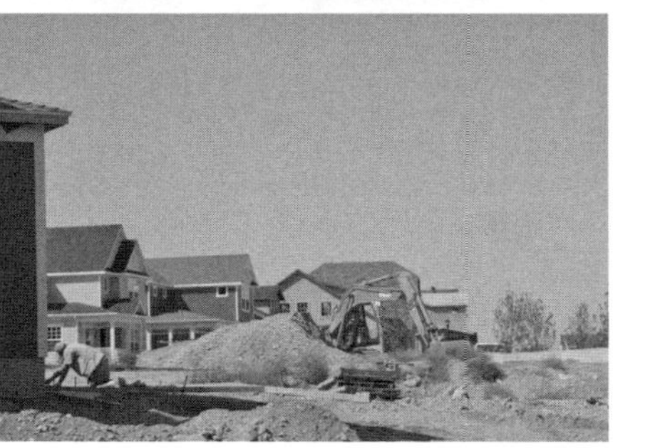

Eighteen miles south of Salt Lake City, in the suburb of South Jordan, Kennecott Land is building Daybreak, a twenty-thousand-home development. When it's completed, Daybreak will be the largest planned community in Utah, and one of the largest in the nation. It will extend twenty miles from South Jordan to the Great Salt Lake, stretching over forty-two hundred acres of "surplus mining land"—formerly mining tailings and settling ponds—bought throughout the 1900s by Kennecott Land's much older sister company, Kennecott Copper. The seven thousand homes of Village One, the first phase of Daybreak's seventy-year master plan, were completed in 2005; a second "village" of equal size is currently under construction.

Bingham Canyon Mine, owned by Kennecott Copper, is known as "the richest hole on earth." It is also one of the biggest holes on earth, visible— along with the Great Wall of China—from the moon. Open-pit mining was invented at Bingham more than a hundred years ago, and the mine has been in operation ever since, producing more copper than any other in history. Today, Bingham is the nation's second-largest copper producer, running twenty-four hours a day, seven days a week, about six miles from what is now Daybreak.

In mining, they say something valuable is a head; a tail is waste. Bingham's tailings impoundment, having been moved several times to accommodate its ever-widening girth, stretches for several miles along the Great Salt Lake and is about 99 percent as large in mass as the volume of the empty pit. Since copper ore was first recovered at Bingham in 1903, Kennecott has methodically purchased sizable tracts of land surrounding the mine as environmental liability: the deeper the pit, the more space needed for the removal, isolation, and neutralization of the millions of tons of overburden and toxic waste produced each year. Today, Kennecott owns more than ninety-three thousand acres of land in the Salt Lake Valley.

When the British-Australian mining megacorporation Rio Tinto bought Kennecott in 1989 during a depression in metal prices, surveying teams taking stock of the company's new real estate saw an alternate vision for its use. In 2001, Rio Tinto launched Kennecott Land, which immediately began planning Daybreak—a suburb that would be subsidized by the heads of the mine and built atop its tails.

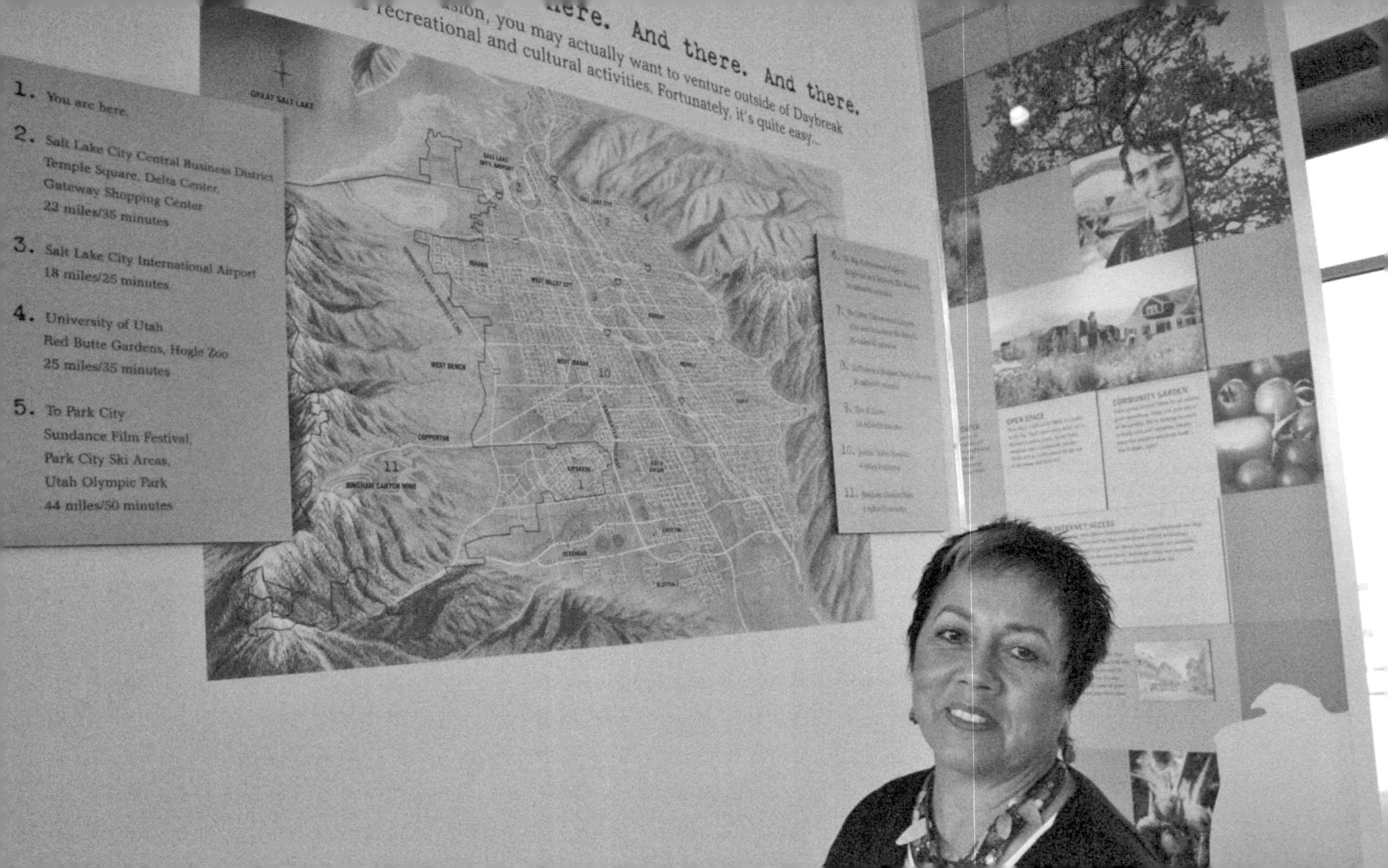
here. And there. And there.
...sion, you may actually want to venture outside of Daybreak
recreational and cultural activities. Fortunately, it's quite easy...
GREAT SALT LAKE
1. You are here.
2. Salt Lake City Central Business District
Temple Square, Delta Center,
Gateway Shopping Center
22 miles/35 minutes
3. Salt Lake City International Airport
18 miles/25 minutes
4. University of Utah
Red Butte Gardens, Hogle Zoo
25 miles/35 minutes
5. To Park City
Sundance Film Festival,
Park City Ski Areas,
Utah Olympic Park
44 miles/50 minutes
OPEN SPACE
COMMUNITY GARDEN

MAKE YOURSELF AT HOME

In the center of Daybreak stands the glass-walled Information Pavilion, where Kennecott Land representative Myranda Baxter welcomes prospective homeowners and tells them about the development. Despite the mine's constant operation, the Information Pavilion is focused exclusively on Kennecott Copper's *postmining* legacy. The term adorns a poster marking an out-of-the-way vitrine stocked with rusted artifacts of old-time mining—the only place in the pavilion where the mine itself is mentioned. If the display of pickaxes and century-old headlamps harks back to an earlier time, the designs of Daybreak's model homes embody many earlier times at once. Kennecott boasts ten different "Guest Builders," each working under separate contracts with individual home buyers. The result is a mélange of styles that transport residents from one age to the next as they walk down the block. Facades jump from Arts and Crafts to Colonial Revival, from Victorian to Tudor shingle.

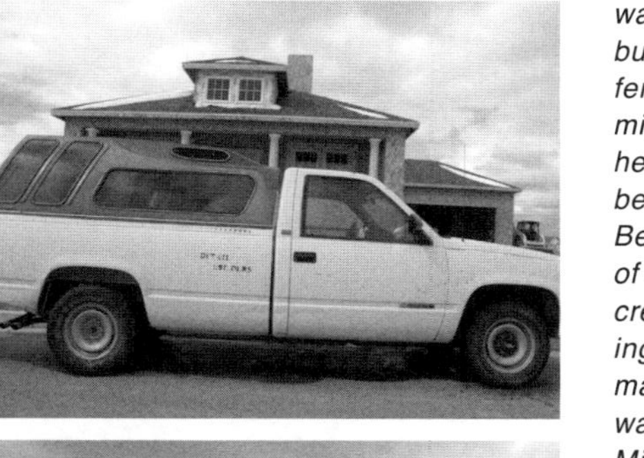

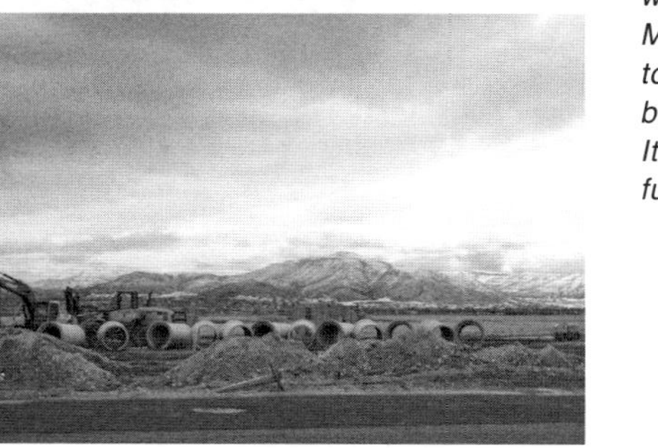

Notice all the architecture here. It's all classic architecture from the 1800s up to the 1920s or 30s. Your Arts and Crafts, they all feature porches in front, and the garages are either set back from the side of the house or on an alley. They want to encourage people to get to know each other, so they positioned the homes closer to the sidewalk than normal, so that we have a chance to see our neighbors as they walk by, wave to them, get to know them. You know, they decided they didn't want a cookie-cutter concept here. Each builder offers between four and eight different styles of homes. You won't make a mistake going into your neighbor's house here, which does happen in some areas, because they just all look so much alike. Because Kennecott Copper has a history of over a hundred years, they wanted to create a theme that reflects the old mining industry, and the homes they built so many years ago. That particular home was built in Salt Lake, but it's from the Midwest. It comes right out of Illinois, so to speak. Even the brickwork—notice the brickwork—emulates the old-style brick. It's not that new, squared-off look. It's a fun concept.

—Myranda Baxter

VILLAGE CENTER

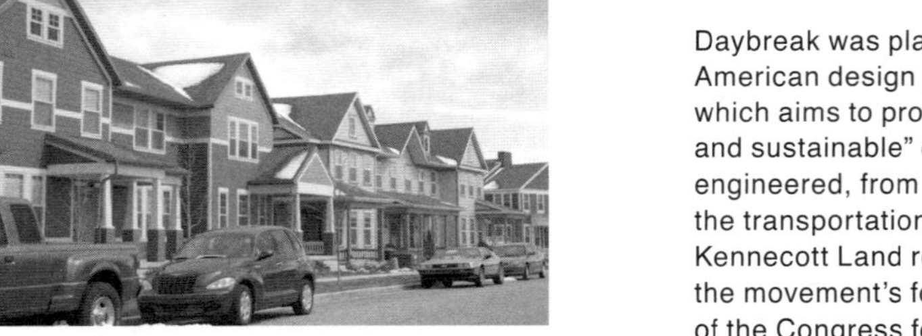

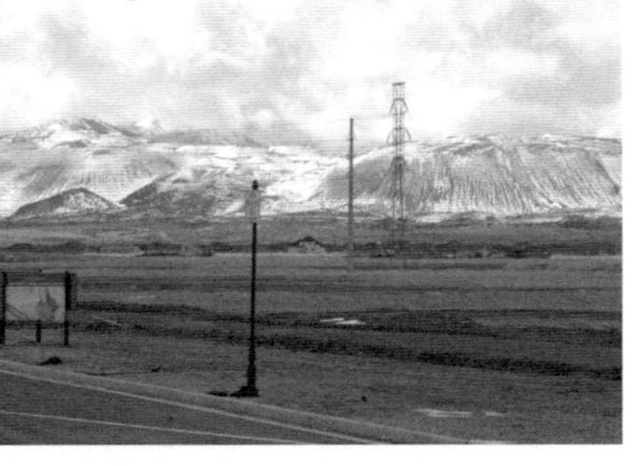

Daybreak was planned in accordance with the American design philosophy of New Urbanism, which aims to produce "walkable, diverse, and sustainable" communities that are fully engineered, from the sidewalks and homes to the transportation routes and civic structures. Kennecott Land recruited Peter Calthorpe, one of the movement's founders and the first president of the Congress for New Urbanism, to act as Daybreak's chief planner. He has provided residents not only with houses constructed by their choice of builder—prices range from the hundred thousands to more than one million dollars—but with the plans, at least, for a complete urban experience, including workplaces and recreational areas.

Daybreak includes an elementary school, a community and fitness center, sports fields, and a sixty-thousand-square-foot temple of the Church of Jesus Christ of Latter Day Saints built on a sprawling eleven-acre lot. A second church is under construction, as are a host of commercial centers that will one day house big-box retail outlets, smaller franchises, and a smattering of "Mom & Pop" shops. Bright signs hanging from a chain-link fence on the edge of Village Two promise a light-rail system for commuters who work in Salt Lake City, a University of Utah satellite campus, and twenty thousand new jobs. After work and on the weekends, Daybreakers can retreat to the sixty-acre lake, take the kids to the community pool, or enjoy movie nights in the park. The only thing missing is a cemetery; despite all the far-reaching plans, there is none in the works.

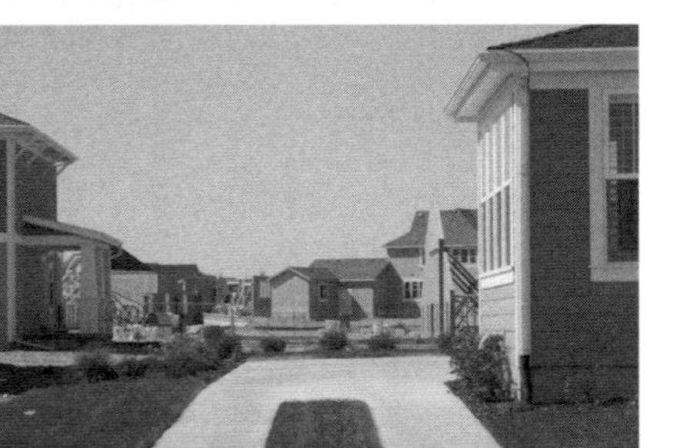

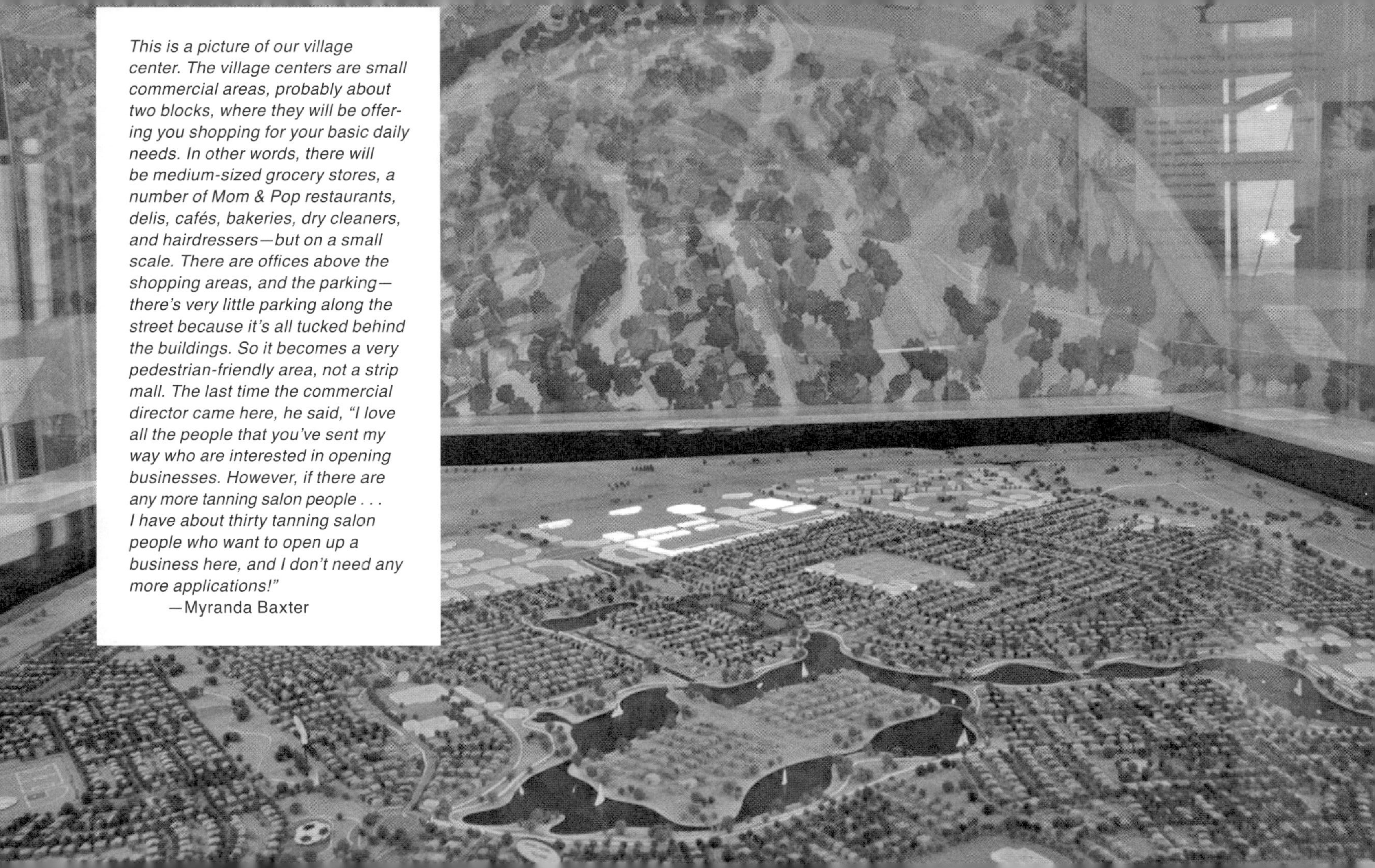

This is a picture of our village center. The village centers are small commercial areas, probably about two blocks, where they will be offering you shopping for your basic daily needs. In other words, there will be medium-sized grocery stores, a number of Mom & Pop restaurants, delis, cafés, bakeries, dry cleaners, and hairdressers—but on a small scale. There are offices above the shopping areas, and the parking—there's very little parking along the street because it's all tucked behind the buildings. So it becomes a very pedestrian-friendly area, not a strip mall. The last time the commercial director came here, he said, "I love all the people that you've sent my way who are interested in opening businesses. However, if there are any more tanning salon people . . . I have about thirty tanning salon people who want to open up a business here, and I don't need any more applications!"

—Myranda Baxter

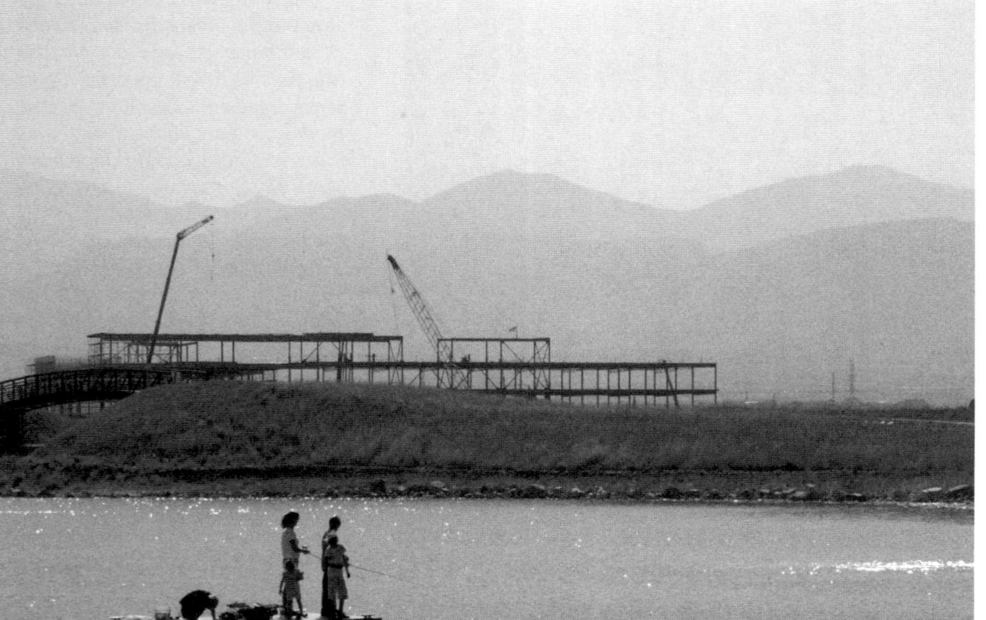

AS MUCH THOUGHT AS WATER

We've put more thinking into the design of this lake than any I've seen.
> —Russell Sanford, vice president of land development, Kennecott Land

Oquirrh Lake is the centerpiece of Daybreak's commitment to leisure time. The sixty-acre man-made body of water is framed by a perimeter of lush natural grasses and lined with a multimillion-dollar synthetic sheeting system that seals it from the contaminated soil below. As the ground beneath Oquirrh Lake is still a brownfield, swimming is not permitted, but there are ducks to feed, and there is catch-and-release fishing (the lake is regularly restocked with tens of thousands of local species). The lake is currently in the first of three phases of construction, and its acreage will eventually be tripled.

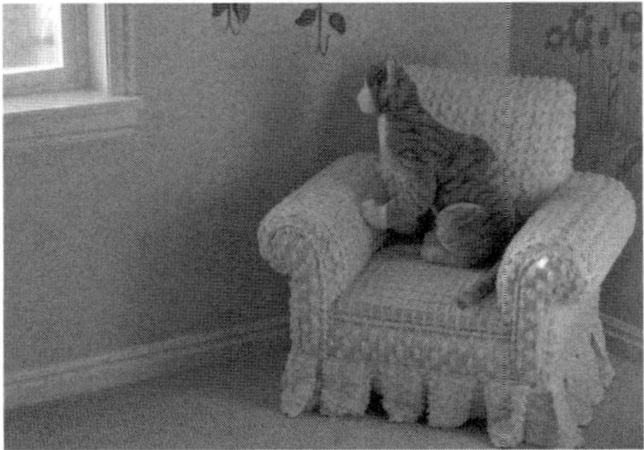

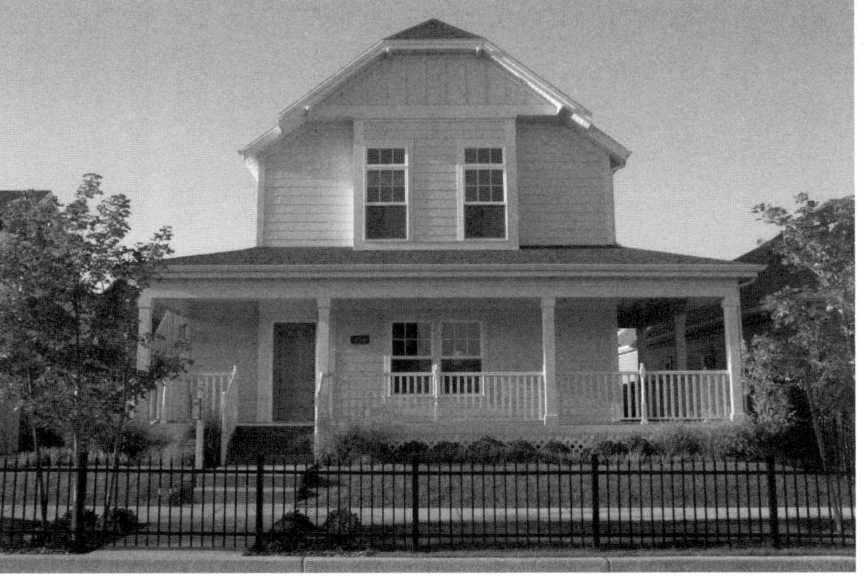

SUSTAINABILITY

Construction on Daybreak began in 2004, at the peak of the housing bubble. As in the rest of the country, the market's crash has devastated the suburbs of Salt Lake City, and Rio Tinto is now reconsidering the size and scope of its development. In the meantime, it's turned its attention to expanding the Bingham pit's digging operations in order to extend the mine's future beyond its prospective closure date of 2018. Engineers are studying the possibility of building a deep underground mine around the edge of the pit, which at its center descends three-quarters of a mile, in order to recover new ore deposits once surface mining has been exhausted. Exploratory drilling (on land earmarked for Daybreak) has shown deposits of high-grade ore.

Without issuing one of the customary press releases that accompany every new development in Daybreak, Kennecott Land shortened its master plan last year from seventy to twenty years. As the profitability of industrial-scale real estate development in the West has collapsed, with no recovery in sight, the allure of regular old mining has grown. But nothing is certain, and plans for Kennecott's mining and real estate operations still change month by month. Meanwhile, inside Daybreak's thousand inhabited homes, life goes on much as it did before.

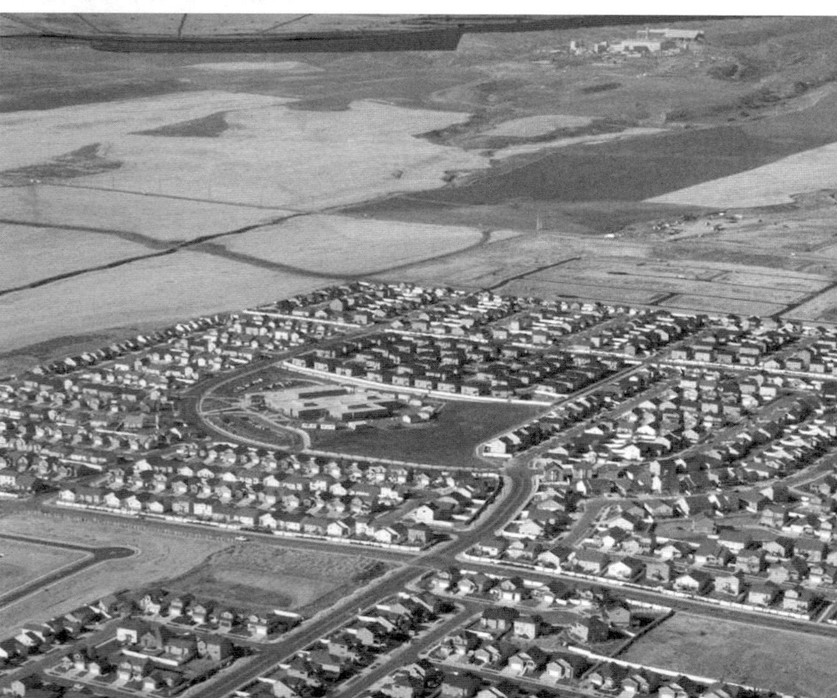

IT'S ALL HERE

The Kennecott Land calendar, available as a free-bie at the Information Pavilion, tells prospective residents what they can expect life in Daybreak to bring each month.

July: "What could go better with Stars and Stripes than some honest-to-goodness Colonial architecture?"

September: "Dramatic sunsets can cause great indecision: fish or kayak? Or go out in the canoe? Or the paddleboat? Or just walk around the lake? Or . . ."

October: "Whoever has the most outdoor furniture wins."

November: "They provide shade, oxygen, and, this time of year, gorgeous color. Who wouldn't want 100,000 of these guys in the neighborhood?"

December: "You'll have no trouble finding Daybreak. Even if you're in a sleigh flying thou-sands of feet above the ground."

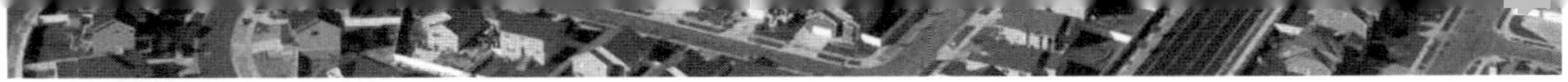

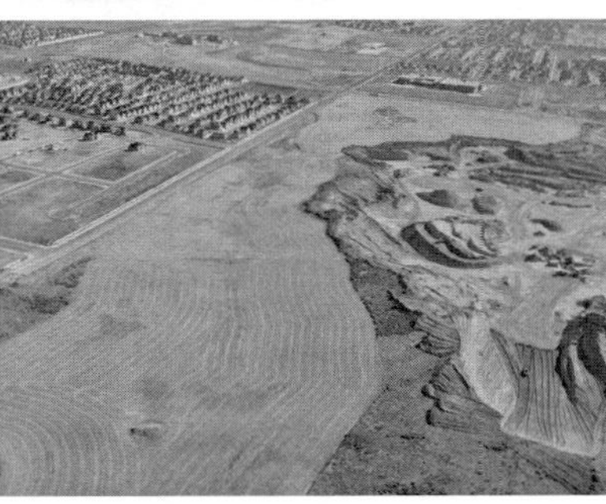

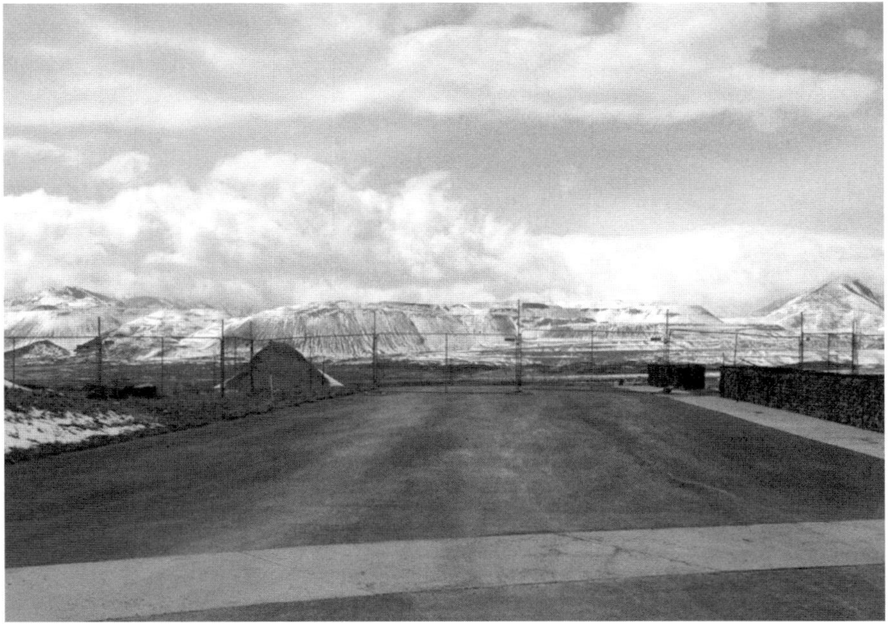

WELCOME TO THE NEIGHBORHOOD

One of Daybreak's signatures is the absence of street-level power and gas lines. The town's system of wires and pipes, made from copper bought on the global market from a variety of international suppliers and distributors, is buried beneath neighborhoods funded by the extraction of ore just down the street. Elsewhere, too, the armature of construction, maintenance, and control is barely visible: The lawns of occupied and empty houses alike are all manicured to an exacting standard; public facilities are neatly maintained regardless of how often they're utilized; security cars circulate soundlessly, patrolling day and night. The porch of every completed home is decorated with a wreath and some form of seating for two. The blinds are almost always drawn. On a recent visit, many of Daybreak's homes seemed as vacant as the unbuilt lots surrounding them. The more elaborate the "vintage" architecture, the more each structure resembled a headstone, with each facade a freshly inscribed epitaph for the boom-and-bust company town, signaling a new day breaking on the waste heap of our postindustrial—but not quite postmining—economy. ⌧

INVALID FORMAT 2 — ISSUE 7 2009

DIVINE WILDERNESS

From Thomas Aquinas and John the Baptist to cellular automata and intelligent design: How God taught us planning, and where we went wrong.

by Nathan Schneider
published November 5, 2009

PLANNING IS SOMETHING that people learned from God. The lesson might be said to have begun with the prescriptions God laid out for his earthly habitation among the Israelites: the Tabernacle that housed him in the desert, and then the Temple that was his residence in Jerusalem. The dimensions of these structures were dictated by a divine blueprint. The Temple gave birth to a city, and from it emerged a civilization. We are descendants of this tradition, irrespective of such trivialities as whether one identifies as a "believer."

Its most obvious inheritors are those who shout of "God's plan for you" from street corners and write "purpose-driven" books, people for whom the blueprint—and our basic need to follow it—is a raft in the ocean of time. But this tradition also finds resonance in something as ordinary as the practical virtue of prudence: the present's responsible response to the uncertainties of the future, which Thomas Aquinas considered the highest of the cardinal virtues.

The philosopher Jacques Maritain spent his life bringing Aquinas's philosophy to bear on the modern world. In a 1988 interview, the priest-turned-radical Ivan Illich recalls a 1957 encounter with Maritain. Illich wondered why there was no reference "to the concept of planning" in his work.

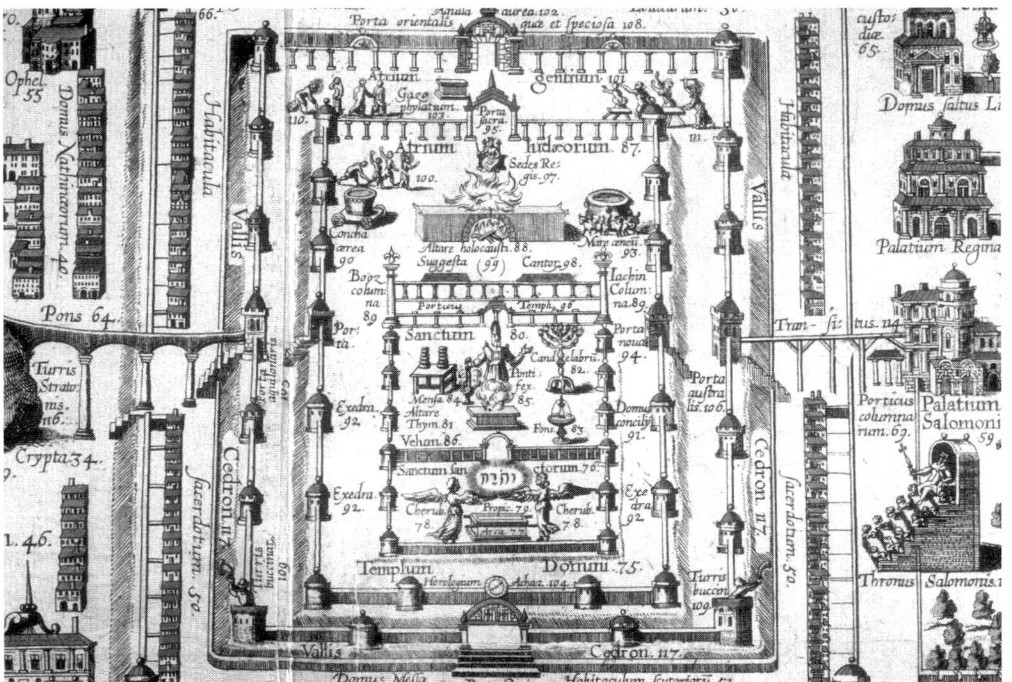

Christiaan van Adrichem,
The Temple of Solomon (detail), 1584.

[Maritain] asked me if this was an English word for "accounting," and I told him no . . . if it was for "engineering," and I said no . . . and then at a certain moment he said to me, "Ah! *Je comprends, mon cher ami, maintenant je comprends.* Now I finally understand. *C'est une nouvelle espèce du péché de présomption.* Planning is a new variety of the sin of pride."

For Aquinas, pride was the worst of sins, the root from which all others spring, the most basic rebellion against God. Maritain suggests that we have exaggerated prudence to the point of its inversion. Planning, despite its origins, has come to lie at the center of the predicaments that face our world at present.

PEOPLE LEARNED TO PLAN FROM GOD, but this is not all that God does, nor is it the only discipline that he taught our forebearers. The Tabernacle's design emerged during the Israelites' sojourn in the wilderness after their escape from Egypt. The subsequent prophets returned to the wilderness again and again to discover God's plan for them. "The voice of him that crieth in the wilderness," it was said of John the Baptist. "Prepare ye the way of the Lord, make straight in the desert a highway for our God." The Lord that John beckoned—Jesus, the embodiment of God himself—also set off for the wild, where he fasted and was tempted by the devil before beginning to preach.

The God who provides only order and plans is not only a fallacy but a heresy, one that has passed into secular assumptions uncorrected.

HUMAN BEINGS ARE MADE in God's image, and God's creative powers, including the capacity to plan, all find expression in us. These powers are gifts; on their own, they cannot be considered rebellion. All of civilization is their yield. But civilization yields its own horrific rebellions, abominations of acedia, greed, and wrath inflicted against people and the planet. Our own success (spreading across vast territories and propagating our species at a feverish pace) has ushered in an age of mass extinction. By planning ourselves out of creation's wilderness, we have consigned it to destruction.

For most of human history, settlements centered on a site of worship and ritual and expanded organically, haphazardly, until they were abandoned or destroyed. The first city plans, proposed for the Greek towns of Peiraeus and Miletus, were drafted by Hippodamus in the fifth century BC. These uncompromising grids made allowances for temples and forums; they oriented life around the sites where people met the gods as well as those where citizens determined their own future. Now, only two hundred years after the juggernaut of mechanized industry was put at our disposal, we are forced to question the utopian idea that arose in ancient Greece: that there can never be too much order. The supply of wilderness once seemed inexhaustible, but now, as it disappears,

we are beginning to recognize that order has depended on the wild all along.

All the trust that the Greeks placed in their planners would later become the dominion of Christianity's God. The Puritan ethic at the heart of the American psyche taught that, as long as people's sexual and social behavior follows a regimented moral order, an unseen force will take care of the affairs of society as a whole, according to benevolent, inscrutable plans. We need only worry about our personal habits. We could make it just fine "by obeying His voice and cleaving to Him," John Winthrop declared in 1630 during his journey across the Atlantic. "He is our life and our prosperity." This mind-set facilitated our laissez-faire economy, which entrusted the distribution of resources to a market so far beyond human control as to resemble the theological concept of grace. Yet with the rise of modern industry, the unseen forces governing our affairs became plainly visible. We no longer entrusted ourselves to God, but to the plans of "corporate citizens."

Modern times, for better or worse, have put people in the position previously occupied by God; the governance of the world has become a human concern. The plans that once issued from heaven now come from high up in office buildings. Yet we remain in the thrall of ancient habits.

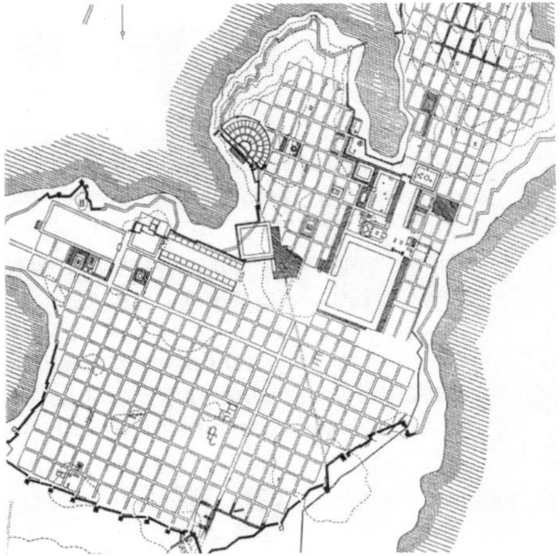

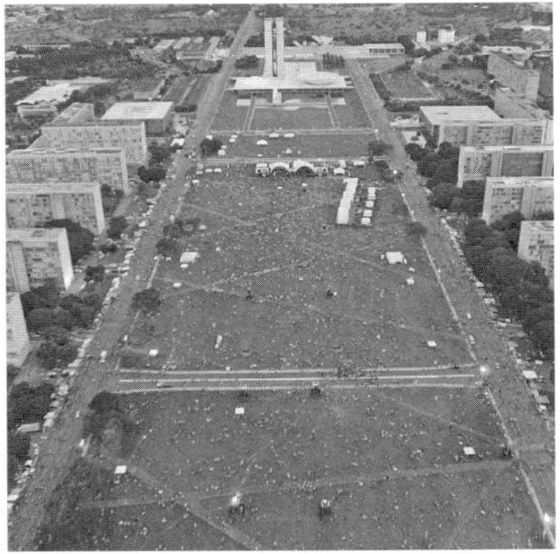

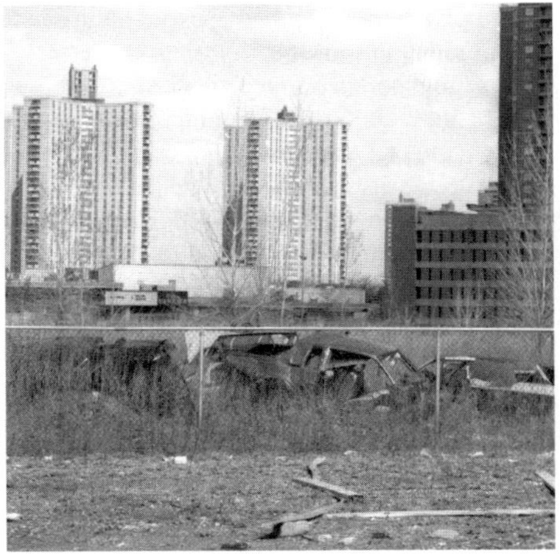

THE GREAT MEDIUM OF MODERN PLANNING, embryonic at the time of Illich's conversation with Maritain, is the electronic computer. Computers organize, calculate, and simulate. They extend the reach of planning far beyond any earlier tool; they not only draft blueprints and run financial markets but also manage personal relationships and usher in new forms of intelligence. Computers themselves are vast, meticulous plans, inscribed in circuit boards, microprocessors, and programming code. The companies that produce them ensure they operate as planned: predictably, orderly, and hypnotically.

Receiving our plans from computers has become routine; computers have colonized and secularized the theological story of the divine planner. Theology was once a sufficient language for orchestrating human affairs, but now only the language of the machine—of predictive models, of vast data sets, of algorithms—will do. Both theology and computing have been mistaken for sources of order alone, antidotes to wilderness.

First we invented computers. Then we realized that, all along, we have been—as cognitive science all but assumes—computers ourselves, carrying hardware and software, responding to inputs with outputs. All that we encounter can be transcribed into quantifiable information; we've been living inside a universe-computer. God is no longer a king, a father, or a mother, but a master programmer. "So might a carpenter, looking at the moon, suppose that it is made of wood," the physicist Steven Weinberg has written. But here we stand. We can do no other.

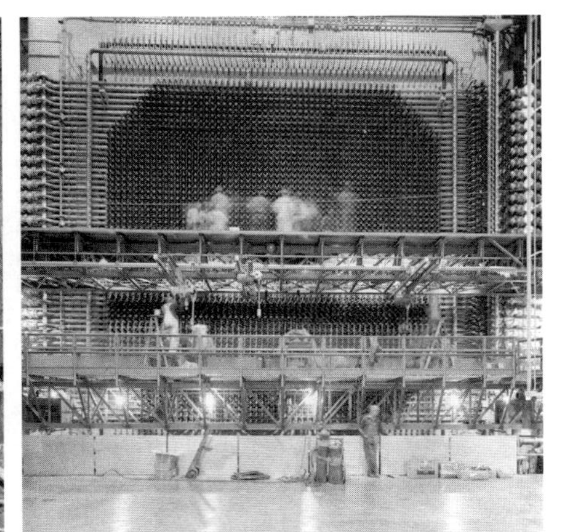

Clockwise from top left: Hippodamus's urban plan for Peiraeus, fifth century BC; Brasília, Brazil; nuclear reactor, Hanford, Washington; projects in the South Bronx, New York.

IN TIMES LIKE THESE, the easiest way to understand where theology went wrong is to look at a computer program.

What follows is a very simple simulation, a cellular automaton, consisting of a one-dimensional line of binary cells that are either on or off—1 or 0, white or black. With each iteration, the simulation applies a rule to the present line of cells, and from that rule the next line blossoms. The rules are sets of procedures that determine what a particular cell in the new line will be, given the conditions of its predecessor and its two neighbors on the last line.

As an example, we'll take one especially famous rule, Stephen Wolfram's Rule 110, and the simplest starting condition: a single cell turned on.

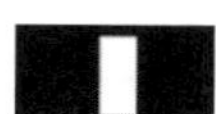

According to the rule, whichever of the eight possible patterns precedes the new cell determines its state. Here is our Rule 110:

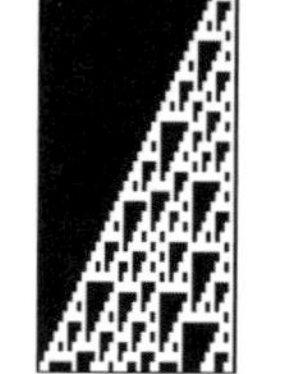

When the simulation applies this rule to our simple starting condition, the output looks like this:

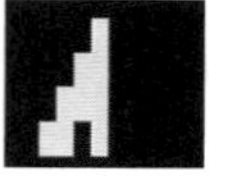

And, two later:

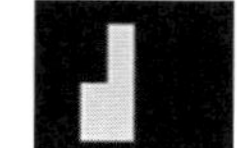

Though every part of the simulation is planned, the results defy prediction. By the forty-first iteration of the rule, an intriguing pattern emerges, one that is neither random nor repetitive. A very simple plan has produced an enormously complex structure:

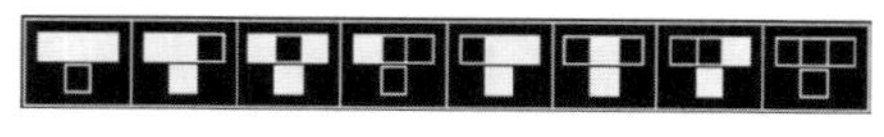

The output of rules like this can be remarkable, resembling complex arrangements in nature such as snowflakes and the human nervous system. Theorists call them universal computers because they produce an infinite number of localized patterns that interact with each other as the iterations unfold.

Not all one-dimensional rules are as interesting as Rule 110, and many result in empty or repetitive patterns. But this is not an isolated incident, and it suggests a general principle:

Patterned complexity—wildlife, that is—can come about in the dance of utter simplicity.

Rule 110:

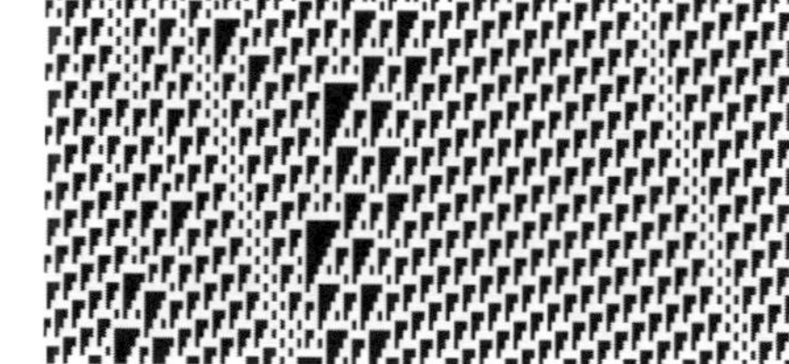

Rule 150:

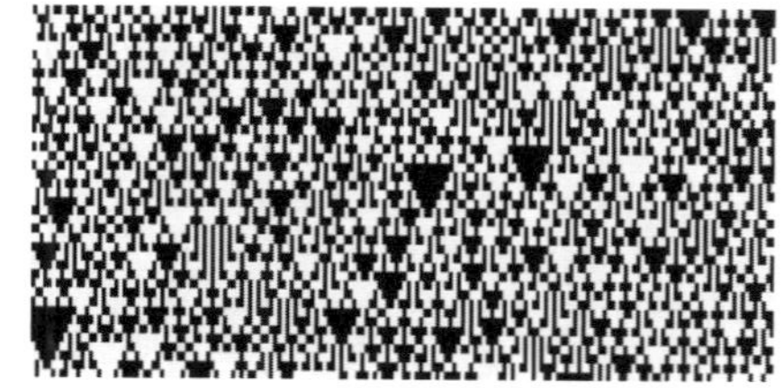

INVALID FORMAT 2 · ISSUE 7 · 2009

Later, Maimonides adds that God "fully knows His unchangeable essence, and thus a knowledge of all that results from any of His acts." But when it is said that God is omnipotent, better to think of a simulation than a blueprint: God constitutes the life-giving rules, iterations, and imagination of our universe simulator.

Thomas Aquinas was Maimonides's closest counterpart in the Christian world. He, too, thought of God in Aristotelian terms, as a generative power. He stood by the "simplicity" of God, despite the rich complexity of creation. Complexity, he somehow knew, could and would emerge from the most orderly of sources.

"WHERE WERE YOU WHEN I laid the earth's foundation?" God asks in the book of Job. "Tell me, if you understand. Who marked off its dimensions? Surely you know! Who stretched a measuring line across it? On what were its footings set, or who laid its cornerstone while the morning stars sang together and all the angels shouted for joy?" God appears to Job in the form of a whirlwind, as if the natural embodiment of his perfect simplicity is fearsome chaos.

Job had been upstanding, law-abiding, prosperous, and pious. Yet he lost all his possessions, witnessed the death of all his children, and saw his body deformed. Refusing to accept that there could be justice in his punishment, he complains to God that he has been wronged: "Does He not see my ways and count my every step?"

God doesn't reply directly. Instead, the whirlwind holds forth on a subject familiar to those who

"undirected" and "random" processes of nature, that God is responsible only for order, and that order can only come about through God.

The lesson of the cellular automata, however, shows that order doesn't have to depend on obsessive intervention; it can emerge through burgeoning iteration. Planning can give rise to a semblance of order without minutely prescribing it, without intelligent design theory's autocratic tinkerer. In earlier times, when the existence of a cosmic principle named God was generally accepted and theologians could focus their energies on his essence and meaning, the Discovery Institute's assumptions would have seemed awfully impoverished.

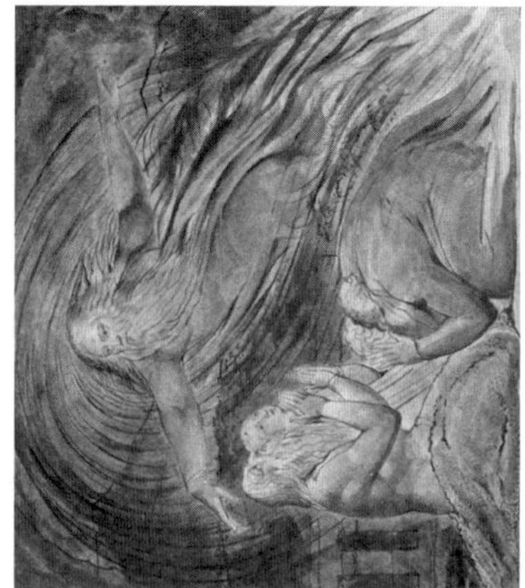

William Blake, *Illustrations of the Book of Job*, 1825.

TWO-THIRDS OF THE WAY through his definitive medieval primer on the philosophy of Judaism, *Guide for the Perplexed*, Moses Maimonides sets out to clear up confusion about how God acts in the world. The Bible's description of the deity commanding clouds to rain and directing armies to march, Maimonides writes, is shorthand for a richer reality. God provides the conditions of possibility for these events, but he doesn't fiddle with the universe. Through human will, natural forces, and the interactions between the two, God's sustaining presence and existential gift makes his plans unfold in the wildness of the world.

Following Aristotle, Maimonides sees every event as having a hierarchy of causes; God works in and through material things, not against or around them, as intelligent design theorists suppose.

IT HAS BECOME COMMON to speak of divine planning in terms of "intelligent design," which some religious apologists take to represent a corrective to Darwinian evolution. The Seattle-based Discovery Institute, whose objective is to find evidence of divine intervention in nature, is the most prominent proponent of this concept. The institute's website explains:

Intelligent-design theory is simply an effort to empirically detect whether the "apparent design" in nature acknowledged by virtually all biologists is genuine design (the product of an intelligent cause) or is simply the product of an undirected process such as natural selection acting on random variations.

This formulation is particular to a culture paranoid about its own atheism. It assumes that God has no relationship whatsoever to the

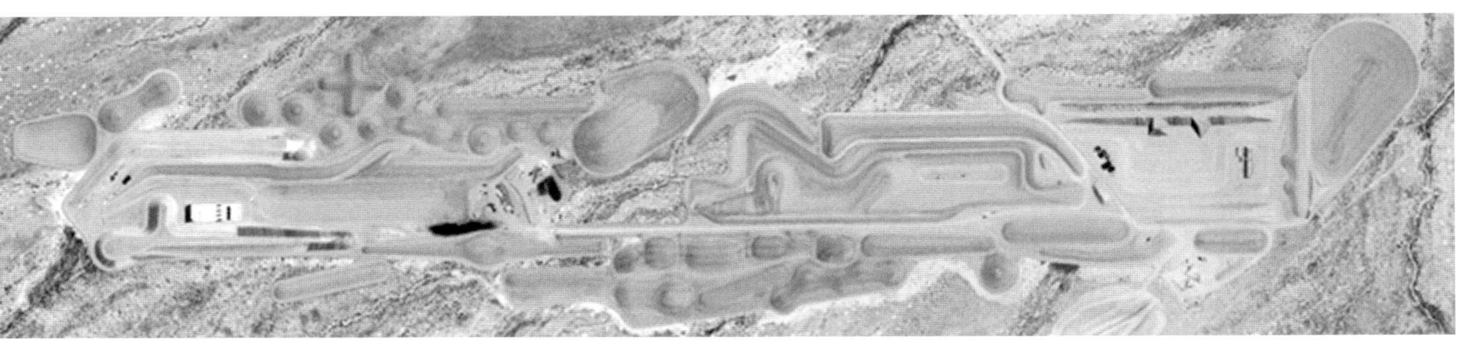

Michael Heizer, *City*, 1972–, Lincoln County, Nevada, .

work with cellular automata: initial conditions. From simple plans in the cosmic simulation, endless permutations play out in the divine iterations of time. Job's complaint is beside the point. Just as we trust our computers, he trusted that God would enforce a comfortable order for him, forgetting God's penchant for wildlife.

Intelligent design, a theory to which more than half of Americans subscribe, represents an all too prevalent heresy of contemporary theology—in both its secular and religious varieties. In misunderstanding the kind of planning that brought about the richness of creation, it also wrongly implies the kind of planning that people, made in the divine image, should undertake. (This mistake did not originate with the Discovery Institute and its allies but has found its most telling expression among them.) By taking it to heart, we have learned to hatch our plans as interventions on nature and history and to think of ourselves as purveyors of order in a world of chaos.

We have long trusted the plans of economists, diplomats, doctors, accountants, engineers, demographers, generals, and experts of all kinds. Shouldn't we? I would be terrified to say we shouldn't. But they are all treacherously wrong. Though we may no longer express confidence in the bureaucratic order, we still entrust our lives to its plans and models and procedures. We turn the plans that come from above into idols.

Life in the divine image does not merely follow plans. It erupts from them, wildly and creatively, then goes on to make plans of its own.

AT A DECISIVE MOMENT in the film *The Dark Knight*, when Harvey Dent transforms into chance-obsessed Two-Face, the Joker, clad in a nurse's uniform, looms above the maimed politician's hospital bed. "Do I really look like a guy with a plan, Harvey?" he asks. "I don't have a plan. The Mob has plans, the cops have plans." He continues, reflecting on the plans at work all around them:

You know what I am, Harvey? I'm a dog chasing cars. I wouldn't know what to do with one if I caught it. I just do things. I'm just the wrench in the gears. I hate plans. Yours, theirs, everyone's. Maroni has plans. Gordon has plans: schemers trying to control their worlds. I'm not a schemer; I show the schemers how pathetic their attempts to control things really are.

Just as Maritain, the existential medievalist, and Illich, the defrocked anarchist, spoke of heretical planning as the crux of modernity's rebellion against God, the Joker recognizes the obsession with order as the petty, futile origin of every lie. We cling to our images of immutable plans, mistaking them for reality. But they are the ultimate joke.

Thus Woody Allen's remark, a Yiddish proverb now lost to pious cliché: If you want to make God laugh, tell him about your plans. ⊠

LEARNING FROM TIJUANA

From the graveyards of corporate architecture to the informal settlements of Latin America.

by Teddy Cruz with
Caleb Waldorf
published November 19, 2009

INVALID FORMAT 2

ISSUE 7

2009

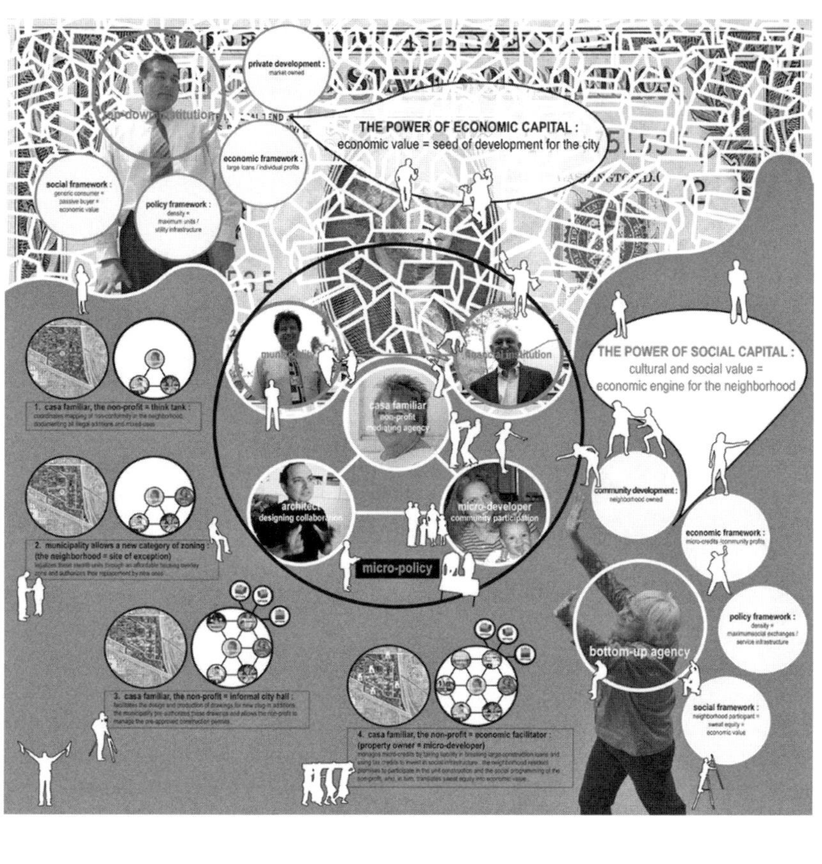

Estudio Teddy Cruz, *Neighborhood Micro-Politics and Economics: Strategies between the Top-Down and the Bottom-Up*, 2007.

Architect and activist Teddy Cruz has been stationed along the border of the US and Mexico for the past decade, traversing the territory between San Diego and Tijuana, observing the social structures and urban formations. He has developed an architectural practice that is rooted in the realities of informal settlements and immigrant suburbs, and that is equally engaged with the needs—and innovations—of their residents and the exigencies of local bureaucracies. Cruz spoke with Triple Canopy's Caleb Waldorf over the course of the past six months.

CALEB WALDORF: You've been doing work on informal architecture and cross-border urbanism for many years. How has the relevance of your practice shifted since the economic collapse?

TEDDY CRUZ: I've always operated in the context of crisis. Over the last few decades, the physical manifestations of capital—corporate high-rises and luxury condos—have become the laboratories of the avant-garde in architecture (though calling them *laboratories* grants them too much credibility). This was a sad thing to witness. Many of the manifestos that inspired me when I was in school in the early '80s

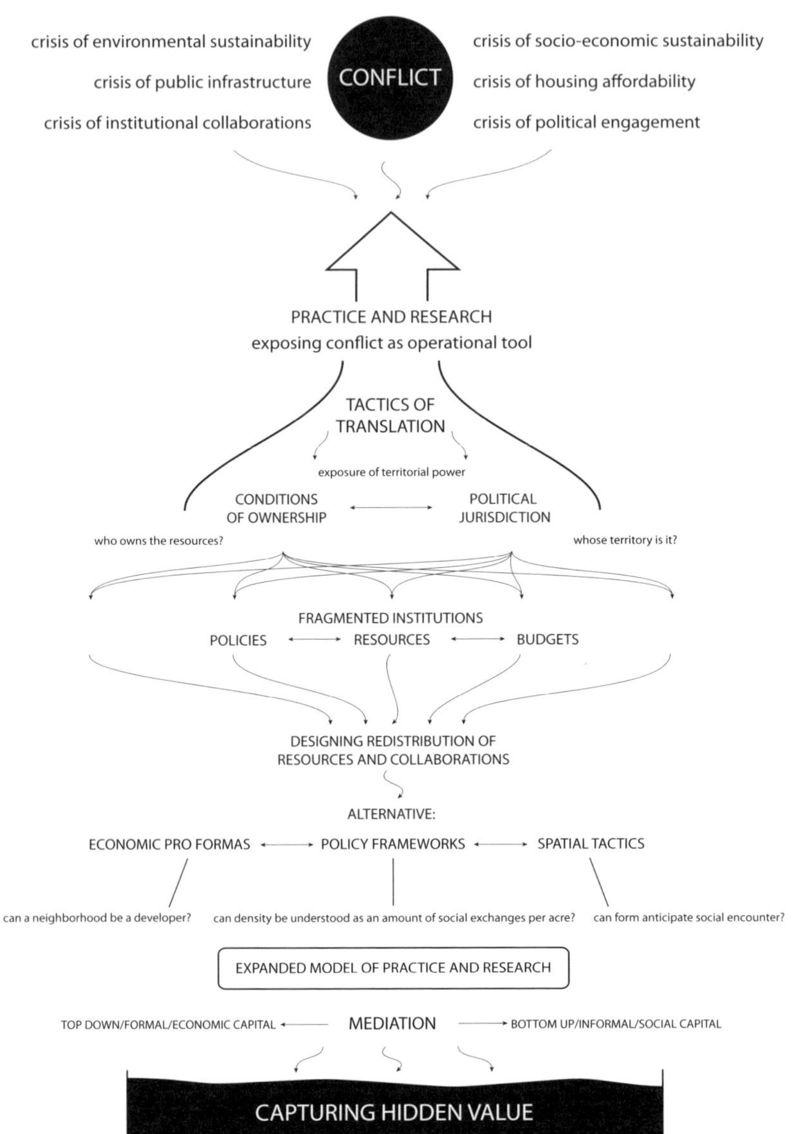

Estudio Teddy Cruz, *Practice Diagram*, 2008.

were truly trivialized in this context. But now architects are shifting focus from those sites of abundance to sites of scarcity.

I've been trying to make this case for years: The most inventive, progressive, experimental projects have not happened in China or the Emirates (where architecture is so often treated as an object or icon), but within the context of infrastructure, in Latin America. Architects and politicians such as Jaime Lerner in Curitiba, Brazil, Antanas Mockus and Enrique Peñalosa in Bogotá, and Sergio Fajardo in Medellín, Colombia, are rethinking the meaning of infrastructure on many registers: suggesting how to negotiate a new relationship between top-down and bottom-up dynamics;

blending top-down industry and economic power with bottom-up social networks and activism. The idea is that urban pedagogy can generate a new type and scale—and suggest a very different kind of awareness—of infrastructure and transportation.

cw: In what ways is this kind of pedagogy manifest in the "sites of scarcity" you mention?

tc: Fajardo, the mayor of Medellín, reinvented certain public spaces by envisioning them not just as manicured gardens, but as hybrids of knowledge and leisure. He believed that public spaces could be infused with knowledge, so he invented library-parks. For him, the site of intervention was not the center of the city but rather the shantytowns, where Fajardo built many of these library-parks. Mockus, the mayor of Bogotá, institutionalized a unique form of interface with public culture as a foundation for urbanization. Mockus's urban pedagogy elevated a sense of civic awareness and participation that paved the way for Peñalosa, the subsequent mayor, to create one of the most progressive transportation systems in the world, threading pedestrian, bicycle, and bus infrastructure with libraries and public spaces. These projects began with a renewed engagement with the public: They're not just one-off experiments, but attempts to establish a social platform through a kind of *eco-literacy and urban pedagogy.*

The effectiveness of this sort of approach has, in the last few years, been more widely acknowledged, which can be vindicating:

It suggests that true experimental architectures can emerge from the intelligence of social networks and dynamics of informal settlements. Because of my belief in the potential of these conditions to facilitate more experimental planning processes, I had come to be known in many circles as this Mr. Do-Gooder architect forcing a social and political agenda. Actually, I'm not interested in the romanticization of the precariousness of the shantytown. I am simply suggesting that behind those dynamics there is a certain intelligence.

cw: It seems clear that we need to approach urbanism from the bottom up, looking at how molecular design solutions can effect the larger urban fabric. This model requires many people working independently, with a DIY attitude; I find it difficult to imagine this actually happening. But given that such a possibility is fundamental to your practice, I'm wondering how you see this molecular approach becoming an institutional model. What are the risks of institutionalizing DIY tactics?

tc: That's something I often ask myself. We all depend on particular ideologies: You have the formalists versus the infrastructuralists, those who support largeness in architecture versus those who are interested in the microscale. But in Latin America, these projects actually came from the top down; progressive governments implemented them. Latin America is the only place in the world where governments have attempted to harness the potential of social networks and the dynamics of informal economies in order to rethink urbanization.

I'm interested in the informal, but I'm not suggesting that it's only interesting now that the large-scale top-down model has failed. We don't always have to turn to the bottom-up, DIY model. One should work on a small scale but always with the idea of retrofitting and challenging top-down institutions. In order for these projects to produce a trickle-up effect that results in the rethinking of those institutions, they need to be reproduced and translated in different environments and at different scales.

CW: What are some examples of this approach being employed in the US, specifically in the work you've done in California?

TC: There are grassroots efforts in the US, but they're minuscule, and not much has trickled up. I think the future of urbanization in California depends on the pixilation of the large and the small. The idea is, of course, to develop an alternative to the oil-hungry urbanism-on-steroids model that defines the sprawl of Southern California. The political and economic frameworks that have supported and promoted this selfish urbanization need to be called into question. One project we've developed that does this is *Non-Stop Sprawl, McMansion Retrofitted*: a plastic model of the ubiquitous tract home, placed in a box with mirrors that reflect it into infinity. The house is accompanied by two monitors, which display a video diptych. On one monitor, a series of immigrants talk about

how they imagine transforming this McMansion to accommodate two families, or a small business in the garage. On the other monitor, an animation shows the house transforming.

Originally, the project was a satirical play meant to speculate on the transformation of American suburbs. In conditions of environmental and economic emergency, the current model of urbanization is not sustainable, and alternative uses must be developed. This is not a fantastical idea: It's been happening for decades. Look at the first ring of suburbs in San Diego, Los Angeles, or Chicago, and you'll see Levittown-style subdivisions that have been radically transformed in the last thirty or forty years. As immigrant communities have taken root, densities have increased and informal economic ties have grown.

Today this phenomenon is being accelerated: Because of the mortgage crisis, people are changing the way they use these large residences, whether it's owners dividing them into two or three units with a small business in the garage, or immigrants turning them into multigenerational family homes. As a result, we're beginning to think of density differently: not as a number of units per square mile, but as a measure of socioeconomic exchanges in an area.

When I talk about trickle-up, it's not to suggest a homogenizing effect of the informal—or that the bottom-up model will now be the only official approach to development—but rather that we need to come up with hybrid approaches, and generate abstract frameworks and informational models.

Studying the patterns of stealth urbanism found in immigrant communities can help us create policies that allow each neighborhood to take its own course of development, in accordance with its own history; that enable people to transform neighborhoods in response to demographic shifts.

I was at a talk recently where Jim Kunstler, the author of *The Geography of Nowhere*, observed that, because of the crisis, people today are really clamoring for solutions to some of these problems. But he also said that he was really pissed off because he feels that solutions are being sought just so that people can maintain a certain lifestyle. This isn't only an environmental crisis and an economic crisis; primarily, it's a cultural crisis. It calls for reengaging the public and suggesting—not in a patronizing way—that people shouldn't live on the periphery and enjoy their McMansions and big lawns anymore. Given that, it's amazing that the Obama administration is suggesting that the way to invest in infrastructure is to fix roads and add more lanes to the freeway.

cw: How do you start the process of generating these abstract frameworks and information models?

tc: Many of my studio's projects begin by highlighting the way in which economic policies have failed. The crisis of affordable housing in San Diego is partly due to a conflict between land use and lending. Subsidies do not support small projects or owner-occupied duplexes or fourplexes. In many depressed and disenfranchised

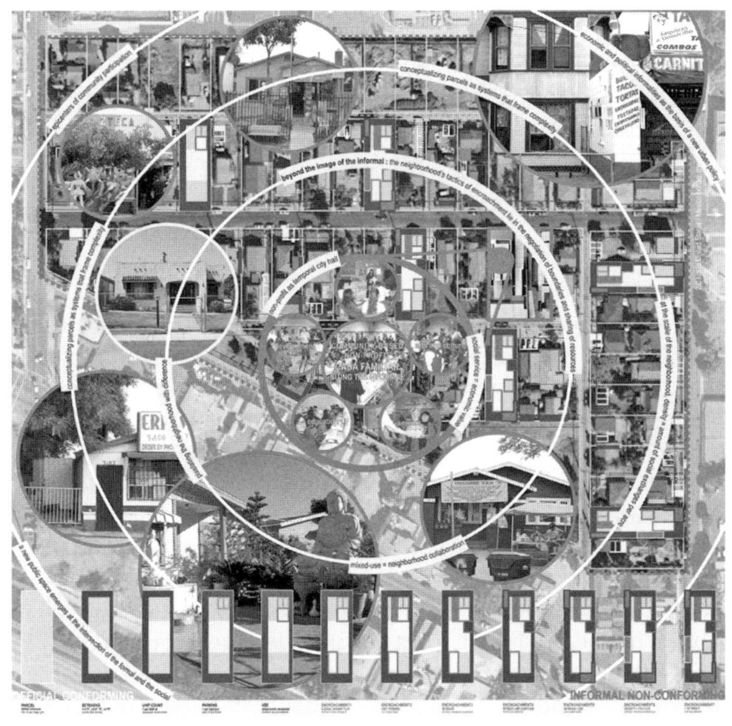

Estudio Teddy Cruz, *Neighborhood Urbanism: The Informal as a Tool to Transform Policy*, 2008.

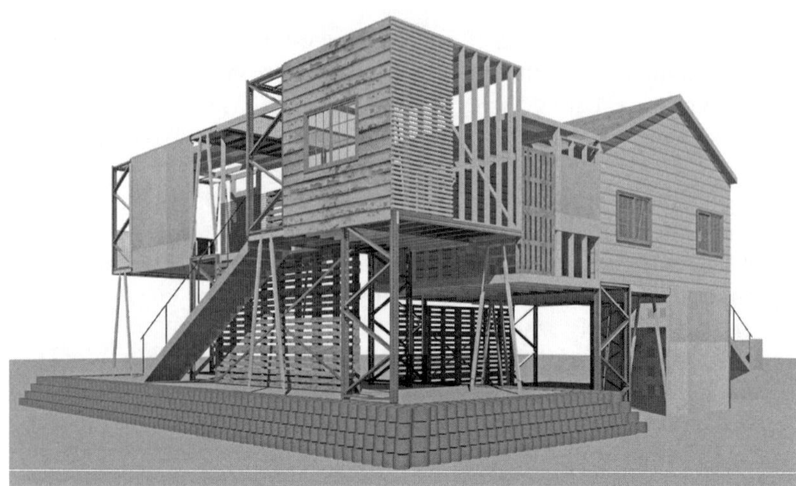

Estudio Teddy Cruz, *Manufactured Sites: A Housing Urbanism Made of Waste*, 2005.

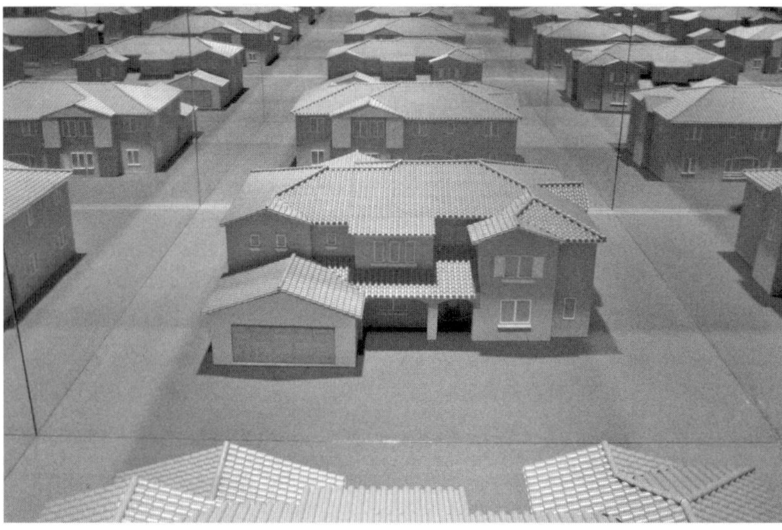

Estudio Teddy Cruz, *Non-Stop Sprawl, McMansion Retrofitted*, 2008.

neighborhoods, subsidized afford-able-housing projects must have a density of at least fifty units; but many of those neighborhoods pro-hibit such a high density (as well as mixed-use constructions), so private developers are stymied.

In order to come up with a dif-ferent model of affordable housing, we had to rethink how tax credits and subsidies were being employed; consider how to collaborate with community-based NGOs, which are developing many of the unconven-tional projects; and suggest how and why the municipality might adopt different models of density and mixed-use. We also had to con-vince them that social participation by people in the neighborhood has an economic value.

My aim is to open up institu-tions, turning their mechanisms into material to be reconfigured.

There's a certain misunderstanding of the meaning of research in the context of architecture and art—a perceived separation between research and product. But the language of research can itself function as artistic material.

The best moments in my practice occur when a research question becomes so volatile that it looses itself from architecture and art and engenders its own facts, which reconfigure the original conversation. Many such research questions are, of course, quite mundane. For the last seven years I've been working with Casa Familiar, a nonprofit in San Ysidro, a town just north of the border. Casa Familiar works in education, advocacy, service programming, housing, and community economic development. Our research question has been this: How do you create a situation in which the local government is compelled to share its power with this grassroots organization? How do you convince this institution that such a group is well-equipped to manage resources and interpret building regulations, and that the government actually benefits from enabling it to do so?

cw: You've been looking at barrios, nomadic settlements, and informal architecture in Tijuana for many years now, taking things you've learned from these case studies and turning them into a template for people in the North. But there's a romantic quality to this process: People come to these places to consume an idealized image of informal urbanism, and then they leave. What emerges is a sort of disaster-tourism dynamic. You run the risk of rationalizing poverty, even venerating it.

tc: This has been part of the criticism of my work. Since I live in San Diego, people in Tijuana see me as articulating a position in relation to the border but not engaging physically with that city. I dislike it when artists become the border patrol of ideas and authorship: I don't live there, so I'm not supposed to talk about it? Who cares where the ideas come from as long as they're furthering the debate around the conditions of urbanity? Who cares, as long as I'm working to uncover the dynamics that exist in these places?

At the same time, I'm aware that one walks a strange, fine line between trivializing oneself and becoming a patronizing tourist. To me, it's a risk worth taking. I've always said that a lot of the fear of seeming patronizing derives from American and European guilt. I've been trying to understand these things incrementally. I'm documenting the environment of Tijuana, but I'm not just producing an image. I'm not interested in the image of the informal, but rather what's behind it: the procedural, political, social, and economic characteristics of a place, and the process of translating them into operational devices that enable us to rethink urbanization. Oftentimes the role of art is only to amplify a problem, to make us "aware" of these issues, whether through metaphor or symbolism. But what happens afterward? As the artist Tania Bruguera said to me recently: I think it is time now to return Duchamp's urinal to the bathroom! ⊠

IT HAD JUST ENTERED OUR VALLEYS

A new translation of a story by the famed Armenian author, alongside a current-day landscape.

"The Construction of the Railway" by Hovhannes Tumanyan, translated by Meline Toumani; photographs by Vahram Aghasyan published November 24, 2009

INVALID FORMAT 2

ISSUE 7 2009

202

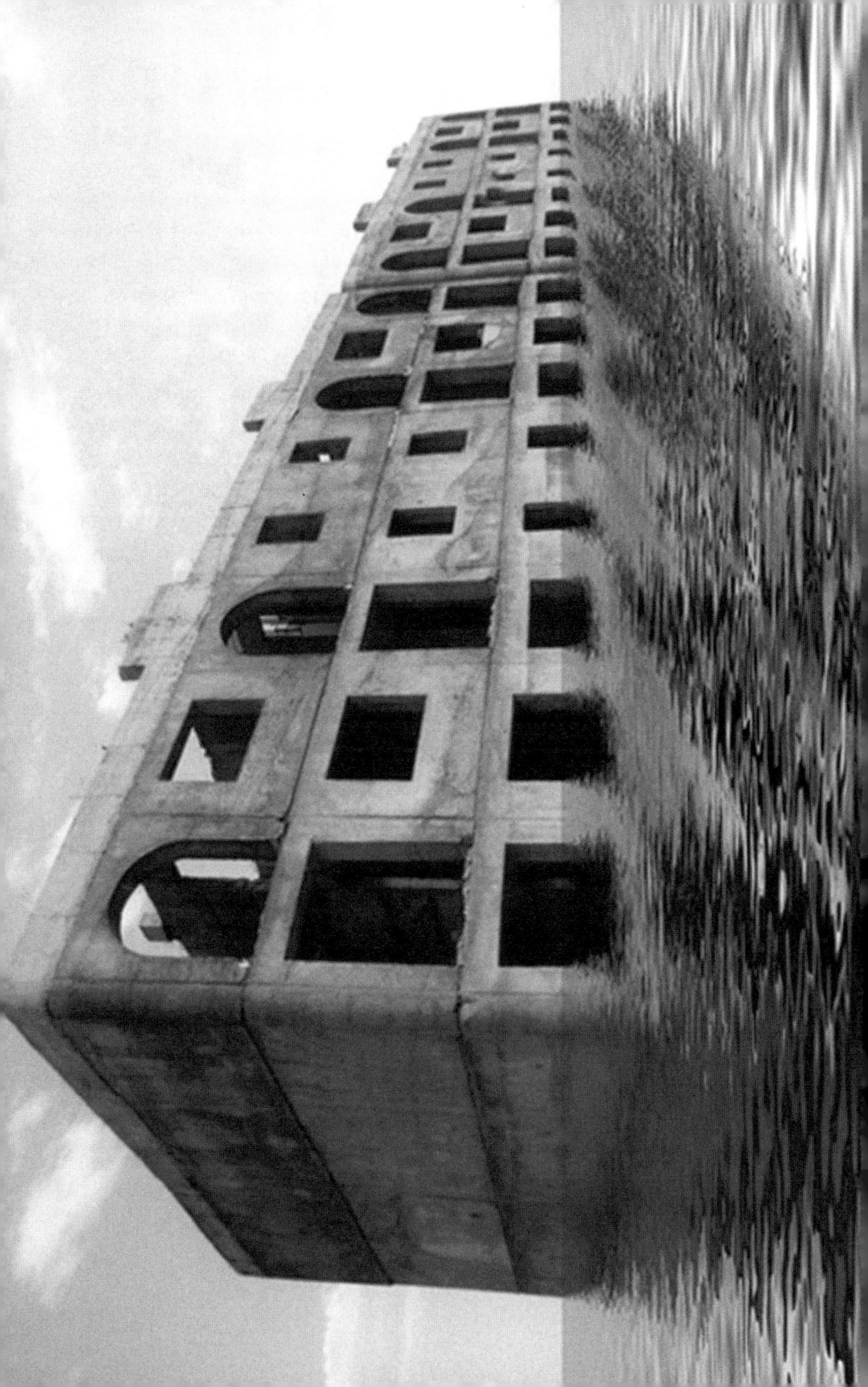

INVALID FORMAT 2

ISSUE 7 2009

HOVANNESS TUMANYAN, the most beloved of Armenian writers, was born in 1869 in the northern village of Dsegh, Armenia. Tumanyan witnessed the First World War, the dissolution of the Ottoman Empire, the genocidal campaign against Ottoman Armenians, the Russian Revolution, and the annexation of Armenia by the Soviet Union.

The railway described in Tumanyan's 1898 story "The Construction of the Railway," newly translated here, would be dismantled a century later. Perennial conflicts have left the borders with Azerbaijan and Turkey sealed since the early 1990s; last year, a rail link between Armenia and Georgia was ruined by an explosion during the war between Russia and Georgia. A recent agreement between Turkey and Armenia to work toward the establishment of diplomatic relations could be transformative; yet a new railway connecting Turkey, Georgia, and Azerbaijan, under construction since 2007, is set to bypass Armenia completely.

Of course, unrelenting tragedy is the oldest theme of Armenian history and literature. With the collapse of the Soviet Union, the signs of progress that had come with empire faltered; now, driving through the Armenian countryside, you can see unfinished construction projects from the final days of the Soviet era.

In 2006, Vahram Aghasyan photographed the remains of one abandoned Soviet housing development in northwestern Armenia called Mush, named for a town in Turkey from which Armenians were expelled at the end of the Ottoman era. The modular concrete buildings were intended to house victims of the December 7, 1988 earthquake, which claimed twenty-five thousand lives and leveled portions of nearby Gyumri, Armenia's second-largest city. Construction began and ended in 1989. The remaining husks are mirrored in pristine pools of water—an apocalyptic scene that no one is likely to ever encounter, as no one travels to that part of northern Armenia these days.

—*Meline Toumani*

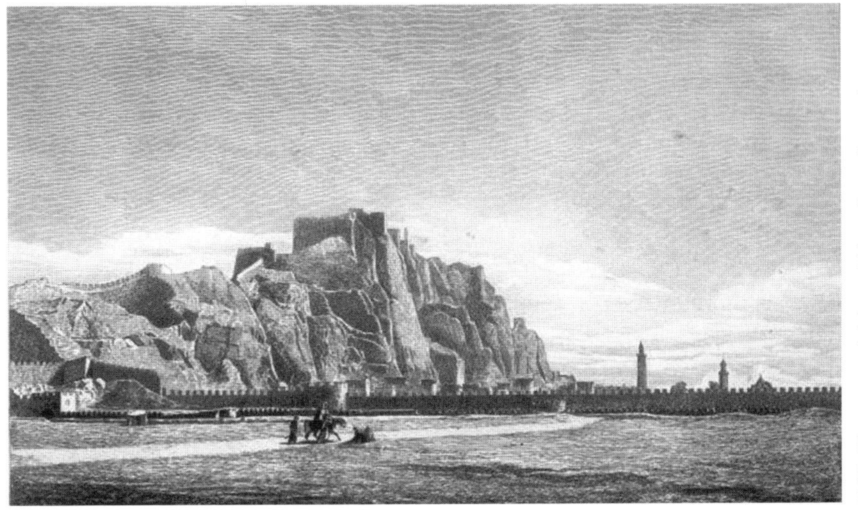

THE CONSTRUCTION OF THE RAILWAY

IN 1898, the railway running from Tiflis to Kars had just opened. We were sitting around on logs in front of the house of Master Ohaness in one of the villages in the Lori region, having a chat. Master Ohaness was telling us how the construction of the railway had gotten started.

"One day, me and our Simon here were out chopping wood in the lower valley by the river"—he was telling it like this.

"Suddenly we saw a few men wearing white worker's caps making their way along the bank. I said, 'Well, Simon.'

"'What is it?'

"'There's something going on here,' I say.

"'Why should there be something going on? They're just travelers going on their way. They could be lost.'

"I say, 'No, something's going on here. You'll see.'

"When we get back to the village we see that someone has stuck a white pole on the roof of Tersan's flour mill. 'Well, Simon,' I say.

"'What is it?'

"I say, 'Now you see?'

"'See what?'

"'Wait a little longer.' I say. 'You'll see.'

"Not long after that, a newspaper comes, and wouldn't you know it, we find out they're taking the railway through here! 'Well, well, Simon,' I say.

"'What is it?'

"'Now do you see how right I was?' I say."

INVALID FORMAT

2

ISSUE

7

2009

"OH, IF ONLY YOU WEREN'T," cried the hunter Ovsep, interrupting Master Ohaness's story.

"Come on, man, why are you talking like that? What harm is there in a railway?" some of the villagers chimed in.

"What is there but harm! Why, it came howling into the valleys and before you knew it the deer got scared and ran away. It's as if they never existed," complained Ovsep.

"It's more than just the deer, believe me," said a shepherd who was leaning on his stick. "When I go and stand near the edge of the cliff and look into the valley and see them blasting the rocks, my heart aches as if my own child is having his guts taken out by the enemy and I can't do anything to stop them."

"A lot of things will be destroyed," some sighed in agreement.

And the argument went on. The railway will bring some benefits, the railway will bring some problems, and so on.

DURING THIS ARGUMENT, there came up from the valley one of the foreign men who was working on the railway tracks. He approached us.

"Good evening," he said.

"A blessed evening, master!"

"I need some flour. Can any of you sell me some?" the stranger asked, addressing us all.

"Where are you from?" asked Master Ohaness.
"I am from Ottoman lands."

"Master Ohaness, ask him what town he's from," said one of the villagers.

"What's the name of your town, my friend?" Master Ohaness asked again.

"Sivas."

"Sivasss!" Master Ohaness repeated knowingly, drawing out the last syllable.

"What did he say, Master Ohaness?"

"Sivas."

"May your house remain standing!" cried some of the villagers, clapping their hands and laughing.

"How many months' journey is it from there to here?" Master Ohaness continued his questioning.

"Three months."

"Oh, my. . ." everyone exclaimed in unison.

"Welcome, wandering brother. Sit down and join us. They'll bring out some food, and please enjoy it."

"No, thanks, I'm in a hurry. If someone will just sell me some flour, I'll take it and be going."

"Hey in there, girls! Bring out a pot of flour," Master Ohaness called into the door. "And fill it all the way up to the top!"

One of the women brought out a pot of flour and went to pour it into the stranger's bag, but he stopped her.

"How much does this cost?" he asked.

"Well, pour it into your bag for starters," said Master Ohaness.

"No. First let's know the price."

"Go on and pour it in, and then we'll tell you. If it's too expensive you can always pour some back."

The stranger opened his bag, and the woman poured the flour in and went away. "So how much do I owe you?" asked the stranger, pulling out his purse from under his belt.

"Nothing, master. That won't be necessary. It's a gift. In our part of the world they don't take the money of travelers for food. There's no such habit," said Master Ohaness, and then went back to puffing on his pipe.

The stranger was a little embarrassed, gave a bit of a protest, and then left.

IT WAS QUIET FOR A FEW MOMENTS, then one of the villagers spoke up. "A few days ago, one of them came and asked for yogurt. The women gave him some. He eats it, then he gets up and asks how much it costs. 'What?' I ask him.

"The yogurt," he says.

'Come on, man, are you kidding me? Don't talk that way or the sheep's milk might just dry up altogether!' I say."

"Fine, gentleman, but then what are we supposed to do? Is that right that whoever comes along just eats all he wants and then takes off?" This was the younger brother of Master Ohaness talking. "Do you have any idea how many more of them are going to come after that one? Just the other day, I myself poured out a pot of flour for one of them and handed it over. Where does it end?"

"If he comes again, give him another," said Master Ohaness calmly, raising his head.

"May your home always be joyous," some of the older men called out.

"I should be so lucky," said the younger brother. "You're telling me that whoever comes, from Sivas or wherever, that I should serve them all as if I work for them? Whoever comes, welcome, a thousand welcomes! But if you want food, pay first and then take it!"

And they began to argue. Master Ohaness got all worked up and the noise got louder and louder.

Chooo-chooooo . . . From down below came the whistle of the train.

It had just entered our valleys. ⊠

THE INVISIBLE GRAMMAR

**A TRIBUTE TO ASPEN ON
ITS FORTY-SECOND ANNIVERSARY
PS 1 CONTEMPORARY ART CENTER,
22-25 JACKSON AVENUE, LONG ISLAND CITY, NY
OCTOBER 4, 2009 (NY ART BOOK FAIR)**

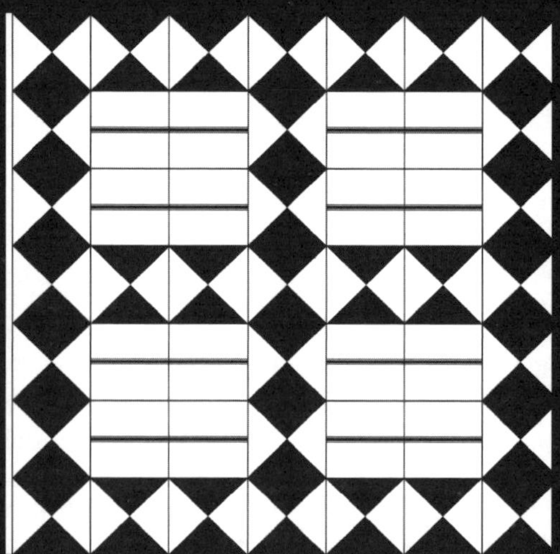

1	3	5	7	5	3	1
3	0	0	5	0	0	3
5	0	0	3	0	0	5
7	5	3	1	3	5	7
5	0	0	3	0	0	5
3	0	0	5	0	0	3
1	3	5	7	5	3	1

Adam Helms's interpretation of "Seven Translucent Tiers," by Mel Bochner.

Date: September 23, 2009
Subject: Join Triple Canopy at the Printed Matter Book Fair

Dear local contributors and friends,

On Sunday, October 4, from 2:30 till 3:30, we'll be presenting "The Invisible Grammar: A Tribute to *Aspen*'s Time, Silence and Reduction, and Language Issue on Its Forty-Second Anniversary" as part of The Classroom, the programming component of Printed Matter's annual book fair. We'd like you to participate. For those of you who don't know *Aspen*, its an incredible "multimedia magazine in a box" that was published from 1965 to 1971 and has been a continuing source of inspiration for Triple Canopy. For this event, we'll be reading, interpreting, performing, playing, and otherwise subjecting fairgoers—in hallways, exhibition spaces, as well as the main "classroom"—to texts and artworks and recordings and films published in this issue—actually two issues, five and six—of the magazine, edited and designed by Brian O'Doherty. The entire run of *Aspen* is catalogued, and all media files are available, here: ubu.com/aspen.

It will all be very casual and require minimal preparation. As a bonus, there will be a TC-hosted after-party in the environs of Long Island City, as this year's fair is being held at PS1. And feel free to invite friends.

Regards,
The Editors

Tom Roberge: "The Death of the Author," by Roland Barthes · Catherine Czacki: "Text for Nothing #8," by Samuel Beckett · Adam Helms: "Seven Translucent Tiers," by Mel Bochner · Nicole Russo: "Nova Express," by William Burroughs · Molly Kleiman: "Conditionnement," by Michel Butor · Dan Torop & Alexander Provan: "Fontana Mix-Feed," by John Cage · Georgia Sagri: "Space, Time and Dance," by Merce Cunningham · Nolan Simon & Oliver Newton: "The Creative Act," by Marcel Duchamp · Summer Guthery: "*A L'infinitif*," by Marcel Duchamp · Nathan Gwynne: "The King of Denmark," by Morton Feldman · Peter Simensky: "The Realistic Manifesto," by Naum Gabo · Caolan Madden: "Poem, March 1966," by Dan Graham · Julia Weist: "Jealousy," by Alain Robbe-Grillet · Forté Magazine: "Phantastische Gebete," by Richard Huelsenbeck · Nadja Millner-Larsen: "Style and the Representation of Historical Time," by George Kubler · Kate Shepherd: "Serial Project #1," by Sol Lewitt · Andrea Merkx: "The Russian Desert: A Note on Our State of Knowledge," by Douglas MacAgy · Natalie Campbell & Bridget Lewis: "Lightplay: Black-White-Grey," by László Moholy-Nagy · Zack Rockhill: "Site," by Robert Morris & Stan VanDerBeek · Hannah Whitaker & Sam Frank: "Structural Play #3," by Brian O'Doherty · Andres Laracuente: "Linoleum," by Robert Rauschenberg · Jessie Stead: "Rhythm 21," by Hans Richter · Rachel Owens: "The Maze," by Tony Smith · Alexander Provan: "The Aesthetics of Silence," by Susan Sontag

In my opinion, the myths of silence and emptiness are about as nourishing and viable as one could hope to see devised in an "unwholesome" time—which is, of necessity, a time in which "unwholesome" psychic states furnish the energies for most superior work in the arts today. At the same time, one can't deny the pathos of these myths.
　　—Susan Sontag, "The Aesthetics of Silence," *Aspen* no. 5+6, 1967

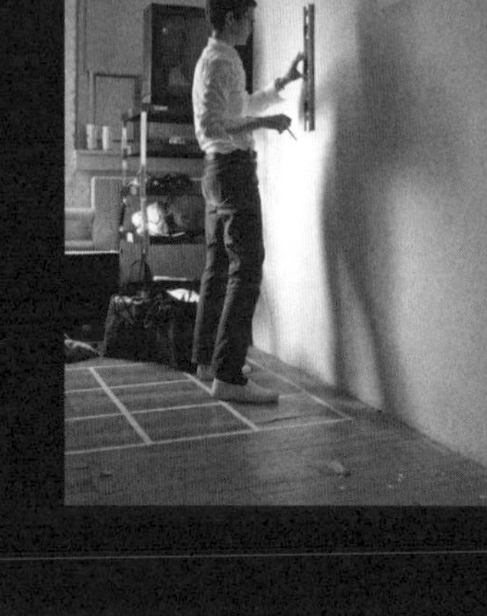
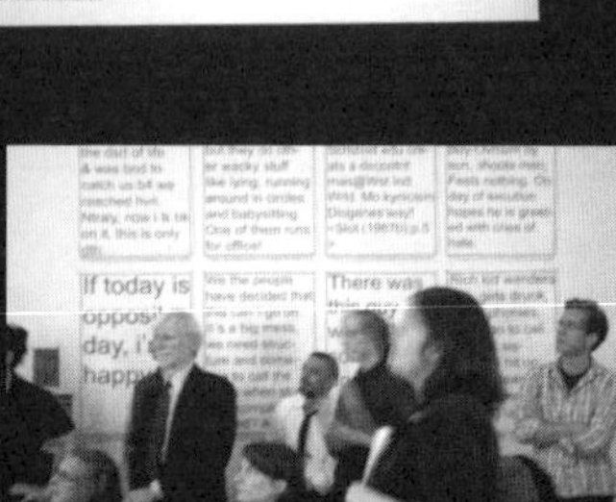
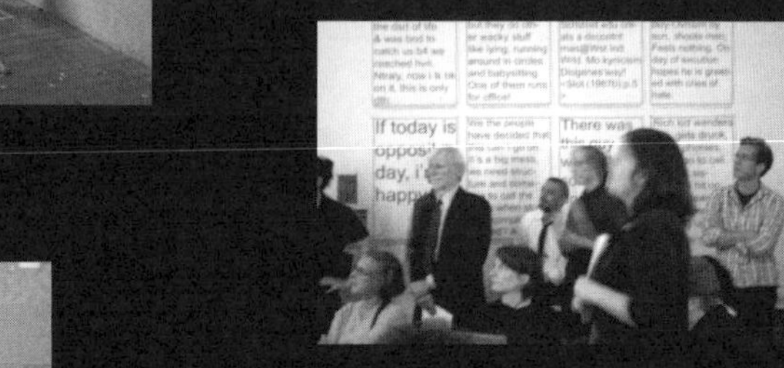
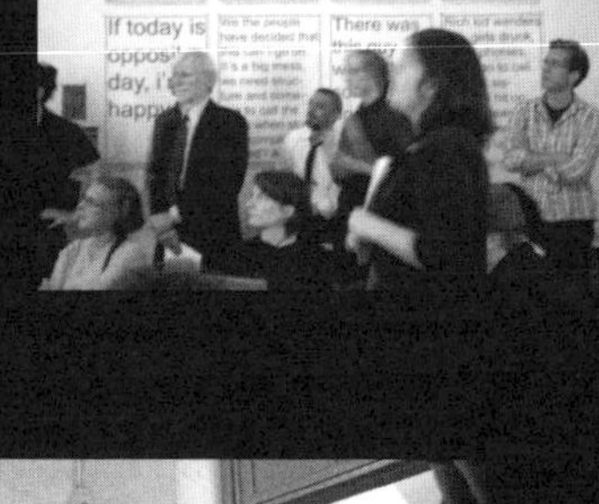
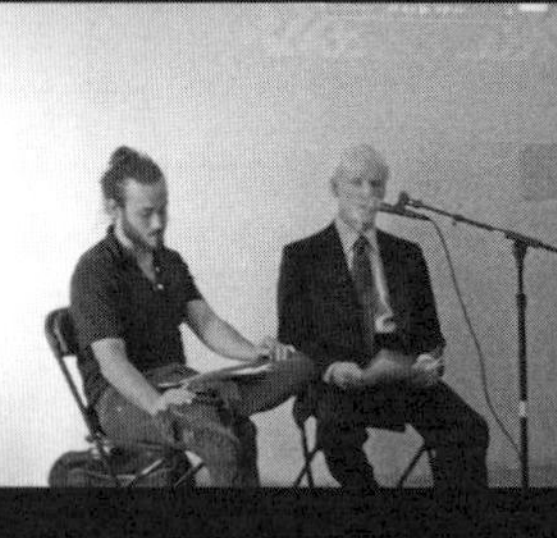
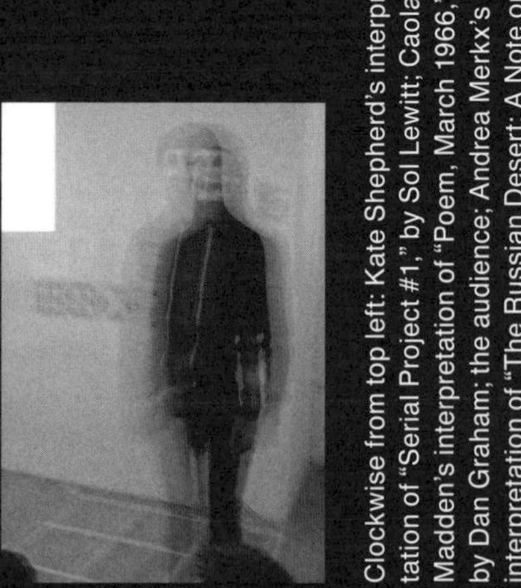

Clockwise from top left: Kate Shepherd's interpretation of "Serial Project #1," by Sol Lewitt; Caolan Madden's interpretation of "Poem, March 1966," by Dan Graham; the audience; Andrea Merkx's interpretation of "The Russian Desert: A Note on Hannah Whitaker and Sam Frank's interpretation of "Structural Play #3," by Brian O'Doherty; Jessie Stead's interpretation of "Rhythm 21," by Hans Richter; Catherine Czacki's interpretation of "Text for Nothing #8," by Samuel Beckett; Georgia by Merce Cunningham; Andres Laracuente's interpretation of "Linoleum," by Robert Rauschenberg. Opposite page: Nolan Simon and Oliver Newton's interpretation of "The Creative Act," by Marcel interpretation of "The Creative Act," by Marcel Duchamp, and Adam Helms's interpretation of

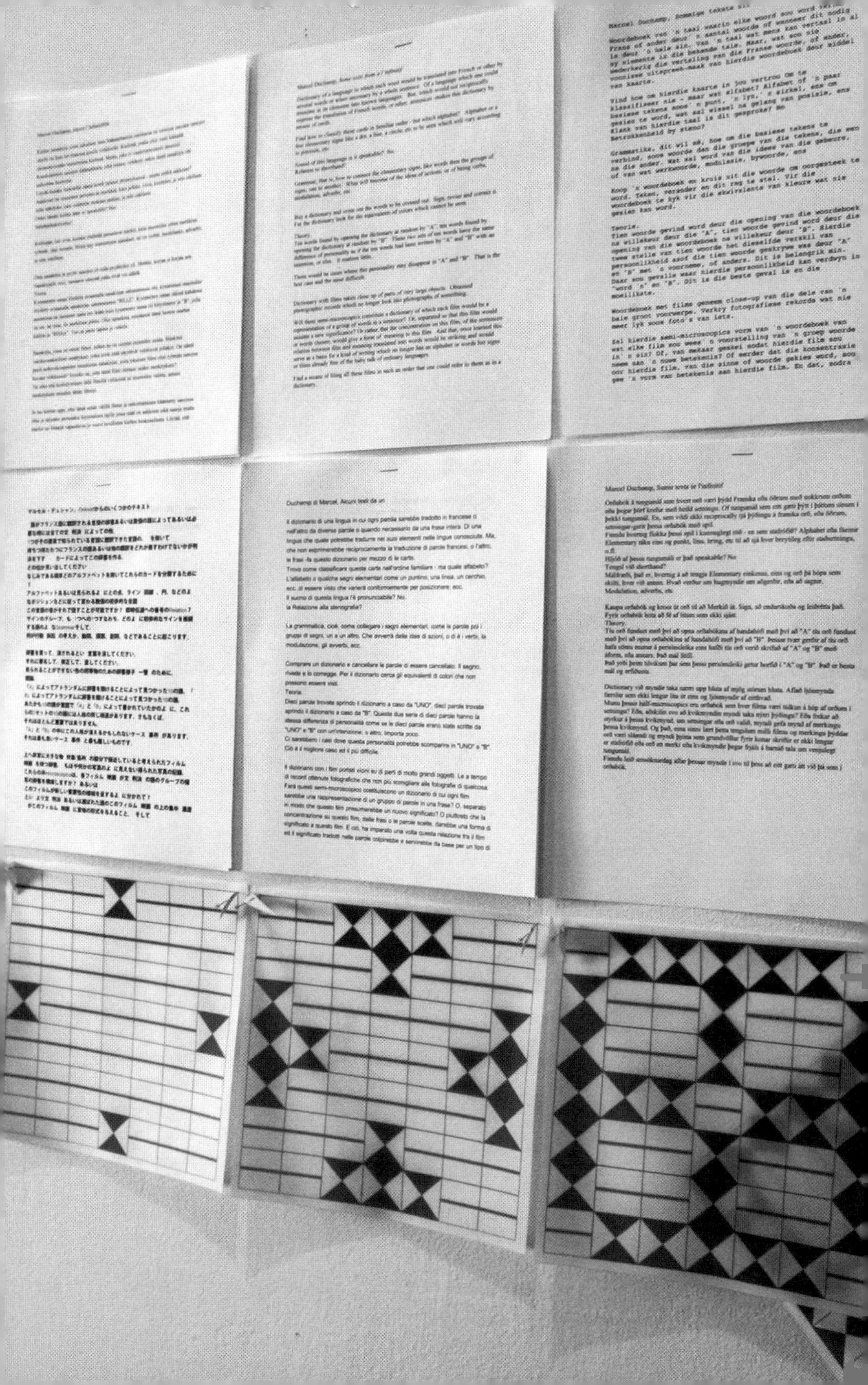

Marcel Duchamp, Some texts from a l'infinitif

Dictionary of a language in which each word would be translated into French or other by several words or when necessary by a whole sentence. Of a language which one could translate in its elements into known languages. But, which would not reciprocally express the translation of French words, of these sentences makes this dictionary by means of cards.

Find how to classify these cards in familiar order, but which alphabet? Alphabet or a few elementary signs like a dot, a line, a circle, etc. to be seen which will vary according to position, etc.

Sound of this language, is it speakable? No. Relation to shorthand?

Grammar, that is, how to connect the elementary signs, like words then the group of signs, one to another. What will become of the idea of actions, or of being (verbs, modulation, adverbs, etc.

But a dictionary and cross out the words to be crossed out. Sign, revise and correct it. For the dictionary look for the equivalents of colors which cannot be seen.

Theory.
Ten words found by opening the dictionary at random by "A", ten words found by opening the dictionary at random by "B". These two sets of ten words have the same difference of personality as if the ten words had been written by "A" and "B" with an intention, or else. It matters little.

There would be cases where this personality may disappear in "A" and "B". That is the best case and the most difficult.

Dictionary with films taken close up of parts of very large objects. Obtained photographic records which no longer look like photographs of something.

Will these semi-microscopics constitute a dictionary of which each film would be a representation of a group of words in a sentence? Or, separated so that this film would include a new significance? Or rather that the concentration on this film, of the successive of words chosen, would give a form of meaning to this film. And that, once learned this relation between film and meaning translated into words would be striking and would serve as a basis for a kind of writing which no longer has an alphabet or words but signs of films already free of the baby talk of ordinary languages.

Find a means of filing all these films in such an order that one could refer to them as in a dictionary.

Marcel Duchamp, Sommige tekste uit

Woordeboek van 'n taal waarin elke woord sou word vertaal in Frans of ander deur 'n aantal woorde of wanneer dit nodig is deur 'n hele sin. Van 'n taal wat mens kan vertaal in sy elemente in die bekende tale. Maar, wat sou nie onderkerig die vertaling van die Franse woorde, of ander, voorlesse uitspreek-maak van hierdie woordeboek deur middel van kaarte.

Vind hoe om hierdie kaarte in jou vertrou om te klassifiseer nie - maar wat alfabet? Alfabet of 'n paar basiese tekens soos 'n punt, 'n lyn, 'n sirkel, ens om gesien te word, wat sal wissel na gelang van posisie, ens Klank van hierdie taal is dit gesproke? No Betrokkenheid by steno?

Grammatika, dit wil sê, hoe om die basiese tekens te verbind, soos woorde dan die groepe van die tekens, die een na die ander. Wat sal word van die idees van die gebeure, of van wat werkwoorde, modulasie, bywoorde, ens

Koop 'n woordeboek en kruis uit die woorde om oorgesteek word. Tekens, verander en dit reg te stel. Vir die woordeboek te kyk vir die ekwivalente van kleure wat nie gesien kan word.

Teorie.
Tien woorde gevind word deur die opening van die woordeboek na willekeur deur die "A", tien woorde gevind word deur die opening van die woordeboek na willekeur deur "B". Hierdie twee stelle van tien woorde het dieselfde verskil van persoonlikheid asof die tien woorde geskrywe was deur "A" en "B" met 'n voorneme, of anders. Dit is belangrik sin. Daar sou gevalle waar hierdie persoonlikheid kan verdwyn in "word 'n" en "B". Dit is die beste geval is en die moeilikste.

Woordeboek met films geneem close-up van die dele van 'n baie groot voorwerpe. Verkry fotografiese rekords wat nie meer lyk soos foto's van iets.

Sal hierdie semi-microscopics vorm van 'n woordeboek van wat elke film sou wees 'n voorstelling van 'n groep woorde in 'n sin? Of, van mekaar geskei sodat hierdie film sou neem aan 'n nuwe betekenis? Of eerder dat die konsentrasie oor hierdie film, van die sinne of woorde gekies word, sou gee 'n vorm van betekenis aan hierdie film. En dat, sodra

---

マルセル・デュシャン、l'infinitifからのいくつかのテキスト

Duchamp di Marcel, Alcuni testi da un

Il dizionario di una lingua in cui ogni parola sarebbe tradotto in francese o nell'altro da diverse parole o quando necessario da una frase intera. Di una lingua che quale potrebbe tradurre nei suoi elementi nelle lingue conosciute. Ma, che non esprimerebbe reciprocamente la traduzione di parole francesi, o l'altro, le frasi -fa questo dizionario per mezzo di le carte.
Trova come classificare queste carte nell'ordine familiare - ma quale alfabeto? L'alfabeto o qualche segni elementari come un puntino, una linea, un cerchio, ecc. di essere visto che varierà conformemente per posizionare; ecc.
Il suono di questa lingua l'è pronunciabile? No.
la Relazione alla stenografia?

La grammatica, cioè, come collegare i segni elementari, come le parole poi i gruppi di segni, un a un altro. Che avverrà delle idee di azioni, o di 4 i verbi; la modulazione, gli avverbi, ecc.

Comprare un dizionario e cancellare le parole di essere cancellato. Il segno, rivede e lo corregge. Per il dizionario cerca gli equivalenti di colori che non possono essere visti.
Teoria.
Dieci parole trovate aprindo il dizionario a caso da "UNO", dieci parole trovate aprindo il dizionario a caso da "B". Queste due serie di dieci parole hanno la stessa differenza di personalità come se le dieci parole erano state scritte da "UNO" e "B" con un'intenzione, o altro, importa poco.
Ci sarebbero i casi dove questa personalità potrebbe scomparire in "UNO" e "B".
Ciò è il migliore caso ed il più difficile.

Il dizionario con i film portati vicini su di parti di molto grandi oggetti. Le a tempo di record ottenute fotografiche che non più somigliare alle fotografie di qualcosa
Farà questi semi-microscopico costituiscono un dizionario di cui ogni film
sarebbe una rappresentazione di un gruppo di parole in una frase? O, separato
in modo che questo film presumerebbe un nuovo significato? O piuttosto che la
concentrazione su questo film, delle frasi o le parole scelte, darebbe una forma di
significato a questo film. E ciò, ha imparato una volta questa relazione tra il film
ed il significato tradotti nelle parole colpirebbe e servirebbe da base per un tipo di

---

Marcel Duchamp, Sumir textar úr l'infinitif

WANG BING: CRUDE OIL

LIGHT INDUSTRY, 220 36TH STREET, 5TH FLOOR, BROOKLYN, NY
NOVEMBER 4–8, 2009
COPRESENTED BY LIGHT INDUSTRY

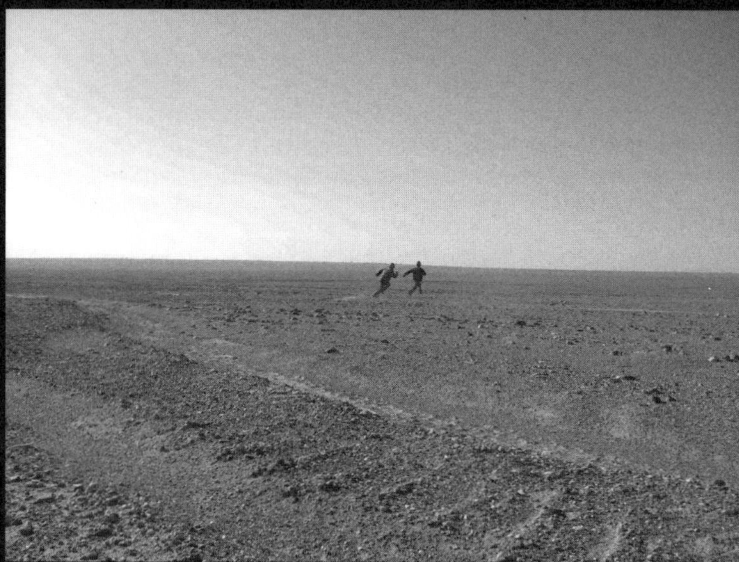

Wang Bing, *Crude Oil*, 2008, still from a color video, 14 hours.

TRIPLE CANOPY and Light Industry presented the East Coast premiere of Wang Bing's *Crude Oil* (2008), a fourteen-hour film installation tracking a fourteen-hour workday of crude-oil extraction in northwest China's Qinghai province. The film was on view from 9 a.m. until 11 p.m. each day, running five times in its entirety.

Accompanying *Crude Oil*, in an adjacent room, will be a film program by Matthew Coolidge, of the Center for Land Use Interpretation, and Lucy Raven, followed by a discussion with the artists; and screenings of Wang Bing's *Coal Money* and *West of the Tracks*, followed by a discussion with Rebecca Karl (Associate Professor, History and East Asian Studies, NYU) and Zhen Zhang (Associate Professor, Cinema Studies, NYU). A curated DVD library of related films was available for viewing throughout the week.

A RECENT *New York Times* article on arbitrage in oil futures began: "Its superfast, supersecret oil trading software was called the Hammer. . . . Founded in 1986 by an options trader named Johann Kaemingk, Optiver has grown far beyond its roots in Amsterdam to trade on exchanges all over the world . . . . It deploys a sophisticated software system called F1 that can process information and make a trade in 0.5 milliseconds—using complex algorithms that let its computers think like a trader."

What movie could capture these black-boxed, microscopic moments? The world outraces art: the sheer speed, placelessness, and impersonality of global finance, if not its crises, defeat our ability even to think it. And yet—work still has a time, a place, and a person. Each day, oil comes up from the ground and flows cross-country; coal is trucked day and night from mine to market; copper is mined, smelted, refined, wired; on plateaus and in pits, in deserts and on mountains, in cities and factories, in China, in America—by people. And here film can catch up. In *Crude Oil*, art-time and work-time coincide, and the film's workers, in breakrooms and on oil fields, enter our space as equals.

Yet the time of reality needn't always be "real time." A

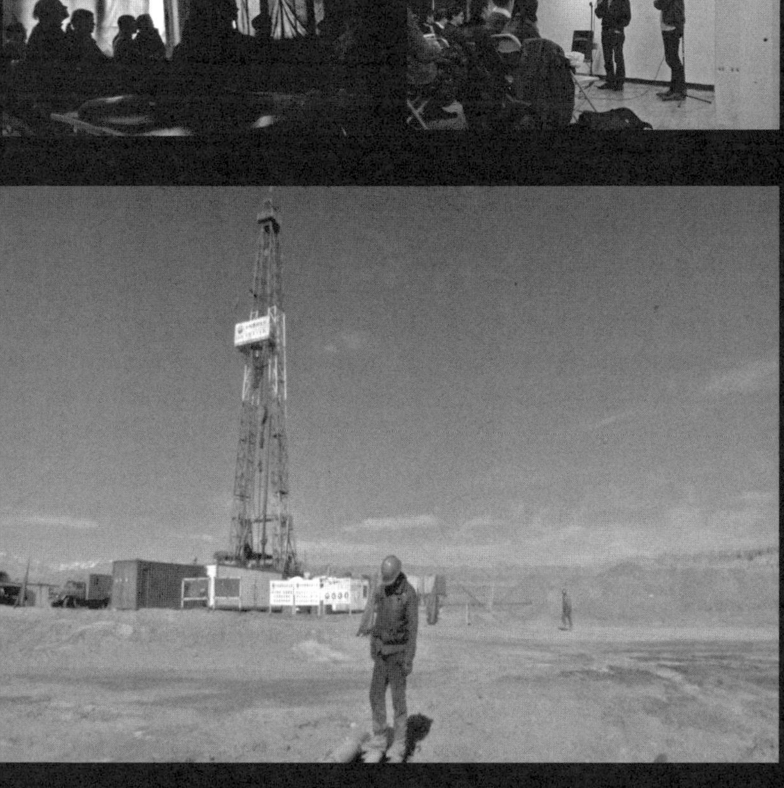

diversity of forms can be found for work, workers, workplaces, and the landscapes of labor: the uninflected duration of *Crude Oil* and the Center for Land Use Interpretation's topographical "landscans"; but also the still-frame animation of Lucy Raven's *China Town* (2009) and the

long-take montage of Wang's *West of the Tracks* (2003). This week, please join us in Sunset Park's Industry City, an active industrial complex built at the turn of the twentieth century, as we map not superfast, supersecret oil futures, but the oil-industrial present.
—Sam Frank, Triple Canopy

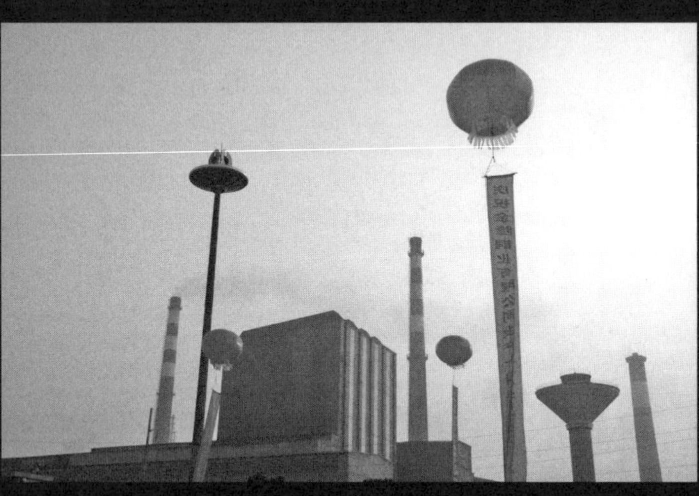

WANG BING'S overwhelming *West of the Tracks* presents us with the panoramic spectacle of progress collapsing. Industry folds and empties its plants; workers lose their jobs and their benefits; people are idle and demoralized, and then they are unhoused, and they demolish their own former dwellings to cash in on their value as scrap; people scavenge among gargantuan ruins that loom like the remnants of a forgotten civilization of giants. It is every twentieth-century mural depiction of the struggle for the good life—socialist or capitalist—viewed in reverse. *West of the Tracks* is at once epic and intimate: epic because of the sheer scale of the factories and the long, straight railroad-tracking shots Wang employs to render the

film's geography; intimate because of the focus on the daily life of the last workers, soon to be displaced. Wang's film is not journalistic in that it does not show us, for example, the bureaucrats who made the various life-altering decisions. It depicts the Teixi District of Shenyang, where industry has failed, but not the rest of the city, not the bourgeois neighborhoods, shops, hotels, highways. There are few motor vehicles in the film, few paved streets, seemingly no structures built since the 1950s. The chief signs of modern life, which is to say the only things the people can afford to consume, are clothing and pop songs. In his nine-hour film, Wang brings us inside the world he is chronicling so thoroughly that, if you watch it in one go, you're apt to lose track of what things outside are like.

You begin to wonder what his shooting ratio might have been—whether, that is, he shot for so long that his subjects forgot that he was there. Maybe he stood there for weeks and months with his camera, not shooting until every so often something struck him. Maybe the concept of being filmed was so foreign to his subjects that they accepted his activity without complaint or self-consciousness. Maybe his personality was such that he soon blended in with the surroundings. In any case, Wang manages to get an enormous amount of footage of people with their guards down, displaying frustration or drunkenness or jealousy or pettiness or sentimentality or even, as in one extraordinary sequence near the end, breaking down altogether. Maybe his

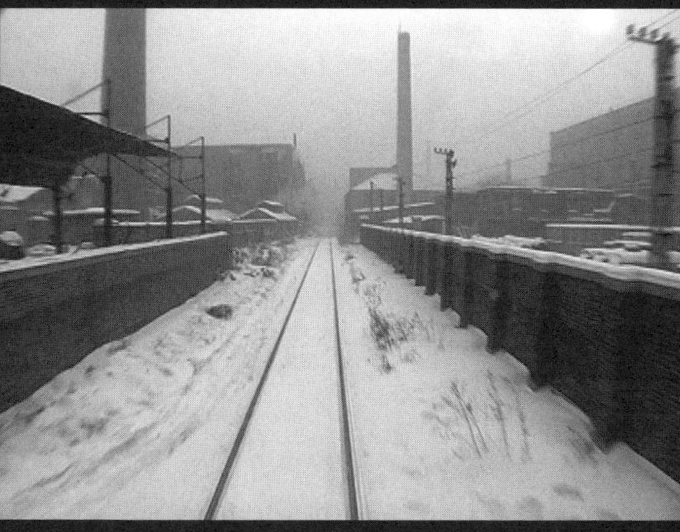

Wang Bing, *West of the Tracks*, 2003, still from a color video, 9 hours.

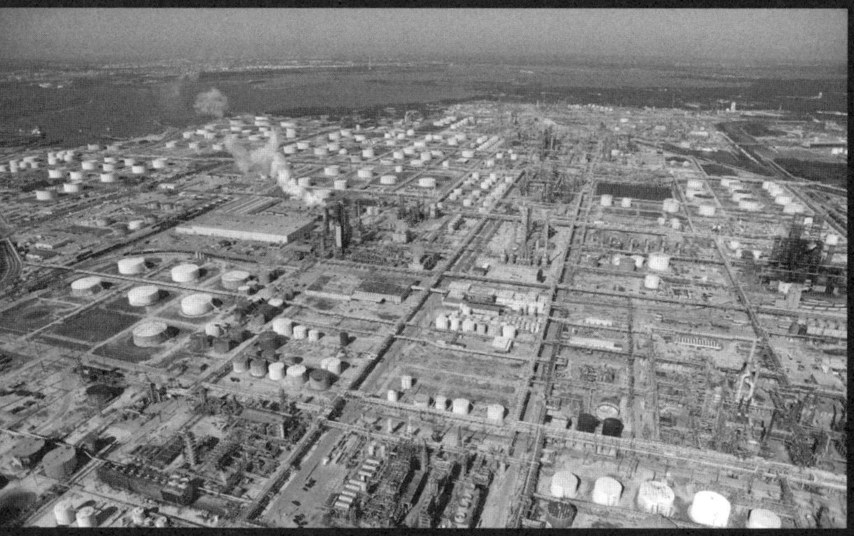

Center for Land Use Interpretation, *Houston Petrochemical Corridor*, 2008, still from a landscan, 12 minutes.

subjects have had their emotions so thoroughly abraded that any amount of self-protection would seem foolish, like putting on airs. As a consequence, there is very little emotional distance between them and us. When this is combined with that strange phenomenon that occurs when watching very long movies with subtitles—you begin to imagine that you are actually understanding speeches in a language you do not know, rather than reading skeletal translations—the immersion is complete.

Wang thrusts us into the small talk and sniping and grousing of the break room as well as the labor of the factory floor. The scenes of work and downtime are interspersed with segments in which Wang travels, camera in hand, down endless corridors and into vast sheds, some of them seeming abandoned until he takes us into the corner where the work goes on. You realize that each of these places once employed thousands and are now down to dozens. Then the plants close, one by one. The workers are taken out to the country for a last shakedown inspection at the hospital. They are there for a few weeks, doing little but having their blood tested, so that their stay takes on the lineaments of a bleak vacation. They drink, play cards, watch porn videos, and take brief jaunts outdoors; one of them manages to drown in a pond. It is a valediction and, of course, a muted death sentence, since the visit can do little but confirm that they have been poisoned by their labor.

Trains that once plied the tracks between the factories, hauling raw materials to the plants and hauling away the finished product, now appear to do little but assist the scavenging of their remaining employees. We get the sense that they will not be running for long. Eventually Wang focuses on Old Du and his son, who have been professional scavengers for some time, and who are allowed to live in a trackside shack by railroad workers. Old Du, plainspoken and canny, has survived many reversals and seems likely to withstand his eventual eviction, but his son, much more fragile, falls apart on camera.

The astonishing intimacy of this final part of the film is somehow emphasized by the strangeness of the physical setting. The mammoth shells of the factories look not just like outsize ruins but deeply alien, like vestiges of some science-fictional race that has no interest in or sympathy for the human cause. But a measure of the greatness of Wang's film is that it does not allow the viewer to sink into the comforting numbness of despair. Humans will somehow carry on in the bleakest of circumstances.

–Luc Sante, *Leaving the Factory: Wang Bing's* Tie Xi Qu: West of the Tracks, 2009

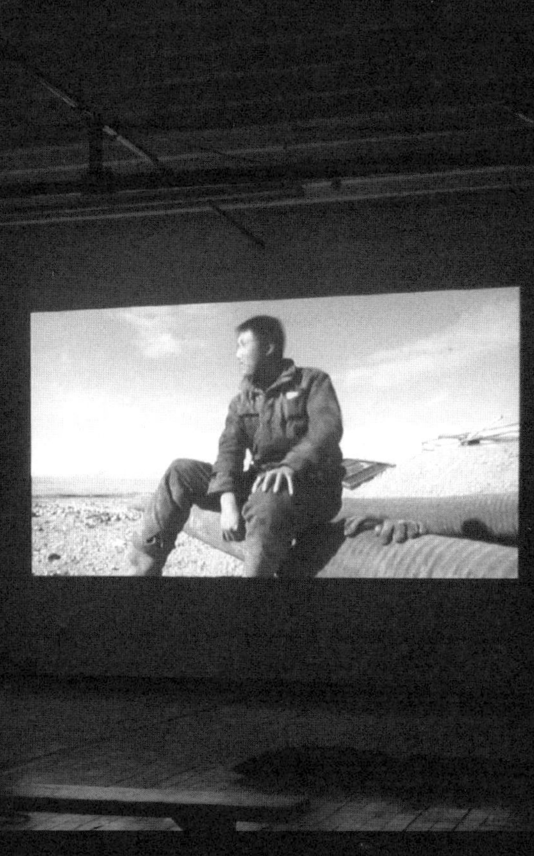

ISSUE 8
HUE AND CRY

published March 17, 2010

CANOPYCANOPYCANOPY.COM/8

DE TRIBUS IMPOSTORIBUS

An Internet play inspired by the eponymous book (which was neither written nor published). Three dialogues on the limits and imperfections of language.

by Victoria Miguel
published March 17, 2010

In its original form, "De Tribus Impostoribus" features video, slide shows, a sound track, a script read aloud, character studies hovering in pop-up windows, and a live video feed of the reader. Bill Weeden is X and M. D.; H. Johnson is C. Ryan Falkowitz conceived of the character studies; Lara Kohl, Matthew Lusk, and C. S. Stevens each conceived of an unrealized set. Jacob Carpenter Morris composed the theme, "VWB 373," and the intro and coda. Lynn Wright and Tony Maimone are listeners. Seth Erickson realized the play for the Internet. Lara Kohl, Victoria Miguel, and Lynn Wright are responsible for the sound. The producers are Adam Helms, Melanie Koch, and Victoria Miguel. What follows is one of three dialogues, Ryan Falkowitz's three character studies, and images from Lara Kohl's unrealized set.

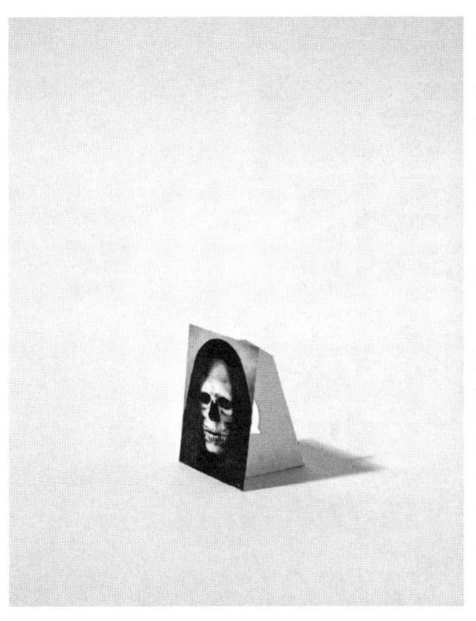

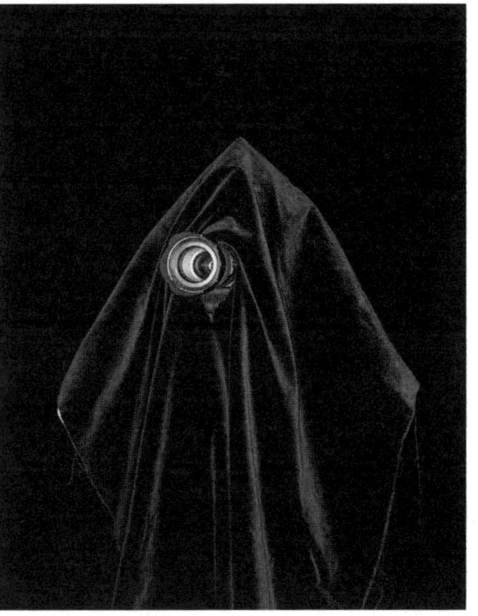

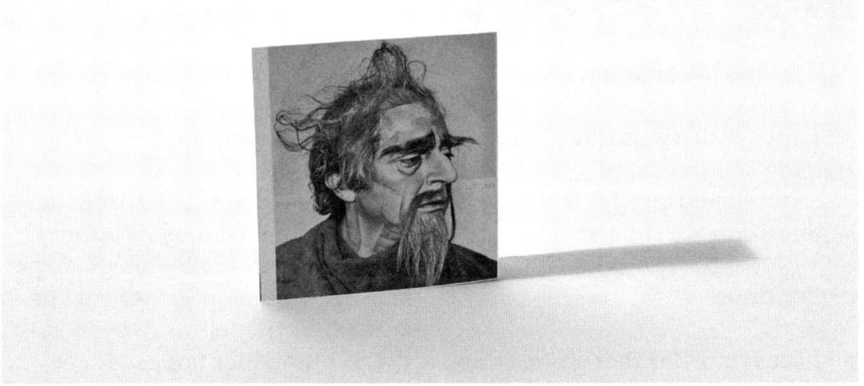

ᴍ Middle-aged man—tends towards warm, jovial, playful

ᴄ Middle-aged man—tends towards cold, preaching, austere

ʟ Listener—tacet

sᴏᴜɴᴅs: *[Listener {aleatoric}; books—rustling through pages]*

sᴜʀʀᴏᴜɴᴅɪɴɢs: *none*

ᴍ: [Authoritatively] But you, faulty logician, whose sad foolishness
    Dares to reassure them in the path of crime,
    What fruit do you expect to reap from your fine arguments?
    Will your children be more obedient to your voice?
    Your friends, at time of need, more useful and reliable?
    Your wife more honest? And your new renter,
    For not believing in God, will he pay you better?
    Alas! Let's leave intact human belief in fear and hope.

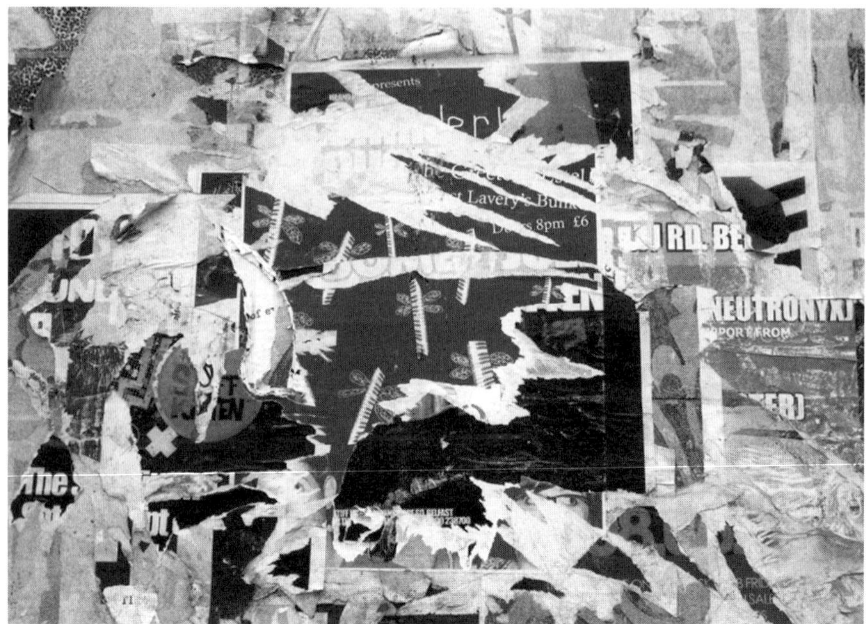

C: [Quietly] Fear and hope

M: I always distinguished between religion
    And the misery bred of superstition.

C: Continue

M: I see from afar that era coming, those happy days,
    When philosophy, enlightening humanity,
    Must lead them in peace to the feet of the common master;
    Frightful fanaticism will tremble to appear there:
    There will be less dogma with more virtue.

C: The end?

M: The end

C: I can't agree. Can he mean it?

M: I have no idea

C: It hardly seems to equivocate

M: Sarcastic perhaps?

C: That is my hope. [Short pause] There are two modes of knowledge, through argument and experience. Argument brings conclusions and compels us to concede them, but it does not cause certainty nor remove doubts in order that the mind may remain at rest in truth, unless this is provided by experience.

M: We can't have the experience

C: Look it up

M: Experience?

C: [Matter of fact] Experience

M: [Short pause] [*Book being opened, page found*] Noun or verb?

C: Noun of course!

M: [Authoritatively] Experience. French expérience, Latin experientia or experiri, to try, to put to the test. The action of putting to the test. A tentative procedure, an operation performed in order to ascertain or illustrate some truth; an experiment . . .

C: [Interrupting] From the Latin experiri—to try.

M: [Authoritatively] Experiment {experimentum, Latin.} Trial of anything; something done in order to discover an uncertain or unknown effect. The 1755.

C: [Pleased] We can experience and experiment

M: We can try

C: [Disapproving] Yes. Faulty logician, whose sad foolishness dares to reassure them in the path of crime, what fruit do you expect to reap from your fine arguments?

M: The basic of logic is the syllogism, consisting of a major and a minor premise and a conclusion.

C: Faulty though? [Pause] [A little playfully] Illogical, alogic, alogical, alogy?

M: [*Book being opened, page found*] Alogism. An illogical or irrational statement. Alogical. Non-logical; not based upon reason or formed by an act of judgment; opposed to logic. Alogy. Obs. Absurdity unreasonableness.

C: And analogy?

M: [*Book being opened, page found*] Latin. Analogia. Equality of ratios, proportion. Origin: a term of mathematics. Due proportion; correspondence or adaptation of one thing to another. Equivalency or likeness of relations; resemblance of things with regard to some circumstances or effects. More vaguely, agreement between things, similarity.

C: The parts and the etymology are revealing

M: Etymology is a science in which the consonants count for very little and the vowels for nothing at all.

C: Same?

M: Same wit. The Phoenix of all great wits

C: Not quite.

M: In the etymological sense: the art of measuring ground.

C: What is?

M: Geometry.

C: And because arithmetic science and geometric science are connected, and support one another, the full knowledge of numbers cannot be presented without encountering some geometry, or without seeing that operating in this way on numbers is close to geometry. I submit it to your correction.

M: I think I agree

INVALID FORMAT

2

ISSUE 8 2010

C: [Pensive] Similarity and division. The etymological sense indicates original meaning. This was also the ancient meaning of etymology but now

M: [Interrupting] The process of tracing out and describing the elements of a word with their modifications of form and sense. That branch of linguistic science, which is concerned with determining the origin of

C: [Interrupting] [Impatient] Yes of course.

M: [Singsong] Illogical, alogic, alogical, alogy—is that alliteration?

C: [Sarcastic] It's a list

M: [Sarcastic] I trouble myself about no worldly things, said the Master, nor do I wish to hear about them.

C: Contrary to the etymological

argument, the evolution of meaning, is the design argument; that language is purposeful, that its purpose is reflected in design, that it is invented, that its parts are suited to its function, that it would not work otherwise, and that to use it you must understand the design.

M: [Quizzical] Designed by whom?

C: The Name-Maker, from *Onoma*.

M: That seems

C: [Interrupting] The maxim, by which we commonly conduct ourselves in our reasonings, is, that the objects, of which we have no experience, resemble those, of which we have; that what we have found to be most usual is always most probable; and that where there is an opposition of arguments, we ought to give the preference to such as are founded on the greatest number of past

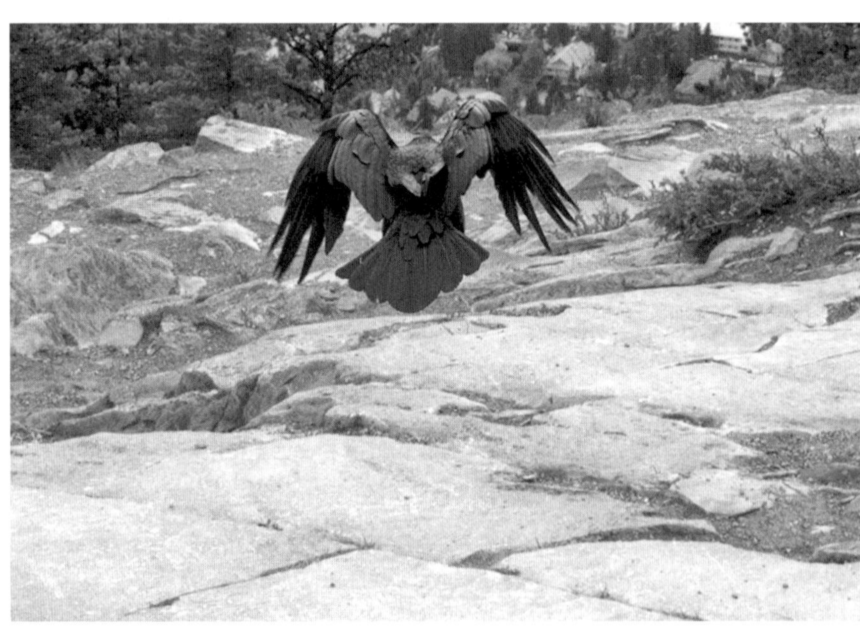

observations. But though, in proceeding by this rule, we readily reject any fact which is unusual and incredible in an ordinary degree; yet in advancing farther, the mind observes not always the same rule; but when anything is affirmed utterly absurd and miraculous, it rather the more readily admits of such a fact, upon account of that very circumstance, which ought to destroy all its authority. The passion of surprise and wonder, arising from miracles, being an agreeable emotion, gives a sensible tendency towards the belief of those events, from which it is derived.

M: But still

C: [Forcefully] It forms a strong presumption against all supernatural and miraculous relations, that they are observed chiefly to abound among ignorant and barbarous nations; or if a civilized people has ever given admission to any of them, that people will be found to have received them from ignorant and barbarous ancestors, who transmitted them with that inviolable sanction and authority, which always attends received opinions. When we peruse the first histories of all nations, we are apt to imagine ourselves transported into some new world; where the whole frame of nature is disjointed, and every element performs its operations in a different manner from what it does at present. Battles, revolutions, pestilence, famine and death, are never the effect of those natural causes, which we experience. Prodigies, omens, oracles, judgments, quite obscure the few natural events that are intermingled with them.

M: I see

C: [Matter of fact] All proceeds from the usual propensity of mankind towards the marvelous, and that, though this inclination may at intervals receive a check from

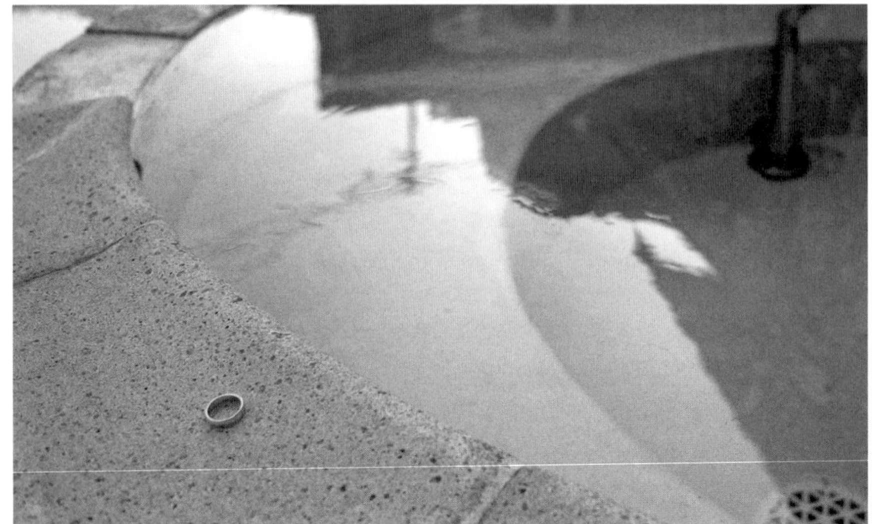

sense and learning, it can never be thoroughly extirpated from human nature.

M: But we shall try it nonetheless?

C: Exactly. The author of language applied, by letters and syllables, its own proper symbol to every object. The L

M: [Interrupting] Illogical, alogic, alogical, alogy

C: The L. He observed that in this letter the tongue glides most smoothly, and so he used this letter for the imitation of whatever is smooth and gliding.

M: L, L, L, L

C: While the G, which arrests this gliding movement, signifies whatever is viscous and sweet.

M: L, L, L. G. L, G. [Short pause] [Drag out] Al-og-y. Obs. Absurdity unreasonableness.

C: Perhaps. D and T, meanwhile, produce a compression of the tongue and are suited to the expression of bondage. Since N kept the voice inwards he used this letter for the word in.

M: N, N, N

C: The letter I

M: [Interrupting] N, N, I

C: I expresses what is fine and subtle and fitted to penetrate through all things, so it is used to imitate the action of going.

M: Going?

C: Clearer in the Greek I think. R was considered appropriate to express every kind of movement since it most agitated the tongue and O the perfect expression of roundness.

M: In the beginning, there was the word

From: ------1@aol.com
Date: April 5, 2009 6:05 p.m.
Subject: SPAM -> (no subject)

Hello:

I never heard of you before. i was researching the mercenary
army called "Triple Canopy" which was, I believe, formed in
2007, using Special Forces veterans:
        Presumably, veterans of the VietNam War, which ended
in 1971 I believe, with the fall of Saigon. However, before
then, Nixon had expanded the Vietnam war into Cambodia and
Laos.
        The term "triple canopy" was first used to describe
the foliage--if you could call it that--which prevented our
bombers from truly laying waste to the place; not that they
didn't do enough damage. Triple canopy was what the jungles
of Southeast Asia were made of: first the ground vegetation;
tall tall 'tiger' grasses (so named because their tough,
tall growth effectively hid the tigers which flourished
during Vietnam), then the interim growth which was mango,
bamboo, orchid vines and the like, and then taller trees .
        Like I said, "Triple Canopy" always meant Southeast
Asia, to me. That is, before we defoliated the place,
killing plants, native Southeast Asians, and of course,
Americans serving in Southeast Asia. Our defoliants--
official dismissals to the contrary--did harm our soldiers,
and the military's still denying it.
        For Shame.
        Meanwhile, what are you? Some kind of lit magazine--
but what kind? War stories from the Johnson/Nixon era? What?
    Cause, if war stories, I got something you'd be
interested in. If I can get through the online copyright
ick--I think they call it "Creative Commons" or something,
LOL! If interested, reply to Val at: ------1@aol.com ⊠

CONTRIBUTORS

Vahram Aghasyan lives and works in Yerevan, Armenia. He has exhibited at the Istanbul Biennial, the Museum Kiasma in Helsinki, and the Contemporary Art Biennale of Thessaloniki, Greece. He recently completed a residency at Künstlerstätte Schloss Bleckede in Germany.

Manal Al Dowayan is an artist based in Saudi Arabia. Her work focuses on the social status of women in her country. She is represented by Cuadro Gallery in Dubai.

Sophia Al-Maria is based in Doha, Qatar, where she works at Mathaf: Arab Museum of Modern Art. Her first book, *The Girl Who Fell to Earth*, will be published in December 2012 by Harper Perennial.

Bidisha Banerjee is a program director at Dalai Lama Fellows, where she created the Head, Heart, and Hands curriculum. She is codesigning an interactive game with the Red Cross Climate Centre and working on a memoir about misremembering the river Ganges.

Joshua Bauchner is an editor and writer living in Brooklyn.

Gil Blank is a photographer and writer based in Portage Bay, Washington. His latest book, *35 Images / The Odyssey*, coauthored with Matthew Stadler, was released by Publication Studio in 2010.

Lev Bratishenko is an architectural journalist and classical-music critic based in Montreal. He is the author of the illustrated guide *How to Eat the Rich*.

José León Cerrillo is an artist living in Mexico City. His work has been shown at Dispatch Projects, New York; Tensta Konsthall, Sweden; Galeria Nara Roesler, São Paulo; East Side Projects, Birmingham, England; Circuit, Lausanne, Switzerland; Proyectos Monclova, Mexico City; and Museo Rufino Tamayo, Mexico City.

Joseph Clarke is an architectural historian. He has taught at the University of Cincinnati and worked at the firms of Eisenman Architects and Skidmore, Owings & Merrill.

Joshua Cohen is the author of *Four New Messages*, *Witz*, *A Heaven of Others*, and *Cadenza for the Schneidermann Violin Concerto*.

George Collins is currently setting thirty-three thousand years of environmental indicators to music and writing three one-act plays about Simon Magus.

Teddy Cruz is an architect and professor of public culture and urbanism at the University of California-San Diego. He recently represented the US at the Venice Architecture Biennale and received the Ford Foundation Visionaries Award. He is the cofounder of the Center for Urban Ecologies.

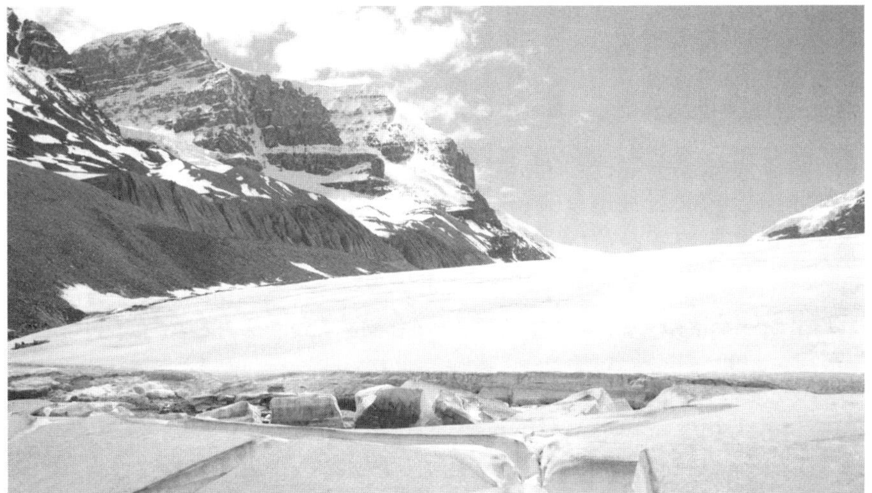

God should not suffer for the stupidity of the priest:
Let us recognize this God, although he is poorly served.

c: There is also our author with whom he disagrees. [Short pause] And himself.

m: [Interrupting] [Dramatically] My lodging is filled with lizards and rats;
But the architect exists, and anyone who denies it
Is touched with madness under the guise of wisdom.
Consult Zoroaster, and Minos, and Solon,
And the martyr Socrates, and the great Cicero:
They all adored a master, a judge, a father.

c: Cicero justly laughs at those who take the poets for good security for any thing they say, when there is so great a difference between the conditions of a poem and that of a history.

m: This sublime system is necessary to man.
It is the sacred tie that binds society,
The first foundation of the holy equity,
The bridle to the wicked, the hope of the just.

c: If every author is a Name-Maker then he himself has three.

m: If the heavens, stripped of his noble imprint,
Could ever cease to attest to his being,
If God did not exist, it would be necessary to invent him.

c: What we have said of miracles may be applied, without any variation, to prophecies; and indeed, all prophecies are real miracles, and as such only, can be admitted as proofs of any revelation. If it did not exceed the capacity of human nature to foretell future events, it would be absurd to employ any prophecy as an argument for a divine mission or authority from heaven. ☒

INVALID FORMAT 2

INSIDE THE MUNDANEUM

Snail mail Google and a card catalogue Web: a fin de siècle Belgian information scientist's proto-Internet.

by Molly Springfield
published March 17, 2010

ISSUE 8 2010

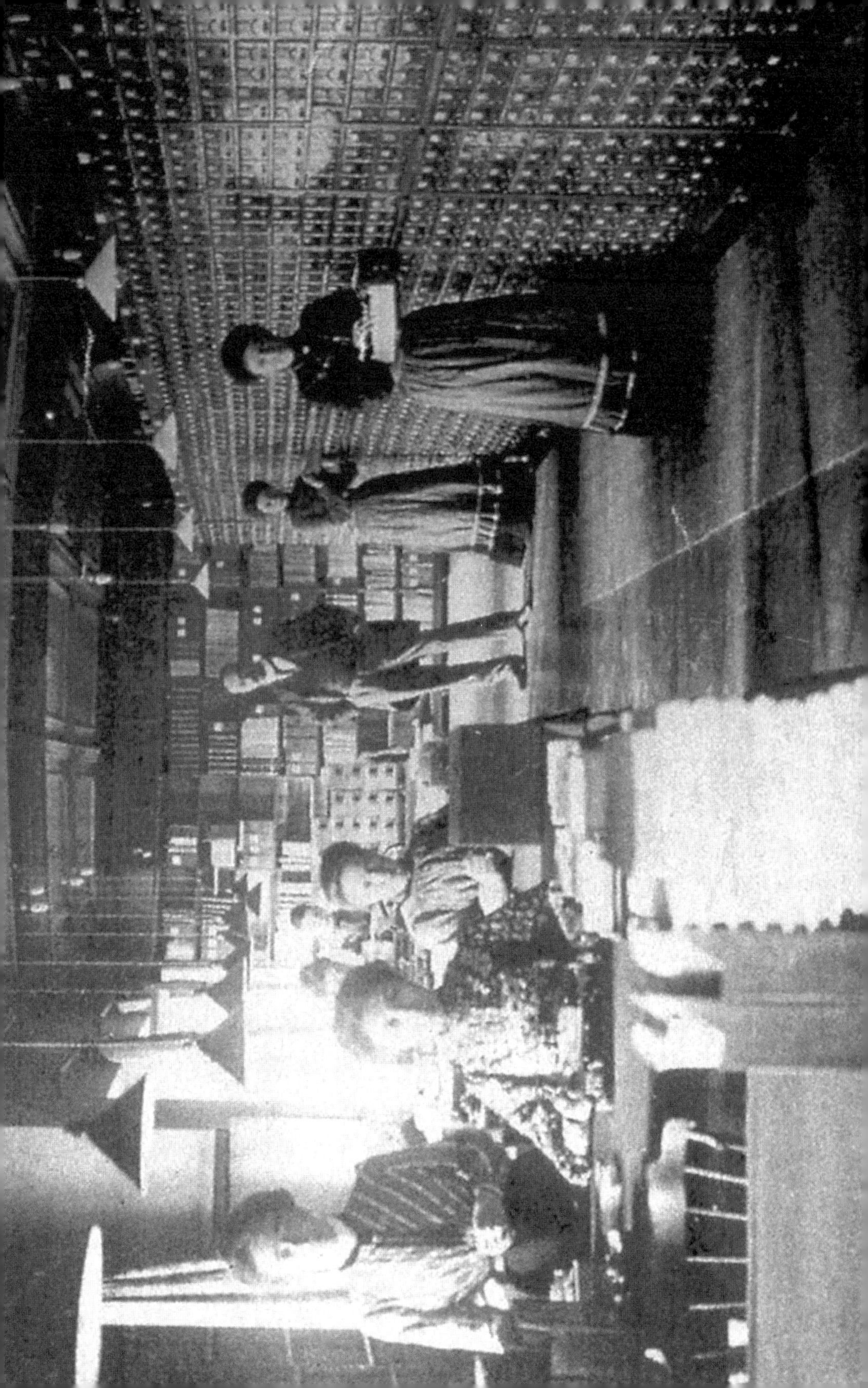

ON THE NIGHT OF JUNE 1, 1934, a Belgian information scientist named Paul Otlet sat in silent, peaceful protest outside the locked doors of a government building in Brussels from which he had just been evicted. Inside was his life's work: a vast archive of more than twelve million bibliographic three-by-five-inch index cards, which attempted to catalogue and cross-reference the relationships among all the world's published information. For Otlet, the archive was at the center of a plan to universalize human knowledge. He called it the Mundaneum, and he believed it would usher in a new era of peace and progress. The Belgian government, however, had come to view Otlet and his fine mess of papers, dusty boxes, and customized filing cabinets as a financial and political nuisance.

Thirteen years earlier, Otlet's Mundaneum—then called the Palais Mondial—had occupied 150 gleaming rooms in the Palais du Cinquatenaire in Brussels. Thousands of visitors a day filed through, marveling at the seven-foot-high card catalogue cabinets lining the walls of an eighty-foot-long room. Otlet and other scholars delivered lectures on topics such as "The Problems of Language" and "The Necessity for Dental Hygiene" in a thousand-seat auditorium. Scores of workers operated the Mundaneum's search service, which employed the card catalogue to answer questions from the public. The queries fielded by Otlet's snail mail Google, writes biographer W. Boyd Rayward, "ranged from intelligence to coagulation of the blood, from Bulgarian finances and comparative statistics for European public debts to the titles of collections of maxims and proverbs from different countries, from the philosophy of mathematics to the boomerang."

Otlet was the first to imagine all the world's knowledge as one vast "web," connected by "links," and accessed remotely through desktop screens, and because of this he can be seen as the kooky grandfather of the Internet. From the beginning of his career as a lawyer and bibliographer, Otlet wrote prolifically and prophetically about how information could be organized and transmitted. He developed the universal decimal classification system, an expanded form of the Dewey decimal classification system that assigned individual numerical subject codes to documents, allowing them to be searched and cross-referenced in a standardized manner. His later writings on information science examined the technological advancements of his time that he regarded as potential substitutes for the book: the radio, television, telephone, and telegraph, sound recordings, cinema, and microfilm (which he developed alongside Robert Goldschmidt). In doing so, Otlet pre-figured the work of computer science pioneers Vannevar Bush, Douglas Engelbart, and Ted Nelson.

The solutions to centrally organizing and disseminating information remained out of Otlet's grasp, as he never lived to see the promises of these technologies fulfilled. He had convinced the Belgian government of the worthiness of his grand endeavor and, perhaps more importantly, that its support would help the country's bid to host the League of Nations. But after losing to Geneva in 1920, expending resources on an enterprise that occupied so much physical space while generating no tangible rewards became less and less appealing to a government in financial straits. Otlet was forced to give up the 150-room suite and move his twelve million index cards to a series of successively more humble quarters, until finally he was thrown out of the Palais.

After his eviction, Otlet moved the Mundaneum to his home, and the paid professional staff gave way to a small band of loyal volunteers. Otlet's wife graciously sold off jewelry and dipped into her personal savings to help finance the upkeep of the archive's dwindling holdings. In his final years, Otlet was reduced to preserving a mountain of paper that nobody wanted. He died the night of December 10, 1944, after working in the Mundaneum well into the evening.

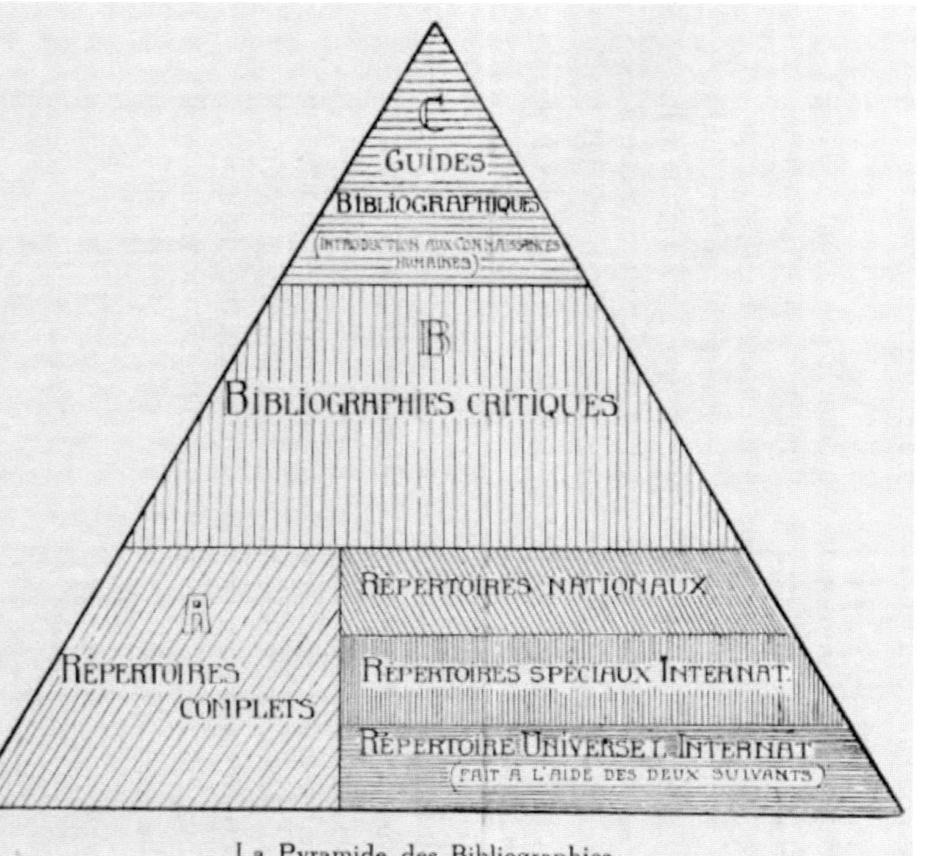

La Pyramide des Bibliographies.

THE BEST GRAIN

In 1883, when Otlet was just fifteen years old, he began classifying his papers and notes into categories such as "Literature," "Personal," and "Sciences." He was an earnest and sensitive young man who hoped to perform "some magnanimous and useful task for society" and believed he could accomplish that goal by practicing law. Soon after graduating from the Free University, he installed himself in Brussels and found work as a law clerk. But legal practice didn't satisfy his intellectual or altruistic goals. In 1891, he met Henri La Fontaine, who was directing the bibliography division of a newly formed professional association of prominent Belgian political- and social-science scholars. In La Fontaine, Otlet found the intellectual companionship he lacked in his professional life, and the two men became lifelong friends and collaborators.

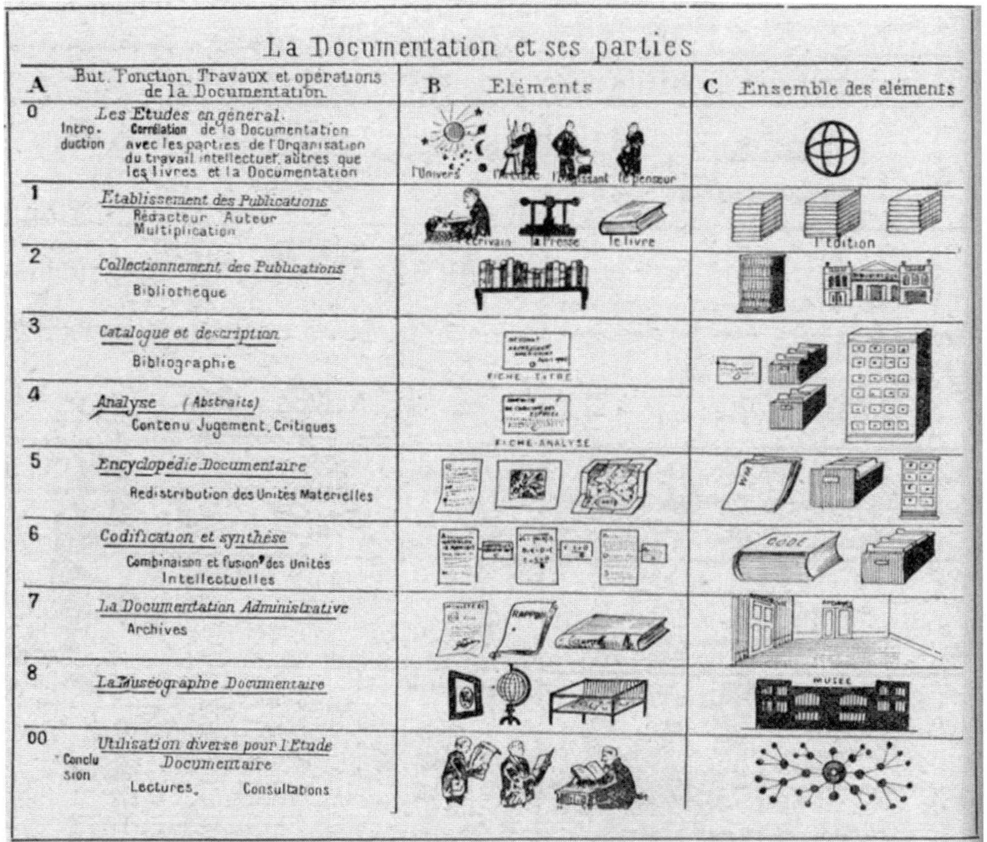

La Documentation et ses parties

A — But. Fonction. Travaux et opérations de la Documentation	B — Eléments	C — Ensemble des éléments
0 Intro-duction — *Les Etudes en géneral.* **Corrélation** de la Documentation avec les parties de l'Organisation du travail intellectuel, autres que les livres et la Documentation	l'Univers … le penseur	
1 *Etablissement des Publications* — Rédacteur Auteur Multiplication	l'Ecrivain — la Presse — le livre	l'Edition
2 *Collectionnement des Publications* — Bibliothèque		
3 *Catalogue et description* — Bibliographie	FICHE-TITRE	
4 *Analyse (Abstraits)* — Contenu Jugement. Critiques	FICHE-ANALYSE	
5 *Encyclopédie Documentaire* — Redistribution des Unités Materielles		
6 *Codification et synthèse* — Combinaison et fusion des Unités Intellectuelles		CODE
7 *La Documentation Administrative* — Archives	RAPPORT	
8 *La Museographie Documentaire*		MUSEE
00 Conclu-sion — *Utilisation diverse pour l'Etude Documentaire* — Lectures. Consultations		

La Documentation et ses parties

During this time, Otlet laid out what would be the guiding principles of his career in an article titled "Something about Bibliography." He believed that to make sense of the rapid accumulation of published material, avoid redundant research, and facilitate the creation of new scholarship it was vital to establish a definitive system of classification, "so that anyone can retrieve [documents] immediately in order to use them and to push ahead, to know at every moment what has been done and what remains to be done."

Central to this belief was Otlet's concept of the document, which extended beyond the written or printed word to include anything with evidentiary value—a photograph, a piece of music, a painting. Any document, whatever its form, should be "winnow[ed] to conserve the best grain."

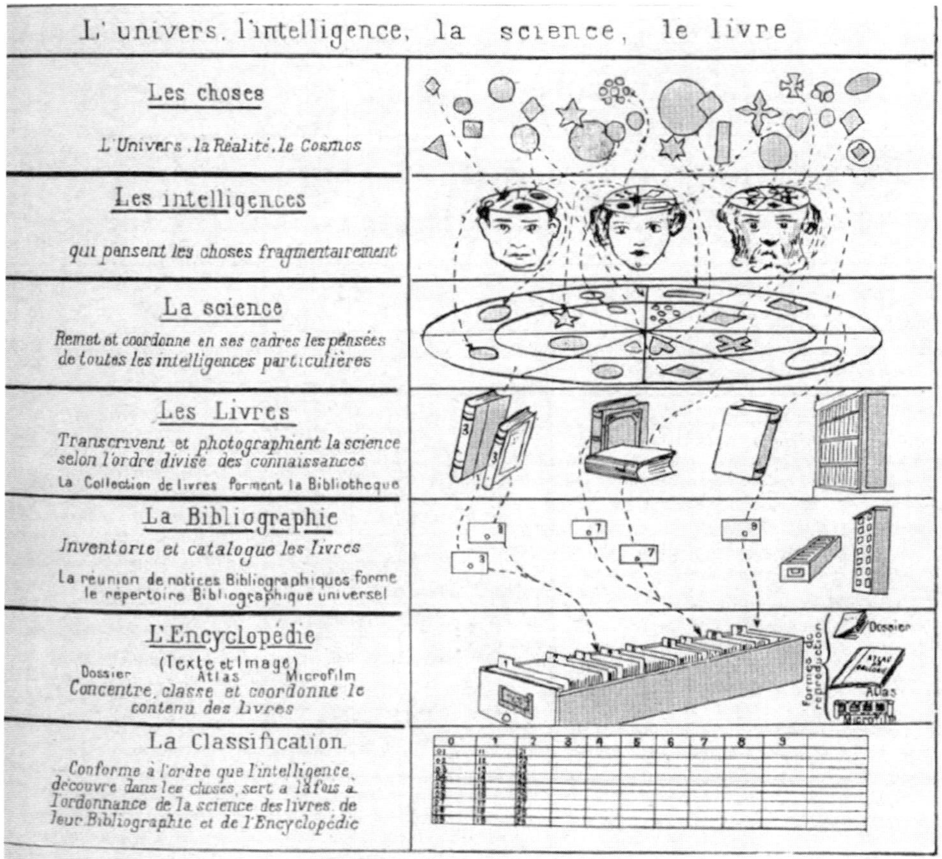

L'univers, l'intelligence, la science, le livre

L'Univers, l'Intelligence, la Science, le Livre

Ideas and facts would then be independent of their physical medium, allowing them to be organized into an easily searchable, universal system. In practical terms, this would be accomplished by extracting the substance of all of the world's documents and recording it on standardized three-by-five-inch cards, either by cutting and pasting from the original document or copying by hand. The cards would then be placed in a general bibliographic card repertory and divided and subdivided by general and specific subjects.

By 1894, Otlet had amassed more than one hundred thousand cards in his bibliographic repertory, and he went in search of an efficient management structure for his collection. After obtaining and studying a copy of Melvil Dewey's decimal classification system, originally published in 1876, Otlet wrote to Dewey asking for the European translation rights and permission to adapt his existing system to the needs of the International Institute of Bibliography, which Otlet and La Fontaine had founded in 1893.

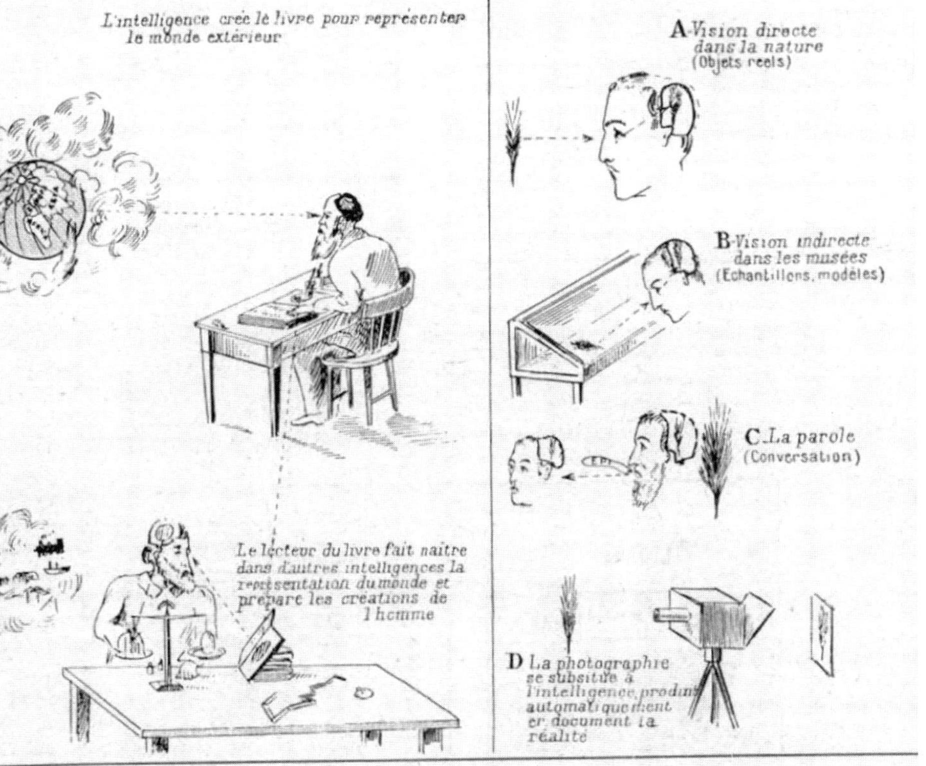

Dewey agreed to both requests, and Otlet and La Fontaine quickly set to work, hosting the first International Conference of Bibliography in Brussels in September of 1895. The librarians, bibliographers, and scholars in attendance unanimously passed a series of resolutions formally establishing the institute and adopting decimal classification as their standard.

In Otlet's view, the rational, scientific language of numbers and symbols used in decimal classification was the ideal way to express the "links, the genealogy even, of ideas and objects, their relationships of dependence and subordination, of similarity and difference." Whatever could not be expressed numerically—whatever Otlet considered "conventional and arbitrary"—would be eliminated.

WHY SHOULD IT NOT BE POSSIBLE?

Otlet's creation of the Mundaneum is one of those rare, transformative moments in history—a point when some visionary fundamentally reimagines the way we organize, reproduce, and experience information. In the preceding centuries, others had envisioned memory theaters, curiosity cabinets, and various classification systems to collect and organize cultural artifacts. But Otlet's vision was focused on pure information, not objects, and was distinguished by its universality and its emphasis on establishing the connections between bodies of knowledge, thus providing a blueprint for today's Internet.

Over the past few years, I have searched out such transformative moments and attempted to visualize them through drawings and installations. I found one in William Henry Fox Talbot's invention of negative-positive photography, which revolutionized the ways that images and text could be reproduced. In *The Pencil of Nature* (1844), the world's first book of photographic reproductions, Talbot relates the revelation that sparked his scientific accomplishment. Photography, it turns out, began its life as a substitute for drawing. In 1833, on his honeymoon in Italy, Talbot had tried to sketch the landscape surrounding Lake Como with the aid of a camera lucida. Unhappy with his "melancholy" results, he speculated, "How charming it would be if it were possible to cause these natural images to imprint themselves durably, and remain fixed upon the paper! And why should it not be possible?" He went on to develop the chemistry necessary to produce photographic negatives, but his invention began as an epiphanic vision—an artistic impulse to permanently capture light and shadow. He called it "photogenic drawing."

While Talbot was inspired to preserve an objective image of nature, one that would not be disfigured immediately by the hand or later by the mind, the narrator of Marcel Proust's *In Search of Lost Time* suggests the impossibility of such an endeavor when he dips his madeleine into a cup of tea, stirring the well of memory. Involuntary memory of the sort Proust describes gives you back everything—"all of Combray and its surroundings, all of this, acquiring form and solidity, emerged, town and gardens alike, from my cup of tea." But the narrator's mental photograph of Combray is a subjective one, unique to him alone.

Proust exalted art's ability to reveal and express our hidden, interior worlds. By immersing yourself in and reflecting deeply on your mental impressions, aided by physical objects, you could access "the book inside." All the information you need, and all the tools to access it, are contained within you. What Proust shared with Talbot and Otlet was a fervent desire to establish dominion over how we experience information about the world—whether through a photograph, a memory, or a numerical code. But unlike Talbot, whose solutions could be realized using available technology, or even Proust, whose technology of the self requires only time and a willingness to engage in reflection, Otlet left us not with blueprints for action so much as science-fictional fantasies—more H. G. Wells than Thomas Edison. (Indeed, Wells, just a few years after Otlet, conceived of a "world brain" that would be accessed through an "information highway.") Otlet's published writings and personal notebooks contain strange, charming illustrations of telecommunicative desks and spiraling structures that would house the archive. Such visions of the future rarely coincide with reality, but they are necessary because they enable later generations to expand the parameters of the possible.

THE MOVING IMAGE OF THE WORLD

The universal decimal classification was published in stages between 1904 and 1907. By 1907, it was more than two thousand pages. (Today, the UDC's core version has 65,000 subdivisions and is available in a database format called the Master Reference File; the full version has 220,000 subdivisions.) As the universal decimal classification's tables and card catalogues grew, so did Otlet's ambitions. He began to see the Mundaneum "as an encyclopedic survey of human knowledge, as an enormous intellectual warehouse of books, documents, catalogs, and scientific objects" that would "tend progressively to constitute a permanent and complete representation of the entire world." The archive would become the center of a utopian "city of the intellect," where all the world's knowledge would be collected and preserved, and where the free exchange of information and ideas would foster world peace. He collaborated with architects and urban planners to draw up plans for the city; when Brussels lost its bid for the League of Nations to Geneva in 1920, Otlet commissioned Le Corbusier to design a Mundaneum for that city. Though actual plans for the Geneva Mundaneum never materialized, achieving peace remained more than an abstract goal for Otlet, who experienced the heartbreak of war personally: In 1914, his older son, Marcel, was captured and held prisoner by German troops; Jean, his other son, was lost in the Battle of the Yser. Otlet searched the battlefield for Jean's body, but it was never recovered.

Gradually, as he fell out of favor with the Belgian government, Otlet became less concerned with the practical functions of the various bureaucratic institutions he had helped create. He focused obsessively on sustaining the Mundaneum's collections and working on his own scholarship, which grew more and more abstract. In 1935, ten years before Vannevar Bush published his seminal *Atlantic* essay describing his memex machine, "As We May Think," Otlet published *Monde*, a further distillation of the concepts embodied in the Mundaneum. In it, he also described a communications system that "would combine . . . radio, x-rays, cinema and microscopic photography" and that approximates the dreams of the Internet's pioneers:

> All the things of the universe and all those of man would be registered from afar as they were produced. Thus the moving image of the world would be established—its memory, its true duplicate. From afar anyone would be able to read the passage, expanded or

limited to the desired subject, that could be projected on his individual screen. Thus, in his armchair, anyone would be able to contemplate the whole of creation.

The previous year, as the Belgian government was shuttering the Mundaneum, Otlet had published *Traité de documentation*, the first modern treatise on information science. In it, he writes of the "radical assumption" that

all knowledge, all information could be so condensed that it could be contained in a limited number of works placed on a desk.... The Universal Book created from all books would become very approximately an annex to the brain, a substratum even of memory, an external mechanism and instrument of the mind but so close to it, so apt to its use that it would truly be a sort of appended organ, an exodermic appendage.

He goes on to describe a kind of steampunk Jeffersonian cabinet, a "scholar's work station" constructed of multiple movable surfaces and screens connected to a movable filing cabinet. From this tricked-out desk, scholars could connect remotely via a telephone-based system—something like a facsimile transmission network—to a central database.

Today's universal book—the Internet—is not the "true duplicate" of our world. But it has become an "annex to the brain," a supplemental memory, at the individual and communal level. It is both a place where the contents of the

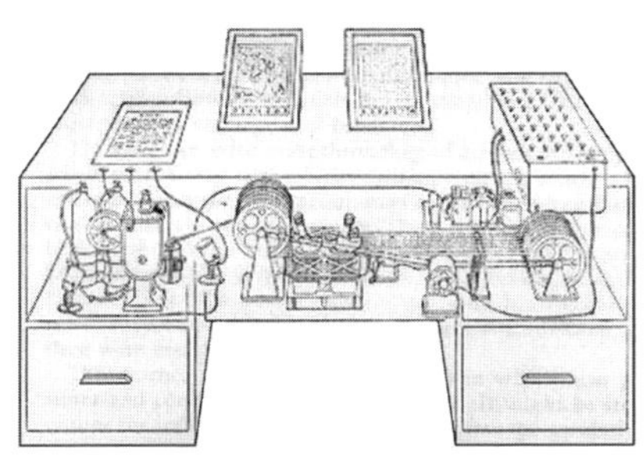

Drawing of Vannevar Bush's Memex machine.

world's libraries are being meticulously preserved and one where anyone can chronicle their thoughts and feelings on nothing in particular, for no one in particular. The former fits within the boundaries of searchable codes and terms; the latter cannot be assigned a universal decimal classification number. It is often in these indefinable, unclassifiable places, like the margins of a page, where new ideas are found.

People have a limitless capacity to shake off established categories and forge previously overlooked connections between ideas. Otlet's tendency to neglect these possibilities—his unyielding devotion to universal classification—was his greatest limitation.

After Otlet's death, what remained of the Mundaneum's collections was stored in an old, damp, leaky room in an anatomy building in the Free University of Brussels. There it moldered, until it was discovered in the late 1970s. Now the Mundaneum is permanently installed as a museum in Mons, Belgium, where it is open to the public. Researchers are scanning the remaining documents. Eventually, you will be able to do what Otlet intended: contemplate the whole of creation—or at least the limited slice contained in the Mundaneum—from the comfort of your armchair.

THE MARGINALIA ARCHIVE

We live in a world where Otlet's vision has been realized, at least in part. The information we consume is increasingly dematerialized; many of the world's printed texts now have digital twins that are instantly available and searchable. We no longer have to reread a book to find a single quotation; plugging a few keywords into a search engine will call it from the ether.

In the *Phaedrus*, Socrates worried that reliance on the new technology of writing would lead to intellectual laziness. Rather than depending on our own memories to store knowledge, we would let ink and paper hold our personal and cultural histories and, in the process, sacrifice real understanding for the appearance of it. Socrates was right:

Writing (and Googling) does make us less reliant on our own stores of knowledge. But the larger point to be drawn from the *Phaedrus* is that information technologies change culture ineradicably. What will happen to our intimate relationships with texts when their tactile, material forms are eliminated entirely?

A few years ago, I began sending letters to friends and family asking them to send me photocopies of texts they had annotated. Enclosed with my letter was a form asking for basic bibliographic information on the chosen text and why it was chosen. I was interested in exploring how the relationship readers have with a text manifests itself physically in the form of handwritten marginalia. Long before Internet-based social networking, marginalia enabled readers to share responses to texts with one another, and a distinctive literary culture grew up around the practice.

An eighteenth-century reader's marginalia might have referenced other sources and preserved the successive layers of commentary left by previous readers. Here is marginalia scholar H. J. Jackson on the culture of annotation in the eighteenth century: "Writers of marginalia at this time usually worked with an audience in mind, not a nebulous scholarly community merely, but known individuals in their own social circles."

As contributions trickled in, I began to wonder whether I could use the accumulating submissions to populate a kind of library of marginalia in which, contra Otlet, the "best grains" would be the material traces (the underlines, doodles, and notes) of reader's reactions, both immediate and considered. Instead of classifying the submissions by subject, I plan to organize my archive around the participants' personal and idiosyncratic reasons for choosing and annotating a particular text. As a library, the result won't be much use to anyone, but perhaps it will make us think about the way we record, catalogue, and exchange our thoughts in an era of incessant communication, when the material products of our reading and writing are increasingly overlooked. ⊠

ISSUE 8 2010   INVALID FORMAT 2

THIRTY-SIX SHADES OF PRUSSIAN BLUE

Reading the world's first artificial color.

by Joshua Cohen
published March 17, 2010

ARTISTS IN THE WEST had no reliable blue until the early eighteenth century. Ultramarine, extracted from the blue stone called lapis lazuli, was said to have once been more expensive than gold, and Renaissance artists had to negotiate with their patrons for individual drops of blue upon receiving their commissions (*ultramarine* means, literally, "over the sea," because most lapis was imported from Afghanistan). Indigo, derived from plants of the *Indigofera* genus, tended to blacken, and was not lightfast, while azurite, derived from the mineral of the same name, turned green when mixed with water, and so was unusable for frescoes, which were painted *affresco*, translating to "fresh," with the implication of "wet." Smalt, a ground glass colored with cobalt, would fade, and the chemical properties of copper were not yet understood; there was no way to consistently create blue from that metal, as opposed to green, or a tint somewhere between. It is commonly agreed that "Prussian blue"—the painter's first stable blue—was the palette's first synthesized color: $Fe(CN)_{18}(H_2O)_x$, where $14 \leq x \leq 16$ . . .

What follows is a portrait of that color—or a "blueprint" of its origins and use—through chemistry, painting, photography, industry, warfare, Holocaust, and nuclear terrorism.

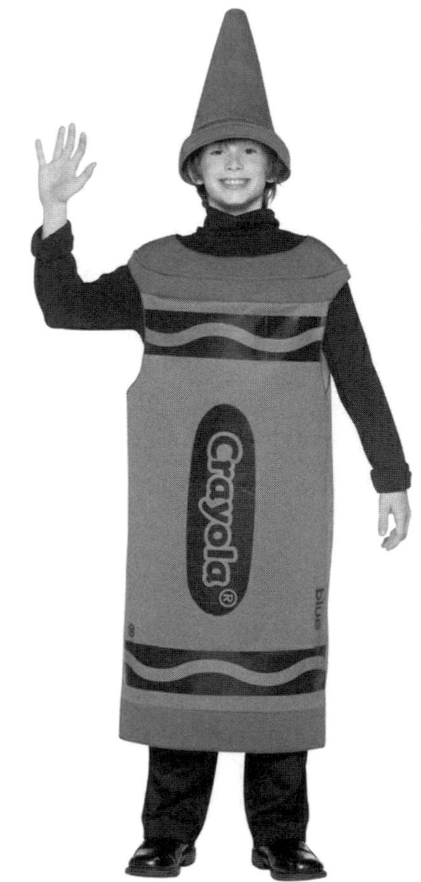

blue *n.* The hue of that portion of the visible spectrum lying between green and indigo, evoked in the human observer by radiant energy with wavelengths of approximately 420 to 490 nanometers; any of a group of colors that may vary in lightness and saturation, whose hue is that of a clear daytime sky; one of the additive or light primaries; one of the psychological primary hues.
—*American Heritage Dictionary of the English Language*, 4th ed.

Dippel's Animal Oil: Johann Konrad Dippel (1673–1734) was born at Castle Frankenstein near Darmstadt, the son of a Lutheran pastor. He became a master theologian, publishing under the name *Christianus Democritus*, but succumbed to the lure of alchemy, signing himself *Frankensteinensis*. Having failed to make gold, he launched his *elixir vitae*—a medicinal "animal oil"—upon an unsuspecting public in 1700. Dippel's oil was a malodorous distillate of the unconsidered residues of animal carcasses—blood, bones and offal. His predilection for body parts may have later inspired Mary Shelley, when she visited Castle Frankenstein in 1814, on her elopement with Percy. We now know Dippel's oil to consist of a mixture of nitrogenous organic bases such as pyrrole, and several alkyl cyanides. At the time it was hailed as a panacea—presumably sustained by the widely-held belief that anything so obnoxious must be beneficial. In 1704 Dippel supplied the artists' colourmaker, Heinrich Diesbach of Berlin, with an impure sample of alkali that was contaminated with his oil. By chance, this provided the essential ingredient—cyanide—to enable Diesbach's serendipitous discovery of the first synthetic pigment, Prussian blue or Turnbull's blue. All painters thereafter have reason to be grateful to this unscrupulous alchemist, who, after numerous scrapes with European royalty, died at Castle Wittgenstein, possibly a victim of his own elixir.
—Roger Jones, *What's Who? A Dictionary of Things Named After People and the People They Are Named After*

Prussian Blue: *Turnbull's Blue—Antwerp Blue—Berlin Blue—Prussiate of Iron—Chinese Blue—Saxon Blue—Bleu de Berlin—Pariser-blau*
—Arthur Herbert Church, *The Chemistry of Paints and Painting*

It has been alleged, that the ancients were acquainted with Prussian blue, which they employed in painting; but Landriani has shown, in his dissertation on this substance, from the evidence of Theophrastus and Pliny, and from the analysis of an Egyptian mummy, that the ancients employed ultramarine blue and the smalt or azure of cobalt; and that Prussian blue, which is readily acted on by the substances to which it must have been exposed in these countries, could not have resisted their influence for so many ages, and retain the beautiful colours, which are admired in the paintings of Herculaneum.

Stahl relates, in his 300 experiments, that the discovery of Prussian blue was owing to an accident. About the beginning of the 18th century, Diesbach, a chemist of Berlin, wishing to precipitate a decoction of cochineal with an alkali, borrowed from Dippel some potash, on which he had distilled several times his animal oil; but as there was some sulphate of iron in the decoction of cochineal, the liquor instantly exhibited a beautiful blue in place of a red precipitate. Reflecting on the circumstances which had taken place, he found that it was easy to produce at pleasure the same substance, which afterwards became an object of commerce.

The pigment was accepted by artists much earlier than previously assumed, as can be proven on the basis of a number of examples. To date, the painting *Entombment of Christ* (Picture Gallery, Sanssouci, Potsdam, dated 1709) by Pieter van der Werff is the oldest known painting that makes use of Prussian blue. Around 1710, painters at the Prussian court such as Pesne, Gericke, Manyóki, and Weidemann were already using the pigment to a surprisingly large extent. At around the same time, Prussian blue arrived in Paris, where Watteau and later his successors Lancret and Pater used it in their paintings.
—Jens Bartoll, *The Early Use of Prussian Blue in Paintings*

Dry thoroughly in an iron vessel and powder grossly, any quantity of fresh blood. Dry thoroughly and powder also a quantity of pearl ash equal to the powdered blood. Mix them, and calcine them in a low red heat in a crucible with a loose cover until all smoke and flame ceases: then make the cover fit close, and calcine in a full red or nearly white heat for half an hour. The crucible should not be more than two thirds full, as the mixture is apt to swell. Empty the contents of the crucible into warm water in the proportion of a quart to four oz. of the mixture. Pour on again as much warm water: mix and filter the solutions. Dissolve of sulphat of iron (green vitriol) and of alum, of each a quantity equal to one half of the pearl ash employed. Pour the solution of alum and green vitriol mixt together, gradually into the solution of blood and alkali: both solutions are better for being warm, but not boiling hot. Stir it well. Let the sediment settle. It will be of a dirty greenish colour: wash it. Then digest it for 2 or 3 days in diluted muriatic acid (spirit of salt one part, water two parts). The colour by this means gradually becomes blue, because the muriatic acid dissolves the yellow oxyd of iron which is not combined with the prussic acid. Wash it repeatedly. Dry it on chalk stones, paper, linen, or any other mode of draining off the water. Spread it thin to expose it to the air. I have kept the lixivium of blood and alkali (prussiat of potash) for a year and a half in bottles, and used it to make prussian blue with equal success as at first. Chippings of hoofs answer equally well with blood.
—John Redman Coxe and Thomas Cooper, *The Emporium of Arts and Sciences*

A number of apparently old paintings have been betrayed by the presence of Prussian Blue: and *Entrance to the Cannaregio* once firmly attributed to Francesco Guardi was hurriedly relabeled "Imitator of Guardi" when it was found to contain Cobalt Blue, invented nine years after Guardi's death.
—David Bomford, *The History of Colour in Art*

The earliest painting on which De Wilde reports [Prussian blue] is one by J. E. La Farque, dated 1770.
—Rutherford John Gettens and George Leslie Stout, *Painting Materials: A Short Encyclopedia*

Shall the names of so many of
our colors continue to be derived
from those of obscure foreign
localities, as Naples yellow,
Prussian blue, raw Sienna,
burnt Umber, Gamboge? (surely
the Tyrian purple must have
faded by this time), or from
comparatively trivial articles of
commerce,—chocolate, lemon,
coffee, cinnamon, claret? (shall
we compare our hickory to a
lemon, or a lemon to a hickory?)
or from ores and oxides which
few ever see?
—Henry David Thoreau,
Autumnal Tints

Rossetti walked round Ruskin's class-room one evening, when the latter was absent. "How's this?"
he said; "nothing but blue studies—can't any of you see any colour but blue?" "It was by Mr. Ruskin's
directions," one of the students answered. "Well, where do you get all this Prussian blue from?" asked
Rossetti; and then, opening a cupboard, "Well, I declare, here's a packet with several dozen cakes of
this fearful colour. Oh, I can't allow it; Mr. Ruskin will spoil everybody's eye for colour—I shall confis-
cate the whole lot; I must do it, in the interests of his and my pupils. You must tell him that I've taken
them all away." When a few evenings later Ruskin was told what had happened, he "burst into one of
those boisterous laughs in which he indulged whenever anything very much amused him."
—Edward Cook, *The Life of John Ruskin*

Prooshan Blue. A term of great endear-
ment. After the battle of Waterloo the
Prussians were immensely popular
in England, and in connection with
the Loyal True Blue Club gave rise to
the toasts, "The True Blue" and the
"Prussian Blue." Sam Weller [Dickens's
Pickwick Papers] addresses his father
with "Vell, my Prooshan Blue."
—*Brewer's Dictionary*

The colours which approach the dark side, and conse-
quently, blue in particular, can be made to approximate to
black; in fact, a very perfect Prussian blue, or an indigo
acted on by vitriolic acid appears almost as a black.
—Johann Wolfgang von Goethe, *Theory of Colors*

As a manufactured color, Prussian blue,
like Naples yellow, Turner's yellow, and
Scheele's green, involved materials and
production methods that crossed the
traditional boundaries of several groups:
colormakers, apothecaries, drysalters, and
manufacturing chemists. Production rights
were frequently in dispute. In France, sale
of painters' materials was a responsibility of the painters' guild (the Académie de
St-Luc). Manufactured colors, when they
did not use traditional coloring materials
or did not use them in traditional ways,
threatened this closely guarded right. In
1764, masters from the Académie de St-Luc
seized the Prussian blue factory of sieurs
Gly and d'Heure. The owners turned to
the Paris Academy of Sciences, asking for
a determination of the nature of Prussian
blue. Gly and d'Heure argued that theirs
was a chemical factory with no connection
to the art of painting, even though painters
used their product. Jean Hellot examined
the problem on behalf of the Academy, and
agreed with the manufacturers. Prussian
blue is a product of chemistry and should
not be controlled by the painters' guild.
The factory in the faubourg Saint-Marcel
was allowed to reopen and continued to
make Prussian blue through the next four
decades; theirs was often considered the
best that was made in Paris.
—Sarah Lowengard, *The Creation of Color
in Eighteenth-Century Europe*

A simple blue sky: Prussian Blue,
Antwerp Blue or Cobalt Blue.
Grass in shadow: Prussian Blue and
Indian Red; or Prussian Blue and
Burnt Sienna. Aurora Yellow and
Prussian Blue gives a green color
similar to Emerald.
—*Cyclopedia of Drawing,*
ed. Alfred E. Zapf

And that is how I caught Cézanne off guard,
coming along bent over in thought. His face
like a potter's, sun-burned, looked startled
as the shadow of nearby leaves played over
it. He had a small, bony head with rosy skin,
lively eyes, and a white mustache, carelessly
smeared with prussian blue.
—Jules Borély, *Conversations with Cézanne*

I find Prussian blue
is the only blue that
retains its exact color-
cast under *artificial
light*, and since a
picture is so often
seen in such light, I
deem this worthy of
consideration.
—John F. Carlson,
*Elementary Principles
of Landscape Painting*

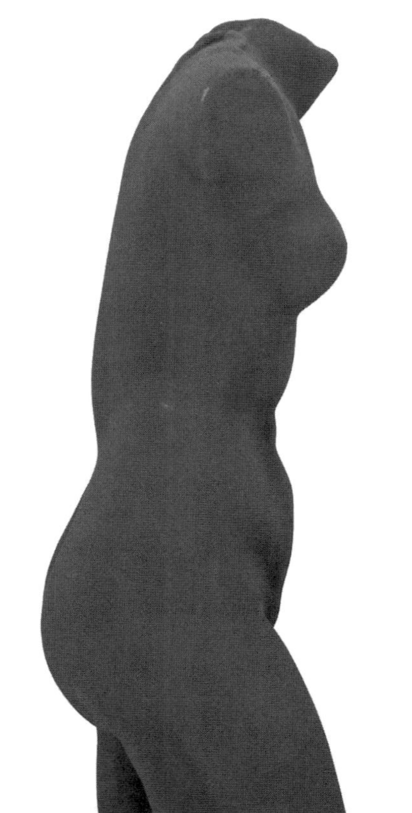

This Prussian blue is the most subtle and invading color
on the palette. It is like those articles marked "made in
Germany," which go everywhere. It was the cause of the
ruder manifestations of French *esprit* being abandoned in the
Atelier Picot. This is the tradition: A new student one day was
stripped, tied to a ladder, painted all over with Prussian blue,
and then set out in the street, leaning against a wall. One can
easily imagine how the police went into the matter, and one
acquainted with Prussian blue can imagine how they came
out. The whole quarter must have been tinged with blue.
—Elihu Vedder, *Reminiscences of an American Painter*

Mr. Wordsworth loved
all that was rich and
picturesque, light and
free, in clothing. A deep
Prussian blue, or purple,
was one of his favourite
colours for a silk dress.
—*Memoirs of Sara
Coleridge*

One should not work Prussian blue into one's
drawing of a face; for then it ceases to be
flesh and becomes wood.
—Vincent van Gogh, letter to his brother Theo

Paper simply washed with a solution of this salt is highly sensitive to the action of light. Prussian blue is deposited (the base being necessarily supplied by the destruction of one portion of the acid, and the acid by decomposition of another). After half an hour or an hour's exposure to sunshine, a very beautiful negative photograph is the result, to fix which, all that is necessary is to soak it in water in which a little sulphate of soda is dissolved, to insure the fixity of the Prussian blue deposited. While dry the impression is dove colour or lavender-blue, which has a curious and striking effect on the greenish-yellow ground of the paper, produced by the saline solution. After washing, the ground colour disappears, and the photograph becomes bright blue on a white ground. If too long exposed, it gets "over-sunned," and the tint has a brownish or yellowish tendency, which however is removed in fixing; but no increase of intensity beyond a certain point is obtained by continuance of exposure.
—Sir J. F. W. Herschel, *On the Action of the Rays of the Solar Spectrum on Vegetable Colours, and on some new Photographic Processes*

"You only need three colours, you know. Very simple." "Which colours are they?" I inquire ignorantly. "Why, you know of course," he says surprised. "Burnt sienna, cadmium yellow, and—er—there! I can't think of it. I know it as well as I know my own face. So do you. Well, that's stupid of me."
Or, his worn eyes dwelling benignantly upon my duffle-bag, he warns me (in a low voice) of Prussian Blue.
—E. E. Cummings, *The Enormous Room*

Your hair's a mass of Prussian blue,
The helmet of an amazon—
No thought has ever broken through,
No blush was ever seen upon
That brow, encased in Prussian blue.
—Charles Baudelaire, *Rara Avis, or, The Nymphomaniad*

Ah, yes—on the darkened parade square there was still a ring of torches and, surprisingly, the strains of military music. There was but one silence, the same for all the skies of prussian blue, and indeed for the plains as well. The dark is so uniquely uniform, so unifying in its uniformity!
—Max Jacob, *The Bouchaballe Property*

National uniform color was simply tradition. At a distance, an army's colors proved incomprehensible save for the Austrians who wore white and the British who wore red. At cannon shot, Prussian blue was much like French blue, and the Russian green was not distinguishable from either of them. Cavalry regiments were particularly difficult to distinguish at longer range, and friendly fire was a constant threat from enthusiastic gunners.
—Roman Jarymowycz, *Cavalry from Hoof to Track*

You are a hundred thousand times welcome, old wort-sampler, hellbeit you're just about as culpable as my woolfell merger would be. In effect I could engage in an energument over you till you were republicly royally toobally prussic blue in the shirt after. Trionfante di bestia!
—James Joyce, *Finnegans Wake*

If, for instance, you were ordered to paint a particular shade of blue called "Prussian Blue," you might have to use a table to lead you from the word "Prussian Blue," to a sample of the color, which would serve you as your copy.
—Ludwig Wittgenstein, *The Blue Book*

If it is the middle of the day, however, discard the use of umber as a substitute for Prussian blue.
—Larry Rivers and Frank O'Hara, *How to Proceed in the Arts*

Morally Chichikov was hardly guilty of any special crime in attempting to buy up dead men in a country where live men were lawfully purchased and pawned. If I paint my face with home made Prussian Blue instead of applying the Prussian Blue which is sold by the state and cannot be manufactured by private persons, my crime will be hardly worth a passing smile and no writer will make of it a Prussian tragedy. But if I have surrounded the whole business with a good deal of mystery and flaunted a cleverness that presupposed most intricate difficulties in perpetrating a crime of that kind, and if owing to my letting a garrulous neighbor peep at my pots of home-brewn paint I get arrested and am roughly handled by men with authentic blue faces, then the laugh for what it is worth is on me.
—Vladimir Nabokov, *Nikolai Gogol*

Blue, *Prussian* (usually with black—with yellow for special greens)
Avoid blue in mixtures because of its imbecile atmospheric tendency
—Marcel Duchamp, *The Bride's Veil*

Perhaps the most spectacular secret ink is Prussian blue, which forms by means of a chemical reaction between ferric sulfate and potassium ferrocyanide. Generally, a message written with ferric sulfate solution will be revealed when it is sprayed with ferrocyanide. A spy can soak fabric with each of these solutions and transport secret information without detection. During World War II a German spy named George Vaux Bacon made notations on his socks and cloth buttons with the secret ink reagents. He, too, was caught and executed.
—Joe Schwarcz, *The Genie in the Bottle, 67 All-New Commentaries on the Fascinating Chemistry of Everyday Life*

Forensic samples were taken from the visited sites. A control sample was removed from delousing facility 1 at Birkenau. It was postulated that because of the high iron content of the building materials at these camps the presence of hydrogen cyanide gas [Zyklon-B] would result in a ferric-ferro-cyanide compound being formed, as evidenced by the Prussian Blue staining on the walls in the delousing facilities.

A detailed analysis of the thirty-two samples taken at the Auschwitz-Birkenau complexes showed 1,050 mg/kg of cyanide and 6,170 mg/kg of iron. Higher iron results were found at all of the alleged gas chambers but no significant cyanide traces. This would be impossible if these sites were exposed to hydrogen cyanide gas, because the alleged gas chambers supposedly were exposed to much greater quantities of gas than the delousing facility. Thus, chemical analysis supports the fact that these facilities were never utilized as gas execution facilities.
—Fred A. Leuchter Jr., *The Leuchter Report*

People may have blue feces (stool) during the time that they are taking Prussian blue.
—Centers for Disease Control and Prevention, fact sheet on Prussian blue

Hydrogen cyanide (HCN), also known as hydrocyanic acid, prussic acid or *Blausäure* was the toxic agent in Zyklon-B. Strictly speaking, the term hydrogen cyanide should be used for the pure compound and the term hydrocyanic acid reserved for its aqueous solutions, but this convention has been ignored so much that it is pointless to insist upon it. HCN is a high vapor pressure liquid; the Merck index lists its boiling point as 25.6 degrees Celsius (78.8 degrees Fahrenheit), significantly less than human body temperature. At room temperature (25 d C, 77 d F) the equilibrium vapor pressure of HCN is 750 Torr (760 Torr = 1 atmosphere), corresponding to 987,000 ppm. At 0 C (32 F) it is 260 Torr corresponding to 342,000 ppm. The Merck index warns, "Exposure to 150 ppm for 1/2 to 1 hr may endanger life. Death may result from a few min exposure to 300 ppm." Clearly, it is not necessary to reach equilibrium vapor pressure in order for the fumes of the liquid to be quite deadly. . . .

Leuchter's primary mistake is his initial assumption that exposure to HCN must result in the formation of Prussian blue. Another error is his claim that the delousing facilities were exposed to less HCN than the homicidal chambers. It turns out that it is more difficult to kill lice than it is to kill humans.
—Richard J. Green, "The Chemistry of Auschwitz"

What has the Food and Drug Administration (FDA) determined about Prussian blue?
The FDA has determined that the 500 mg Prussian blue capsules . . . can be found safe and effective for the treatment of known or suspected internal contamination with radioactive cesium, radioactive thallium, or non-radioactive thallium. . . .

How does Prussian blue work?
Prussian blue works using a mechanism known as ion exchange. Cesium or thallium that have been absorbed into the body are removed by the liver and passed into the intestine and are then re-absorbed into the body (entero-hepatic circulation). Prussian blue works by trapping thallium and cesium in the intestine, so that they can be passed out of the body in the stool rather than be re-absorbed. If persons are exposed to radioactive cesium, radioactive thallium, or non-radioactive thallium, taking Prussian blue may reduce the risk of death and major illness from radiation or poisoning.
—FDA/Center for Drug Evaluation and Research, "Questions and Answers on Prussian Blue"

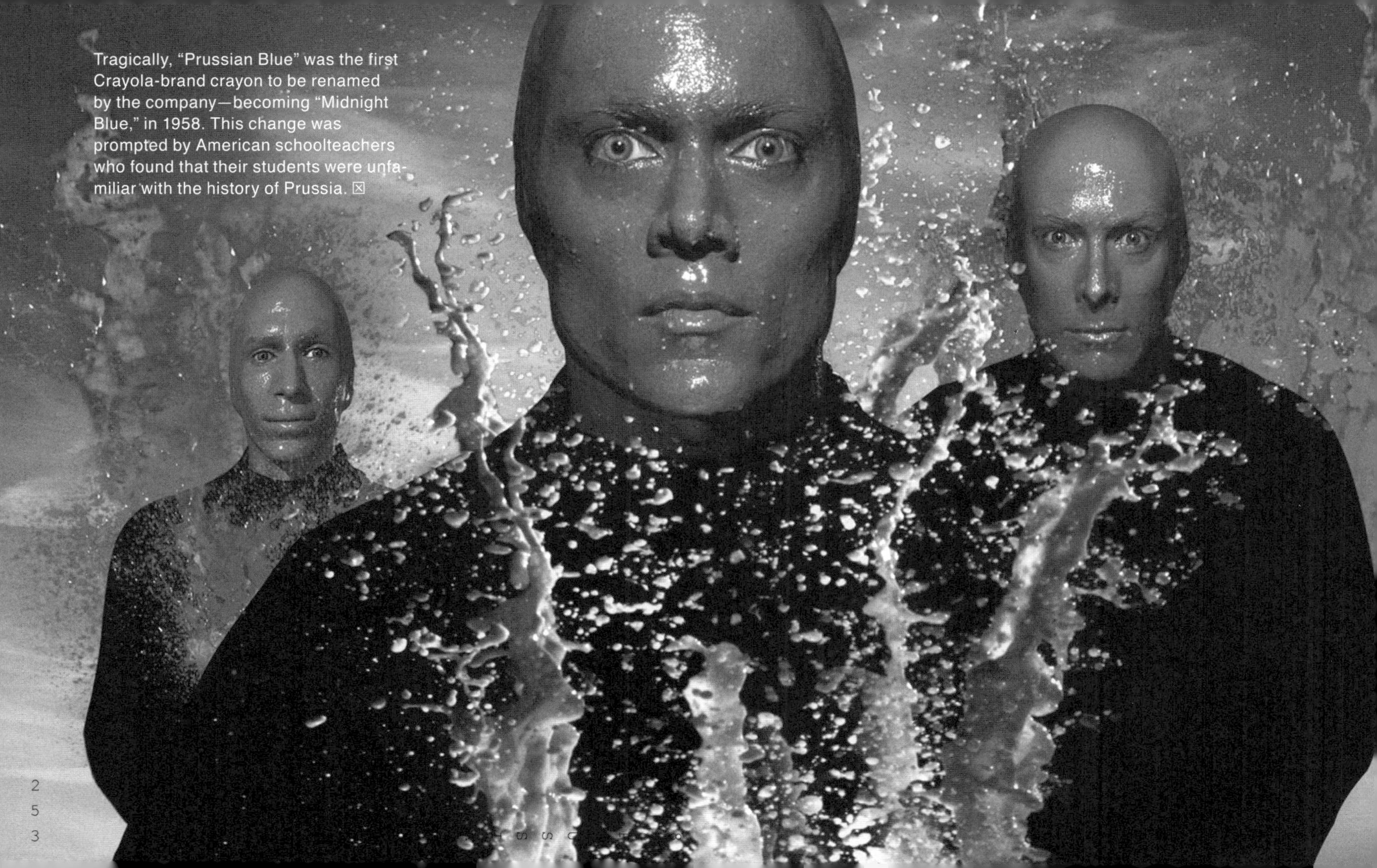

Tragically, "Prussian Blue" was the first Crayola-brand crayon to be renamed by the company—becoming "Midnight Blue," in 1958. This change was prompted by American schoolteachers who found that their students were unfamiliar with the history of Prussia. ☒

EVERGLADE

"A story in which I explain": *a collage and prose poem.*

by Lucy Ives
published March 24, 2010

INVALID FORMAT 2

ISSUE 8 2010

254

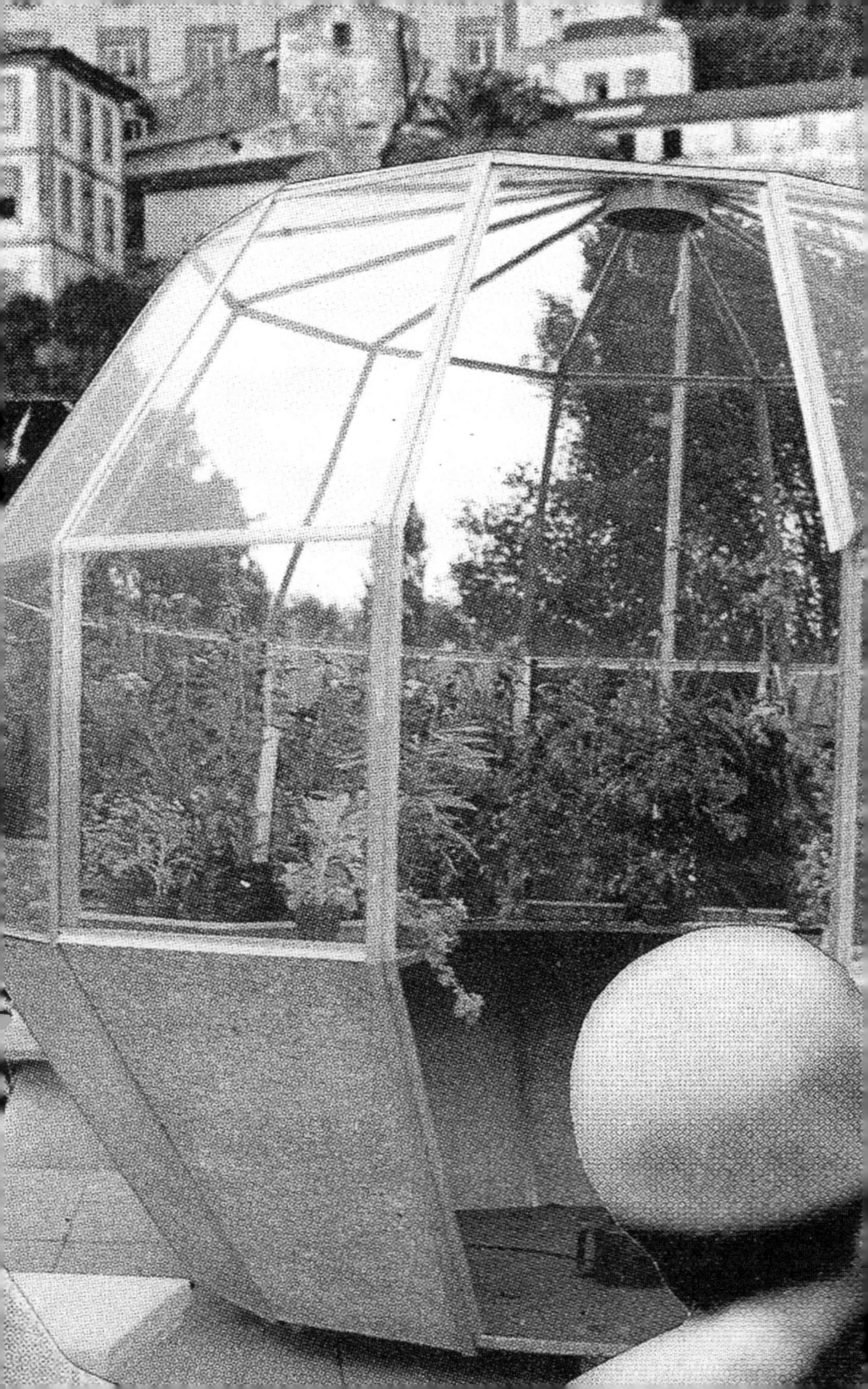

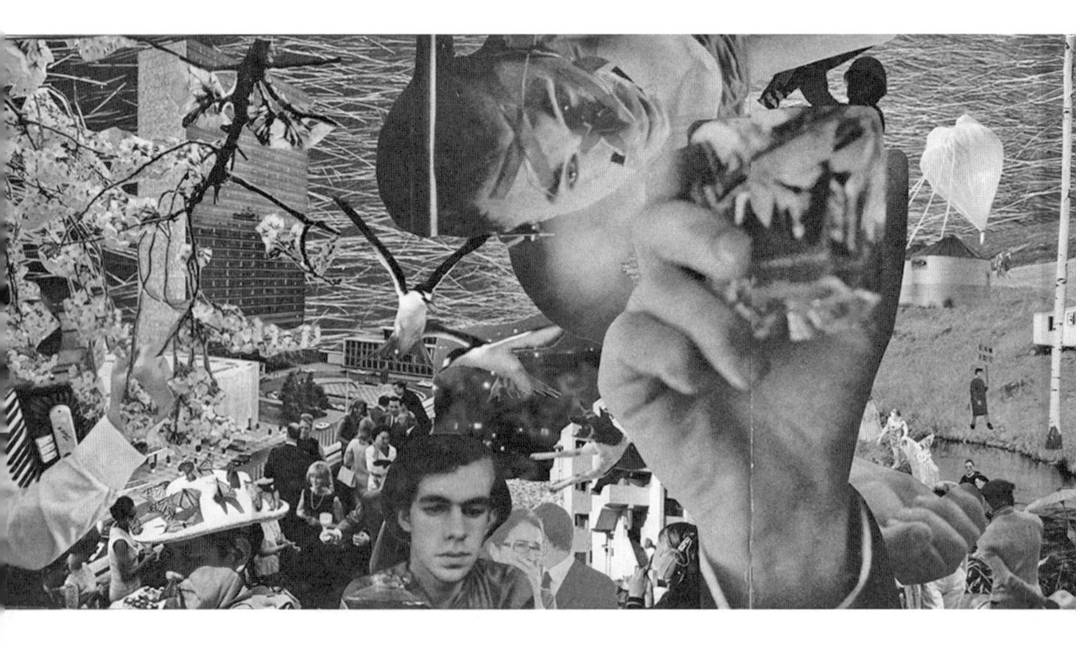

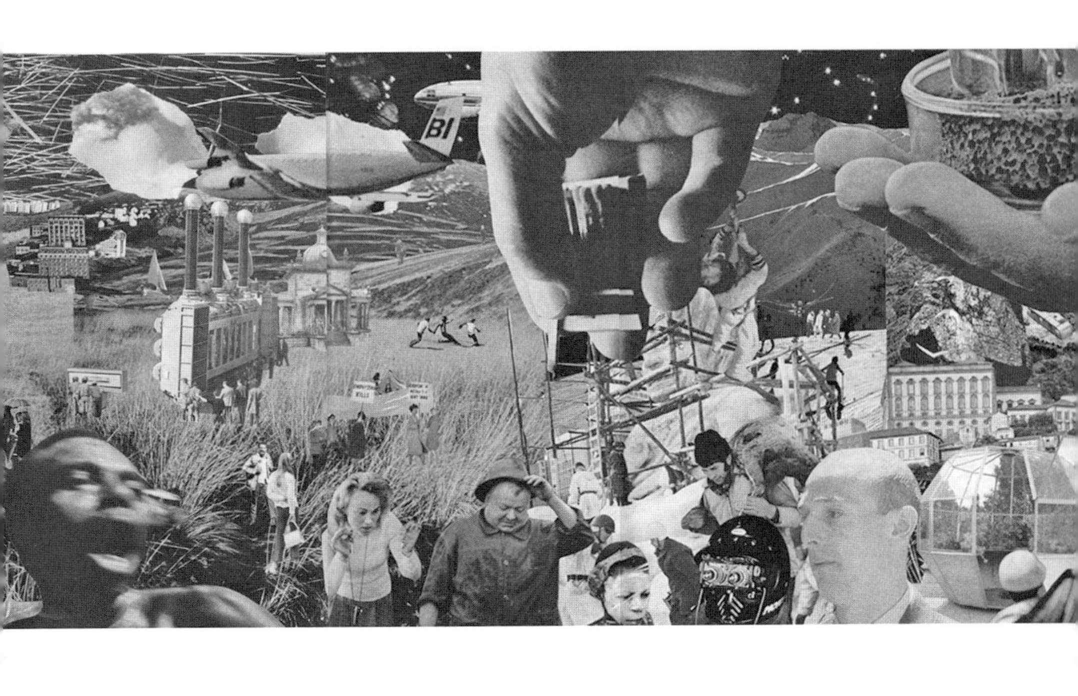

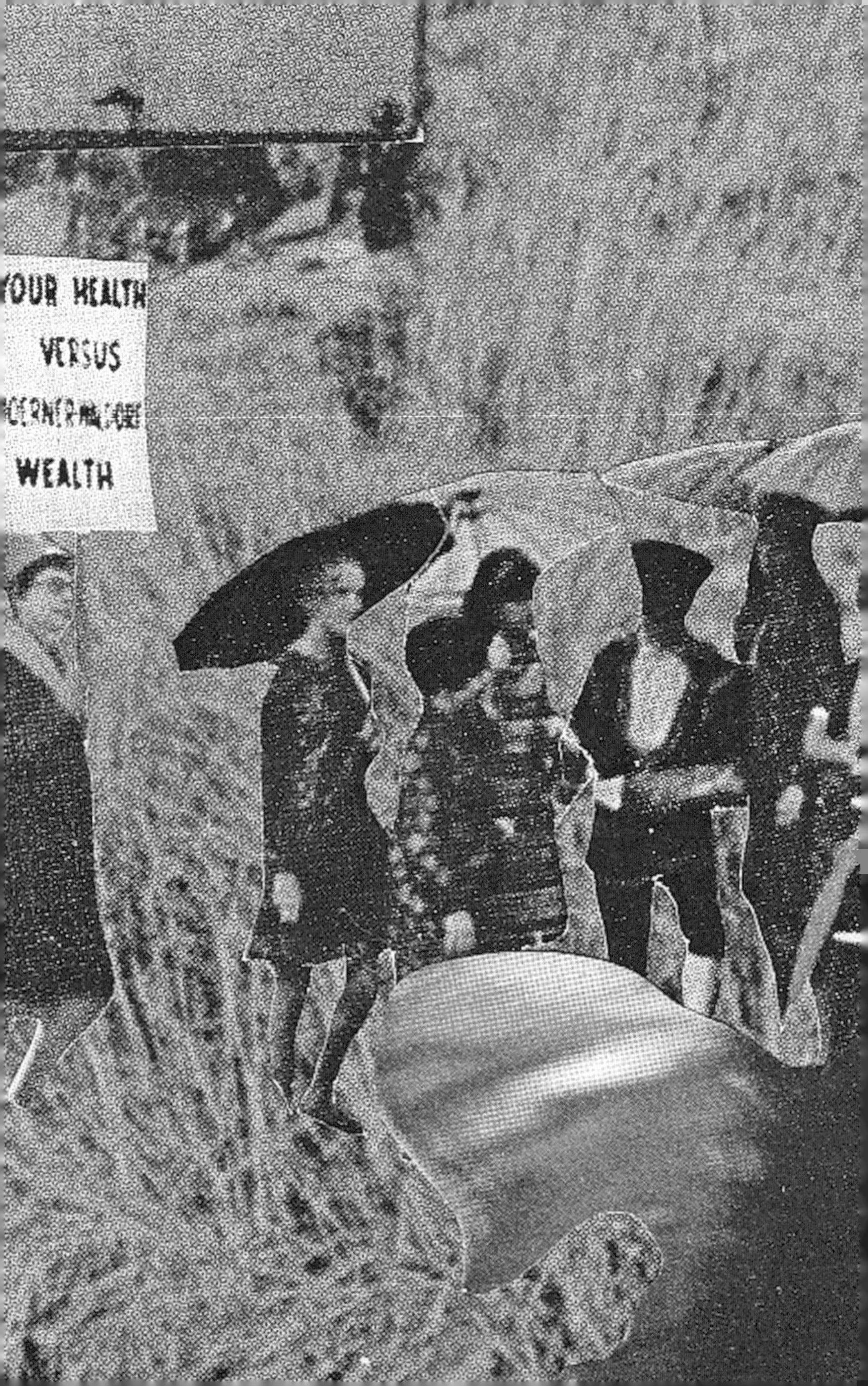
YOUR HEALTH
VERSUS
WEALTH

Now I will tell you a story. It will explain what you are about to see

Now I will tell you a story. A branch tumbled through space. Blossoms on the branch winked and strained. A man looked up. He made his hand into a shape. A man stood still, and he looked upon a crowd. As far as anyone can tell, there has always been that building, those offices, just before the river; a red dot, a sun. We see cars. We see lots, vans, white signage

It is my ancestor. He never stops leaning into the scene. He hangs there, actually. He is a lamp, a letter. Seconds hurry to hide in the shade of a raised glass, behind an illustration of the tense wings of rising gulls. You hide your face. You only rest your face in your hand. Light is gliding down a stair. It is a story about heroes. No, it is a story about a single ancestor

Now we come to a field. Now we come to see actors at the edge of a lake. Where the foot meets its reflection is a line. Now we follow land to the horizon. Where field meets evening is an edge. In the image is a future. A satellite will rise. Meanwhile, somewhere there is a page, which implies another, though there is nothing yet behind or underneath this sentence

You have kept on walking. In the story, someone rings a bell. She says three words, "As though virtually," but we cannot hear the rest of what she's saying. Meanwhile, work goes on. Boys chase one another around ruins. Above them, clouds have left the sky. Clouds have left the sky and descended to live as humans

Perhaps you are like me

Perhaps you are like me. You are waiting to see if you will learn. It is worth it to you to seek out a monument, to give away matches in snow. When one desires to see, is this or is this not like tying a knot, is this or is this not an image

Anyway, it's time. Now we may walk back into the hills. The bird that falls into view is a kite. You want me to say something about cities, about nations and the arts they produce, but I am not talking. In the forest are crags and pines, silver moss and lichen. You strain to see the distance. Now when you see, what distance

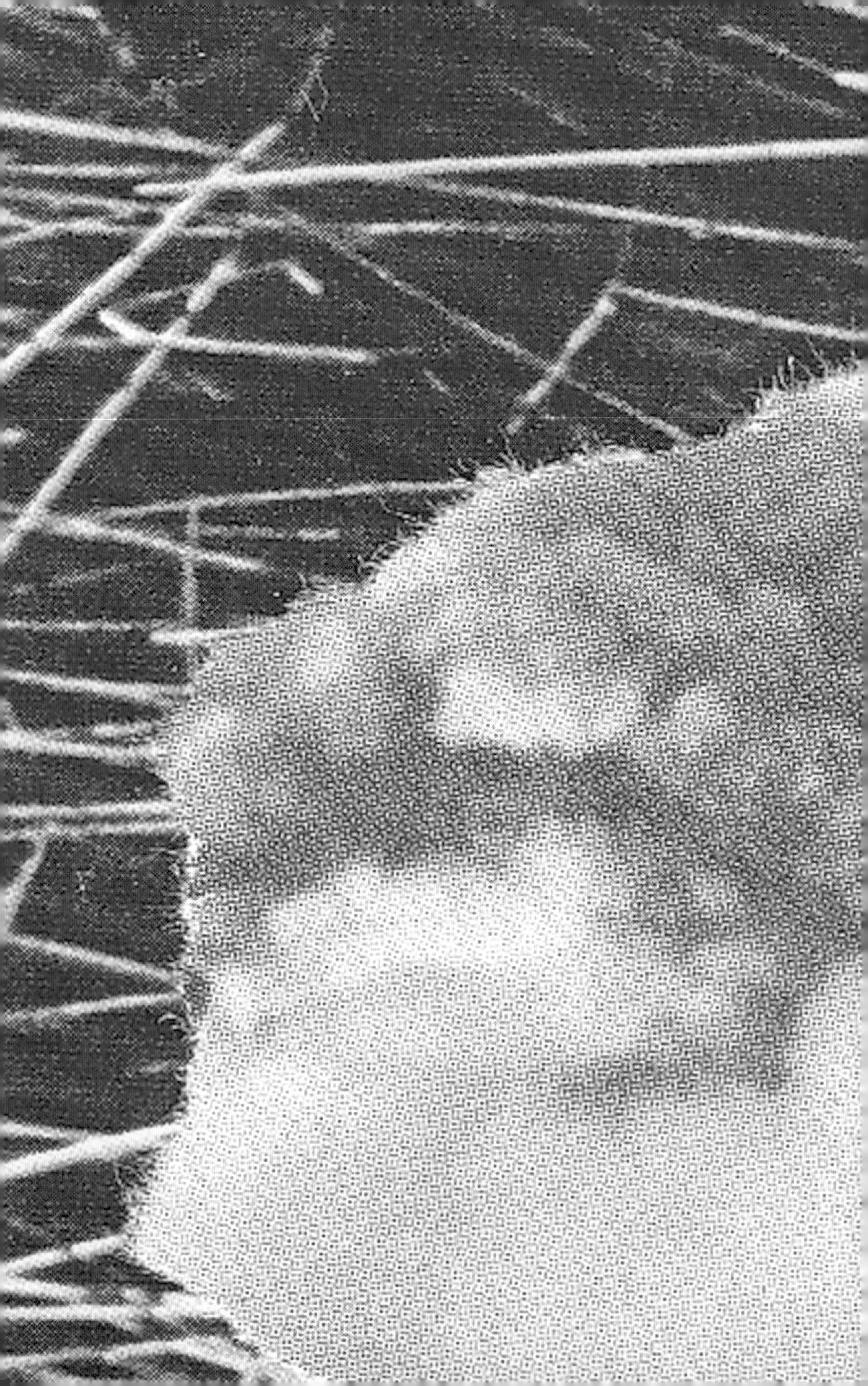

R, ADIEU

The primal violence and utopian trill of the rolled r, *the most rrresilient of locutions.*

by Joe Milutis
published March 26, 2010

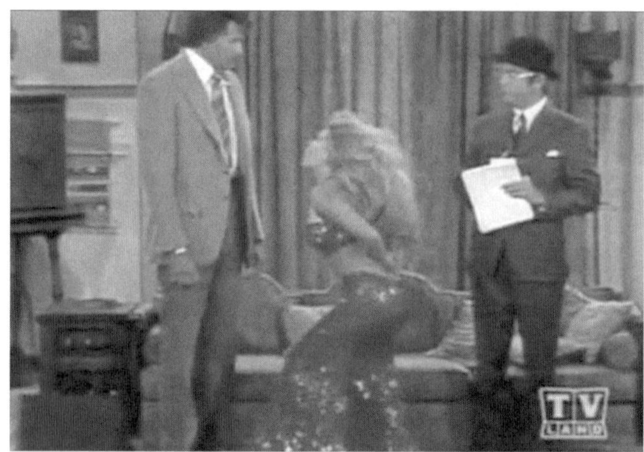

Charo on *The Carol Burnett Show*, 1973. She enters the room preceded by her trill. It is no longer an *r*, but a pure phonic abstract force.

FOR A LONG TIME, I thought that in order to have any business doing what gets called "sound poetry," I had to sound like Charo. Any Latin bombshell—like the bombardiers of the phoneme in Futurism and dada—knows that the rolled *r* is central to the arsenal, and this *r* I cannot muster. Over the years, I have been similarly shamed by the butterfly stroke and by my inability to produce Oscar Peterson–like runs up and down the keyboard. Unable to marshal such combinations of coordination, focus, and energy for what seemed merely ornamental, yet seductive, excess, I learned (for example) to do scales more like a drunk stumbling up the stairs of his flat only to be kicked back down by the landlord. My tongue, when faced with the *r*, is not even that mobile. It goes nowhere when *buon giorno* attempts to rouse it and thus, embarrassedly, tends toward *ciao*.

They say you can learn to roll your *r*'s—what's called the alveolar trill. Why, then, does my tongue remain incorrigible? While English does not require this trill, sound poetry—a sub-subgenre of poetry and sound art— seems to demand it, especially as an efficient way to energize the sonic properties of language at the particulate level of the letter. From the first dadaist simultaneous poem in 1916—which included, according to Hugo Ball, "an *rrrrr* drawn out for minutes"—to today's *arrière-garde* heritage-dadas, the hyperextended *r* is well nigh inescapable. Poet-performers like Jaap Blonk and Christian Bök have brought this doggedly underground practice to a larger public, by reinterpreting its earliest works and creating new ones with a crowd-pleasing vigor to compete, avowedly or not, with hip-hop—sound poetry's estranged, affluent, and amped-up brother. In doing so, Blonk and Bök have recalibrated the levels for hearing sound poetry; rolling their *r*'s with such a preternatural intensity, they can't help but create new performative standards, which sanctify the rolled *r* as a sine qua non. I say with tongue only halfway in cheek that latter-day sound poets do a disservice to the form by maintaining such gaudy *r*'s and other apoplectic athleticisms, ensuring that sound poetry forever will be only the literary equivalent of a loopy guest on *The Merv Griffin Show*.

I am, then, suspicious of this *r* drawn out, not for minutes, but for almost a hundred years, without a good examining. While sound poetry has always been a scarce, ephemeral practice, new archives allow for reconsiderations, recontextualizations, and rereadings, and of these archives I have availed myself, resurrecting the rolled *r* from various historical and contemporary instances by editing performance recordings and stringing their *r*'s together. Both with the morbid curiosity about what would result from the monstrous reanimation of these amputations and with the properly scientific attitude a new form of media analysis warrants, I proceeded to assay the unique properties of this remnant as it has passed from artist to artist. As perhaps a shibboleth of loyalty to the first sound poems, these *r*'s could be the sonic sigil of a secret society. Or they could be merely an unquestioned gimmick, pure cabaret corn from our avant-garde forebears. Notwithstanding, since this *r* trundles between the dark corridors of the avant-garde and the ostensibly sunnier avenues of culture at large, as a backdrop to these art *r*'s I will unscroll a historical panorama of popularly rolled *r*'s and of *r* itself, in the hopes that our *histoire* will serve as an appropriate distraction from my less wholesome body-snatching activities.

INVALID FORMAT 2

ISSUE 8 2010

THE R HAS NOT ALWAYS BEEN ENSCONCED in the affections of the avant-garde, or those of poetry generally. Oulipian writer Georges Perec called the *r* a "non-letter," and in his "History of the Lipogram" (1969) he points out that "in the eighteenth century, the letter R was renounced by poets." On the tradition of the *R sbandita*—texts with the *r* "disbanded"—he says that "the whole of the Italian school evinced a profound distaste for the letter R, and most often for that letter only." The Italian disdain for the *r* here is surprising, not only because of the rolled *r*'s Mediterranean pedigree but also because of the importance of the *r* to the Italian Futurists (of whom, more later). Some clue as to the meaning of this prohibition might be found in an odd eighteenth-century biography called *Hesperus; or, Forty-Five Dog-Post-Days*, which uses the *R sbandita* in a outrageously elaborate metaphor about finding love in the alienating city, prickly with *r*'s:

> In the noisy foundery and mill of the city he felt as if
> in a dreary forest. Accustomed as he was to tender

souls, the city ones appeared to him all so thorny and unpolished; for love had, like tragedy, purified his passions in exciting them. All hung over so ruinous and moss-grown as if on the verge of a collapse, whereas the clean mirror-walls of Maïenthal rose firm and radiant. For love is the only thing which fills the heart of man to the brim, although with a nectar-foam that soon sinks again; it alone composes a poem of some thousand minutes without the rattling repetitions of the letter R, as the Dominican Cardone executed a poem upon it quite as long under the name *L'R-sbandita* without a single R,—hence, like crabs, it is finest in the months without an R in their name.

Perec's own fascination with these forgotten prohibitions goes to the core of his writerly identity. This distasteful letter lucky-pierres between the two *e*'s of his patronym, an apt conjunction for a writer who in *A Void* absented the *e* into thin air, formally mirroring a more fundamental disappearance of the self.

Next those ars, rrrr!
those ars all bellical,
the highpriest's hiero-
glyph of kettletom
and oddsbones . . .

IF THE ABSENCE OF THE E in *A Void* stands for the absence of the self, the *e* even when *there* tends toward silent but ubiquitous presence—like the void, perhaps more etherized. The *r*, in contrast, is naturally self-assertive, both of itself and of the self, if only because of the energy it requires to articulate. David Sacks, in his history of the alphabet, says that "R takes effort to say: It has a relatively demanding pronunciation, requiring a stiff tongue tip." Charo can enter the room with the *r* as her avatar, the *moi* in her hummingbird oscillation between flamenco self-assertion and cuchi-cuchi maternalism. James Joyce, in the section of *Finnegans Wake* that parodies the alphabet, goes as far as to attribute to the ontological "stiffness" of *r* a militant fervor; as well, Virginia Woolf, in her imagining of an alphabetical scale of being through the agency of Mr. Ramsey in *To the Lighthouse*, posits *r* as that level of dubious excellence that would serve one when leading troops into battle. When Joyce writes, "Next those ars, rrrr! those ars all bellical, the highpriest's hieroglyph of kettletom and oddsbones," he is extending this militancy of *r* even to the priesthood, since the ecclesiastical symbol for Christ is a Greek *r* with an *x* over it—a high priest's "skull and cross-bones." While it refers to the first two letters of *christos*, this combination also implies the mystery and paradox of Christ's human status. To put it crudely, his individuality is "crossed out," or, in a more theoretical idiom, the *x* over the *r* puts being *sous-rature*.

If the *r* encourages reflections on being and, by association, the peremptory status of identity in language, it may be because, historically, it represents a quite literal localization of being specifically in the apparatus of the head.

Immigrant laborers in ancient Egypt got it into their head to translate the Egyptian hieroglyph for "head" into a reverse *P*—the Phoenician *resh*, which, continued in Hebrew, would be the transitional mark between this ancient head and our contemporary *r*. If, then, this historical memory of the human head slowly whittled down to mere *r* still impinges on our consciousness, could we not also say that when one rolls the *r*, the tongue rattles a head within the head, and within that head is another head rattling, and within that head . . . etc., etc.? The rolled *r* instigates the infinite regress of language reflecting back on its origins. Could that be what Roland Barthes was saying, in "The Grain of the Voice" (1972), when he seemed to hallucinate "voices within the voice" set off by the *r* of an opera singer who

> carried his *r*'s beyond the norms of the singer—without denying those norms. His *r* was of course rolled, as in

every classic art of singing, but the roll had nothing
peasant-like or Canadian about it; it was an artificial
roll, the paradoxical state of a letter-sound at once
totally abstract (by its metallic brevity of vibration)
and totally material (by its manifest deep-rootedness
in the action of the throat). This phonetics—am I alone
in perceiving it? am I hearing voices within the voice?
but isn't it the truth of the voice to be hallucinated?
isn't the entire space of the voice an infinite one?

R contains within it—in the secret channels between
demotic Egyptian and Barthes's pleasure of the text—the
movement of language itself. Resh is the atomic particle
of language that means "all movement, good or bad, [the]
original sign of renewal," as Johanna Drucker puts it. But
what do we do if this movement, this change, is a hallucinated reality, the fundamental and total hallucination of language entering its own "head space" and rematerializing as
pure vibration? Could we also add that *r* is movement both
real and irreal, both a clacking of the tongue in the hollow of
the mouth and the ghost of whole being left out when resh is
beheaded?

For language to truly move, after all, the head might
be the very source of congestion. Well before his infamous
suppressed radio broadcast—which would attempt to extir-
pate all being in the quest for a radiophonic body without
organs—Antonin Artaud claimed in "Position of the Flesh"
(1925) that "with each vibration of my tongue I retrace all
the paths of my thought within my flesh." For this to work,
the *r* must rid itself of head, even becoming *k* in the caca-
phony of the world's arse, or—as it would be pronounced on
French radio—go on-"*r*" to shake the body out of its automa-
tisms. Without *r* rolling, the insistence, instead, of Artaud's
k's in "To Have Done with the Judgment of God" (1947)
opens up a literally scatological critique of being. "Hearing
death in the voice"—as Allen Weiss describes this radio
excoriation—would require not the infinite self-referential
regress of a trill rolling up the centuries, but rather the

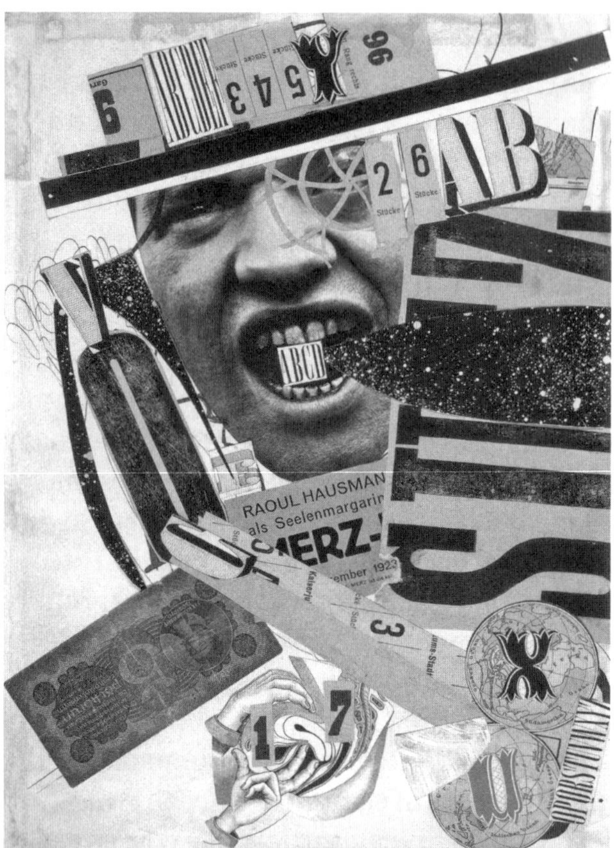

Raoul Hausmann, *ABCD: Portrait of the Artist* (detail), 1923–4, photocollage.

tongue replaced by the anus, *r* blocked by *k*, what's left out of Being challenging what is (or *are*).

Whether the *r* is present becomes an unconscious "To be or not to be" for the speaker, an attitude or a stance regarding the way one inhabits language. The simple fact that rhotic—or *r*-emphasizing—language requires an extra expenditure of energy draws attention to the nonindifferent act of speaking itself when the *r* rings out. This exertion, which whole linguistic communities in the southern US, New York, and New England have chosen to opt out of, asserts a modern nomadic self; when we don't hear the *r*, as in phrases like "the Waah between the States," "Pahk the cah in Hahvahd Yahd," and even "The city's clamour can never spoil / The dreams of a boy and goil," we can imagine it's inaudible because of long-standing sociolinguistic ties that are suspicious of those who are too ambitiously individualistic. Old

boys from, say, Brooklyn or South Philly become odd provincial confreres to Artaud's antihuman shaman.

Yet while the *r* posits an energetic self-presence, its
hyperextension heralds the opposite—a dissolution of self
in pure vibration. Nowhere is this conflicted *r* trill more
evident than in the *r*'s of F. T. Marinetti. To our ears, his
disarticulated *r*'s may sound bubbly and light; but his rolling
tongue in its day was a particularly militant linguini, clearly
a celebration of the vibrational machines—the machine gun,
the radio, the rotoriferous universe of the gas engine—that
inspired the Futurist desire for immolation of a coherent
self, local language, and spatial boundedness. At the same
time, though, in his *r* he has the cockiness of one classi-
cally trained in elocution, perhaps even opera. In contrast,
a sound poet like Raoul Hausmann—perhaps because of
the more pacifist orientation of dada, or its more anarchic
aesthetic, or because many of its practitioners, Hausmann
included, gravitated toward the visual arts rather than
poetry and music—has *r*'s that collapse in on themselves,
flail like hooked fish, try to get started like old jalopies. His
tongue is dead matter enlivened so as to carry out his sce-
nario of "language wreaking revenge on poets."

Hausmann's *r*'s:
dead fish, old jalopy . . .
the material instantiation
of "language wreaking
revenge on poets."

OUR CURRENT ARS POETICA seems to have forgotten
these collapsing *r*'s, these failed *r*'s that don't extend the
Übermensch's dominance across the linguistic terrain or
reenergize the quest for a cosmic over-soul, but rather
revert to the body, the prelinguistic, the monstrous, or
the animalic. The *r* is sometimes called the dog's letter
because of the sound it makes alone when extended but not
trilled, and this sound should be one of many with which
a performer could interpret the dadaist/Futurist cliché

of *rrrrrrrr* typed in boldface across the page of a poetic score. However, only one series of *r*'s comes off as a pit-bull growl in Blonk's version of Kurt Schwitters's Dadaist masterpiece *Ursonata* (1922–32); there is a sequence of barks at the end, but those are from short triple and double *r*'s, the lyric extension of being here again blocked by the caca *k*: "EkeEke ekeEke ekeEke ekeeKe / EkeEke ekeEke ekeEke ekeeKe / EkeEke ekeEke Rrrumm! / EkeEke ekeEke Rrrumm! / EkeEke ekeEke Rrum Rrum / EkeEke ekeEke Rrum Rrum." In Blonk's defense, this paucity of the *littera canina* is an accurate interpretation of the original, although Schwitters's own recording of *Ursonata* is much mellower.

Ursonata, inspired by some of Hausmann's work, is in more ways than one the ur-text of sound poetry. Nevertheless, in its virtuosity it's also a well-groomed Jazz Age compromise of the form, its flight out of being disguising a restitution of being in the new world of machines and speed, rather than a pointed critique. Schwitters's riff on an earlier typographic deconstruction by Hausmann is thus closer to the Futurist Marinetti's output than to that of fellow dadas, albeit bringing with it the symbolist mysticism that Marinetti disavowed. Sound poetry, whether engaging the Futurist or the primitive imagination, has always carried within it the dream of reinventing sacred language or creating a common global tongue; the sounding of the rolled *r*'s in *Ursonata* takes the performer on a utopian-mystical flight into the firmament of a vibrational cosmos, and as such may be the source of some Dadaists' disdain for Schwitters as too bourgeois. (Or maybe it's the fact that he performed *Ursonata* at military garden parties.)

Blonk and Bök's punker versions may avoid the bourgeois tonalities of the original, of which, according to Julian Cowley, Hausmann "disapproved [because] of the classical mould into which the subversive implications of his act of provocation had been channelled." But Blonk and Bök's reinstatement of a tightly crafted trill continues a legacy that subsumes more anarchic tongues.

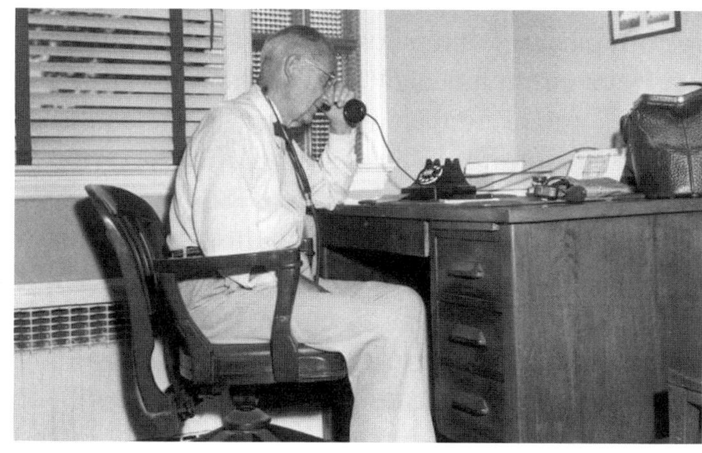

Photograph of William Carlos Williams dressed as doctor, 1967.

Bachelard: "In the resonance we hear the poem, in the reverberations we speak it, it is our own."

Williams: More multiculti than he let on?

Since no theater of the *r* is complete without a "return of the repressed," the spirit of the Hausmannic flailing *r* has had to emerge, albeit somewhat more covertly, in something like the "Poème-partition H1+H2, or 'Le Quatrième Plan'" (1963) of Bernard Heidsieck, who unfortunately has largely disappeared from any detectable scene. Heidsieck asserts the limitations of the tongue; when repeating the words *plus vite* ("faster"), he gets close to the same motion as the rolled *r*, ironically slowed down even as the words repeat faster and faster. Yet "plus vite, plus vite, plus vite," straining toward the purr of easy mechanical speed—more feline than canine, after all—never jump-starts into some cosmic vibration machine but remains rooted in an inexpert tongue. *Plus vite* does not stage an escape from language, but rather exemplifies, as in Giorgio Agamben's description of the poetry of Giovanni Pascoli, "the site in which he can capture language in the instant it sinks again, dying, into the voice, and at which the voice, emerging from mere sound, passes (that is, dies) into signification."

This site between what Agamben calls "the infinite sea of mere sound" and articulate speech is the particularly generative, albeit ambiguous, site of sound poetry, if not of poetry itself. Yet sometime around 1950 (for poet Steve McCaffery), or even at the turn of the twentieth century (for media theorist Friedrich Kittler), something happened to take poetry away from the word, and by extension the letters that compose it, as recording technology allowed for an aestheticization of "mere sound." Indeed, the rolled *r*—puncturing the line through its pure sounding—promised this return to the infinite sea of the real, presaging more effective disruptions of symbolic networks by way of the proliferation of reproduced sound. This *r* was resolutely *avant la lettre*.

However, with the growth of recording and transmission technologies, such rhotic acrobatics would no longer be necessary to explode or deform word-based practices. Phonograph and radio would create a network of voices realized beyond their written materializations; later, tape manipulations would open up a veritable subatomic universe beyond the letter. So, why is the rolled *r* so . . . rrrrrresilient?

PEASANTLIKE, CANADIAN

I HAD A DREAM ABOUT MY GRANDMOTHER. I was trying to make pasta and beans, but it wasn't pasta and beans, was it? It was *pasta e fagioli*, but who spoke Italian anymore so it was pastafajole . . . no, pasta *fazool*, but I was calling her from my freshman dorm so I was embarrassed that this was perhaps the wrong way to say it. I'm grown up now and this is just baby talk right? But I can't look it up anywhere. Is it pasta fazoola, basta vazul, pastafazoo? I see it in print for the first time—some smart-ass named Thomas McGuane (not even Italian) has it in *The Bushwhacked Piano* as "pasta fazoula," but still I am having trouble making it and the recipe eludes me, when my grandfather takes the phone and tells me how the Sicilians cut off the French's balls if they weren't able to pronounce the word for "chickpea." And as he says the word *CHEY-CHED-DEE* in a way I know can't be right, the line goes dead. This all happened in the thirteenth century.

Correct language: dream or hallucination? Is it based on earth sounds and mother tongue, or is it the inhuman correctness that allows for flight but also bureaucracy and separation from lived reality? Official language falls apart, or rather softens, becomes linguini or just plain lazy when localized. Witness the disappearance of the *r* up and down the East Coast, especially in, as David Sacks says, "long-time local families of traditionally lower income." There is something comforting and seductive in the entropy of immigrant patois, but this comfort could easily be a trap. Marinetti was faced with something similar when he placed his poetic practice in conflict with an Italy insufficiently modern, too in love with its multiple unstandardized dialects to accede to the world stage. His rolled *r*, then, is a performance of linguistic energy and forward-looking uprightness, standing in for his hatred of all pastas and pastafazoolas, those heavy, deadening noodles of dreams.

But here is where I get confused. Because it seems to me that while the rolled *r* is a cultured skill that Henry Higgins might have tortured Eliza Doolittle into mastering, it also comes to my ear as emerging from the very peasant culture and dialect practices that Marinetti was shaming by his ripping *r*. The rolled *r* is correctness itself, but relative to what? In France, we can speculate that the whole history of the Revolution can be read in the *parler gras*, or "fat talking," characterized by a more guttural (nonrolled) *r* sound. An 1806 manual of oratory by Gilbert Austin tells us that a trilled *r* is desirable to counter this guttural, or uvular, *r*, "an imperfection which it was formerly the fashion in France for *pétit maitres* to affect." At first an affectation of the court, this throaty *r* has taken hold as the official French *r*, notwithstanding any elocution manuals— a subtle victory for the royalists. Yet the trilled *r* holds out, in all its "peasantlike, Canadian" splendor. A "Petite

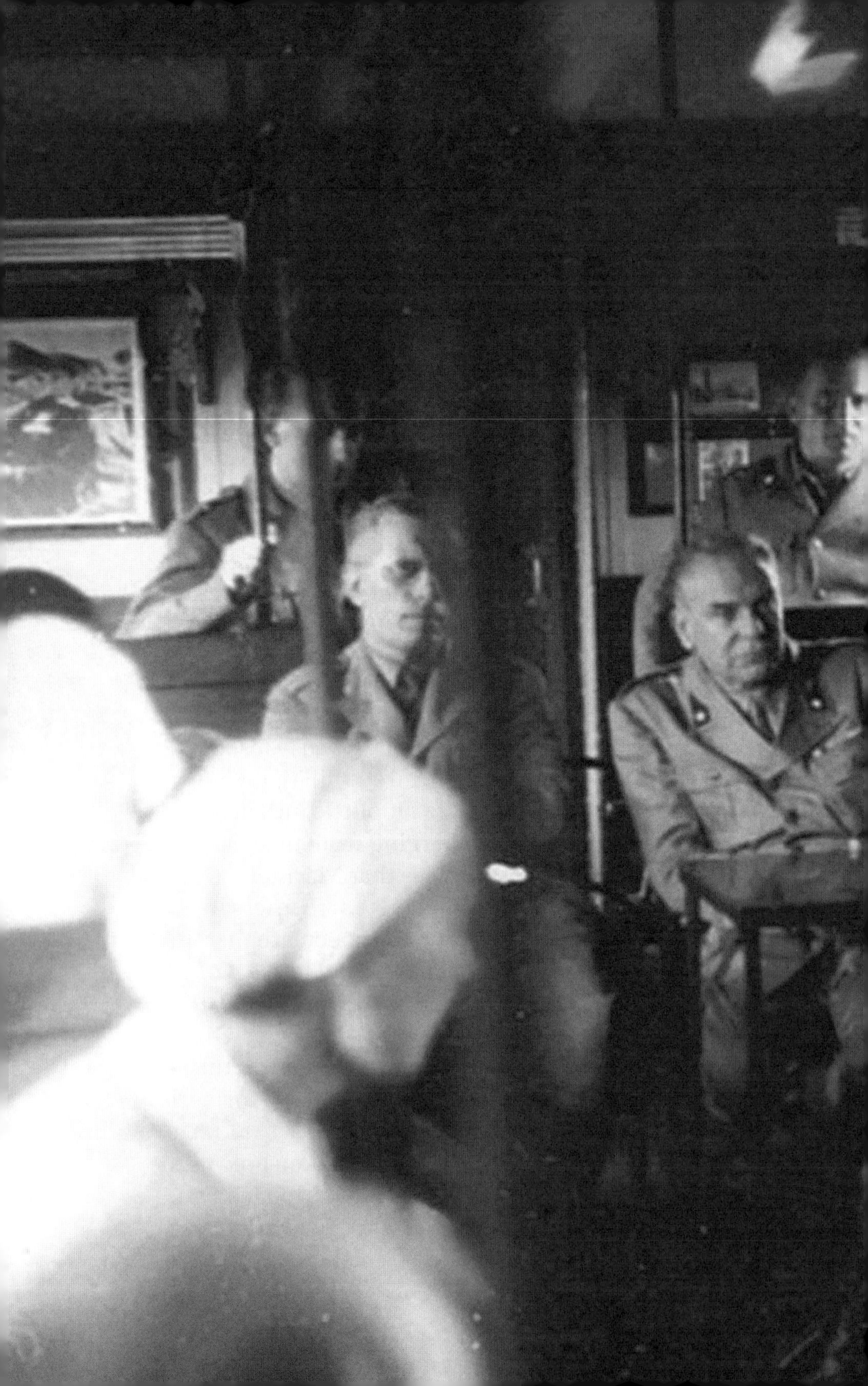

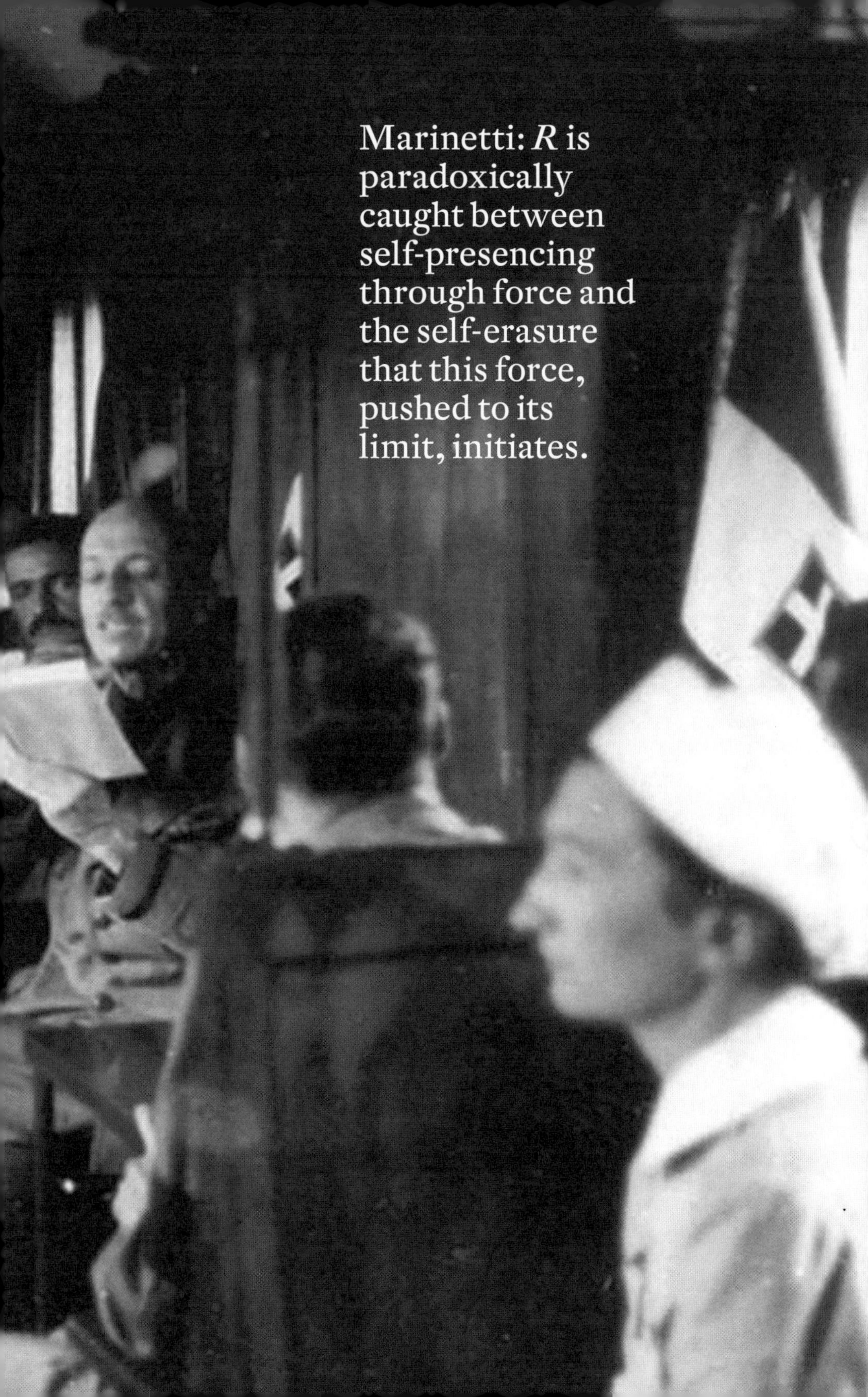

Marinetti: *R* is paradoxically caught between self-presencing through force and the self-erasure that this force, pushed to its limit, initiates.

Histoire de r" from the Web tells us, "One attributes to the rolled r properly irrational virtues: linked to the past of the rural, the provincial, the peasant, the rolled r becomes the guarantor of an ancestral pronunciation exempt of all metropolitan, intellectual, and Parisian defilement, a metric of authenticity and innocent beauty dating back to the crack of time! The mythification of the rolled r would assure neighborhoods of nobility for the speaker, which would be anchored in his earth and in his family history."

We can surmise, then, that the rolled *r* would be particularly important to the phenomenologist, and the same website tells us Gaston Bachelard was a big roller of *r*'s. Imagine him saying this with a few ripe ones!

> In the resonance we hear the poem, in the reverberations we speak it, it is our own. The reverberations bring about a change of being . . . . This grip that poetry acquires on our very being bears a phenomenological mark that is unmistakable. The exuberance and depth of a poem are always phenomena of the resonance-reverberation doublet.

Yet the "properly irrational virtues" of the rolled *r* also bring to mind the aestheticization of the *Volk* in fascism. Poor Ezra Pound, his rolled *r*'s had to have been an affectation, for a Pennsylvania boy does not roll them naturally. What could have started as a simple putting on of European "airs" got caught up in a genocidal gambit for the heart and soul of Europe. Imagine his pal William Carlos Williams back in Rutherford rolling his *r*'s, with a Spanish mother looming in the background of his heroic modernism; think what that would have meant for poetry! The pure energy of *r* would not only have made Williams more multiculti than he let on; if, for Hugo Ball, "reality only begins at the point where things peter out," an indefatigable *r* would have left Williams no time to seek out a clear image of reality, his famous "no ideas but in things."

WHETHER WE ARE EZRA POUND OR CHARO, the *r* when rolled encourages a kind of sonic deformation of a language. Whether this deformation is seen as correct (yet outmoded) or déclassé (yet virtuous), a harbinger of the future or an echo from the past, when we follow the *r* we see how language moves—that is, a continual deformation in the unfolding of time. Deracinating forces caused the Phoenicians to take a hieroglyph that stood in for their very selves and produce a glyph much more mobile, thus attuned to their nomadic existence. But the move from hieroglyph to alphabetic script, as a movement from a language based on visible resemblance to something more abstract and manipulable, dramatizes how in order to represent ourselves, we engage with inhuman materials. What in ancient times were the discrete and motile properties of the alphabet are today those of the digital, which, while increasing the speed and efficiency of communication, also produce vast amounts of unreadable posthuman compositions emerging from the data fallout of the Web (much like the typographic flarf of Hausmann's that Schwitters ran with). Subsequently, our own nomadism is a function of the lettristic motility in this particular system, unhinged from its connection to a sensible world.

Could the *r* and all it might mean for holding on to identity, for "keeping one's head" in the digital maelstrom, be an anxiety formation, and would it be better to err than *r* in our ear? Or is our *belle*-(or *bête*-)*lettre* the first that helped us understand where we were *heading*? While the modernist *r*'s ostensible purpose was to highlight the materiality of language, we're now faced with the apocalyptic notion that writing is so beyond us, its material totality so vast and unthinkable (yet at the same time instantly searchable), that the rolled *r* is a puny alphabetic nothing on the lips of a supermaterialist data god. In the age of the easily produced and accessible MP3—a writing by other encoded means—a whole poem, nay, a whole database, can be shot through with a single energetic trill.

Because all poetry, and even all text, must tend toward *poesie sonore* in order to call attention to itself in this context, obsessive sonorization on the Web might be a return to authentic, essentialist being by another name. Yet if one wishes to maintain a concept of a practice specific to poetry, sound or otherwise, it may be useful to keep in mind our incommensurable noodles. Charles Bernstein, in his "Poetics of the Americas" (1996), describes the field of poetic experimentation as existing between work that embraces unofficial dialect—our local varieties of the p. fazoo—and work that, evading complacent identity categories, creates its own ideolect, or "ideologically informed nonstandard language practice." These two poles of experimental poetics are akin to the arrows of a rolled *r*—one direction goes to the heart of self-identification in rooted communality, the other toward an invented future: a future that may, dangerously, be without humanity or community. But what form could sound poetry take without this *r*—for that matter, in the absence of recognizable letters *in general*, each with its sordid and conflicted attachments—if the genre wanted to remain separate from the "mere sound" of music and sound art?

BECAUSE SOUND POETRY is, above all, as McCaffery points out, "a practice of freedom," the flight of the *r* escapes a deadening ersatz reality that encroaches on our movements, poetic and otherwise. But if with colder eyes we look at the actual means of this flight, the lowercase *r* is the letter most resembling a Luger. In 1920, Richard Huelsenbeck wrote, "To make literature with a gun in hand had, for a time, been my dream." As an important weapon in the dadaist "congenial hatred" toward static language practices, and notwithstanding the perceived funniness of sound-poetry antics, *r* is a particularly humorless letter. In its trill, however, the archaic, primal violence of *r* risks dissipation. Vibrating through and past the alphabetic into some finer-grained reality, we are, after *r*, left comically abandoned—in the air, as it were—to our own devices. ⊠

SACRIFICE OF THE BANANA

*An ecstatic bestiary. A prequel to 2012.
Shot by the temple police. Performed
for the video camera. A film.*

by Karthik Pandian
published March 30, 2010

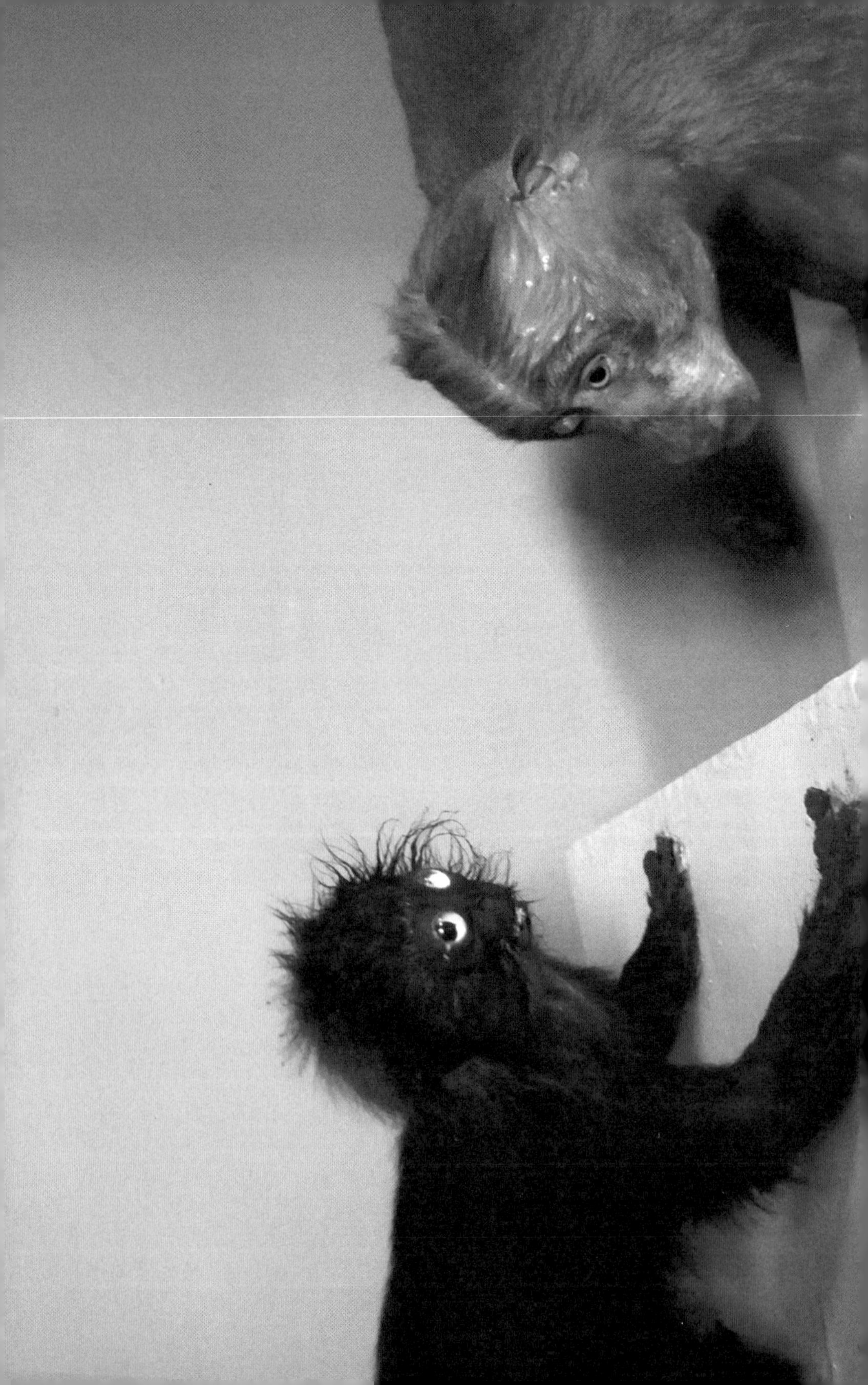

Every animal is in the world like water in water.
—Georges Bataille, *Theory of Religion*

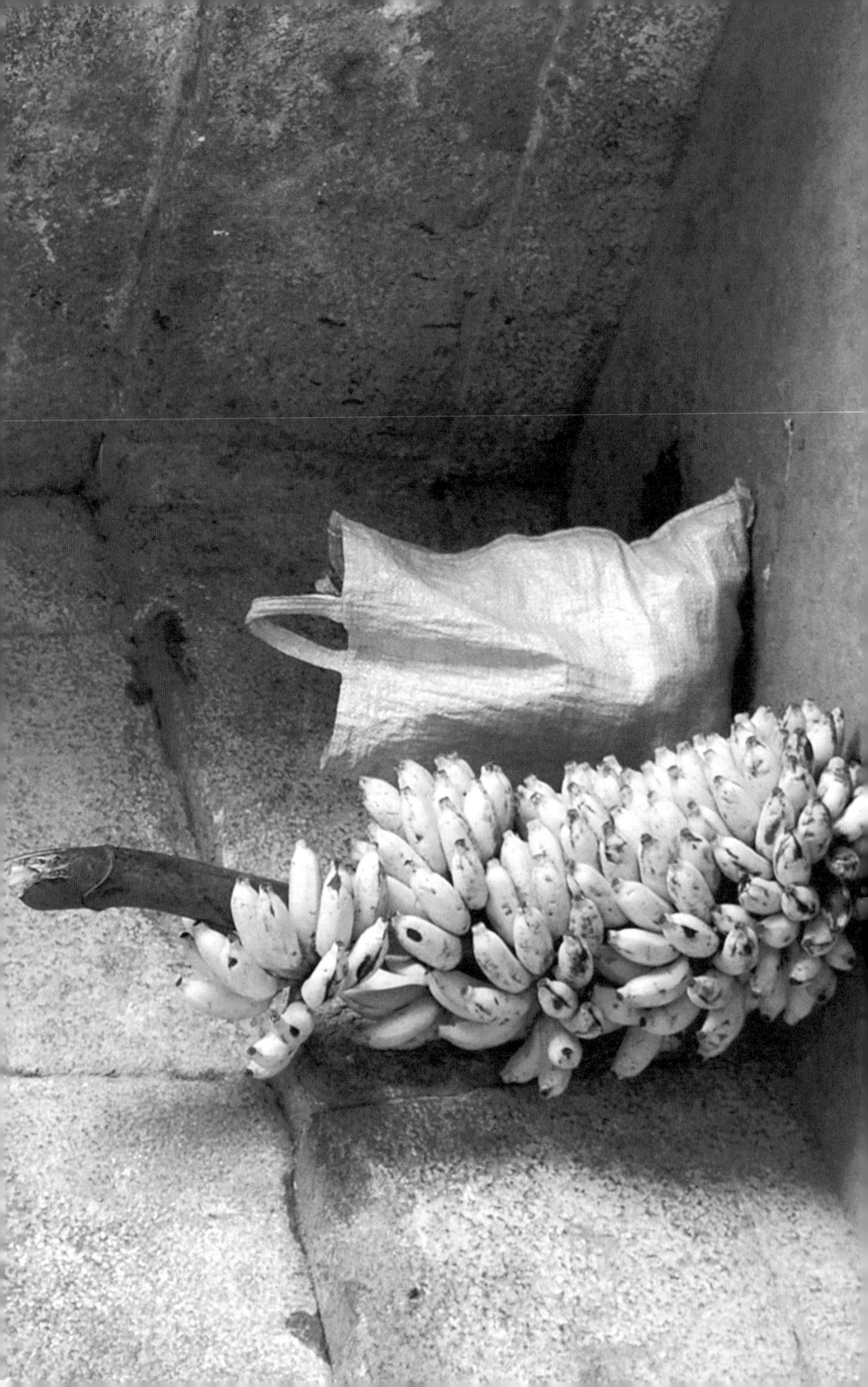

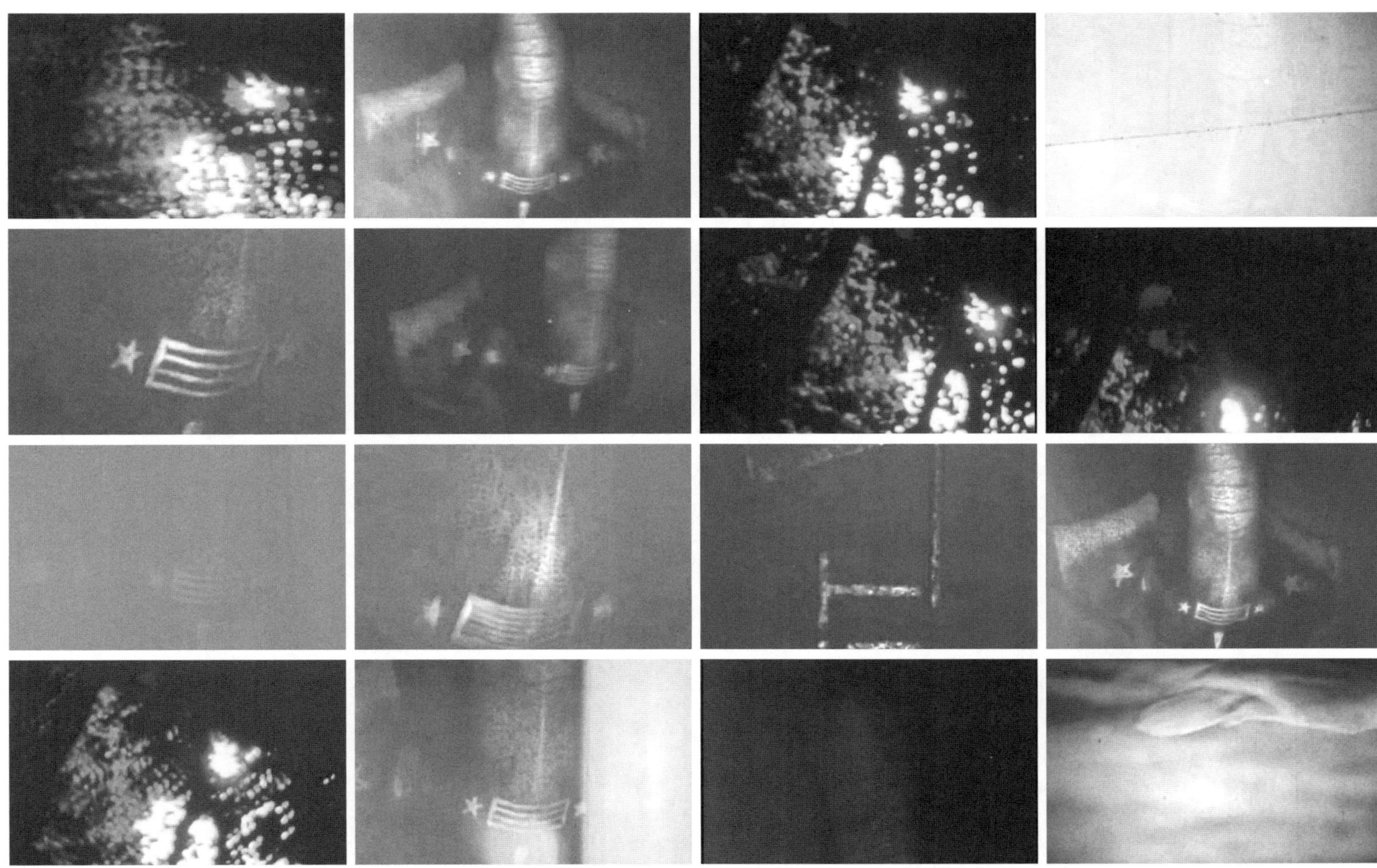

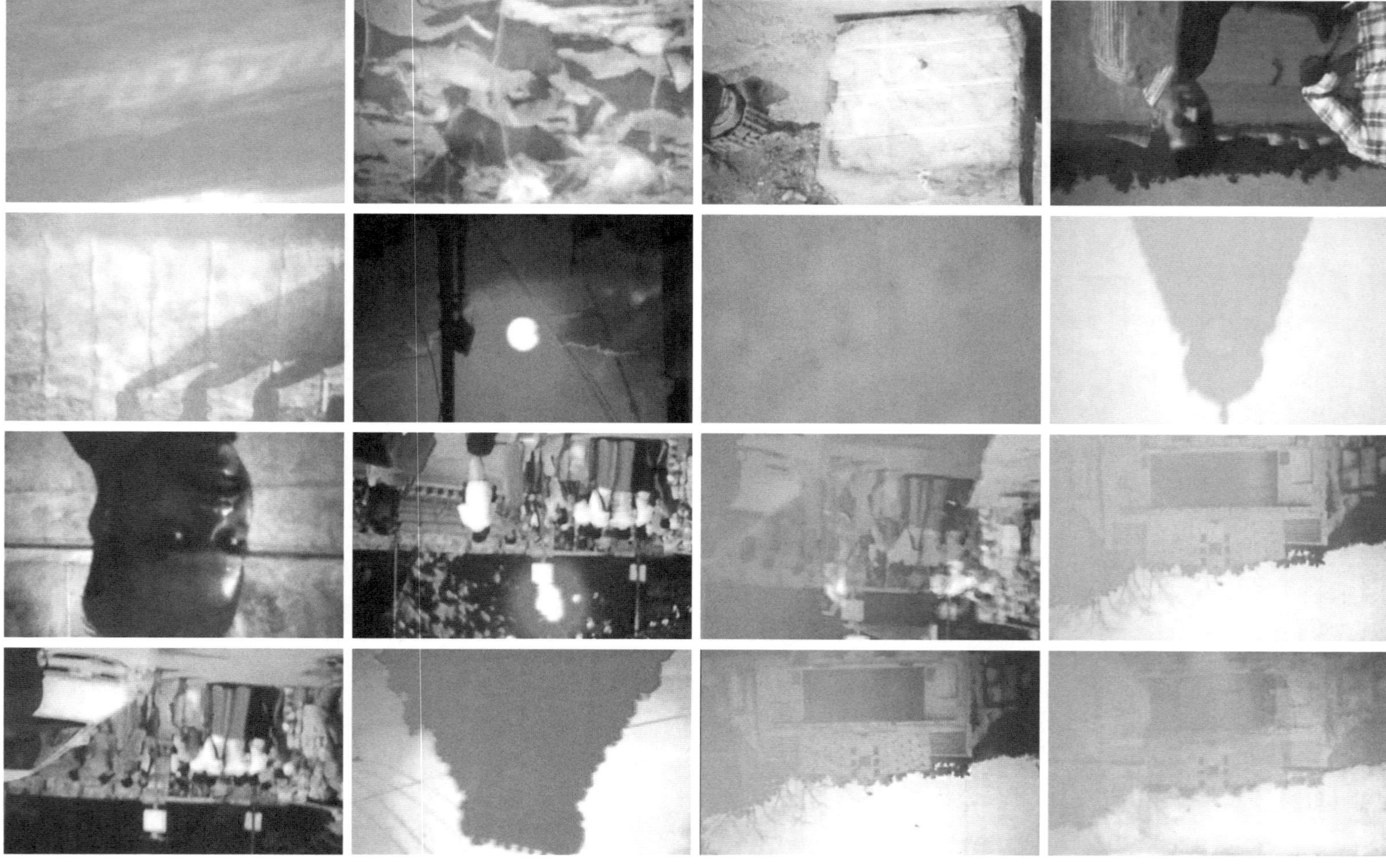

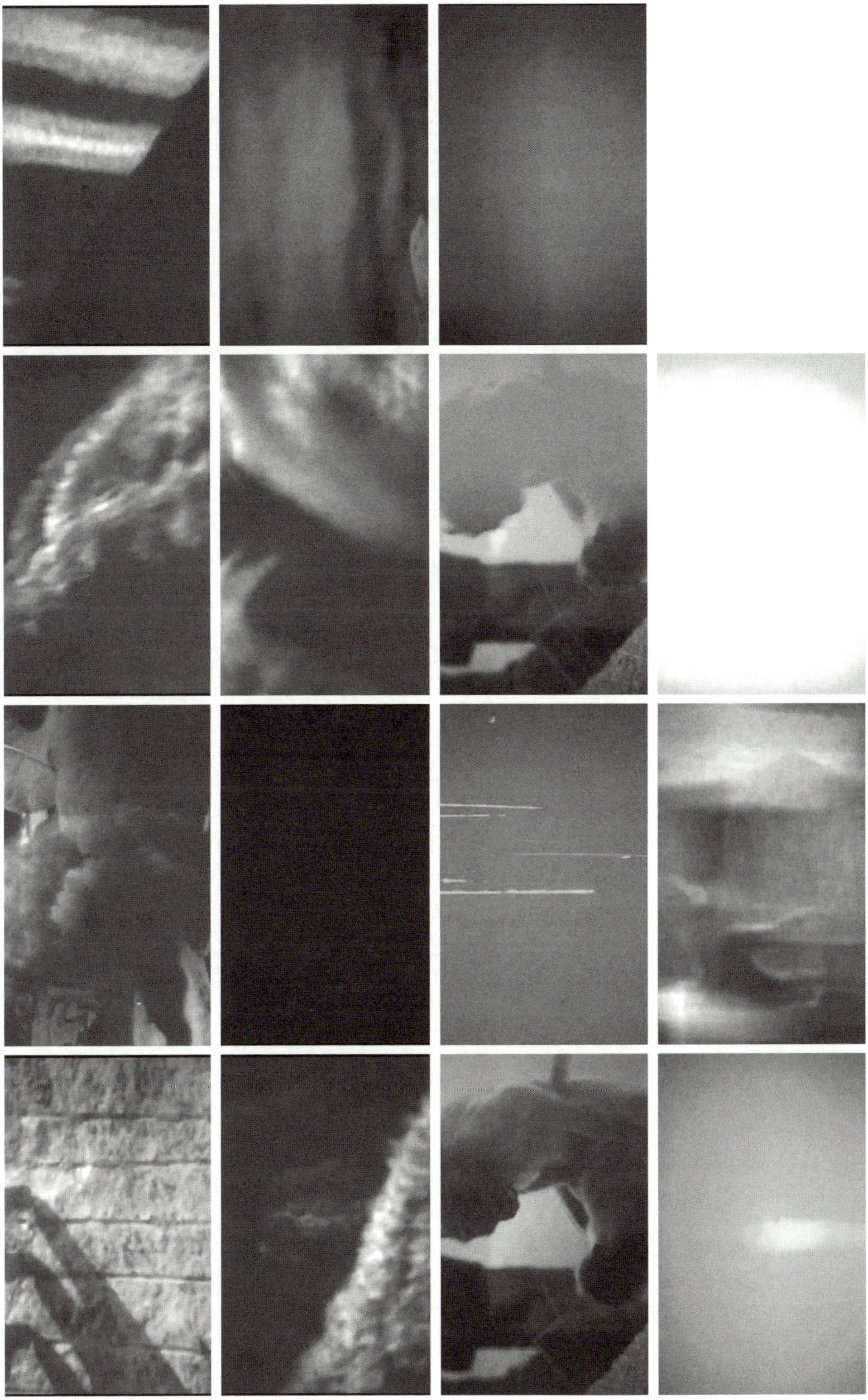

PANDIAN

8/SACRIFICE_BANANA

Keelavalavu is one of the largest mining operations of the PRP Group.
It produces the most popular colours: Madura Gold, Ivory Fantasy & Kashmir White.
—PRP Exports website (www.prpexports.com)

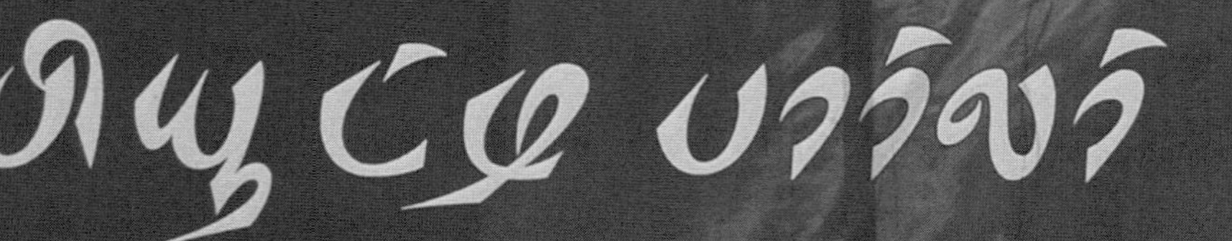
நியூ
ராஜா
சலூன்
பியூட்டி பார்லர்
NEW WORLD DIGITAL
9655818828
அன்னவாசல் ரோடு, திருவப்பூர்.
செல் : 99421-32507

Yes, it dazzles like a billion suns.
—Karur Thevar on the Big Temple, Thanjavur

CRUDE MERIDIAN

"The desert of Arabia is America's last frontier." The story of the cowboy oilmen who branded the Gulf and the Bedouin who followed in their footsteps.

by Sophia Al-Maria
with Manal Al Dowayan
published May 15, 2010

Sooner or later the Middle East equivalent of the western is bound to show up on the gravel plains and sand dunes of the desert. Arab desert lore is filled with the great deeds of Bedouin heroes, and the vast desert itself offers possibilities of breathtaking panoramic backgrounds for some great chase scenes.
—*Saudi Aramco World*, May 1963

MUZAHMIAH WAS A BEDU HICK TOWN in 1968, when my father was nine years old, and it's a Bedu hick town now. The one-truck farming outpost twenty-five miles west of Riyadh is best known as the home of the Reem International Circuit, Saudi Arabia's answer to the Daytona International Speedway. But back in 1968, it was not even that. My father, Mohamed, remembers that winter as "the season of the television," when his world was dilated by the arrival of a black-and-white Sears set on a ledge overlooking my great-uncle Saleh's courtyard.

In my father's telling of the seasons, that winter was preceded by "the season of the hell," when he'd encountered his first oil flare. He and Uncle Ali were hitching a ride to a relative's camp near al-Hassa on the back of a postman's truck. It was dusk, and the sun had settled deep into the reddening west. But oddly, there was also light coming from the east: a clean, yellow, too-bright light that threatened to bring the morning out to meet the night. My father and Ali climbed up from behind the shield of the cab and into the open, where they were buffeted by sandy gales. On the horizon there appeared a roaring flame, more brilliant than the sun. It was unfathomably large and impossibly high off the ground, exactly like a mirage—only there was no way this was an illusion.

This strange, unflagging flame was silent at first. But soon the wind lapped at Mohamed's and Ali's ears, and they heard its growl and felt its heat, if only for a whipping second. After half an hour the postman steered his truck north and left the roiling stacks of fire behind. My father and Ali would for the rest of their lives be drawn back to this desert, where at certain times of day, depending on which way you face, it is at once twilight and dusk.

BY THE TIME THE SEASON OF THE TELEVISION arrived in Muzahmiah, Dhahran TV had already been on air throughout the Gulf for more than five years. In those early days of broadcasting, a village ritual (punctuated by two breaks for prayer) was formed around the sequence of programming carefully calibrated by Saudi Aramco, the oil company founded in 1933 by Standard Oil of California with a concession from King Ibn Saud. Below is an early television schedule, as recounted by my father and uncles:

17:30 Maghrib prayer. By the time the *kahraba* (electricity) was switched on, the animals had gone silent, and the crackling hum of a generator filled the courtyard of Saleh's house. If the *kahraba* kicked in early enough, the viewers would see the beginning of the broadcast: a screen of illuminated text and a Koranic recitation.

18:00 Cartoons, *Looney Tunes* or *Popeye*. Zeitoonah (Olive Oyl) became a common nickname for clumsy, lanky, cow-hawked girls.

18:30 Children's hour: *Mr. Ed*, *Lassie*, or both. A few years later came *Little House on the Prairie*, which was a runaway hit. The settling traumas of the Ingalls girls struck a chord with Bedu kids being relocated to villages like Muzahmiah from scattered camps that had been caught in the drill lights of oil derricks.

19:30 News, with auspicious tidings of King Saud's good health as the lead item.

20:00 Asha prayer, more Koran.

20:15 *Perry Mason* or *Rawhide*, the root of my father's fascination with Clint Eastwood.

I S S U E   8   2 0 1 0

21:15   Musical interlude, sung by beehived Kuwaitis. One of them—but not just one of them—was the Syrian beauty Samirah Tawfiq, whose heart-shaped face and "cowgirl braids," as my father called them, had every boy in the kingdom rearing. Her signature move was a wink directed at the camera—or, as it seemed, at the viewer. Each momentarily shuttered eyelid provoked a territorial skirmish between my father and his friends, all of whom believed she was theirs alone.

Years later, during a family gathering in the *salah* (ladies' parlor) of my grandmother's house, a favorite Samirah clip came on; my father walked into the room, caught a glimpse of her, and began automatically forecasting each wink and wiggle the second before it happened. Recently, I found the video on YouTube and sent it to my father. He called me on the phone and let out a dreamy sigh: "Samirah . . . *helwa*." Samirah . . . sweet.

24:00   Midnight marked the cutoff. The broadcast would fizzle into static with cool finality, whether or not the film had ended.

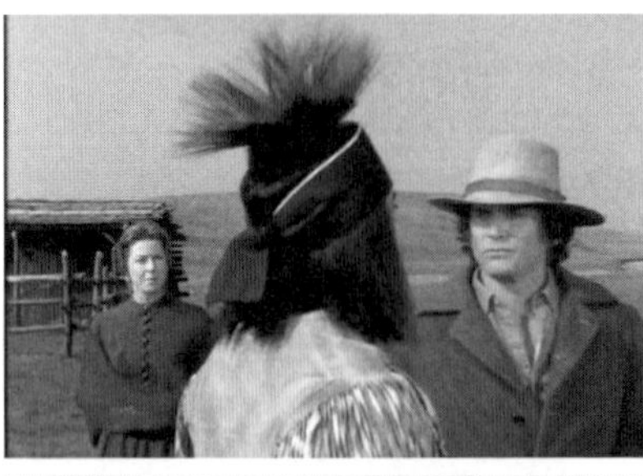
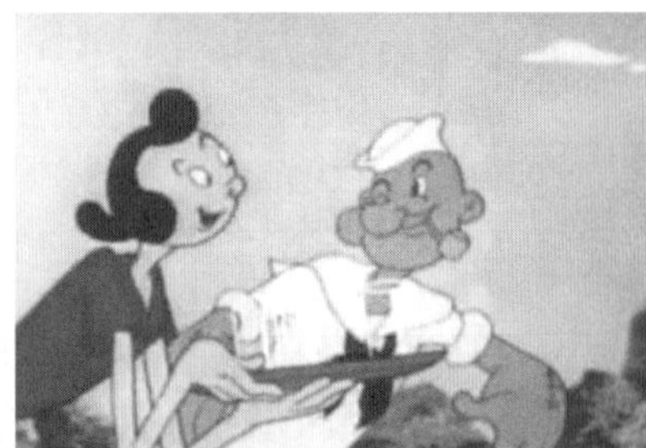
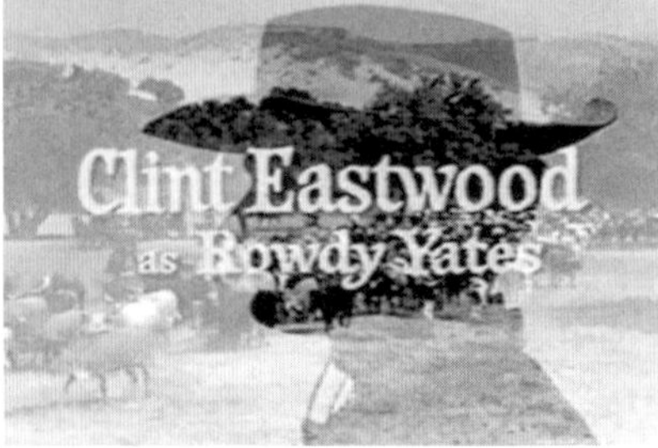

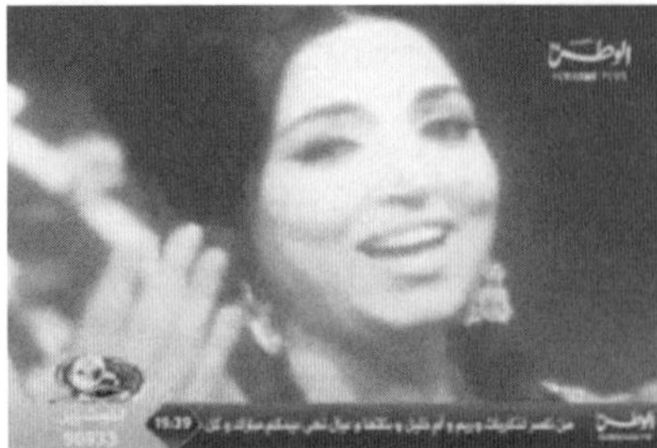

Clockwise from top left: *Little House on the Prairie*, *Popeye the Sailor*, *Rawhide*, and Syrian singer Samirah Tawfiq, stills from YouTube videos.

*That universal hero, the cowboy, has found a home
in the desert with an assist from TV. Saudi Arabs,
like Londoners, Parisians and Romans, have taken
enthusiastically to American horse operas.*
—*Saudi Aramco World*, May 1963

THE TELEVISION WAS ALWAYS the sole appliance in the village that stayed on right until the electricity curfew. By the time the tube's rubber band of black-and-white had disappeared, the rest of the desert was blanketed in darkness. Any firelight in nearby camps was canceled out by the wattage of the stars. The adults had all gone to bed hours before, leaving an array of boys and girls splayed across the gritty carpet of Saleh's courtyard, long braids spread over bare feet. Some had been out cold since before Lassie had saved Timmy; some had zoned out during the Battle of the Little Bighorn; the littlest ones had begun roughhousing after Yosemite Sam plunged down a mineshaft and had long since curled up in dog piles and fallen asleep. The elder children would each sling a sibling around a hip—my father taking Hamendi, Ali with little Saleh, Nora with Jameela—and shuffle along the moonlit treads of their uncle Saleh's truck, a path strewn with camel tracks and barely dry goat turds, until they reached their two-room cinderblock huts.

Each night after my father crawled into his bed of wool blankets and jumbled brothers and sisters, he would imagine, through his bleary eyes, a silhouette loping toward him. This *khayal*, or shadow, stood over him all night, keeping watch from the back of his steed, distinguished from a Bedu only by the sharp slash of the Stetson's brim cutting across the head. My father called him cowboy.

IN NOVEMBER 1955, A PLANE NAMED "the flying camel" touched down in Dhahran with the dean of western writers, Wallace Stegner, aboard. Aramco had flown Stegner and his wife to the kingdom to chronicle the discovery of oil and the latter-day American frontiersmen who had traveled there to extract it. The Stegners were transplanted

INVALID FORMAT 2

ISSUE 8 2010

to Aramco's camp at Dhahran, a soundstage replica of Anytown, America, replete with town houses and palm trees—a corporate state within a state. The author set to writing *Discovery! The Search for Arabian Oil*, published serially in *Saudi Aramco World* magazine in 1970 and '71. The book chronicles Stegner's tours of the dunes with the "old-timers and pioneers of the 1930s."

Stegner's Arabia echoed the desert Southwest, "with its flat crestlines, its dry clarity of air, its silence. But it felt more mysterious than that." The oilmen called to this virgin territory recalled the cowboys of yore, all grit and humility. "Seen in retrospect," the job they came to do "has the nostalgic, almost mythic quality of an action from the age of giants."

Bringing on Stegner as a hired pen was a masterful move by Aramco's PR men. Though they were later called out for their reliance on "unctuous and cloying language," which produced a landscape "tainted by sentimental illusions," they succeeded in rebranding Arabia in the image of the Old West. The American frontier, by then vanishing beneath the sprawl of Phoenix and Las Vegas, was in the Gulf imagined anew, albeit in a landscape so dazing that even Stegner eventually deemed it "unreality." But what better place than unreality to stage an encounter between the Aramco pioneers and the land that guarded their destiny?

> *Oh, friend, a little of the cold tea, please.*
> —Dhahran TV translation of "Hey pardner, gimme a whiskey."

MUZAHMIAH'S IMAM, ALWAYS SUSPICIOUS of the broadcasts emanating from the American Dhahran Camp—surely they were meant to make his town's children love the deserts of America more than their own—began an assault on the television after someone modified its antenna with a latticework of jury-rigged wires and metal scraps, which caused it to surpass the mosque's minaret. At Friday

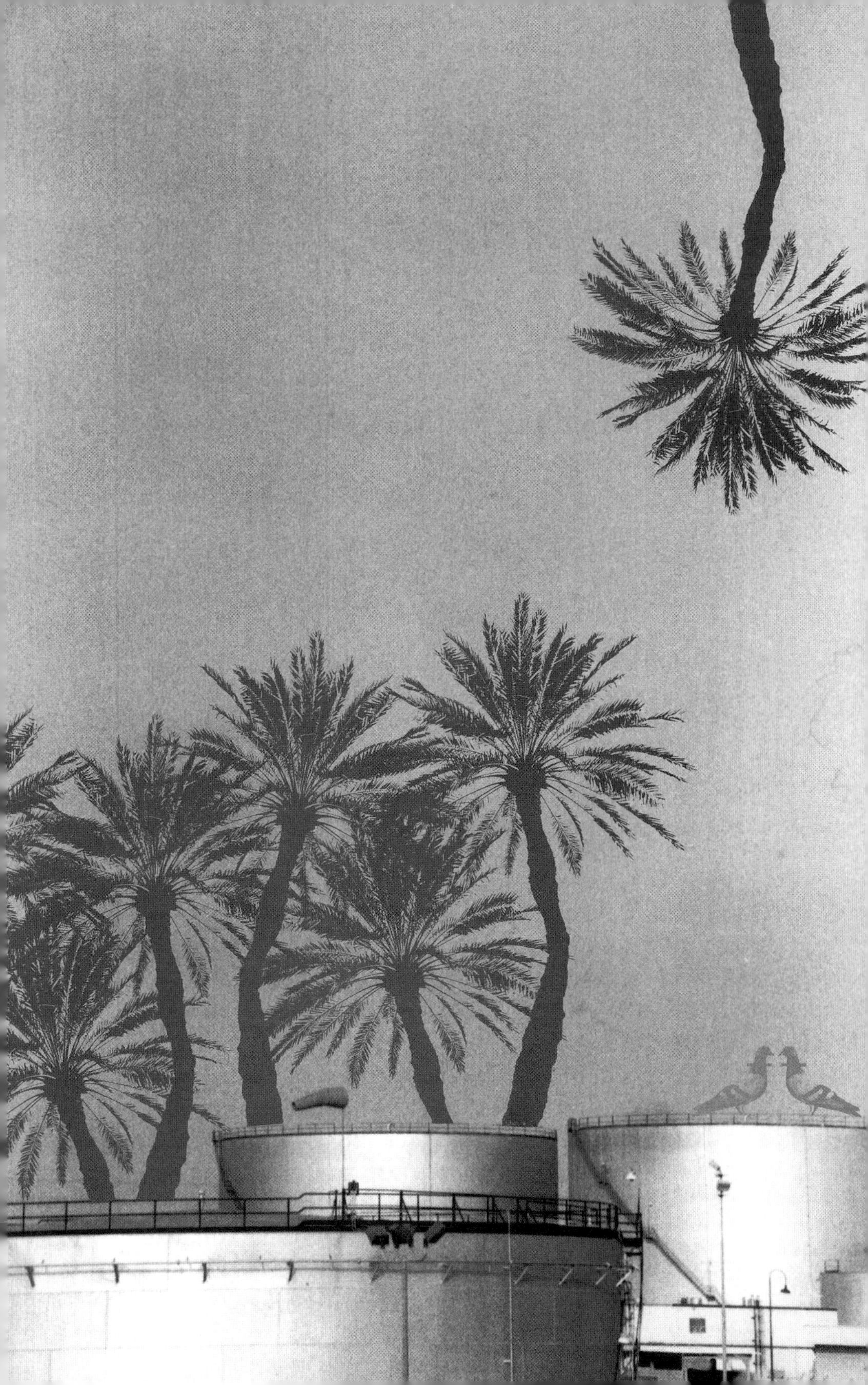

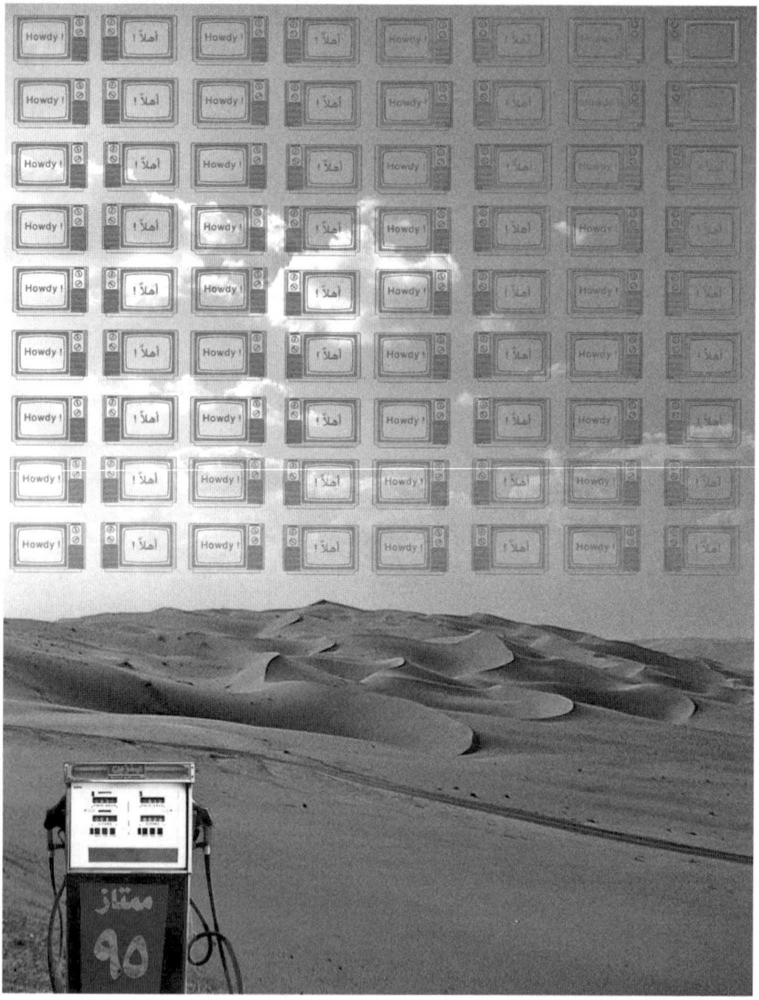

Manal Al Dowayan, *Howdy*, 2010, mixed media on paper.
From the series "Landscapes of the Mind," 2009–10.

prayer—and in social calls to village *majlises*, or men's parlors, every other day of the week—the imam preached against "the flag of evil" flying over Muzahmiah.

Nevertheless, he, too, made the occasional pilgrimage to Saleh's courtyard to watch the cowboys and Indians do battle. He smoldered at the perimeter of the TV's blue-gray devil ray and secretly marveled at the similarities between his tribe and the bands of *hinood hamr*—"red Indians"—corralled by railways and mining camps, ambushing the white man from outcroppings and rock formations just like those surrounding his own town.

Before him sat the children of Al-Murrah, who were described in a 1964 issue of *Saudi Aramco World* as "the tribe of nomads which more than any other has given birth—and considerable substance—to the colorful image of the desert Bedouins." The imam must have known that these children were unknowingly reliving the same tired arc played out nightly on the television. After all, the bulk of the oil found in the early years of exploration lay directly under the tribe's migratory routes; Aramco bought off the various clans with the twentieth-century equivalent of shiny beads and a beaver pelt: sacks of riyal coins and cinderblock huts on the outskirts of a town hundreds of miles from their ancestral hunting grounds. And yet the children cast their lots with the cowboys.

In the summer of 1978, a decade after the season of the television, and long after the cathode ray cowboy had ceased haunting him, my father headed to "Montana, America," to see how he measured up. He flew west into the sunset from Dhahran, traveling with the edge of night. He was wearing pants for the first time, and they were ill fitting; he carried nothing but a briefcase with his *sirwal* (long underwear) and some traveler's checks. Ten, eighteen, twenty-four hours passed—Dhahran to New York to San Francisco to Missoula—and it was still night. He spoke no English and navigated JFK by matching the airline logo on his ticket with the logos on the gates. Jet lag set in. He later told me, "I thought the sun would never rise again."

FORTY-FOUR YEARS BEFORE my father flew out West, Max Steineke abandoned it for the unbounded deserts of Arabia. He served as Aramco's chief geologist between 1936 and '46, discovering more than ten billion barrels of proven reserves during his tenure. "He was no son of a bitch for civilization," Stegner wrote, describing him in a drawling panegyric fit for the campfire. "Burly, big-jawed, hearty, enthusiastic, profane, indefatigable, careless of irrelevant details and implacable in tracking down a line of scientific inquiry, he made men like him, and won their confidence. He was a very pure example of a very American type and heir to every quality that America had learned while settling and conquering a continent." In other words, he was what all the boys gathered around Saleh's courtyard hoped to become.

Steineke responded to the call put out by Aramco's public-relations-and-marketing apparatus in the early '30s, when the company began modeling Saudi Arabia after a John Ford set, a place where boyhood fantasies could be indulged and fortunes made. The groundwork for this romancing of Americans had been laid by Harry St. John Philby, the British explorer, Arabist, and confidante of Ibn Saud. Long before Aramco became a hundred-billion-barrel giant, it was a figment of Philby's fertile imagination. He convinced the king that Arabia was "a man sleeping atop buried treasure" and that extracting it required the California-Arabian Standard Oil Company (which later begat Aramco). "Arabia is a mirror image of the Old West," Philby wrote, "a wide, unfenced land where nature is unsubdued, religion is simple and fundamental, and the law of the gun prevails—the desert of Arabia is America's last frontier."

And so the American geologists and hydrologists and their wives began to fill the compound at Dhahran. The men trekked into the desert with guides who measured distance in "camel days," while the women partook of the leisure activities delineated in *Desert Venture* (1958), a Technicolor treat of a corporate film produced by Standard Oil, which called for men who possessed the "pioneering spirit" to partake of this "venture by American capital in a strange and ancient land." By the time my father landed in Missoula, there were ten thousand of them there.

WHEN MY FATHER FINALLY MADE IT to Montana, he bought a white Stetson and headed to the Billings rodeo. He bellied up to the bar, doffed his hat, and asked for "a little of the cold tea." Right then and there, fate dealt him my mother. She was tall, blond, and blue-eyed—a berry farmer's daughter, milkfed and tough; Slue-Foot Sue to his Pecos Bill. He lied and told her it was his birthday; she bought him a celebratory drink.

His English needed fixing, so she fixed it. He couldn't cut it as a cowboy, so she steered him toward trucking. Within a month he was driving a cab-over-truck Mack up and down I-5, through the Cascades and all along Snake River, singing along to Red Sovine and Waylon Jennings. Now, when the sun is low in the sky over Al Riwais, he'll gather the family into our Suburban and steer the car in the direction of Al-Hassa. When the road opens up before us, he'll take a deep breath, adopt his best American drawl, and belt out a song by Tom T. Hall:

> *I love little baby ducks,*
> *Old pickup trucks,*
> *Slow-moving trains*
> *And rain.*
>
> *I love coffee in a cup,*
> *Little fuzzy pups,*
> *Bourbon in a glass*
> *And grass.*

Toward the end of his stay in big-sky country—where, it seems, he never took off his white Stetson—a drunk old woman gave him a piece of her mind that struck him hard and low: "Hunny, yer too short to be a cowboy." Not long after, he packed his saddlebags, bid farewell to my mother and me, and headed back toward the rising sun, back to the oil derricks, back to the flares of hell.

In 1985, Abu Dhabi was a boomtown in full swing, its skyline rising in glass and steel. My father had swapped the shadow man's Stetson for his father's red-and-white-checked *ghutra*, but even if he looked the part, he was too late to be a Bedouin; he had hoped to continue driving trucks—the Mercedes eighteen-wheelers that connected the ports and hubs of the Gulf—but was undersold by harder-up Bedu who had just left their own families in *al bar*, the wilderness.

He headed out again, this time to the sea, by helicopter, without expectations. He took up work as a watchstander on a rig twenty kilometers off the shore of Abu Dhabi, an eternity from the desert but with the same lonely vistas. Beyond the expanse of the sun's splintered reflection, he glimpsed his future: the outline of the Sheraton, a gently eroded sand castle installed on the shore; the Corniche, with its volcano-shaped fountain spewing sandalwood-scented magma-colored water into the air; and angled mushroom shadecasters marking every few yards for the weary workers. Here the desert venture was being consecrated, the Gulf visions of the Aramco ad men carved in stone. And here, finally, he had a role to play.

As with any folklore, there are untold stories buried beneath tradition. Some of the Al-Murrah boys fled the season of the television, rode off into the desert, disappeared into the widow-making dunes of the Empty Quarter. In a 1969 issue of *Saudi Aramco World*, photographer and writer Tor Eigeland captured these "castaways in the sand":

> There they were, a boy and his camel, drifting along like castaways from a disappearing past and vanishing into a future where he, like stray gypsies, old prospectors and wandering cowboys, will have no deserts to cross, no plains to ride, no more open roads to tread. ☒

JUKEBOXES ON THE MOON

*Stardom is martyrdom:
India arrives in the
American imagination.*

by Rafil Kroll-Zaidi
published July 1, 2010

CANOPYCANOPYCANOPY.COM/8/JUKEBOXES_ON_THE_MOON

LATE IN NOVEMBER OF 2008, making their way through Mumbai's Victoria Terminus, two young Muslim men became famous. One was Jamal Malik, a fictional orphan in a movie. The other was Ajmal Amir Kasab, said to be from a clan of butchers in small-town Pakistani Punjab. The former, in the closing scenes of the film, is weedy, gawky; lets his mouth hang open in a pantomime of nervous exhilaration; is newly rich from winning a game show; kisses the girl and then dances with the rest of the cast. The latter, in the most widely seen photo, is stout, steroidal; wears too-short cargo pants, a knockoff VERSACE T-shirt, two backpacks filled with ammunition and snacks; carries a double-banana-clipped AK-47 that blurs as it swings through the depopulated space before him. On May 6, 2010, he was sentenced to be hanged.

"THE SAME LEGENDARY rail terminal that's the setting for the movie's joyously Bollywoodized finale . . . was on the news as a massacre site. Yet," asserted *GQ,* "that only gave Jamal's very secular defiance a new edge of triumph." Let us return, then, to Victoria Terminus—a shooting location twice over—and to the anti-Jamal, the complement to his physical weakness, political insensibility, and inherent Westernness, the other South Asian Muslim who rose to fame at the same time: Ajmal Amir Kasab.

Years from now, the magazine went on to say, "we won't have forgotten the scads of anonymous dancers who show up to shake their collective booty . . . behind Jamal and his honey in *Slumdog*'s euphoric train-platform finale. Just think of them as the Mumbai victims' posthumous revenge on the gunmen." If *terrorist* sounds a note of pejoration while *insurgent* concedes certain autochthonous rights, *gunman,* the American media's epithet of choice for the Mumbai attackers (and for the use of which the *New York Times* was called out and couldn't explain itself), seemed tinged with near-approbationary awe.

All ten gunmen were superlatively competent. They remained sharp; the police assumed they must have taken

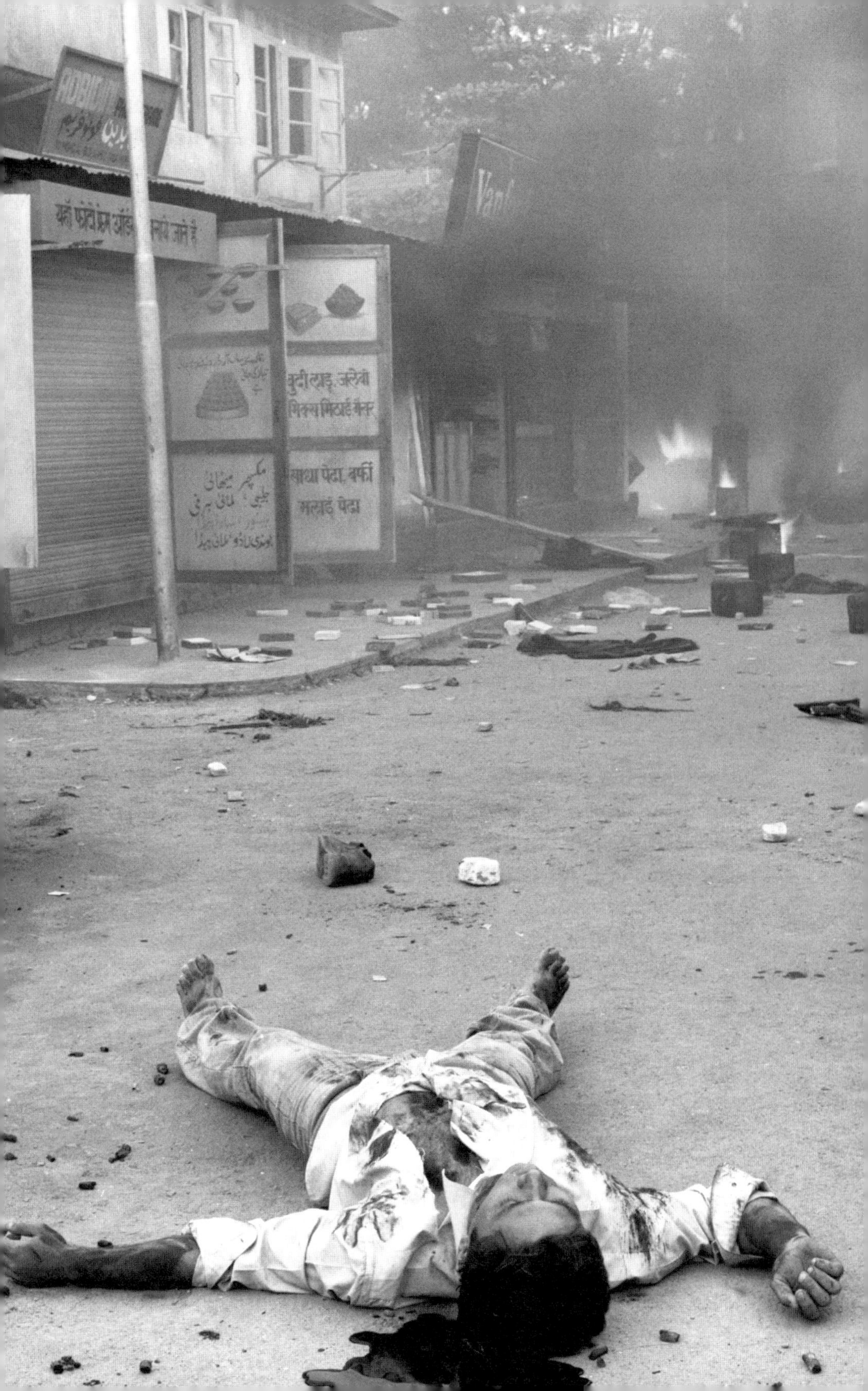

amphetamines, cocaine, LSD to stay awake. (Autopsies showed they had not.) The police seemed almost vaudevillian in their uselessness. Some of them were armed with muskets, others had no ammunition. Those who were armed couldn't shoot to save their lives. One cop tried throwing a plastic stacking chair at Kasab and his partner, Ismail Khan. All teams save Kasab's (which attacked Victoria Terminus and a hospital) made for locations where foreigners and wealthy Indians congregate (a backpackers' café, a Chabad Lubavich center, two five-star hotels). "If you speak to the media," one of the gunmen was advised, via cell phone, by his handler, "tell them this is only the trailer. The film is yet to come."

Kasab was perfectly cast. At VT, he and Khan racked up fifty-eight kills (a third of the final toll) in what was by far the most efficient phase of the three-day-long operation. Kasab had no handler; he "strolled." "They were like angels of death," said a newspaper photographer who shadowed Kasab and Khan through the station and whose photo of Kasab—clean-cut in back-to-school clothes, one-handing his AK-47—was universally disseminated. "When they hit someone they didn't even look back. They were so sure." The pair inexplicably passed over some of those caught in the station, doing them no harm. They went on to storm an obstetric and children's hospital, outside of which they shot the state's top antiterror cop; they stole his SUV, shot at people outside a cinema, stole a sedan, and ran into a roadblock, and then Khan was killed and Kasab pretended to surrender but then shot another cop before he was overpowered and arrested.

Kasab was captured on 26/11 itself, and by November 30 he had become "the lone surviving gunman." One of his first interrogators spoke of a "muscular, well-trained body" and a face that was "very calm but has a blank, cold stare all the time." The police asked him who he was supposed to kill. "People." Where was he supposed to go after completing the operation? "We were supposed to die."

He had no surname, so the criminal-justice bureaucracy

used his family's caste, Kasai—butchers. (*If you have never seen a tiger, look at a cat. If you have never seen a thug, look at a Kasai.*) Some said he spoke fluent English. He had extensive Koranic instruction, or knew nothing of the Koran. His age was unclear. His vagueness construed his villainy.

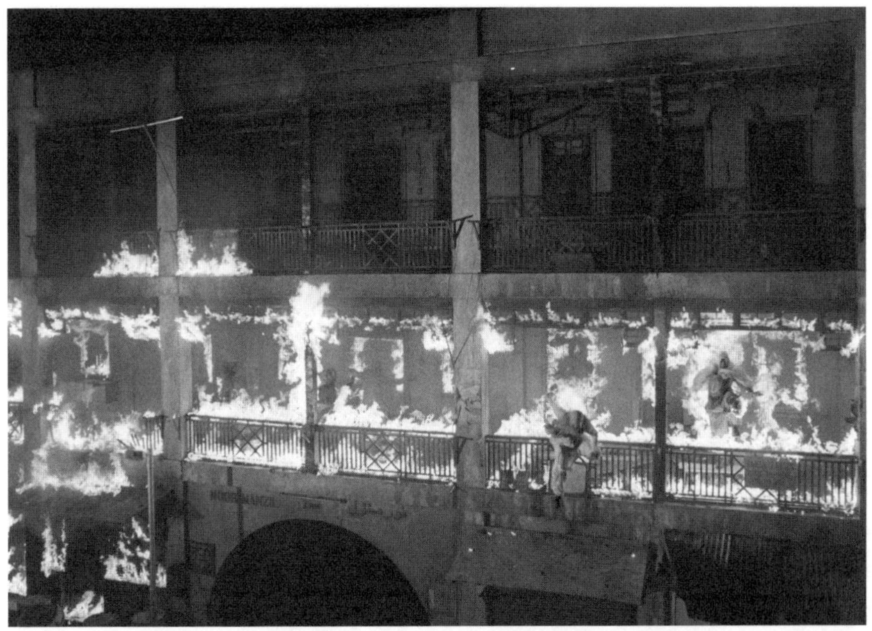

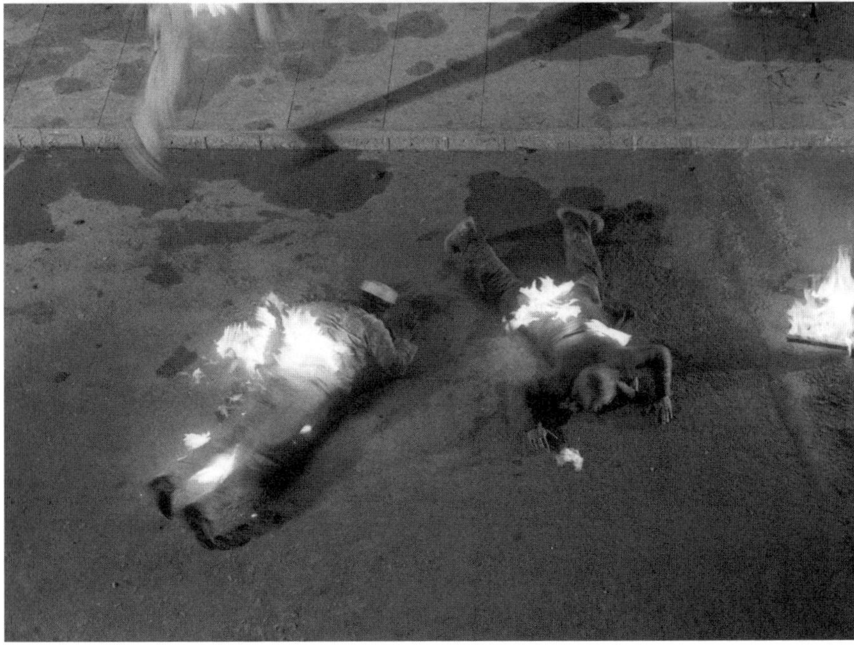

I N V A L I D   F O R M A T   2

I S S U E   8   2 0 1 0

THE ONLY SCENE in *Slumdog Millionaire* that connects Jamal to Islam is the pogrom in which his mother is killed. This event—which should be the seminal moment of his life—becomes but one more answer to one more trivial question. ("Trifles," as *David Copperfield* has it, "make the

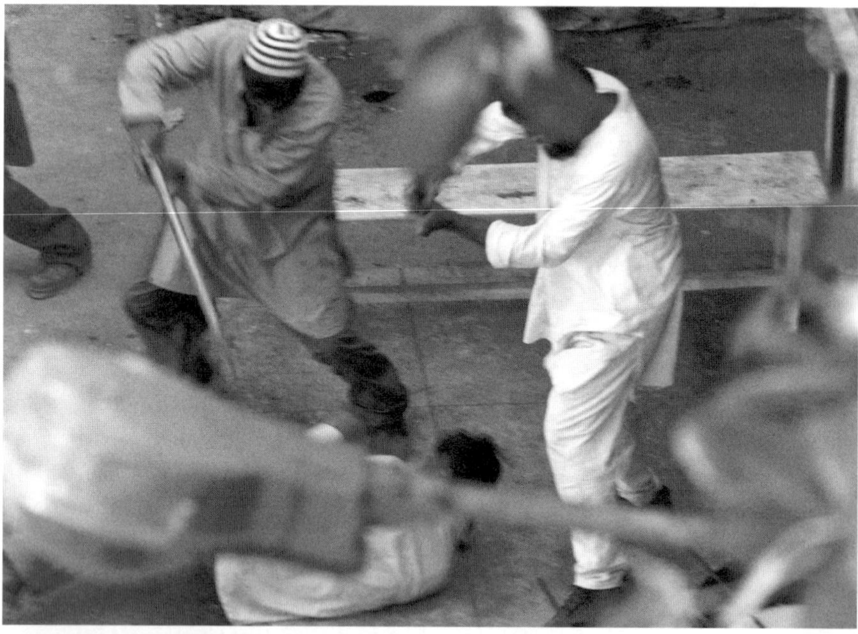

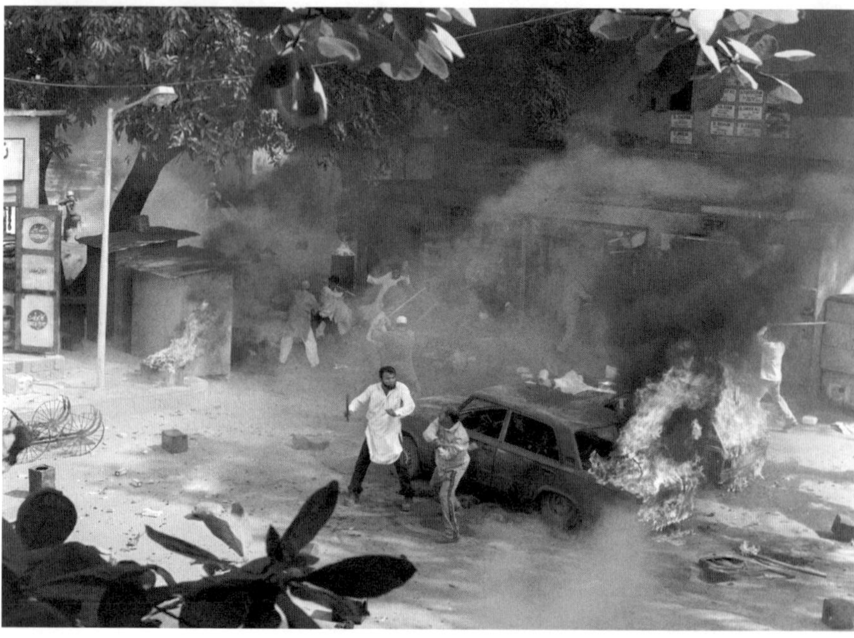

sum of life.") In the riot scene, a six-year-old Jamal and his older brother, Salim, splash in a shallow concrete cistern while their mother and a dozen other launderers go about their Indically polychromatic business; the mother glances with portentous washerwoman unease toward trains rumbling past on nearby tracks; the train traffic clears to reveal an onrushing Hindu mob (the white noise of their roar subtitled, "They're Muslims, get them!"); she is felled by a fanatic's rebar; the brothers, fleeing amid further rout, happen upon a young boy elaborately kitted out as a blue-skinned Hindu god who stares at them as he stands frozen in the posture of the relevant iconography. The little blue boy provides Jamal a crucial piece of knowledge about the god Ram ("Hindoo Deities for $100"). Having related this anecdote to police interrogators years later, Jamal concludes, with husky piety, "If it wasn't for Ram and Allah, I'd still have a mother."

One stage beyond progressive skepticism, Jamal's faux truism is full of unspoken repudiation. (Salim, a small-time gangster who prays mornings for the forgiveness of his sins, seems meant as a soft example of a *bad man*, with worse lurking beyond the frame.) Jamal's heroism, in short, is his gormlessness. "Agreeable enough if vague" was the *Times'* description. As a putative Muslim, he is made courageous and principled by his very lack of these qualities.

FOR A LONG TIME, there were no new photos of Kasab. Then he was pictured sitting in a police station on a plastic stacking chair, his wrists in handcuffs and bandages. He looked bored. His T-shirt now said "sports." In February 2009, the police filed against him a charge sheet that ran to eleven thousand pages. He was indicted for belligeration, for murder actual and attempted, for entering the train station without a ticket; connected to physical evidence that included leftover grenades, scraps of paper reading "This is a pointer to war," and a large bottle of Mountain Dew. Hundreds of witnesses testified against him. *He killed my sir. . . . This short man shot at my boss. How can I forget? He is*

INVALID FORMAT 2

ISSUE 8 2010

the one. She was my only daughter. He was carrying a bag. She died in front of my eyes. That shorty!

In the months following his apprehension and during the trial, Kasab remained opaque but became much more pedestrian. In court he smiled, laughed, and cried; in which acts he was called "baby-faced," "childlike," "college student"–like, "fresh-faced," "very good-looking," "sullen," "curious"; a patsy, a monster, an expert in the production of crocodile tears. His lawyer, Abbas Kazmi, claimed the accused was a minor, but Kasab himself slipped up and told the court he was twenty-one. ("The cat," said Kazmi, "has now come out of the bag.") Still, serologic and radiologic testing was carried out to establish Kasab's majority. (His clavicle had fused; he could be tried as an adult.)

Kasab had left school at age twelve. He worked as a laborer. At some point he may have had a falling out with his father, who had refused to buy him new clothes for the festival of Eid. He possibly became involved in petty banditry and with a friend sought out Lashkar-e-Taiba in order to acquire better weapons and thereby improve their brigandage. In another version of the story (*A Kasai never tells the truth; if he did he would not be a Kasai*), Kasab said his father encouraged him to seek out the group: "He said, 'Look, son, we're very poor. Other people live the good life, and so can you. You won't have to do anything difficult. We'll have money, we'll no longer be poor. Your brothers and sisters will be able to get married. Look at how well these other people live [lit. "eat"].'" Reporters tracked down Kasab's father and asked him whether it was true that he'd handed Kasab over to Lashkar-e-Taiba for money. He denied it. "I don't sell my sons."

MANY NOTED THAT the romantic young man cared nothing for money:

> "There's something much more interesting, of course, that steps outside the show, in a way, is that he is not interested in the money, really. Which is strange. His

reason for being on the show is very different." "His goal isn't money, it's to raise his profile in hopes of finding the girl he lost." "She's the only thing of real value he sees in the swirl of riches and rags around him." "I wanted to make it about more than money."

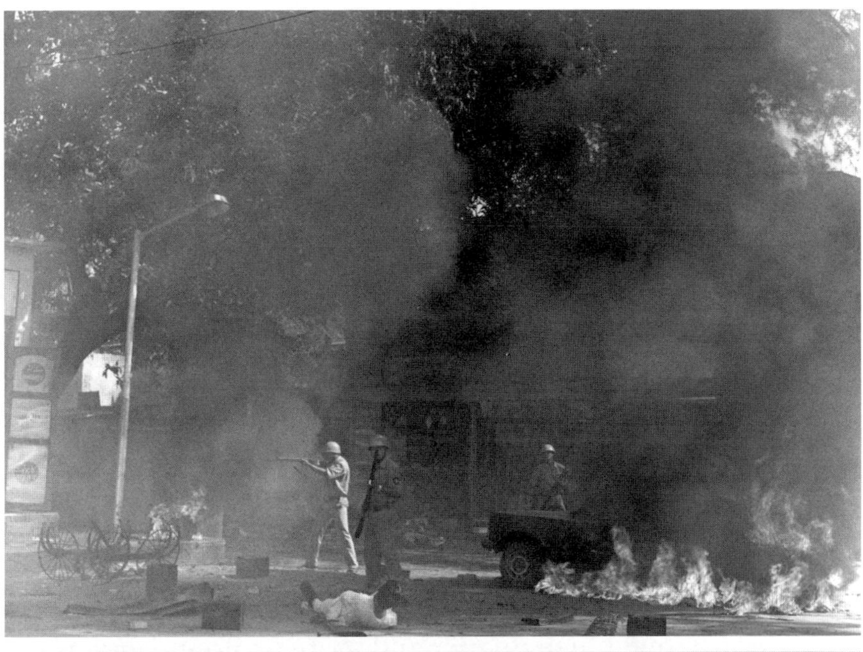

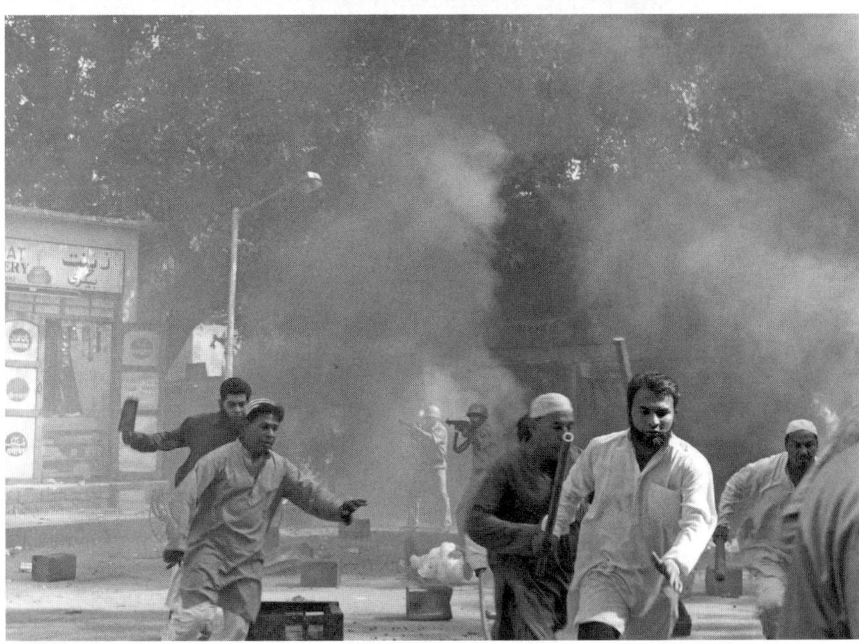

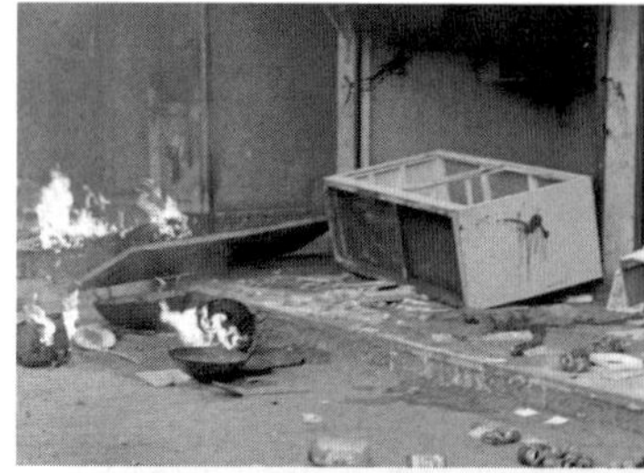
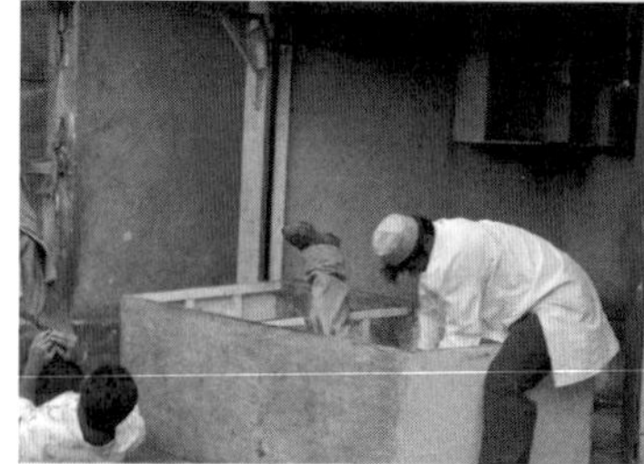
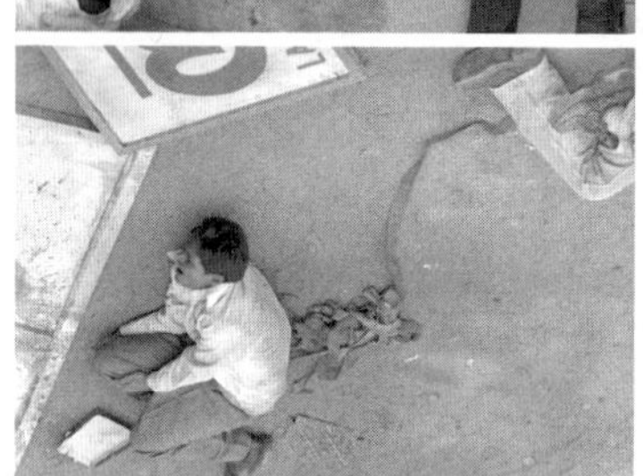
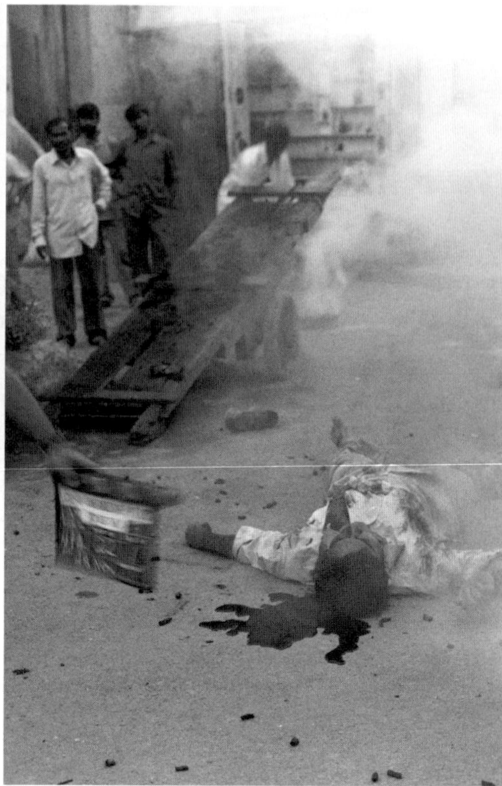

"The love story, which is much stronger than a television show, much deeper and more profound and more recognizable and more lovable and more timeless than a game show." "I didn't want to make it a story about a slum dweller who drives off with a Rolex watch on his wrist in a Bentley at the end." "'Cause I don't think getting rich . . . is necessarily a great way to end a film." "Someone who finally finds the love of their life after finding her and losing her and finding her again, *that's* something I will applaud." ♫ "Just a humble slum-dog / Sittin' in the chair, of a millionaire. / What will I be holding in the end? / What's my final answer? / Is it written there, do I really care? / I'm only here so I can phone a friend. / And if I thought I could find equivalence / I would swim a sea of human excrement!" ♫ "Salim is in a bath of money at the end, so the only one who gets rich in this film ends up dead." "And that's struck a chord with people, I think, right now, in an era where we've suddenly turned around and gone, 'Wait a minute; this money thing, it's been shown to be a real false idol.'" "People in early screenings wanted to know, Did he get the money? Well, he got the girl." "Have they got no soul?"

What a relief that it might be not about the money, at least for Jamal and for his people. For Americans, of course, the absence of money as the presence of virtue is a bit of a hard sell. Better if the hero chooses virtue over money and for his virtue is rewarded with—money.

There is a holy dread of those for whom it's truly not about the money. Those who know that death is no commodity, who do not count their lives cheap. Those princes among the bought off, for whom there is no boredom, no seduction by honeyed zealotry, but instead a willful reverse trajectory: millionaire to slumdog. Those who would give up a quarter-billion-dollar construction fortune to live in a cave near the Khyber Pass.

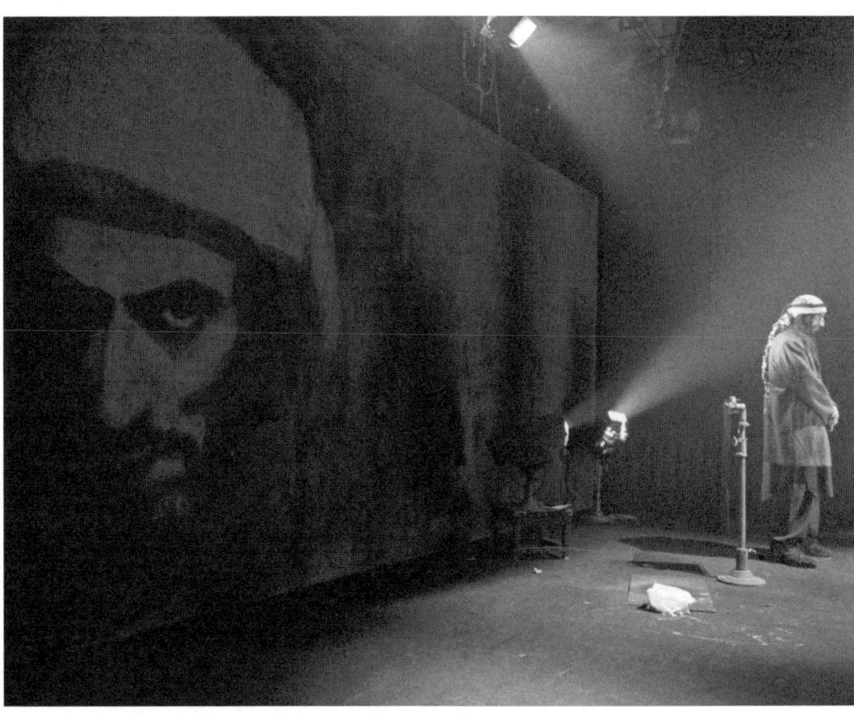

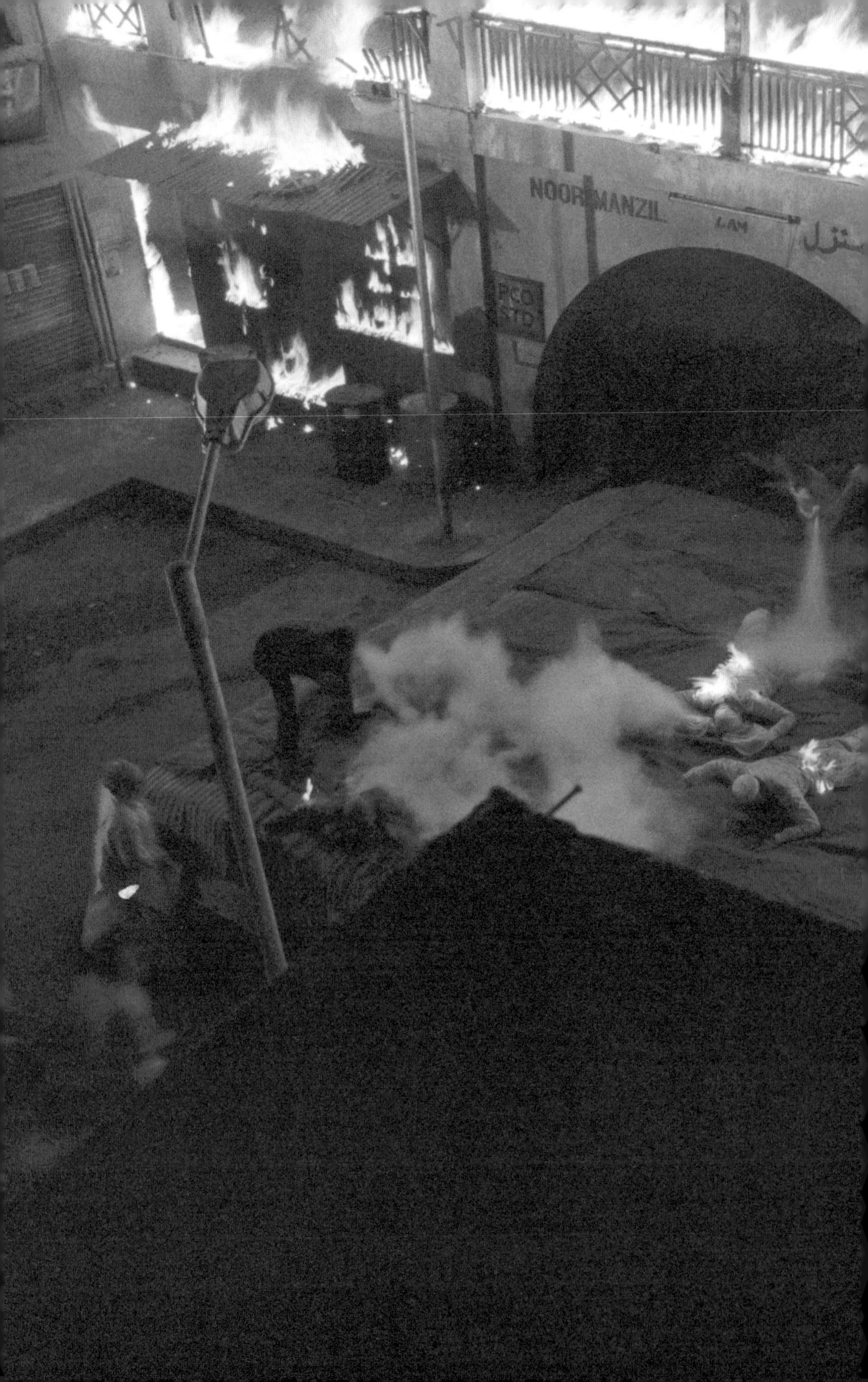

NOOR MANZIL
PCO
STD
منزل

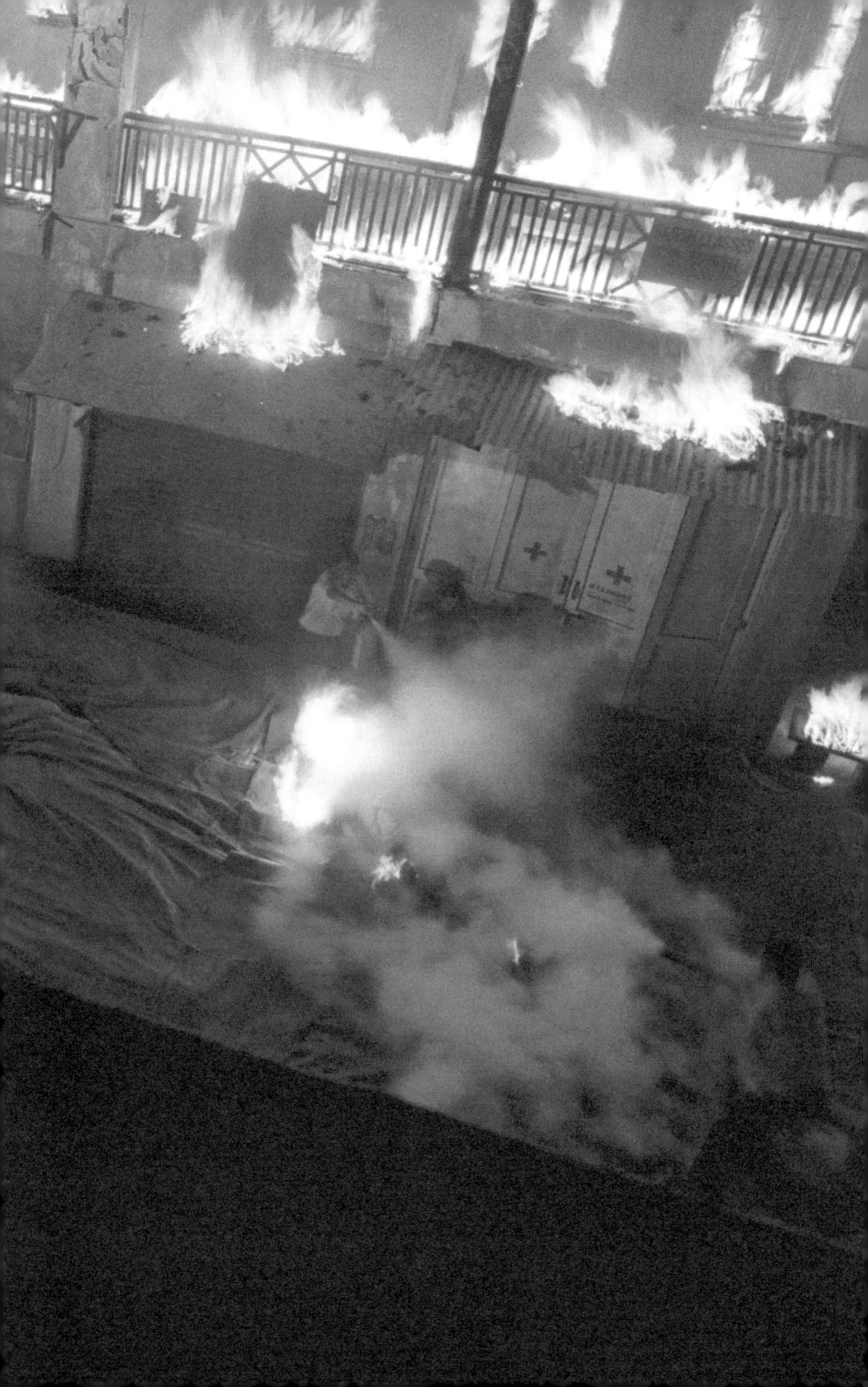

THE WESTERN MEDIA'S interest in Ajmal Kasab waned long before the trial began; his romance had faded. In India, though, the coverage remained intense. "Kasab seems as interested in the journalists as they are in him." He goofed off in court. "Prosecutor Ujjwal Nikam turned to him and said: 'Don't laugh. Be serious. Otherwise I will call Dara Singh,' a reference to the legendary Indian wrestler often invoked by parents to keep their children quiet. Kasab laughed even more." "Nikam condemned Kasab's behaviour saying he was throwing tantrums every now and then." "Kasab's behaviour was brought to the notice of the court after he refused to eat food on Wednesday and banged the utensil against the wall." He offered to sketch Lashkar-e-Taiba leaders whose likenesses were unknown to authorities, but officials found the drawings useless: "When he gave us the sketches we did not know what to say. He had drawn doodles like a small child." The judge scolded him endlessly. "Keep away this casual attitude and show some seriousness." "It is not proper to misbehave in jail." "Why did you throw away your plate of food?" "Are you crying? What is the matter?"

As the prosecution's case wound down, Kasab became quieter, and for much of his time in the dock he slept, awaiting his conviction. (In one Bangladeshi newspaper's imperfect English, he had become the "lonely gunman.") He perked up when it came time for his final statement, in which he denied having been present at any of the attacks and said the police had detained him in Mumbai days before, had shot him in the hand, "just like in the movies," as part of the frame-up. What had he been doing in the city, the judge wanted to know. Kasab's answer can be interpreted two ways: He had come either to watch some films or to break into Bollywood.

Throughout it all, he kept on asking for things he could not have. "I am bored and need books to read," he told the judge. Countered the prosecutor, "Now, what is the use of reading books?" "I need a few things urgently," wrote Kasab to his lawyer. "These are *Urdu Times* newspaper, a perfume bottle and a toothpaste. Also please seek court's direction to police asking them to deposit the amount, seized from my possession, in my jail account." But the seized monies were the property of the court, and so Kasab could not order the one-kilogram cake that it was his right to request from the prison bakery for his twenty-second birthday.

He didn't get anything he wanted, but he asked nevertheless. He wanted to walk on the veranda outside his cell. He wanted, on the Hindu holiday of Raksha Bandhan, when sisters tie bracelets around their brothers' wrists, for someone to tie a *rakhi* on his own. He wanted to meet Amitabh Bachchan. ⊠

All photographs by the author. The photograph on page 311 was taken on the set of an unknown film in Mumbai in 2004. All other photographs were taken on the set of the film *Dev*, directed by Govind Nihalani, in Mumbai in 2003. This essay is excerpted from the original online publication.

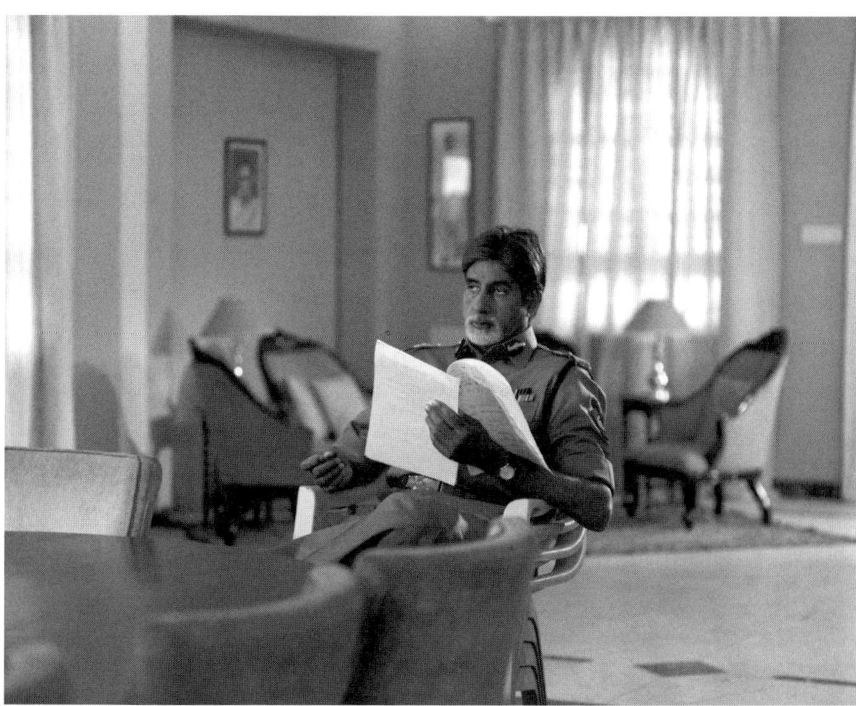

SELECTED CORRESPONDENCE OF TRIPLE CANOPY: THE IRON CAGE

From the annals of incorporation and internal audits. In which we work to find forms to sustain our remaining youthful energies.

From: Alexander Provan
Date: July 6, 2008, 4:13 p.m.
Subject: Re: Meeting

In an attempt to formalize the inchoate process that allows
Triple Canopy to function, and clarify the roles and
responsibilities of all involved, we're asking everyone
to honestly address his or her ideal commitment level and
choose an appropriate position. Mainly, we want to determine
who will take part in the higher-level conversations about
conceptual issues and the general direction of the entity
in all its facets (no longer just a magazine! see revised
mission statement to be presented on Thursday). This entails
committing to keeping up with a more rigorous (and time-
consuming) dialogue about how we're operating, and reading
and responding thoughtfully to all related emails. It's
one part management, one part meta-conversation, one part
sustained auto-critique.
        This isn't meant to exclude anyone—general issues
and decisions will still be presented to the larger group—
but rather to avoid feeling compelled to solicit everyone's
opinion (and to avoid having people feel compelled to give
their opinion) every time a decision needs to be made, and
to thus establish a more transparent (if less egalitarian)
governance structure. We're realizing it's not feasible to
operate by consensus, and that many people are perfectly
happy contributing more occasionally, or contributing
primarily through soliciting, facilitating, and contributing
projects. This will also help us establish who does what,
and who we can rely on to execute certain regular tasks,
and generally come up with a more concrete distribution of
responsibilities.

From: Caleb Waldorf
Date: July 7, 2008, 4:48 p.m.
Subject: Re: Meeting

One thing I've been thinking about is a more transparent
system of selecting content for the magazine. Right now
it's not totally clear (or consistent). I think if we open
this up a bit and have a system that everyone understands it
might lead to less frustration; I've gotten the impression
that other editors have been perturbed by the lack of
transparency. We need something that balances the roles
of the top tier and the senior-editor tier, like a voting
system. House of Representatives or Senate or Parliament?

From: Sam Frank
Date: July 7, 2008, 5:06 p.m.
Subject: Re: Meeting

The vetting system is a problem for one major reason: we're
not paying people for their pieces, so that by the time
they've put in the work, it's pretty nasty to outright shoot
down the piece (we're not paying a kill fee). I suspect that
the best we'll be able to do is: a) Run proposals by a few

people (though maybe not the whole staff?) before approving them. b) When a draft comes in, the editor and a few readers work on it until they're satisfied. c) Then the whole staff can take a look, point out problems, and try to get them fixed.
    Obviously this isn't a consensus-based way of operating. But I'd maybe prefer that editors be given the freedom to pursue pieces that interest them, with a few safeguards in place. Also we should make an effort to present pieces in progress as early as possible at meetings, or on the email list. Taking a few weeks to get simple approval for a proposal doesn't seem ideal to me. Maybe I'm wrong.

From: Peter J. Russo
Date: May 18, 2008, 9:28 a.m.
Subject: Want to Incorporate but can't decide?

We can start by filing to incorporate in NY State and then apply to the IRS for tax exemption. I'm being told that the IRS can take up to six months and we need that approval in order to move forward with exemption from the state. In addition to the documents I passed along, here are some strong suggestions from Matthew at Free Dimensional (lawyer):

You should begin drafting a two-year budget, bylaws (along with the Articles of Incorporation), and a partnership agreement defining the relationship between indivduals involved with Triple Canopy. The partnership agreement defines the nature and purpose of your business relationship, including the type of business you are starting and your individual roles. It should specify the following sections: capital contributions (how much will you put in and how will you recoup?); profits & losses (how will these be accrued by each person?); authority (who does what?); death of partner (how are interests inherited by surviving partners?); admission of new partners (how do you handle the addition of new execs, employees, and partners as you grow?); buy-outs (there are circumstances that may necessitate a buy-out of a partner's interest, e.g. death, illegal acts, bankruptcy, so how do you effect a buy-out?); signature authority (who has the authority to sign for what?).

From: Alexander Provan
Date: Dec. 16, 2008, 11:03 a.m.
Subject: Digital age (tweet tweet)

Hey everyone. I impulsively signed us up for Twitter. Is this a good idea? I could make a note on our Facebook page that we're on Twitter.

From: Tom Roberge
Date: Dec. 16, 2008, 4:25 p.m.
Subject: Re: Digital age (tweet tweet)

My only reservation is that it seems like something reserved
for teenagers and for those who don't mind derisive comments
in which you're compared to teenagers.

From: Peter J. Russo
Date: March 3, 2009, 8:11 a.m.
Subject: EIN, bylaws

Called the IRS today to check on the status of our EIN: "Do
you spell out Triple?" "Will you be operating any big trucks?"

From: Colby Chamberlain
Date: Dec. 9, 2008, 9:16 a.m.
Subject: Re: Programming

I think the most successful events with independent
publications are those that comprise a number of short
presentations by the magazine's "talent," gathered under
some conceit. And by conceit I don't necessarily mean
theme, but rather some structuring principle that makes
the talks a bit more playful. The now-defunct Topic asked
people to present something in the format of a vacation
slide-show. In some ways that's idiotically simple, but it
worked fantastically well, and gave the event an energy that
approximated what you want from a magazine—some synergy and
verve that exceeds the merits of any individual article.
Regarding the urbanism event at the Kitchen, the world
doesn't need from us some approximation of the architecture/
planning talks that happen all the time in architectural
schools (this is a profession that loves the talks).

From: Peter J. Russo
Date: Dec. 9, 2008, 9:42 a.m.
Subject: Programming

I've always liked the idea that TC programs could be an
extension of the magazine by featuring some of the same
contributors. It's also interesting how the reverse is now
happening: events are feeding back into the magazine. I
think this continued engagement also shows a commitment to
the individuals we choose to work with (and vice versa).
It's also a show of gratitude when no honorarium is yet
possible.

From: Alexander Provan
Date: Dec. 10, 2008, 1:14 a.m.
Subject: Re: Programming

I think we need to take the opportunities presented to us
as chances to represent the magazine, rather than invite
interesting outsiders to give a talk under the auspices of
the magazine. By doing so we can engage a new audience in a
way that clearly and directly establishes what the magazine
is, which will in turn increase interest in TC (and the

possibility of getting grants). And I think material in the magazine can benefit from being reworked for a live setting; events we produce that involve staged conversations, performances, and other types of interactions that aren't normally part of the process of producing the magazine can germinate projects that wouldn't otherwise come into being. (That said, this hasn't happened so much yet; we've mostly been throwing benefit parties.)

From: Sam Frank
Date: Feb. 17, 2009, 11:41 p.m.
Subject: Bug on new Internet Explorer for PC

My friend just told me he's not able to read Ben Tausig's piece on the newest version of Internet Explorer for the PC. He said he's "getting the logo and the +/-, but no images."

From: Adam Florin
Date: Feb. 18, 2009 1:31 p.m.
Subject: Re: Bug on new Internet Explorer for PC

OK! After some hairpulling I have a fix for this. Copying editors as our embed methodology for YouTube videos has changed. Due to an obnoxious bug in IE7 (and our fancypants layout system), we can't just use YouTube embed codes in pieces. The process will now look more like how it does for our audio players. Use this snipped to embed a YouTube video:

```
<div id="soulja_boy_video_player"></div> <script type="text/javascript" charset="utf-8"> window.addEvent('after_column_wrap', function() {init_youtube_video('soulja_boy_video_player', 'http://www.youtube.com/v/mMycfdNdlKA&hl=en&fs=1', '350', '283');}); </script>
```

Each time you paste this in, you must do the following: Make sure the div id matches up with the first param to init_youtube_video (in this case, "soulja_boy_video_player"); extract the full YouTube URL from the YouTube embed code and paste; modify the last two parameters, width and height.

From: Sam Frank
Date: Feb. 18, 2009, 1:36 p.m.
Subject: Re: Bug on new Internet Explorer for PC

Just to clarify, we need to write a new, unique div id (that is, come up for a name for each new div id) for each YouTube video we embed? One we're sure we've never used before?

From: Adam Florin
Date: Feb. 18, 2009, 1:37 p.m.
Subject: Re: Bug on new Internet Explorer for PC

That's correct!

From: Alexander Provan
Date: Feb. 2, 2009, 8:40 p.m.
Subject: Title for issue 5

We need a name for the issue. Here are some overarching
themes: reenactments, reincarnations, peripheries. Idol
Traffic? Revelation of Everyday Life?

From: William Smith
Date: Feb. 3, 2009, 12:01 p.m.
Subject: Re: Title for issue 5

Little Stabs at Happiness, Form into Form, Party Sequence?
"Ow, my balls" might be played out, but how about just
"dildozer" . . . it suggests "periphery" as a condition (our
condition).

Sent from my iPhone.

From: Sam Frank
Date: Feb. 3, 2009, 1:08 p.m.
Subject: Re: Title for issue 5

Ow, My Baseballs; The Diacritic as Artist; -Phile Sharing;
Shit Is Garbage (After Ice-T); Why Me Crank Dat; Public
Access Gibberish.
     "Sent from our iPhone"?

From: Sarah Kessler
Date: Feb. 5, 2009, 10:56 p.m.
Subject: Re: Title for issue 5

Picture Book? Chaff? Outliers? Marginalia? T[V]C[1]5?
Wikipedia: "Bowie's 'TVC 15' was inspired by an episode
in which Iggy Pop, during a drug-fueled period at
Bowie's L.A. home, hallucinated and believed that the
television set was swallowing his girlfriend. Beyond
oblique mentions to absorption via television, the
lyrics are largely nonsensical. Bowie himself hasn't been
able to shed any light on their meaning beyond the Pop
anecdote, having very limited recollection of the Station
to Station sessions, due to his own heavy drug use at the
time." The song is meaningless, nonsensical, but contains
some reference to reality! And: absorption.

From: William Smith
Date: April 12, 2009, 9:20 p.m.
Subject: Re: Board meeting minutes

Management, Communication, and Workflow
Given the variety of projects, it might be necessary to move
beyond the traditional hierarchy of magazines to a cell
model. Molly and Sam pointed out that Google Docs / Dashboard
had been adopted to facilitate easy communication, but that

we did not use them with enough consistency to make it a replacement for the editor email list. Several editors also voiced concerns that Dashboard could be a potential source of confusion in the editing process as different versions of a piece might be worked on simultaneously by different editors. Adam and Caleb discussed the possibility of making our current editor interface more useful for communication and collaboration. To save on labor, it would be easier to use Base Camp, a commercial workflow organization program that would simplify the file sharing process. Although superior to Dashboard, Base Camp is not free.

Peter observed that we need two project management systems for sharing information: one to facilitate an orderly editing process, and another to exchange more general ideas. Sarah commented on how important it is for us to share information about the issue so that we maintain a coherent face for our writers. Peter discussed the need for a community message board. Colby pointed to the frequency of pitches he gets that go nowhere. Lots of wasted time on unserious ideas. A set of guidelines for pitches would be good. Laurence suggested we could point to particularly successful pieces in these guidelines, but Colby disagreed.

Publicity
Publicity is arduous shitwork, but it needs to be done. Interns seem unwilling to do it, so what do we do? Laurence suggested we appoint a director of publicity. Alex said that interns are overqualified for this kind of work, but at the same time it would be hard to find someone outside of the magazine whom we like and would do this for free. Laurence suggested it should be the responsibility of each editor to publicize the piece he or she is working on. Caleb argued that Internet publicity is unique, that we need to use Web 2.0 and Twitter to build networks as a way of publicizing in a more diffuse way. He suggested that we are not using our mass emails as effectively as possible. We could make a template that would be easier to code each time. It should include a digest at the very top, featured content, an article from the archives, etc. Adam also noticed that our publication dates and email messages are not well timed. People get the email, visit the site once, and then miss a lot of content.

Website
Adam wants to brainstorm ways to make our website fresher and webbier. In the past we had resisted a lot of Web stuff that would keep our site "live," but also make it feel slightly more like a blog. But Adam proposed a few ideas that would maintain our identity while also giving people more of a reason to check up on our projects more consistently. Caleb agrees that it's time to refresh our site, which can be confusing. It's hard to find content from the splash page; we need a search function; we need to date our articles. Adam proposed tagging as a way of keeping older content fresh. We would reward people who make it through a piece by giving them related articles tagged in the same way. As with publicity, editors would need to be responsible for tagging their pieces/suggesting related content. We

would need to have some creative tags to link our articles.
Re-blogging is another potentially useful way of keeping
the site fresh and building an online publicity network.
Sarah suggested that we could invite guest re-bloggers who
would function like respondents to an issue by gathering
related content. Re-blogging also means we would be tracked-
back from the sites we blog about, perhaps enticing more
people to visit our site. Peter argues that we shouldn't
include comments or feedback, that we need to maintain our
reputation for editorial heavy-handedness. Blog territory is
not for us. Alex says articles need to be printable so that
old people can read them.

Fundraising
We'd like to start raising more money, but our traffic
is low so ads are unlikely. Grants, auctions, commercial
operations, etc. were discussed. Peter walked us through
the projected budget, which showed increased income
and donations. He also described how we're finalizing
our incorporation as a nonprofit. Adam H. described the
Brown Foundation grant. We talked of getting an intern
specifically for grant writing. Peter discussed the
possibility of a benefit auction with work priced between
$50 and $1000, perhaps with contributors to the magazine
donating work. Laurence suggested that we start a money-
making operation producing events or consulting on websites,
and that we do larger entrepreneurial projects. Colby
brought up the difficulty of covering operating costs
with grant money. Peter talked about the need to develop
an organizational narrative: a 2-10 page document that
describes our history, organization, projects, outlook, etc.
We need a subcommittee to get this going.

From: Alexander Provan
Date: May 20, 2009, 11:27 a.m.
Subject: Issue 6 assignments

What do we actually need in terms of new editors? People who
have a serious interest in complicated, committed writing
and other work on politics, urbanism, etc., but not from
a totally academic perspective—or people who can bring
currents in academic thought to bear on a more popular
level, and have a sense of prose style that will facilitate
that. People who have the connections and sensibilities
to bring in good artists to work on TC-specific projects.
People who aren't white and male and into exactly the same
stuff we are, and who can tap groups that we don't already
(L.A. counts).

From: Caleb Waldorf
Date: May 23, 2009, 1:53 a.m.
Subject: Re: Issue 6 assignments

I'm really interested in thinking more broadly about our
editorial approach in relationship to time and attention.
I was looking at our analytics and the length of visit

information is very interesting. Our main committed audience is on the site for 61–600 seconds. We need to try and get those folks in the 31–60 seconds range to stick around longer. And we need to think carefully about how long it actually takes to read/look at our content and make sure that people are likely to actually do so. This is important for two reasons: If they aren't going to make it through an entire article, it's highly likely they aren't going to make it to other pieces; if this is what is happening—you can see that it is by looking at our top exit pages—there is very little point to spending tons of time carefully sequencing issues and thinking about deployment strategies. So we may benefit from doing more shorter pieces punctuated by longer pieces. The coming redesign will tackle some of this by providing better navigation throughout the site, which will make content more horizontally organized (through keywords and related-content links).

From: Peter J. Russo
Date: May 23, 2009, 12:49 p.m.
Subject: Re: Issue 6 assignments

There's a long learning curve for developing projects with artists who don't generally work in the medium. It's an experiment. And approaching artists with suggestions, having long discussions, finding folks to program the work, etc. is very time consuming. Finding an editor with a specific interest in new media would be ideal; however, I think this requires an understanding that not all artists are interested in building out robust magazine pieces as opposed to shorter Web-specific works. Maybe we should also define "the kind of work we'd be interested in developing" in the submission guidelines and tailor that document to writers and artists.

From: Sam Frank
Date: May 23, 2009, 2:39 p.m.
Subject: Re: Issue 6 assignments

I've been thinking a lot about what I'm actually excited about doing with TC, rather than what I feel a responsibility to do. And one thing is that while I'm glad we've published all these long essays, editing and laying them out saps my will to live. I don't want to put a call out for short pieces. But I do think we've let 5,000-worders become the rule rather than the exception. And they're a drain on all of us. More generally, I need to dial back the work I do on pieces that seem good and important in some general, impersonal way, and focus my energy on a couple pieces an issue that excite me personally. Cutting down on the emails I have to read—that's big.

        I really need to define my role better. (But then I think we all need to define our roles better.) And I want to formally clear time for writing: as much time as possible. So that's kind of my six-month plan. Then I turn 30! Fuck. The main thing I want to avoid is the fuzziness where

suddenly a week off disappears into a TC black hole. Which
is a matter of my inefficiency, but is still a fact. And we
need some money! Just a little bit would make things feel
different.

From: Peter J. Russo
Date: May 23, 2009, 3:42 p.m.
Subject: Re: Issue 6 assignments

I'd like to be doing more design work, helping establish the
style guide, etc. Often, I'm sad not to be more involved in
the layout of each piece and wish I had a firmer grasp on
the back-end work. Either way, unfortunately, I think this
work really requires someone close to the content. You can't
divorce the two. And I feel like we're going to really get
ourselves in a bad spot if we don't begin to think further
ahead about admin stuff, especially now that we're paying
taxes, considering the formation of a board, potentially
holding an auction, etc. This is an area in which I'm
really invested; I'm looking forward to tying up the 501c3
paperwork.

From: Colby Chamberlain
Date: May 12, 2009, 12:33 a.m.
Subject: Re: Meeting

We're interested in generating a boilerplate text about
Triple Canopy for potential grants and funders. Thus,
we're looking for "grant-speak," and not language we would
dream of actually posting on the site. The text should
answer the questions, Who We Are, What We Do, Why It
Matters (from the viewpoint of funders). The text should
list a sampling of What We've Done and Who We Work With,
but history shouldn't be privileged considering we are a
one-year-old organization. The text should be flexible
enough that we could tailor it to two or three different
categories of funders: 1) funders interesting in writing/
literary endeavors, 2) funders interested in the visual
arts, and 3) (maybe) funders interested in various forms of
techno-fetishism.

From: Peter J. Russo
Date: June 18, 2009, 9:52 a.m.
Subject: Re: TC Greatest Hits

As I understand it, for the 501c3 incorporation paperwork
and subsequent grants we need to describe each activity
in terms of seven questions: What is the activity? Who
conducts the activity? When is the activity conducted? Where
is the activity conducted? How does the activity further
TC's exempt purposes? What percentage of your total time is
allocated to the activity? How is the activity funded? (This
should agree with the financial data in Part IX.) The IRS
will be reviewing this with a checklist mentality.

From: Alexander Provan
Date: July 8, 2010, 11:10 a.m.
Subject: Redesign feedback

We discussed the need to eliminate small amounts of text below the larger images, as well as the need for the slide-show tools to be more identifiable. Some editors mentioned the need for "break" and "anchor" tools to control the pace of the reading experience; that this is at the heart of what we do and why many people appreciate the current design. Sarah said she likes that there will be image size options, but also wonders if four is too many; she agreed that the slide-show tools should be more apparent and that we need to eliminate small amounts of text under the image. She prefers the elimination of the page outline. Molly said she appreciates the desire to up the webbiness, but fears that all of the pieces now look very much alike and wants to make sure that flexibility is still built into the system. She likes that the images can pop up for a larger view, but thinks their original sizes should be left to our discretion. Will thinks there should be an option to create a hierarchy of images. Some images we want to emphasize, others are interesting but not that exciting viewed large. The full bleed is a tool that we use now to create these distinctions, and he doesn't see something equivalent in this layout. Having the option to run an image or slide show as a full bleed has been a very effective design tool for the look, feel, and pacing of TC pieces. Will said he doesn't see an easy option for printing yet. What's the status of that? Old people with money really want the site to be printable, and he thinks we should incorporate a nod to our geriatric patrons with some easy-to-find print button they can mash.

From: Alexander Provan
Date: Sept. 30, 2010, 5:52 p.m.
Subject: Meeting notes, 9/29

Some of us have been talking about the need to regroup after the new site launches and the benefit is over and the next issue has been published . . . whew! . . . and have a decent dinner where we can talk more generally about the state of affairs and the future. I know I'm not the only one who's happy that we've accomplished so much, organizationally speaking, in the past months and years (!), but is somewhat frustrated that, as a result, we seem to be having fewer substantive conversations related to the work we're doing. And we seem to be devoting more time to work that is largely administrative and, thus, not sufficiently engaging intellectually. The price of success, I suppose; nevertheless, it would be good to have a real conversation about what we all want for and from Triple Canopy moving forward, and how to ensure that we're engaging each other and the work of the magazine in a meaningful and enjoyable way, etc.

From: ------1@aol.com
Date: April 5, 2009 6:05 p.m.
Subject: SPAM -> (no subject)

 Hello:

I never heard of you before. i was researching the mercenary
army called "Triple Canopy" which was, I believe, formed in
2007, using Special Forces veterans:
         Presumably, veterans of the VietNam War, which ended
in 1971 I believe, with the fall of Saigon. However, before
then, Nixon had expanded the Vietnam war into Cambodia and
Laos.
         The term "triple canopy" was first used to describe
the foliage--if you could call it that--which prevented our
bombers from truly laying waste to the place; not that they
didn't do enough damage. Triple canopy was what the jungles
of Southeast Asia were made of: first the ground vegetation;
tall tall 'tiger' grasses (so named because their tough,
tall growth effectively hid the tigers which flourished
during Vietnam), then the interim growth which was mango,
bamboo, orchid vines and the like, and then taller trees .
         Like I said, "Triple Canopy" always meant Southeast
Asia, to me. That is, before we defoliated the place,
killing plants, native Southeast Asians, and of course,
Americans serving in Southeast Asia. Our defoliants--
official dismissals to the contrary--did harm our soldiers,
and the military's still denying it.
         For Shame.
         Meanwhile, what are you? Some kind of lit magazine--
but what kind? War stories from the Johnson/Nixon era? What?
    Cause, if war stories, I got something you'd be
interested in. If I can get through the online copyright
ick--I think they call it "Creative Commons" or something,
LOL! If interested, reply to Val at: ------1@aol.com ⊠

CONTRIBUTORS

Vahram Aghasyan lives and works in Yerevan, Armenia. He has exhibited at the Istanbul Biennial, the Museum Kiasma in Helsinki, and the Contemporary Art Biennale of Thessaloniki, Greece. He recently completed a residency at Künstlerstätte Schloss Bleckede in Germany.

Manal Al Dowayan is an artist based in Saudi Arabia. Her work focuses on the social status of women in her country. She is represented by Cuadro Gallery in Dubai.

Sophia Al-Maria is based in Doha, Qatar, where she works at Mathaf: Arab Museum of Modern Art. Her first book, *The Girl Who Fell to Earth*, will be published in December 2012 by Harper Perennial.

Bidisha Banerjee is a program director at Dalai Lama Fellows, where she created the Head, Heart, and Hands curriculum. She is codesigning an interactive game with the Red Cross Climate Centre and working on a memoir about misremembering the river Ganges.

Joshua Bauchner is an editor and writer living in Brooklyn.

Gil Blank is a photographer and writer based in Portage Bay, Washington. His latest book, *35 Images / The Odyssey*, coauthored with Matthew Stadler, was released by Publication Studio in 2010.

Lev Bratishenko is an architectural journalist and classical-music critic based in Montreal. He is the author of the illustrated guide *How to Eat the Rich*.

José León Cerrillo is an artist living in Mexico City. His work has been shown at Dispatch Projects, New York; Tensta Konsthall, Sweden; Galeria Nara Roesler, São Paulo; East Side Projects, Birmingham, England; Circuit, Lausanne, Switzerland; Proyectos Monclova, Mexico City; and Museo Rufino Tamayo, Mexico City.

Joseph Clarke is an architectural historian. He has taught at the University of Cincinnati and worked at the firms of Eisenman Architects and Skidmore, Owings & Merrill.

Joshua Cohen is the author of *Four New Messages*, *Witz*, *A Heaven of Others*, and *Cadenza for the Schneidermann Violin Concerto*.

George Collins is currently setting thirty-three thousand years of environmental indicators to music and writing three one-act plays about Simon Magus.

Teddy Cruz is an architect and professor of public culture and urbanism at the University of California, San Diego. He recently represented the US at the Venice Architecture Bienniale and received the Ford Foundation Visionaries Award. He is the cofounder of the Center for Urban Ecologies.

Clare Davies is a doctoral candidate at the Institute of Fine Arts at New York University and writes regularly for contemporary art publications. She lives in Cairo, where she is completing her dissertation on twentieth-century art practices in Egypt.

Neil Greenberg wears many hats in the worlds of public transit and city planning. His projects include Fake Omaha, Freshwater Railway, and U-M airBus.

Ed Halter is a founder and director of Light Industry, a venue for film and electronic art in Brooklyn. His writing has appeared in *Artforum*, the *Believer*, *Frieze*, *Little Joe*, and the *Village Voice*. He cocurated the film and video program for the 2012 Whitney Biennial.

Lucy Ives's *Early Poems* is forthcoming from Ahsahta Press in 2013. She is a senior editor at Triple Canopy.

Matico Josephson is pursuing a doctoral degree in architectural history at the Institute of Fine Arts. He is currently living in a quiet spot in Queens.

Peter Kerlin is a musician, composer, and video maker from Sunset Park, Brooklyn. As a bass player he performs regularly with Chris Forsyth's Paranoid Cat Band, Christy & Emily, Source of Yellow, and others. He has taught at NYU and CCNY.

Hassan Khan is an artist, musician and writer. He lives and works in Cairo.

Rafil Kroll-Zaidi is an editor at *Harper's Magazine*.

John Latta is the author of *Rubbing Torsos* (Ithaca House, 1979) and *Breeze* (University of Notre Dame Press, 2003). Recent poems are in or forthcoming in *Lana Turner*, the *Brooklyn Rail*, *Zoland Poetry*, *Critical Quarterly*, *New American Writing*, and *Chicago Review*. He writes regularly at the website *Isola di Rifiuti*.

Rustam Mehta is an architect living in New Haven.

Victoria Miguel is a Scottish writer based in New York.

Joe Milutis is a writer and media artist. He is the author of numerous multimedia essays and, most recently, *Failure, A Writer's Life*, a catalogue of literary monstrosities.

Thomas Moran is an architect, designer, and educator based in Ann Arbor, Michigan, where he is a lecturer at the University of Michigan's Taubman College of Architecture and Urban Planning. His design work focuses on reclaiming the domestic interior for architectural speculation and has been exhibited at the Center for Architecture, Storefront for Art and Architecture, the Museum of Contemporary Art, Chicago, and the Venice Biennale.

Karthik Pandian is an artist whose work in film and sculpture has been exhibited widely, including as a solo exhibition at the Whitney Museum of American Art, New York, and as part of group exhibitions at the Palais de Tokyo, Paris, and the Hammer Museum, Los Angeles.

Lucy Raven is an artist whose work ranges from sculptural installations and animated films to performative lectures and live television. Raven's work has been exhibited at the Whitney Museum of American Art, MOMA PS1, and the Hammer Museum. She lives and works in Oakland, California, and New York City.

Nathan Schneider is author of *God in Proof: The Story of a Search, from the Ancients to the Internet*, to be published in 2013 by University of California Press.

Anna Sperber is a dancer and choreographer and native of Brooklyn, where she still lives. Her work has been presented at the Kitchen, Dance Theater Workshop, the Baryshnikov Arts Center, and the Brooklyn Museum. She has been an artist in residence at Movement Research, Barnard College, and the Lower Manhattan Cultural Council on Governors Island.

Molly Springfield is a visual artist based in Washington, DC. Her work has been shown widely in museums and galleries throughout the United States, including in solo exhibitions in New York, Chicago, San Francisco, and Washington, DC.

Ben Tausig is a doctoral candidate in ethnomusicology at New York University, studying urban sound and protest music in Bangkok. He lives in Manhattan, where he also writes and edits crossword puzzles for the *Onion*, *Chicago Reader*, and others.

Leslie Thornton is a Brooklyn-based artist working in video, photography, and film. She is best known for her epic project, *Peggy and Fred in Hell*. She teaches media production at Brown University and is represented by Winkleman Gallery.

Dan Torop works with lenses, film, paper, words, vehicles, and computer languages. His *Alkali Desert* exhibition is on view at the Center for Land Use Interpretation's Wendover Exhibit Hall One.

Hovhannes Tumanyan was an Armenian writer of poetry and fiction. He was born in 1869 and died in 1923.

Ian Volner is a writer living in New York.

Caleb Waldorf is an artist living in Berlin. He is a cofounder and currently the creative director of Triple Canopy. Since 2008 he has worked on the open framework for pedagogy the Public School, started in Los Angeles by Telic Arts Exchange. He is also the coeditor of a journal for short-form writing and media work called *Version* and part of the editorial collective Occupy Everything.

Triple Canopy is an online magazine, workspace, and platform for editorial and curatorial activities. Working collaboratively with writers, artists, and researchers, Triple Canopy facilitates projects that engage the Internet's specific characteristics as a public forum and as a medium, one with its own evolving practices of reading and viewing, economies of attention, and modes of interaction. In doing so, Triple Canopy is charting an expanded field of publication, drawing on the history of print culture while acting as a hub for the exploration of emerging forms and the public spaces constituted around them.

Triple Canopy was founded in 2007 as an informal, nonhierarchical, geographically dispersed editorial collective. A nonprofit organization, Triple Canopy currently consists of a staff of writers, artists, researchers, designers, and developers based in New York, Los Angeles, and Berlin. The magazine operates as the locus for the collaborative production of artistic and literary projects, research work, public programs, and print objects that mine the legacies of the artist book, the avant-garde journal, the political pamphlet, the alternative arts space, and the magazine-in-a-box, all the while enriching those forms with new media.

As a magazine, Triple Canopy is dedicated to *slowing down the Internet*. This begins with our design interface, which encourages prolonged, focused engagement. It extends to our methods: We work closely and collaboratively with contributors from the inception of a project to (and often beyond) its publication or public presentation. We consider the editorial process to be a collective enterprise, not a utilitarian transaction; a workspace for testing ideas and cultivating aesthetic experiments that might otherwise lack a critical, nonspecialized context, online or elsewhere. We are committed to learning from past efforts to rethink and renovate the print object and the exhibition space, as well as the literary and artistic forms they have engendered. We are convinced that the Web can act as a proper venue for these endeavors, one with its own materiality and timeliness.

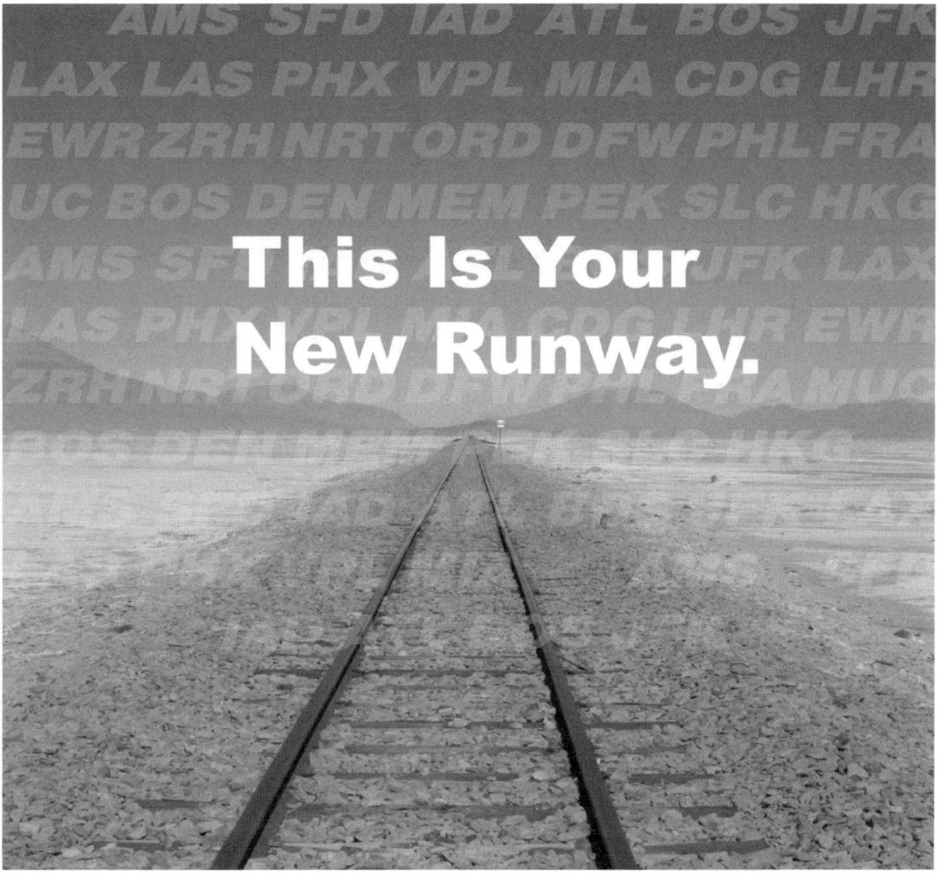

This Is Your New Runway.

Environmental, economic and political obstacles will prevent expansion at major city airports. If we can't add new runways, let's make better use of the ones we have. Linking LAX, LAS and PHX via rail will reduce airport traffic more than adding a runway to each, and at a tenth of the cost. It's time to get smart about the future of air travel—and it begins on the ground. High Speed Rail. Real. Fast.

When is building train tracks the smartest way to add capacity to an airport? When it's the only way.

    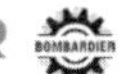 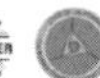    

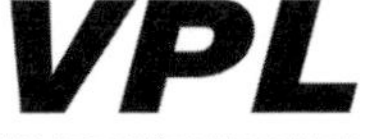
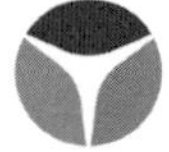

Since it was founded in 1977, the VPL Authority has worked diligently to facilitate growth in the area circumscribed by Las Vegas, Phoenix, and Los Angeles. The private, public-benefit corporation, headquartered in downtown Phoenix, is little known beyond the desert Southwest, in part because it has been so successful: The region's rampant growth has rendered the agency's work all but invisible. But as problems of congestion, irresponsible water use, and unchecked development have begun to plague the region, the VPL Authority has worked to rethink its use of energy and its transportation infrastructure. What we've come up with is a bold new plan for a high-speed rail corridor in the desert Southwest, with a green mega-station at its center. What sets this project apart from so many wish-list ideas of the past decade? It's a pragmatic approach to transforming American infrastructure, appealing to big business and the grassroots alike. It's a plan with a potential constituency as broad as the Mojave Desert. The VPL Authority has already received preliminary funding from the White House thanks to stimulus spending on new rail capacity, but it will take popular support and private investment to make this happen. There's still plenty of time to make your voice heard before construction begins in earnest! Please send your comments to info@ VPLauthority.com, and write your local congressional representatives to voice your support. Tell them you're ready for smart-sprawl.

INVALID FORMAT 2

SUPPORT

Triple Canopy gratefully acknowledges The Andy Warhol Foundation for the Visual Arts, The Brown Foundation, Inc. of Houston, CEC ArtsLink, Chamber Music America, The Doris Duke Charitable Foundation, Experimental TV Center, Foundation for Contemporary Arts, Furthermore: A program of the J. M. Kaplan Fund, Lambent Foundation Fund of Tides Foundation, National Endowment for the Arts, New York City Department of Cultural Affairs, New York Council for the Humanities, New York State Council on the Arts, Office for Contemporary Art Norway, Royal Norwegian Consulate General, and the Orphiflamme Foundation, and the many individuals and in-kind contributors who have generously given their support.

Special thanks to Elizabeth Feidelson, Jessica Lee, and Owen Roberts for their tireless research and dedication to this project.

Major support for *Invalid Format: An Anthology of Triple Canopy, Volume 2* has been provided by Furthermore: a program of the J. M. Kaplan Fund as well as the Publishers Circle, founded to support the development of paperback books, broadsheets, e-books, and other print and digital projects that emerge from and feed into Triple Canopy's online magazine and public programs.

Publishers Circle
Mel Bochner
Christine Burgin
May Castleberry
Lisa Cooley
Zoë & Joel Dictrow
Barbara Epler
Ruth Fine
James Fuentes
Sharon Gallagher
Laurel Gitlen
Wendy Goldberg
Rachel Harrison
Nicholas Harteau
Tom Healy
Christian K. Keesee
David Kiehl
Wynn Kramarsky
Susan Lorence
Gregory R. Miller
Kristian Nammack
Oliver Newton
Barry Rosen
Nicole Russo
Lisa Schiff
Fabienne Stephan
Gretchen Wagner
Tracy Williams

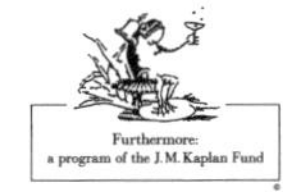

Invalid Format: An Anthology of Triple Canopy, Volume 2, edited by Triple Canopy

Published by Triple Canopy, New York, and Sternberg Press, Berlin, 2012

ISBN 978-3-943365-35-1

Sternberg Press
Caroline Schneider
Karl-Marx-Allee 78
D-10243 Berlin
www.sternberg-press.com

Design concept
Project Projects

Layout and typesetting
Triple Canopy and Alex Lesy in consultation with Project Projects

Printed by fgb. freiburger graphische betriebe

triplecanopy
155 Freeman Street
Brooklyn, NY 11222
www.canopycanopycanopy.com

Triple Canopy is a nonprofit 501(c)3 organization.

For more information, please write to contact@canopycanopycanopy.com.